Creolization as Cultural Creativity

Creolization as Cultural Creativity

Edited by Robert Baron and Ana C. Cara

University Press of Mississippi / Jackson

www.upress.state.ms.us

The University Press of Mississippi is a member of
the Association of American University Presses.

Previous versions of Roger D. Abrahams, "About Face: Rethinking Creolization" appeared as
"Questions of Criolian Contagion" in the *Journal of American Folklore* 116, no. 459 (2003):
73–87, and as "Creolizations" in his *Everyday Life: A Poetics of Vernacular Practices*, University of Pennsylvania Press, 2005: 217–237.

   A previous version of Robert Baron, "Amalgams and Mosaics, Syncretisms and Reinterpretations: Reading Herskovits and Contemporary Creolists for Metaphors of Creolization"
appeared in the *Journal of American Folklore* 116, no. 459 (2003): 73–87.

   A previous version of Ana C. Cara, "The Poetics of Creole Talk" appeared in the *Journal of American Folklore* 116, no. 459 (2003): 36–56.

   A previous version of Lee Haring, "Techniques of Creolization" appeared in the *Journal of American Folklore* 116, no. 459 (2003): 19–35.

   A previous version of Raquel Romberg, "Ritual Piracy: Or Creolization with an Attitude"
appeared as "Ritual Piracy: Or Creolization with an Attitude?" in *New West Indian Guide*
79, no. 3–4 (2005): 175–218.

   A previous version of Nick Spitzer, "*Monde Créole*: The Cultural World of French Louisiana Creoles and the Creolization of World Cultures" appeared as Nicholas R. Spitzer,
"*Monde Créole*: The Cultural World of French Louisiana Creoles and the Creolization of
World Cultures" in the *Journal of American Folklore* 116, no. 459 (2003): 57–72.

   Previous versions of John F. Szwed, "Metaphors of Incommensurability" appeared in the
Journal of American Folklore 116, no. 459 (2003): 9–18, and in his *Crossovers: Essays on Race,
Music and American Culture*, University of Pennsylvania Press, 2005: 223–233.

First printing 2011

∞

Library of Congress Cataloging-in-Publication Data

Creolization as cultural creativity / edited by Robert Baron and Ana C. Cara.
    p. cm.
   Includes bibliographical references and index.
   ISBN 978-1-61703-106-9 (cloth : alk. paper) — ISBN 978-1-61703-107-6 (ebook)
   1. Creoles—Louisiana—Folklore. 2. Creoles—Caribbean Region—Folklore. 3. Creoles—
Argentina—Folklore. 4. Folklore—Performance. I. Baron, Robert A. II. Cara, Ana C.
   GR111.F73C74 2011
   398.209763—dc22   2011001437

British Library Cataloging-in-Publication Data available

To the memory of
Daniel J. Crowley
(1921–1998)

Contents

Contents

Preface

Creolization is never-ending. For the editors, an Argentine *criolla* with Andalusian and Moravian ancestors and a New York Jew with roots in Belarus, Hungary, Lithuania, and Poland, the subject of this volume has deep personal resonance and represents an ongoing intellectual journey. This voyage began when we were graduate students in John Szwed's visionary seminar on creolization in folklore and literature at the University of Pennsylvania during the mid-1970s. Along the way, we were joined by panel participants and a plenary speaker at annual meetings of the American Folklore Society, by contributors to a special issue of the *Journal of American Folklore*, and by the authors included in this volume. They represent an extraordinary variety of scholarly perspectives and personal backgrounds, yet all of us share a view of creolization as a quintessential embodiment of cultural creativity.

This volume includes substantially revised essays from the winter 2003 special issue of the *Journal of American Folklore* along with new contributions written especially for this book. In the years since we first conceived this volume, creolization studies has expanded exponentially from an area of sociolinguistics that challenged received paradigms to a robust field of scholarship that profoundly influences multiple disciplines in the humanities and social sciences. We were privileged to have been students of the late Dell Hymes, whose groundbreaking "ethnography of communication," combined with his work on Creole and pidgin languages, his pioneering research and fieldwork on ethnopoetics, and his explicit recognition of the contribution of folklore to sociolinguistic research (Hymes 1971), decisively shaped our work on creolization.

Over the years, our interest in creolization intensified, with fragrant overtones, through many conversations with Daniel J. Crowley. This volume was to include an article by Dan on carnivals throughout the world as manifestations of creolization. Unable to complete his writing, he worked on it until just prior to his death in 1998 while attending the Carnaval de Oruro in Bolivia. This book is dedicated in loving memory of Dan, a pioneering scholar of creolization for over four decades. He inspired, informed, enlightened, entertained, and delighted all of us interested in creolization, drawing from his extraordinary firsthand experiences and insights about the Creole world. His ongoing work on cultural creolization reached back to the 1950s. As his classic article "Plural and Differential Acculturation in Trinidad" (first published in 1957) attests, Crowley's work on creolization was decades ahead of its time. His essay envisions creolization as a focal cultural process in the Caribbean and is suggestive of how it is a shaping force in social and cultural theory. It is both a historical document and a programmatic account of creolization in the Caribbean, still fresh after more than half a century, resonating with anyone who knows the Caribbean as ethnographer or resident.

A number of other fellow travelers shaped our thinking and contributed to our insights on creolization. These include panelists who joined us at professional meetings over the years and whose presentations and discussions expanded and developed our ideas: Edward Hirsch, Susan Stewart, Michael Aceto, Mary Hope Lee, and Lynda M. Hill. Colleagues who participated in two NEH Summer Seminars conducted by John F. Szwed at the University of Pennsylvania (1980) and at Yale University (1984) also inspired and influenced us. We are especially grateful for the deep understanding of creolization that anthropologist, sociolinguist, and ethnomusicologist Morton Marks and anthropologist, sociolinguist, and James Joyce scholar Karl Reisman brought to the table on those occasions, and for the formative influence of Susan Stewart's poetic sensibility and literary insights into creolization. In Argentina, we want to acknowledge the brilliant graduate students who shared their ideas with Ana Cara in the seminar on creolization and the Caribbean and, particularly, to thank Dr. María Cristina Dalmagro, who administered the Comparative Literature Program at the Universidad Nacional de Córdoba. No less enlightening have been the contributions of Oberlin College students, whose inquisitive minds and creativity are always an inspiration.

We wish to acknowledge the Center for Latin American Studies at the University of California at Berkeley, which generously provided a refuge to Ana Cara for research and writing; and, especially, we thank Dr. Teresa R. Stojkov for making this possible. We are grateful to the W.E.B. Du Bois Institute for African and African American Research of Harvard University, which enabled Robert Baron to benefit from extraordinary library resources and inspiring collegiality as a non-resident fellow. Many thanks also to City Lore, especially Elena Martínez and Steve Zeitlin.

We give our heartfelt thanks to other friends and scholars who lovingly encouraged and challenged us, Alessandra Benedicty, Robert S. Bruch, Henry Lewis Gates Jr., Phyllis Gorfain, Diana Grossman Kahn, Julie Chun Kim, Amy Shuman, and to our devoted and ever-patient family members, who gave us generous and welcome respites from work: Lise Korson and Violet Baron; Rachel, Will, Elizabeth, and Sam Vranick; Maria Walker and Jonathan Allmaier.

Oberlin College provided support for research and for the completion of this manuscript. We are deeply grateful to Dean Sean Decatur for making this funding possible. Elisa Fernández-Arias, a recent graduate of Oberlin and rising Uruguayan American fiction writer, was indispensable in making final edits and in assembling the manuscript. Thanks also go to Karen Johnson for copyediting and to the indexer, Sarah R. Hammond. Our editor at the University Press of Mississippi, Craig Gill, has been everything anyone would want an editor to be, and then some.

Last, but certainly not least, we thank our fellow contributors, whose good company and effervescent dialogue have made this journey a rare privilege.

Creolization as Cultural Creativity

Introduction

Creolization as Cultural Creativity

—ROBERT BARON AND ANA C. CARA

Creolization is cultural creativity in process. When cultures come into contact, expressive forms and performances emerge from their encounter, embodying the sources that shape them yet constituting new and different entities. Fluid in their adaptation to changing circumstances and open to multiple meanings, Creole forms are expressions of culture in transition and transformation. Even as these emergent forms persist and become institutionalized after initial culture contact, they continue to embody multiplicity, render multivocality, and negotiate contestation while also serving as means of national identity and creative expression. Traditionally most closely associated with the New World cultures of Caribbean and Latin American Creole societies, creolization is now increasingly viewed as a universal process that occurs anywhere cultures encounter one another. This process is especially marked in folklore as well as other kinds of expressive culture, explored in this volume through essays by folklorists, cultural anthropologists, ethnomusicologists, and literary scholars.

The concept of creolization was first formulated through the study of languages in colonial situations—especially in the Americas—where people who met speaking mutually unintelligible tongues developed a linguistic medium to communicate among themselves. They restructured the existing languages of the colonizers and colonized, creating new Creole languages with distinctive phonology, morphology, and syntax (see Baker and Mühlhäusler 2007, 102). The emergence of languages, deeply expressive of their corresponding new cultures, pointed not only to new cultural forms but to new power relations and aesthetic dimensions. Both the new languages and new expressive forms embodied resistance to domination and asymmetrical power relations, thus creating and expressing a new, distinct way of being in the world. In response, the study of creolization offered a critical way of conceptualizing the emergence of cultural phenomena borne out of the necessity to negotiate cultural differences and to resist dominance by asserting a new local voice. Today, in the post-colonial world, "Creole" has become a powerful marker of identity in Latin America, the Caribbean, southern Louisiana, Cape Verde, and islands of the southwest Indian Ocean. As "creoleness," "créolité," or "criollismo," it is uniquely manifested through local as well as national expressions.[1] We also contend in this volume that creolization is a potent vehicle for cultural analysis while acknowledging that these premises are contested by some scholars—as we discuss below.

In keeping with the dialogic nature of culture contact in Creole societies, creole forms are never static. Their protean nature continuously adjusts to their immediate interactive context, improvising as they adjust to new situations. Creolization can thus liberate us conceptually from a notion of fixed or "finished" products in culture, whether purportedly "hybrid" or whole. We are freed to focus on cultures in transition, allowing us to grasp the "in-betweens," the ambiguous spaces where cultural boundaries blur and disappear as hierarchical categories collapse into each other. At these interstices in creole societies, groups and individuals combine and restructure cultural entities, thus imagining and formulating Creole expressive forms that defy placement within external analytical categories.

This dynamism in Creole communities, and the impossibility of absolute cultural transparency in favor of fluidity, blurring, and obfuscation, led in the past to the characterization of Creole forms and behavior by outsiders as "impure" (see Szwed, this volume). Too often, Creole expressions have been viewed as manifestations of fragmentation and degeneration, thereby suffering in comparison to supposedly fully formed, reified, and historically sanctioned expressions of a colonial or "Westernized" elite. In sharp contrast, creolists see creolization as creative disorder, as a poetic chaos, thereby challenging simplistic and static notions of center and periphery. The cultural and critical lens of creolization, in other words, allows us to see not simply hybrids of limited fluidity, abstracted from human agency, but new cultures in the making.

Creolization is most vividly manifested and represented in the expressive forms and artistic behaviors of everyday and ceremonial life as folklore. Although creole forms have often become the symbols and instruments of nationalist interests and particular political agendas, the actuality of Creole folklore in lived experience demonstrates that creolization cannot be reduced to an artificial construct, singularly imposed from above by the post-colonial nation state. Everywhere you look in the Caribbean, much of Latin America, southern Louisiana, and the southwest Indian Ocean region, you will find creolized musics, foods, hairstyles, verbal arts, sports, dances, customary behaviors, belief systems, rituals, ceremonies, festivals, material culture, and so much more, thereby rendering idle the question, "Why study creolization?" Jazz, salsa, or calypso; ways of worshipping and making sense of the world through Santería or Vodou; Old World pastries filled with New World fruits and Creole gumbos; the tango, the mambo, the samba; shotgun houses and vernacular architecture informed by Gothic and Baroque models rendered in tropical versions; not to mention the emergence of formerly unheard languages and the verbal art that creolization brings into being—these only begin to eloquently answer this question. To attempt to name all of the expressive manifestations of creolity would fail as an enterprise. For, in every Creole society, writers and artists of all kinds continuously create works of art grounded in, and infused with, Creole expressive culture.

In the expressive interaction shaping Creole forms, a diverse repertoire of strategies are put into play that characterize Creole intercourse: reversals, carnivalization, improvisation, mimicry, obfuscation, double-talk, feigned submission, and many other maneuvers, tactics, and schemes designed to steal power away from "top-down" monolithic impositions. The creolization process is marked by multivocal play throughout a society's cultural manifestations, making possible, as Derek Walcott has indicated, the creation of new expressive forms unlike anything the world had ever seen! (Walcott 1974, 9).

To understand creolization, we must see it on its own terms, recognize its inner workings, and comprehend how it is conceptualized by native scholars, creolist literati, and everyday culture bearers. Indeed, we must recognize that there is no one creolity or single way of being Creole, as several of the contributors to this volume observe, but rather unique creole manifestations that express and represent creole communities around the globe, thereby underscoring the emic dimension of Creole cultures and their expressive forms. Though the creolization process and the dynamics of creolization have common features across the world, each Creole community or nation is shaped and conditioned by different local colonial and post-colonial histories, demography, geography, politics, economics, religious forces, and other influences.

Because of the predominantly face-to-face interaction that brings about creolization, creolity or creoleness is an insider's culture, most commonly (though not exclusively) defined and expressed beyond the gaze of outsiders. At times a "secret" or "masked" culture during periods of conquest and colonization, it is intimate, it is the home culture, the native culture of a people voicing alternative ways of being to those imposed hegemonically by colonial powers and elite cultural forces. Formulated and enacted by folks who historically lacked political power yet aimed to establish autonomy, Creole cultural forms have often been subversive social and political tools. Frequently masking as the dominant other and often provoking and defying elite or dominant powers through mockery, irony, humor, and other subversive measures, Creole formulations nevertheless remain intimately grounded and entwined in the everyday exigencies of their own Creole communities. In this respect, Creole enactments are counterhegemonic in their challenge to cultural dominance, making creolity nothing but revolutionary.

Creolization has always been closely tied to folklore and other forms of artistic production as the creative response of peoples from multiple cultural communities coming in contact with each other. Through creolization, subaltern cultural communities resisted the imposition of mechanistic, systematizing, standardizing norms from official, politically dominant cultures. Without ceasing to be a political force grounded historically and geographically, the success of creolization lies in its native poetic response—in the integrative ethic and aesthetic capacity of communities to confront conflict and harmonize disorder, even if in a subversive manner. Creolization offers scholars and artists in many disciplines a dynamic and contextual base from which to understand culture contact from within and from "below" through the expressive forms of emergent communities, as well as from ongoing, traditional communities that identify with and perpetuate their local or national Creole values.

Being or behaving creole, *criollo*, or *créole* is an outlook on the world in cultures self-identified as Creole—a way of saying who we are as a people. As such, creoleness is also a style, a way or manner of doing things that characterize a community or nation, as exemplified in many of the essays included here.

Although as a concept creolization is increasingly universalized as a key term for practices or means through which cultures meet and create new expressive forms, not all creolists and scholars of creolization agree about whether creolization should be universalized beyond its deeply evocative, politically resonant, and subversive local meanings in Creole societies. These divergent views are reflected in the perspectives of the contributors to this volume. Those who contend that the phenomenon of creolization should be seen as restricted to self-ascribed Creole societies argue that the universalizing view dilutes the political potency of the term "creolization" for societies where "Creole" is constitutive of identity and cultural self-determination, and creolization is a pervasive cultural process. There is an exceptionalism to the Caribbean basin, southwest Indian Ocean region, and much of Latin America that especially suits the concept of creolization. The Caribbean region, as Stuart Hall puts it, is a place where, "after the first century of conquest, all the social forces which created plantation societies came from 'somewhere else.' They did not 'originally' belong" (2003a, 33). The social forces in the Caribbean, Hall notes, were "'conscripted,' whether they wanted to be or not, to a process of indigenization" (33). Hall sees creolization as a process of "'indigenization,' which prevents any of the constituent elements—either colonizing or colonized—from preserving their purity or authenticity" (34). Hall asks whether the "expanded concept" of creolization has "moved so far as to have destroyed all the richness and specificity present in its first, more concrete application" (27).

The term "criollo" (creole) has been employed in the Americas since the sixteenth century, when new, emergent populations and cultures used the rubric to identify and thus distinguish themselves from the European and African Old World cultures and from indigenous cultures. Sidney Mintz stresses that in the Caribbean, creolization "stood for centuries of culture building rather than cultural mixing or cultural blending, by those who became Caribbean people. They were not becoming transnational; they were creating forms by which to live, even while they were being cruelly tested physically and mentally" (1998, 119).

In the universalizing view, creolization as cultural process has the potential to occur anywhere cultures meet in expressive interaction. These interactions are progressively more frequent in this age of globalization as migrations, trade, diasporas, and virtual, electronic communication in cyberspace generate ever more diverse communities and create new and unprecedented affiliations between peoples at an ever-accelerating pace. Creolization in the Caribbean is seen by some as modeling a contemporary global phenomenon. According to Robin Cohen and Paola Toninato, creolization in the Caribbean has been seen as a "master metaphor for comparable historical experiences in other societies and a prefiguring of what was taking place in the contemporary world, where mass migration, increased connectivity, tourism and other aspects of what we can loosely call cultural globalization have breached prior frontiers of identity" (2010, 5). Proponents of the universalizing approach to creolization offer

compelling visions of disparate or apparently incongruent potential relations and creolized boundaries and frontiers worldwide, wherein a plu-
rivocal and genuinely multicultural world might exist on a global scale.
Ulf Hannerz (1987), for example, has spoken of "the world in creolisation"
and sees creolization as a valuable universal concept necessary for a world
constructed on exclusive and racialist terms and marked by constant cultural encounters.[2] Viranjini Munasinghe characterizes Hannerz's view of
the "creole" as "a way of framing global processes associated with heterogeneity, interconnections, and creativity" (2006, 551). Edouard Glissant's
writings also speak to this new globalizing approach. Both in his fiction
and his critical works Glissant's *pensée rhizome* (rhizomous thinking)—
inspired in good measure by Félix Guattari's model of cultural identity—
moves toward a grand vision of the "tout-monde" (Glissant 1993, 1997).

Creolization, a concept so well equipped to handle multiplicity, is itself
conceptualized in multiple ways and used in a variety of discourses about
local and global phenomena. Aisha Khan recognizes the varying conceptualizations of the term "creolization," both on the ground and in academic
discourse, underscoring its instrumental rather than expressive dimension.
She contends that "creolization is basically a floating signifier—a flexible
concept that, despite its common recognition, is interpreted in different
ways in particular relations of power, delivering multiple messages and
being put to many uses: by states to foster certain expressions of nationalist ideology, by scholars, artists and activists to make interventions into
dominant epistemologies in the preparation of new foundational futures,
and by local actors to make more of conditions not of their own making"
(Khan 2007a, 665). Munasinghe sees different conceptualizations of creolization as interacting with one another, with "the term creole operating
in three discursive modes—the lay, the academic, and the political—and
these modes collapsing in on each other at different historical moments"
(2006, 556). As folklorists, we believe that there should be a primary distinction in creolization studies between creolization (whether in academic
or lay discourse) as a phenomenon characteristic of self-ascribed Creole
societies and their native categories of "Creole" cultural forms and processes and creolization as a metaphor or a critical concept applicable to
cultural interactions that occur throughout the world.

Creolization has much to offer folkloristics, which has often been ste-
reotyped as a field centered upon the study of homogeneous, discrete
cultures and their expressive products.[3] A creolization perspective has
engaged, and can continue to engage, folklore more deeply with cultural

complexity, fluidity, ambiguity, and the margins of culture. The dual concerns of creolization with emergence and cultural sources are also highly congenial to folklore studies, engaged since its earliest days with transmission, origins, creativity, native genres, and the dynamics of tradition and innovation.

Conversely, the field of folklore lends valuable insight to our understanding of creolization. The folk practices and other kinds of popular expressive interactions occurring through everyday exchanges and grassroots connections—as opposed to cultural practices which take place in more official or institutional venues—provide arenas for small group negotiations of cultural differences and offer expressive frameworks within which to improvise cultural change, contest dissimilarities, relate divergences, expand or create new cultural expressions, give voice to multivocal interests, and tolerate layers of meaning embodied in a single expressive form. At the same time, Creole encounters simultaneously buttress the local traditional scaffoldings that allow each of the interacting cultures to subsist and maintain their integrity throughout the creolization process and in the resulting new, creolized articulations. Similarly, the contemporary arts (in literature, drama, musical compositions, the plastic arts, choreographed dance, architecture, fashion, to name a few) follow the lead of folklore and also integrate into their creative endeavors new Creole perspectives, thus redefining and creolizing cultures through their aesthetics. In this manner, through both the creative space of everyday folk practices as well as the more staged and stylized arenas of the fine arts, creolity declares its own manifesto: its own politics, its own history (memory), its own poetics and values. Accordingly, Snoopy is no longer (merely) Snoopy, but a guardian and memorialization of deceased loved ones, as Grey Gundaker reveals in her essay in this volume; and the voice—and shape—of the Gumbe square drum, as Kenneth Bilby traces in this volume, survives across space, time, and unimaginable adversity.

As the essays in this volume illustrate, each author's perspective on creolization places folklore and other kinds of expressive interactions at the nexus of culture in formation, rather than as epiphenomena at the periphery of what is deemed important in society and culture. During the last several years, some anthropologists have critiqued creolization both as an analytic concept and as an empirically verifiable phenomenon. These critiques have often focused abstractly upon political and social institutions or the use of the rhetoric of creolization as a tool of political domination, rather than closely examining through an ethnographic lens the on-the-ground processes of cultural formation and representation through expressive culture. Nevertheless, it behooves us to consider seriously the recent critiques of the concept of creolization, bearing in mind its merits and limitations as we offer our defense and affirmation of its analytic and empirical value.

Contemporary critics of creolization see the extrapolation of cultural creolization processes from the creolization of language as unwarranted and contest the theorization of creolization based upon linguistic models. While we acknowledge the value of the linguistic paradigm, which sees the emergence of new, restructured languages growing out of the encounters of two or more peoples in creole societies, we also recognize that the linguistic model has limitations as the exclusive model for cultural creolization. To be sure, it is problematic to assume that linguistic change is determinative of or parallels cultural change. Criticizing "theoretical borrowings" from linguistics to the study of creolization, Stephan Palmié asserts that linguistics should not be used as what Charles Briggs (2002, quoted by Palmié) calls a "magic bullet" for studies of "cultural creolization" (Palmié 2006, 445). The historical sequence assumed in the past regarding the development of creole languages from pidgins (trade vernaculars) is now questioned by linguists, and such assumptions may be viewed today as inherently speculative and overly schematized, with scant possibility for solid justification through the historical record (see Palmié 2006, 444–446; Harris and Rampton 2002; Jourdan 1991; and McWhorter 2000). It is also worth underscoring that language is but one of many expressive means in creolization. Indeed, the expressive *use* of languages to indicate creolity is at least as important as its formal features.

Consequently, rather than embracing outright the more schematic, formal linguistic model uncritically applied to culture, we consider more fruitful the perspectives and tools offered by the ethnography of communication from sociolinguistic research. This approach better addresses the expressive and improvisatory quality of Creole cultures and emphasizes social interaction as much as formal structure, also stressing performance competence. It further accounts for a community's expressive, stylistic, or aesthetic dimensions, the values that inform these, and the social actors communicating with one another in culturally specific speech acts, events, and situations—thus adhering to the premise that there is no language without culture. As Dell Hymes prophetically stated in the early 1970s, "the future of sociolinguistics lies in a . . . concern with the structure of variation, not for its own sake, but as part of human adaptation. It would be a part of the general problem of the social sciences, the maintenance and transformation of social and symbolic order" (Hymes 1971, 5).

Unlike fifteen years ago, when most scholarship couldn't talk about creolization without referring to linguistics, today the uncritical application of linguistic models is largely absent from creolization studies. Creolization substantially informs a remarkably large variety of disciplines, each of which, in turn, embraces creolization within its own disciplinary paradigms. These disciplines include anthropology, Caribbean studies, cultural geography, cultural studies, ethnomusicology, Francophone studies, law, economics, languages and literature, Latin American studies, social history and sociology, as well as folklore and linguistics.

Another criticism of creolization sees it as an emic phenomenon and questions its value as an analytic category. Charles Stewart, for instance, states, "The creole idea has become more of an epigrammatic than an analytic concept" (Stewart 2007, 6). As folklorists, we know not only that our disciplinary theories are largely derived from observing actual behavior in context, but that native categories, folk conceptualizations of the world and their society, and local aesthetic standards produced by the communities we study yield insights and lay theories as important and indispensable as those produced in the ivory towers.

On the other hand, looking at Creole societies exclusively from above has led some critics to stress the use of creolization as an ideological vehicle, manipulated by the nation state for the ends of social and political control and self-interested nationalist ideologies. While, certainly, creolity has at times been used and abused by nationalistic interests, our own research and experiences throughout the Caribbean and Latin America, and those of other contributors to this volume, indicate that peoples, performances, and material culture are repeatedly (self) defined as "Creole" by community members, thus legitimating this native and ever-mutable category. By the same token, it is important to recognize the widely varying meanings of "Creole" throughout its history. As Raquel Romberg points out in this volume, "'Creole,' things Creole, and 'creolization' have become contested terrains not only in academic circles but also within native contexts, reflecting the often contradictory sociopolitical local meanings (e.g., racist, developmental, modernist, or conciliatory) they have gathered during colonization, nation-building, and postcolonial processes." And we well know, in the case of the Caribbean, a "callaloo society," an "all ah we is one" projection of identity is contradicted to various degrees by conflicts between peoples; and Creole encounters may, at times, be asymmetrical and dominated by one or more contributing cultures, as Daniel J. Crowley (1957) noted early on and subsequent scholars have also indicated (see Khan 2007b). To be sure, creole cultural encounters happen all the time, decisively shaping society and culture, with the social actors engaged in creole encounters selectively accepting and rejecting aspects of each other's cultures.

Another well-known critique targets the notion that creolization is an elite phenomenon, promulgated and promoted by an elite literati and intelligentsia (notably in purportedly decreolized Martinique), rather than a multi-layered, dialogic, widespread phenomenon that serves the interest of a range of cultural communities (see Palmié 2006, 442-443, Price and Price 1997). Moreover, such a critique does not adequately recognize that a local phenomenon or a grassroots occurrence cannot have an intellectual counterpart interested in affirming cultural independence from the metropoles by responding to, and within, a native, Creole poetics. Furthermore, the plethora of Creole cultural forms, often explicitly called "Creole," provides abundant evidence to counter the view that creolization is an exclusively elite concept or practice.

Naturally, no introduction to our volume can possibly address all the exciting, provocative, and creative work and research relating to Creole cultures and creolization that scholars, artists, and practitioners of tradition have produced in the past half century and continue to produce today. Instead, we focus here upon how creolization is manifested through expressive culture—especially folklore and literature—through case studies and analyses by folklorists, anthropologists, ethnomusicologists, and literary scholars.

Particularly inspiring, as we first embarked on this project, were our conversations with the late Daniel J. Crowley, whose continuous work on cultural creolization reaches back to the 1950s. In his classic article "Plural and Differential Acculturation in Trinidad" (published in 1957), Crowley demonstrates how, within a social structure organized around contested hierarchies of class and color, groups are distinct from one another yet not sealed off in a "functionally exclusive" or "watertight" manner as has been depicted by social scientists of the 1950s and 1960s. Rather, they maintain selective knowledge of each other's cultures and are often engaged in each other's cultural activities. The cultural domination of Afro-Trinidadians results in other groups "partially acculturated" or "creolized" to the dominant culture. At the same time, through engaging in each other's folklore, speaking a shared Creole language whose lexicon is drawn from the various groups, participating in each other's folk traditions by maintaining syncretic folk beliefs and through sexual relations, Trinidadians learn each other's culture as well as their own. Crowley, like contemporary scholars of creolization, emphasizes that creolization involves selective acceptance or rejection of aspects of one another's culture through a process he calls "differential acculturation." In Trinidad, Crowley asserts, "each individual and each group has been Creolized to a greater or lesser degree in one or another aspect of his culture, while at the same time preserving inviolate the traits and complexes of his parent culture or cultures" (1957, 824).

Over the centuries, significations of "the Creole" have varied substantially, with some notions fundamentally opposed to others. This volume opens with broad historical perspectives provided by John F. Szwed. He points out that for colonizers, defenders of the arts of dominant groups and others favoring purportedly "whole" cultures, creolization—and many other terms for the meeting of unrelated cultures and the new forms that emerge—long signified impure and inferior forms of expression. This perspective is associated with a discredited linkage of race and culture, which has produced terms for racial intermixing to describe the pollution and degradation that result when cultural forms are changed through contact between social groups—especially in circumstances of political domination. The radically different perspective of creolization's proponents transvalues into cultural assets the multiplicity and ambiguity of these mixed, emergent forms, affirming what Szwed sees as the transformative and complex possibilities of culture. He contrasts a single-frame, monologic point of view with the production of new meaning. The openness that goes along with emergent forms and their multiplicity of codes, voices, styles, meanings, and identities shapes movements that cross social levels and strata to achieve new, radical artistic and political ends. Creolization enables us to see cultural encounters as a process of continuous creative exchange. Received views of purity and impurity become less clear-cut, as Szwed asks, with Creole-like ambiguity, if something new is purer than the old, or if it is the essence of corruption.

Creole cultures are worlds at once deeply local and articulated to ever-widening spheres. Nick Spitzer relates how in southern Louisiana Creoles self-identify as *"monde Créole,"* a "small world" that maintains a strong local identity even as it interacts with other small worlds, creolizing from within and in relation to one another on local, regional, national, and global levels. Neither conventionally "Black" nor "White," Creoles in southern Louisiana defy the received idea of a South where African- and European-derived cultures are rigidly separated. They provide a counterexample to commonplace views of diverse, putatively bounded ethnic groups that undergird the premises of both the melting pot and multiculturalism. The Creole folk expressive forms cited by Spitzer—notably, zydeco—lack the "purity" of idealized folk culture and are paradigms of creolization in their multiplicity of sources. In Spitzer's view, creolization is both a local and global phenomenon, critically important for both the continuity and transformation of society and culture. The transformative power of creolization has been particularly palpable in the years since Hurricane Katrina. In the epilogue included here he demonstrates how the local New Orleans community drew upon its own cultural resources while forging new relationships through creolization with New Orleanians from other cultural backgrounds, thereby becoming an indispensable force in the revitalization and recovery of the city.

Creolization brings together old and new, whether or not historical sources are consciously recognized. Grey Gundaker discusses how objects are appropriated by African Americans to memorialize lost loved ones and act as "watcher" guardians that "keep ancestral presences alive." These objects, exemplified in a Snoopy dog figure, have been mislabeled and trivialized as "toys" by outside observers who failed to see their spiritual significance and recognize their serious purpose. She indicates that the African Americans whose practices she discusses do not verbally articulate historical sources—some things, she notes, are "done" rather than "said"—as "echoes of past uses" are invoked in new contexts. The practices described by Gundaker embody the "mixture, emergence, performance, and flexibility" characteristic of creolization. Drawing from Kamau Brathwaite's concept of "negative creolization," entailing rejection of influences from the "other" and a turning toward aspects of an ancestral culture that maintain a group's distinctive identity, she describes creolizing practices that both "mix" and "hold back." Gundaker contrasts the "notion of cultural buckets" with a "fixed corpus of elements" with a fluid approach to creolization, where "multiple resources [are] deployed ever on the fly."

In regions of the Americas that experienced Spanish and Portuguese colonization, the ritual practices of the Roman Catholic Church were appropriated within emergent, creolized belief systems. Coining the term "ritual piracy," Raquel Romberg shows how Puerto Rican *brujos* creatively and "illicitly" transmute Catholic religious symbols and practices for their own purposes. Like other contributors to this volume, she employs a processual approach, focusing upon "production," seen as "processes and power relations," instead of analyzing "end products" apart from the processes that shaped them. In discussing the mimesis occurring in *bru-jería*, Romberg demonstrates that rather than involving the naïve and failed imitation implicit in V. S. Naipaul's mimic men and other distortions by colonial and neocolonial critics of Creole cultures, "sacred mimesis" involves a "simultaneous acceptance and rejection of metropolitan powers." Contesting the view of some scholars of syncretism who contend that the use of Catholicism in Vodou, Candomblé, and Santería was an "ecumenical screen" to conceal the worship of African deities in order to avoid persecution, Romberg reframes it as "the religion of the colonizers: revised, transformed, and appropriated by the oppressed to harness its power within their universes of discourse."

Recent scholarship on Afro-Atlantic cultures has shown that the circulation of cultures has long flowed in both directions between the Americas and Africa. While Africa serves as a baseline for cultures of African heritage in the Americas, New World Black cultures experiencing creolization on this side of the Atlantic have also influenced the culture of the motherland for over two centuries. In his fine-grained study of the adaptation of the Jamaican Maroon Gumbe drum in Africa, Kenneth Bilby discusses how Maroons forcibly removed from Jamaica to Nova Scotia at the end of the eighteenth century brought this drum, its music, and associated traditions to Sierra Leone in 1800. He draws from his earlier research on the topic, as well as the work of Barbara Hampton (1977, 1979–1980, 1983), Jean Rouch (1961), Judith Bettelheim (1979, 310–319), John Collins (2007), Flemming Harrev (2001), and other scholars who researched the diffusion of Gumbe in Africa and the varieties of Gumbe-related musical practice. Bilby discusses how the Gumbe continues to influence African music to this day. Gumbe, "Africa's Creole drum," and its traditions are seen as paradigmatic of continuity and change in creolization. It is both a "fluid social process occurring over time" and a "culture phenomenon [that] always entails some degree of continuity with multiple pasts."

The continuous creative exchange of creolization is made palpable through specific techniques at play in the performance and publication of folklore. Lee Haring demonstrates how these verbal devices work in the Creole societies found in islands of the Southwest Indian Ocean, where African, Asian Indian, and European cultures have interacted since the colonial period. These strategies of creolization include language-mixing, reported speech, framing one story in another, changes in referential content and scene, and parody. As Creole rhetorical dynamics, they serve to indirectly code covert messages with subversive power, much like the folklore of Creole societies half a world away in the Americas. These devices occur in both oral and written media. Oral narrators, collectors, and writers engage in complementary processes of creation, performance, collection, and rewriting that all contribute to the creolization of folktales. In the transition from oral to written text, replication, elaboration, revision, simulation, and the invention of new tales based upon oral folklore are predominant creolization strategies.

Cultures that seem Europeanized on their surface may actually be deeply Creole, masked by camouflages that are themselves "tricks" of creolization. Ana C. Cara reveals Argentina as an exemplar of how creolity is exposed abundantly through folklore and in literature. She discusses the poetics of "Creole talk," existing independently of a full-fledged Creole language, that relays a pervasive Argentine Creole dynamics—it is found in everyday speech, a wide range of folk genres, Argentina's national epic poem, and modernist, groundbreaking writers like Jorge Luis Borges. Cara identifies a Creole style that is integral to Argentine cultural ethos and aesthetics, less concerned with *who* is inherently creole but with *how* and *when* creolity is performed.

Written literature, like folklore and religion, reveals creolization in action. Francophone Caribbean writers render cultural encounters with extraordinary expressive power and remarkable insights about how creolization happens "on the ground" in everyday life. J. Michael Dash employs the conceit of the crossroads to highlight the central role of urban space and its margins in Caribbean creolization. He argues that urban spaces are not zones of alienation and exile but ideal creolizing sites of contemporary transnational contact celebrated in literature, resonating within and beyond the Caribbean. Remarking on the dynamism of Haitian Vodou in the capital (noted by Alfred Métraux) and examining the ethnography and poetics of the *ville* and its *carrefours* (documented by Michel Leiris), Dash goes on to discuss the works of writers who include Edouard Glissant, Magloire St. Aude, Jacques Stephen Alexis, Patrick Chamoiseau, Simone Schwarz-Bart, Ina Césaire, Maryse Condé, and Dany Laferrière. He contrasts the Creole unpredictability and risk of contact and collision in the crossroads space central in certain works with a more nostalgic outlook in others, where the preservation of cultural oppositions seems to duplicate the plantation.

Creolization is a Janus-like process, emergent as it creates something new while embodying references to its historical sources. Robert Baron contends that creolization, like folkloristics, conjoins the analysis of form, content, and process. Baron views Melville J. Herskovits as a proto-creolist who employed both metaphor and schematic social scientific explanations to create a conceptual framework for the study of acculturation and cultural change, based upon his research with New World Black cultures. Contemporary creolists and Herskovits have both used metaphor to convey cultural transformation. Herskovits's metaphors represented various patterns of combination of cultural forms and their transmutation into new entities where cultural elements of different provenance may continue to exist. He also developed the concepts of syncretism and reinterpretation, referring to the reconciliation of cultural elements and beliefs from cultures in contact with one another and the processes that give old meanings to new forms and retain old forms with new meanings.

Roger D. Abrahams believes that universalizing creolization to conceptualize cultural processes occurring anywhere dilutes its power as a folk concept, anchored in the highly specific histories of peoples who experienced conquest, colonial oppression, and slavery. He discusses how Carnival and similar Creole festivals in the New World are infused with historical memory, as "serious play" that incorporates revelry along with the replaying of formative events and foundational stories. Abrahams argues that creolization is best understood through expressive behavior occurring in the "in-between" realm of the marketplace and through festivals where rage, resilience, and cultural adaptability all come together in a cauldron of creativity. These spectacular, improvisatory events refer to a mythologized Africa as well as the experiences of conquest, vanquishment, slavery, and emancipation. For Abrahams, creolization should be seen within the context of historically specific processes of cultural construction. In discussing a current expansive view of creolization, he argues against conflating "cosmopolitanism" and creolization in the rendering of relationships between the local and the global.

Creolization is a powerful concept, whether limited to cultures self-identified as "Creole" and forged through encounters among multiple cultural communities or employed as an exceptionally apt transcultural term for expressive interactions occurring anywhere in an increasingly globalized and hyperconnected world. Regardless of whether one views creolization as a culturally specific or global concept, we see through the abundance of examples in this volume how through creolization expressive forms emerge, at once creating something new and different while sustaining two or more divergent (and even contradictory) traditions that come in contact as people from different cultures interact with one another.

Contrasting sharply with notions of romantic nationalism, so often associated with folklore studies of the past, the concept of creolization resonates with us as folklorists today, letting in new air by moving scholarship away from the celebration of creative genius as expressed only through traditions associated with discrete, rather than with fluid and emergent, cultures. Recognizing creolization as a pervasive vernacular phenomenon forced us in the early 1970s to let go of the now outdated view of cultures as "coherent" and "whole" entities abstracted from encounters with other cultures. It broadened our views of traditional expressive cultures, revealing how they are decisively shaped and creatively reinvigorated through creolization, opening up new vistas in the spaces between cultures. As a result, the study of folklore has disabused itself of blinkered conceptions of authenticity associated with the romantic conceptualization of "authentic culture" as "rooted in a place" (see Eriksen [2003] 2010, 73).

Nevertheless, we must maintain a critical eye on creolization as a model, as Abrahams reminds us in his essay, by looking empirically at how creolization takes place in everyday life. We must be ready to embrace cultural contradictions, blurred genres, contrapuntal and dialogic exchanges between notions of "high" and "low," and numerous other apparent incongruities. Like the concrete phenomenon of creolization itself, we must welcome the destabilization of tidy, discrete notions of culture and explore the extraordinary resourcefulness and creativity that emerge through and from the processes of creolization.

Notes

1. Listing the "localities where people . . . have been called 'creole' (or called themselves thus)," Palmié includes, in addition to the Caribbean and "much of Latin America, . . . parts of the southeastern United States (and Alaska) several island groups off the Atlantic and Pacific coast of Africa, a number of mainland regions on that continent (including Sierra Leone, Equatorial Guinea, Angola, and Mozambique) and a few pockets in the former Portuguese and Dutch colonial spheres in southeast Asia" (Palmié 2006, 435).

2. Hannerz acknowledges the particular significance of the concept of creolization for creole societies but contends that as a "travelling concept" it can "contribute something of value to a cosmopolitan imagination, and that anthropology, not least in its more public version, can play a part in promoting that, even as anthropologists stay

conscious of the fact that something (e.g., detail or subtlety) is likely to be lost in the transition from the sociocultural context of origin" (2006, 564–565).

3. Anthropologists (even when writing critically about creolization) recognize the significance of creolization as a concept suited to a shift in their discipline from the study of putatively "whole" and homogenous cultures, as Palmié indicates:

If the societies and cultures of the Caribbean never quite fit the "savage slot" (Trouillot 1991) so crucial for the development of anthropology's disciplinary identity—if they were never quite "other" enough, but rather perceived as odd and largely uninteresting "hybrid" formations then it should not come as much of a surprise that once we began to abandon the strategies of epistemic purification that had once underwritten our intellectual practice (Latour 1993; compare Maurer 1997, Palmié 2002) their former "hybrid" irrelevance to the discipline's central concerns instantly transformed as well. Once regarded as insufficiently differentiated from the "West" to warrant ethnographic attention, just such attention to the "creolized" cultures of the Caribbean now seems to be warranted, not because these cultures have become any more different from ours in the meantime, but because we feel ours are becoming increasingly similar to theirs: . . . a densely rhizomatic mangrove of potentialities (Bernabé et al. 1989, Glissant 1989) that irreversibly dissolves all rooted certainties into contingent routes toward indeterminate cultural futures (Clifford 1997). (Palmié 2006, 436)

Metaphors of Incommensurability

—JOHN F. SZWED

Notes is good enough for you people, but us likes a mixtery.
—JEANETTE ROBINSON MURPHY,
"The Survival of African Music in America"

The old Black woman who gave Jeanette Robinson Murphy an account of how spirituals were created reminds us that it is "mixture" that lurks behind the vast array of words that have been used over the last four hundred years to describe the processes and products of cultural contact in the Americas and elsewhere in the world: words like *nomadism, deterritorialization, transnationalism, modernism,* and *postmodernism,* all of which attempt to characterize some of the conditions under which people come into contact and produce new cultural forms; or *marronage, border culture, heterogeneity, cosmopolitanism, multiculturalism,* and *pluralism,* terms used to name the social results of such encounters, results that social scientists have also called *trans-culturalization, oppositional culture,* or *contra-acculturation.*

These are only a small part of a field of terminology that is rich to the point of obsession, an obsession that perhaps thinly disguises the fear that race and culture are inextricably—perhaps even causally—linked, a fetishization that sees things, like people, in the process of dissolving and reforming before the eyes. Despite the refutation of just such a linkage by anthropologists since the time of Boas, terms for racial intermixing are still used to describe the pollution and degradation that result when cultural forms are changed through contact between social groups (especially those in which one group is dominant), terms such as *mongrelization, bastardization, corruption, métisage,* or *mestizaje,* and the recent more polite or ironic terms, *symbiosis* and *hybrid.* But this is the terminology of those who speak from positions of dominance; the view from the bottom often yields quite different terms, such as the food and cooking metaphors *gumbo, callaloo, massala,* and *sancocho,* or those of violence and disruption, like *broke-up,* or of mock or transvalued opprobrium, like *bad.* Similarly, the defenders of the arts of the dominant describe the products of the contact between what they perceive as high and low arts as *pastiche, macaronic, aping,* or at best, as *mimicry, ventriloquism, parody,* and *mockery.* (But compare how the same individuals speak of the arts that result from contact of peoples of relatively equal social status, especially across national lines; the words are *borrowing, influence, loan,* and so on.) It is only among the more radical and political elements of the art worlds of the West that we find terms such as *bricolage, détournement, montage, fusion,* and *collage,* words that originally surfaced in art movements like dada, surrealism, and lettrism and that attempt to complicate the nature and sources of creativity. (That those very art movements may also have been inspired by products of such cultural contact should at least be noted in passing.)

In the Americas the oldest known term for these processes is *creole,*[1] itself apparently created in creole fashion from the Portuguese *criar* (to bring up) and *crioulo* (native) and who-knows-what-else and merged into a term with both adjectival and noun forms. The discourse of creolization has continued now for four centuries, an ongoing dialogue that remains remarkably open and inviting of participation. The concept of creole has been used across a great deal of geographical and intellectual territory in the New World (and to a lesser degree even in parts of the Old World). From Cotton Mather's description of Harvard graduates ("shining criolians") to the offspring of Russians and Aleuts in the Bering Strait, from the children of French planters in Louisiana to the children of newly arrived slaves, the concept has always meant a new product, something emergent, something else. It has been fought over and claimed by various peoples, and as such retains a certain residual ambiguity and variability. It has referred to foods, spices, clothing, language, architecture, literature, and styles, as well as to individuals and entire races; it has been said to be an impure state of being, but also the purest state possible. (Is something new purer than the old, or is it the essence of corruption?) But in whatever way it has been used, it has raised questions about the appropriateness of such concepts as "descent," "origins," and the very status of *being* itself.

In spite of a long and widespread history of the folk use of the idea of creole, academic thinking on creolization has until very recently been focused primarily on Afro-Caribbean and African American populations, and more often than not on the languages of these peoples. Some of the highlights of this academic work deserve at least a brief overview, since it has given us our clearest and most sustained view of the concept of creolization, one that ultimately raises fundamental questions about the nature of language and even society itself.

A Brief History

Melville J. Herskovits ([1941] 1958) conceptualized the relations between African and European cultures with a set of processual terms, the key one of which was *reinterpretation*, a concept refined out of an earlier African Americanist concept, *syncretism*. Where *syncretism* was used to describe the situation within which African cultural forms fused with European forms of similar configuration, *reinterpretation* encompassed situations in which a cultural form from one society could be given another society's function or value, or in which a newer alien form could be assimilated to elder functions and values. (The classic case of reinterpretation is the joining of African deities to Catholic saints in Haiti, Brazil, Trinidad, and elsewhere.) Herskovits saw this process as describing the reinterpretation of African forms into European terms. It could work both ways, however, as Alfred Métraux, in *Voodoo in Haiti* (1959), seemed to imply that imposed European forms and values were reinterpreted into African forms and functions.

To this notion of reinterpretation, the linguist Douglas Taylor—himself a native of Dominica in the West Indies—added the concept of *remodeling*, a notion apparently borrowed from classical philology. The essence of this idea was that forms are not only reinterpreted, but also gradually changed and transformed to resemble their cultural environment—African words come to seem Portuguese, Portuguese to seem English, English to seem Dutch, and so on. In an example, Taylor (1964, 436) traced the transformation of the early Surinam maroon language Saramaccan word *sinda* (sit) into *sindo*, the modern Saramaccan word with the same meaning, to *sidon*, the Sranan (the Surinam Creole) term with equivalent meaning. Positing a missing form, *sindon*, the evolutionary sequence then becomes this: sinda > sindo > * sindon > sidon.

Assuming that the original *sinda*, like Haitian Créole *sita* and the Dutch West Indies Papiamentu *sinta*, has its roots in Ibero-Romance (Ptg.

assentar, Sp. sentar, Ptg. Sp. *sentado*), *sidon* ends up resembling the English "sit down." The problem that this presents for historical linguistics is this: At what point did the word change its genetic relationship? That is, at what point did it change from Portuguese to English?

Karl Reisman (1970) later articulated the dynamics of remodeling and reinterpretation as a constant creative process in relations between creole language and lexically similar European languages, permitting a given element, motif, or syllable to take on one cultural garb and context of meaning or another, but to also oscillate (not simply switch) unclearly between forms; he introduced the term *transvaluation* for the point where these movements occur. Reisman put this process within a context of the duality of cultural identities, a theme elaborated by Black writers in the Caribbean and the United States (the theme of *masking* and *doubleness* in writings by W. E. B. Du Bois, Ralph Ellison, and George Lamming) as well as by folklorists (Roger D. Abrahams [1983] on tea meeting in the Anglophonic West Indies, and John Szwed and Morton Marks [1988] on set dances).

The Brazilianist Roger Bastide (1960, 388) refined and extended these ideas by distinguishing between material reinterpretations—those that remain and continue on the same cultural level and thus do not profoundly influence modes of thought (to return to an earlier example, African deities and Catholic saints could be considered as existing in a substitutive, masked relationship) and formal reinterpretations, in which forms are comprehended in light of newly acquired values and conceptions (e.g., mystical trance reinterpreted as a form of spiritualism and then used as a means of upward mobility within a national, organized church setting; such a case is Umbanda in Brazil). Bastide noted that the first and more typical form of reinterpretation occurs in segregated social settings, the latter in more "racially democratic" societies (1960, 389–399).

It is important to remind ourselves that all of these African American cultural developments took place either under slavery or in societies at their fringe, the various maroon communities, and that they were shaped by Africans and their descendants. It was the special historical and social complexities of these societies that next needed to be elaborated in order to show the wider social contexts impinging upon them—that is, to develop a historical model of creolization and relate it to cultural process—and Edward Kamau Brathwaite has been at work on this for some thirty-five years, most notably in *Contradictory Omens* (1974b). He notes that much of the analysis of the West Indies has been caught in the trap of dualism, such as White/Black, or colonizer/colonized, while the creative

force of the creole experience (the interchange and transformation of cultural and social elements) has been slighted. Indeed, these dualities may
have blinded many to the emergent and creative qualities of West Indian
life. One thinks of V. S. Naipaul's assertion that "nothing was ever created
in the West Indies and nothing will ever be created," and Derek Walcott's
response, "Nothing will always be created in the West Indies . . . because
what will come out of there is like nothing one has ever seen," a response
that manages to simultaneously transvalue "nothing" into a positive, a
presence rather than an absence, as well as to perhaps present a basis on
which to challenge received notions of art and mimesis (Walcott 1974, 9).
Yet while Brathwaite emphasizes the emergent quality of creole life, he
also insists (possibly to the distress of some anti-essentialists) that there
remains in all parties to the creole experience an engagement with ancestral relationships, with what he calls *nam*, the apparently irreducible core
or essence that coexists with the cosmopolitan and processual qualities
of creolization. And it is the interplay of these factors, he suggests, which
determines the outcome.

Creole Languages

Though the general features of creole languages have been understood for
some time, the descriptions of them typically have been simplistic. In part
this is the result of premature attempts to universalize them through a
typology, as part of a unilinear evolutionary process wherein pidgin languages always turn into Creole languages; and in part it is a consequence
of attempting to over-systemize languages, to reduce their inherent variation in the name of science. The most widely recognized Creole languages
are found in the Caribbean, in parts of South America, the United States,
Sierra Leone, in what are mistakenly called the pidgins of West Africa, the
islands of the Indian Ocean, and early Afrikaans in South Africa. These languages all coexist in a complex relationship with English, Dutch, French,
or Portuguese in the same areas. All these creoles share common features
in verb system, aspect, syllable remodeling, serial verbs, stress and tone
independence, semantic shift in common words, and a heritage of African words and syntax. Though they may be crudely characterized as the
languages of the enslaved or the conquered because of their origins in the
plantation system, they also have the ability to conquer and have become
the ultimate and folkloric languages of Whites in some areas, the vehicular

language of East Indians and Middle Easterners in others, and have been spread through migration and popular culture to the rest of the world.

These creoles are more than the result of the meeting and interaction of European and African languages. They are also the consequences of the encounter of the different styles, forms of expression, and beliefs associated with these languages. And once in place they exist in opposition to—but also overlapping with—the imposed European languages. The creolized forms thus also came to exist in a peculiar relationship between African systems of stylization and means of interpretation of forms and meaning, on one hand, and their European equivalents, on the other. While never fully resolved in this social state, they are realized in an oscillation of forms, a movement back and forth across the Euro-African scale.

What all this adds up to is that linguistic creolization involves the merging and dissolving of language images, the ambiguous play of language forms and meanings, of forms and styles, all decentered, with no clear sense of which language is primary or foregrounded, all maintained under an apparent merging of languages with no apparent fixed boundaries of distinct linguistic systems, or of nonshared syntaxes.

Of course, all languages may be said to exist between the poles of systematic structural features, on the one hand, and contextual adaptation and creation and the varying valences and ranges of individual items of form and meaning, on the other. Yet if grammar or syntax is conceived of as a relation of form and interpretation, creolized languages seem to create unusual amounts of division between formal systems and meanings. In some cases they seem to be able to move in relative independence from each other, leading to the remodeling of new forms, on the one hand, and the reinterpretation of "Afro-" and "Euro-" forms, on the other.

One of the other results of the creole process is a greater ambiguity in the relation of form and meanings, the production of a multiplicity of meanings beyond that found in most languages. Further, the nature of the search for multiplicity seems to carry certain specifically African-style and some specifically Creole-style features and ways of handling and interpreting meaning (thus paralleling Brathwaite's insistence on the continuity of core ancestral values within the creole experience).

Considered as a whole, creole languages provide one instance of human creativity closely resembling what Umberto Eco calls the "open work" of art, a work that offers an unusually high degree of possibilities in the amount of information provided and in the form of ambiguity entailed. It is a creation susceptible "to countless different interpretations which do not impinge upon its unadulterable specificity," and one that makes every reception of it "both an interpretation of it and a performance of it, because in every reception the work takes on a fresh perspective for itself" (Eco 1962, 4). It is this openness, this ambiguity, this emergent quality, which has made art of the Americas in general (and African American art in particular) seem both perpetually modern and a model of the postmodern (Szwed 1992).

Yet open though they may be, creole forms are not completely indeterminate, and in fact often seem to carry with them cues to interpretation, and, by modeling the process in front of us, even provide the means for understanding the processes that gave rise to them. All art may have such interpretive cues built into it, but creole forms cue the observer/listener/ participant into a position that also dislocates a single-frame, monologic point of view, thus virtually assuring the production of new meanings. If we return again to the woman quoted by Jeanette Robinson Murphy (where "mixtery" creolizes "mixture" and "mystery" at the same time as it asserts a contrast between written and nonwritten forms, i.e., "notes" opposed to a "mix"), we see the creolization process demonstrated for us. Think also of W. E. B. Du Bois's opening chapter in *The Souls of Black Folk* (2009 [1938]), where in delineating double-consciousness among African Americans, he converges at least three distinct threads of meaning: the well-established nineteenth-century meaning of double consciousness as an abnormal condition, a form of multiple personality; the revision of that meaning by transcendentalist and European Romantics into the notion of the artist as exemplar of true understanding warring with "the social forces inhibiting genuine self-realization" (as Ralph Waldo Emerson put it); and the African American folk conception of those born with "double vision," those able to see into both the spiritual and material realms (Gundaker 1998, 22–26).[2] Yet Du Bois, like Murphy's anonymous informant, does not belabor the multiplicities or spell out the possibilities, but leaves them floating, open, free to be interpreted by those who could and would do so.

Creolization, whether called by that name or not, has often been a highly conscious process and has served as the locus of new and radical artistic and political developments in a variety of New World areas. There were, for example, the aesthetic proclamations of the Martin Fierro group in Argentina, or the *Anthropophagous Manifesto* of the Brazilian "cannibals" in the 1920s (Bernabé, Chamoiseau, and Confiant 1990). In more recent times developments in the West Indies and Mexico have led to the examination of their own folklore and a reckoning with creolization that has incited political and artistic potential. Over the last thirty years in Martinique, for example, there has been increasing reaction to implications of the literary politics of negritude as articulated in the work of Aimé Césaire. "Antillanité," a position with which Edouard Glissant (1989) is often associated, stresses creativity rather than preservation as a basis for political and artistic activity. And even if those of Glissant's persuasion view their folkloric background ambivalently, they nonetheless draw strength from the transformative and complex possibilities of their culture. Now we see in Martinique a new movement called "créolité" (as represented by Jean Bernabé, Patrick Chamoiseau, Raphaël Confiant, and others), which expresses renewed interest in folklore (especially in the work of their own folklorists) not so much as a means of reconstructing a real or imaginary past, but as a basis for a new creative openness. It offers them a sense that what they have discovered in their own cultural history provides a model for the world, not in timeless values or the Western notion of universality, but in *diversalité*, "the great opportunity of a world diffracted but recomposed, the conscious harmonization of preserved diversities" (Bernabé, Chamoiseau, and Confiant 1990, 903). Such movements provide us with more than opportunities for the study of exotic folklore. They have much to teach us about our own cultural processes.

Creolization, Mixture, or Something Else?

Perhaps creolization is a concept broad enough to serve parallel phenomena in areas beyond the Americas; perhaps its lessons will reach across historical and linguistic lines. Perhaps other terms might serve just as well. But to my mind, none has yet emerged. True, in recent years the concept of hybridity has attracted an unusually large following. Yet I think its usage has been by and large uncritical and, though superficially open and indefinite, ultimately too limited. The modern use of the term *hybrid* derives from postcolonial studies, especially those concerned with India, and was developed around a particular use of "text," and one that is textual in a rather narrow sense (at least from the perspective of linguistics). "Hybridity" is a biological and sexual metaphor, usually applied oppositionally (though not necessarily as oppositionally as when some West Indian intellectuals many years ago spoke of the power of "mongrelization" in New World art). And, in spite of some writers' interest in ambiguity in hybrid states, there is nonetheless often a crude duality behind the term that distorts the complexity of the process described; worse, there is also the assumption of an essentially pure past for all parties before encounter. In spite of the progressive intentions of its users, hybridity is too often the controlling metaphor of a rather shallow and ahistorical analysis.

This is not to say that *creolization* is always used with precision. Indeed, it, too, often functions as a shallow (and even mystical) metaphor for the merging of previously "untainted" elements into a single new form. For example, it is often said that jazz was created out of the meeting of the harmony of Europe and the rhythm of Africa;[3] or, similarly, that creolized languages are constructed from a European vocabulary imposed on an African syntax. But surely this is oversimplification to the point of ignorance. Who among such commentators knows "African harmony" well enough to be able to show that it had no influence? Would they, for example, rule out the complex and multiparted Ekonda choral music of the Kongo as being nonharmonic? For that matter, who among them knows the array of relevant "European rhythms" well enough to dismiss their influence? And who knows enough of both creole and African languages to make such judgments about the influence of the latter's vocabularies? Even if these characterizations could be shown to be correct, surely such a crude lamination would not resemble jazz or any known creole language. Such simplifications are at best uninformed shorthand descriptions; at worst they are racist projections, Europe always on top.

In fact, if we can generalize from what we know of the creation of creole languages to cultural creations in other domains, we come face to face with this paradox: while it may be possible to identify the history and sources of individual components, when put into use new combinations and totalities come into being that have no apparent specific relationship to their historical sources. In the case of language this means that while particular sounds and words can be traced to particular languages, the total speech that results is a new and emergent product. The same is true of music. Even if one can trace the sources of particular instruments, rhythms, and forms of ensembles, when we hear them combined in performance, their sources are moot at best. The European marching band, for example, has gone through countless transformations in the United States, from James Reese Europe's World War I military show band to their sit-down versions, the swing bands in ballrooms; or from the dancing brass bands on the streets of New Orleans and the flamboyantly spectacular half-time bands of Black universities such as Florida A & M and Grambling. Similarly, the European symphonic string section turned into a virtual rhythm section in Cuba with the *charanga*.

If the virtue of creolization lies in its organic history as a native concept in the Americas, its fault stems from the specificity of its New World history and the timidity of its users in applying it elsewhere. Since it is normally only applied to situations of Black and White contacts in the Americas with their attendant inequities, creolization is often understood as being merely one of the weapons of the weak, the result of raw necessity, a make-do phenomenon, or a function of secrecy. But surely expediency and privacy are secondary to the process of interpretation, not only a result of adjusting to divergent cultural forms, but also an act of mediation between different systems of values and meanings. Such processes are not limited to the oppressed and the abject. As Ralph Ellison once said of African American culture, it surely must amount to more than the sum of its brutalization.

There are, in fact, situations worldwide that seem remarkably parallel to New World creole events. A few brief examples: the cultural contact situations of Europe have for too long been the preserves of historians and literary scholars, groups with vested interests in maintaining certain territorial boundaries and alignments, or, conversely, of those like Milan Kundera, who see all peoples of Europe as sharing the same literary tradition regardless of language and national differences (Kundera 2006, 29–56). Gilles Deleuze and Félix Guattari (1986, 16–27), on the other hand, have demonstrated how European literature can be rethought from the margins by using Franz Kafka's notion of minor languages and literature, in which minority languages such as "Czech German" are seen as functioning to undermine the stability of major languages like German. By simultaneously intensifying and impoverishing the dominant language, deterritorializing it, setting it into motion, turning it into just another dialect, the minor language tends to reduce the major to minor status. In his dialogics, Mikhail Bakhtin (1981), too, came close to approximating a creolist position while using only the languages of Europe from the perspective of what was then a minor language, Russian.

Whatever the terms chosen to encompass the phenomena discussed here, the mixture of cultural materials is ultimately what is of concern, and we need to ask, To what degree and at what levels is mixture possible? Is anything conceivable, everything up for grabs? Or is there some limiting order here, a set of parameters, or at least a range in which mixture takes place? These are big questions, but we might at least make a start by thinking of some of the varieties and possibilities of mixture within one domain, language, since it is the cultural exemplar par excellence and thus a model for culture itself (as well as one of the sites at which it is easiest to see mixture at work). The following might serve as a preliminary list:

1. Mixture within the structure of a language—such as in the cases that we call creoles and pidgins (and though such cases may seem obvious, it is worth remembering how long linguists stubbornly resisted even the idea of the possibility of mixed grammar).
2. Mixture within the repertoires of individual speakers—either by means of mixing various codes together in what is typically called "switching," or by the creation of individualized private codes. Christopher Columbus is said to have used both of these strategies, speaking Mercantile Latin as well as Spanish with Portuguese interference.
3. Mixture in the speech of segments of the population, as in street slang, the vocabulary of literary scholars, and so on.
4. Mixture within the use of different styles of speaking—essentially style-switching (though "switching" is again too simple a designation for what occurs in most instances). The possibilities here include an enormous range of processes, such as parody and mimicry, artificial language construction (as in macaronics), oscillation of languages, and the carnivalization of speech. One literary example is the manner in which Ezra Pound, James Joyce, and T. S. Eliot style-switch within levels of literature and speech in their particular brands of literary modernism (crudely put, Pound creolizes "up" from a Eurocentric perspective, Joyce creolizes "down," and Eliot—at least in "The Waste Land"—moves in both directions).
5. Large, mixed repertoires developed within individuals and groups for use in linguistic navigation, such as in trading, criminal activities, and journalism.

Mixture also implies commingling and crossing of social levels and strata in a variety of circumstances: the local versus the metropolitan, local versus global, the colonized versus the colonizer, the emergent vernacular versus the standard language, the as-yet-unrecognized versus the hegemonic, and so on, for the regional, the religious, and the ethnic. Mixture suggests the presence of a multiplicity of codes, voices, styles, meanings, and identities (all of which, incidentally, surface as part of the development of written literature).

Whatever the ultimate terminology, we will at least always be in debt to creole linguistics for placing into doubt the idea of genetic linguistic models and for having forced our attention toward all languages (not only the "distressed" languages) as being involved in social processes and characterized by high variability. And as a result we benefit from a creolist view of society that rejects monolithic visions (even those that are pluralistic) of society as a sacred, political entity whose principal product is nationality in favor of a notion of peoples in potentially equal, differing cultures, developing distinct ways of being and doing from ancestral sources, but also exchanging and sharing with each other and developing new forms, meanings, and interpretations. *This* is something new.

Notes

1. I am indebted to Karl Reisman for first introducing me to many of the ideas in this essay.

2. Walcott's retort to Naipaul above is yet another example of the demonstration of the creolization process.

3. For an early example of this simplistic musicology, see chapters 8 and 9 of Winthrop Sargeant (1946), *Jazz: Hot and Hybrid*. For a modern continuation of this in textbook form, see Donald D. Megill and Richard S. Demory (1996), *Introduction to Jazz History*, 2–3.

Monde Créole

The Cultural World of French Louisiana Creoles and the Creolization of World Cultures

—NICK SPITZER

Music: "J'ai fait tout le tour du pays" (I Went All Around the Country)

In June of 1934 young Alan Lomax was in pursuit of the oral traditional music of Cajun and Creole Louisiana. His recording of African French singer Jimmy Peters's "J'ai fait tout le tour du pays" in the southwest prairie, rice-farming village of Lake Arthur was recalled by Lomax over forty years later as one of his most "remarkable" field experiences.[1] He was a documentary witness to the intensely creolized music that would evolve to become the now popular zydeco. Deeply West African in impression with rhythmically dense, accented foot percussion and repeated vocal fricatives sung by a second voice, this still resonating Creole performance fuses several genres and realms of meaning and aesthetics. The style is a blend of dance music and a testifying religious genre sans instruments called *juré*. Vocally, it leaps from an apparently Medieval French horseman's verse sung in European melodic form to a responding African chorus, *Les haricots sont pas salés* ("the snap beans are not salted")—a proverbial answer about living through hard times. Unlike the commercial recordings of Creole performers from the same period, "J'ai fait tout le tour du pays" has no accordion or fiddle, with more of an African or Caribbean than French imprint in its rhythm, harmonies, and overall style. Lomax recalled that this series of performances was made near a church and that those who attended danced to the singing and percussion in a "shuffling, body-shaking" fashion he associated with the "shouts" of the Sea Islands.

We may be tempted to label this sort of expression a "blurred genre"—between African and French cultures, between song forms, between sacred and secular styles—using notions of familiar, bounded descriptive categories. Yet for people within the culture at this time, I suggest it is a stable though evolving, creolized form of musical performance whose elements are understood as wholly within the African French aesthetic of Creoles in rural south Louisiana.

"Monde Créole," the title of this address, is intended to summarize a range of interests from the "small world" of Creole culture in rural French Louisiana to the notion of a global society made up of many such small worlds that are constantly creolizing from within and in relation to one another in local, regional, national, and global levels of proximity. Here in French Louisiana, *"monde Créole"* is used by community members in French and French Creole languages to inclusively mean the Creole people, Black Creoles or African French Creoles, and more broadly their social and cultural aesthetics and networks. The word *monde* ("world" in standard French) translates locally in this context as "the people." Part of this presentation will focus on this local—but complex—world of Creole culture on the Louisiana landscape. It is a world that has influenced national and global society and culture out of proportion to other social orders of similar scale, owing to expressive forms like zydeco. It stands as a microcosm of parallel processes of cultural creolization worldwide, in settings where the word *créole* is not part of the local cultural system of meaning as a noun or adjective. In this sense *monde créole* refers, as Ulf Hannerz would, to a "world in creolisation" (1987).

The historically heterogeneous cultural landscape of mostly rural southern Louisiana is unique in the United States for its mix of African, Acadian French (Cajun), Continental French, Spanish, and Native American groups. The contemporary Creole culture of the region was formed primarily through contact between African and French peoples. Alongside the Cajuns, with whom they overlap culturally to a degree, African French Creoles are significant in terms of group size and settlement areas, and, for our purposes, their particularly influential expressive culture. This is the symbolic aesthetic realm that includes zydeco music and dance, foodways, and Mardi Gras celebrations that express the complexities of Creole ethnic identity and consciousness in multiple contexts. "Cultural creolization" is the organizing concept for talking here about Creole arts and ethnicity in this local context and for suggesting how the aesthetics and boundaries of other American and worldwide groups and cultural expressions may be similarly considered.

Cultural creolization in its fullest sense describes the development of new traditions, aesthetics, and group identities out of combinations of formerly separate peoples and cultures, usually where at least one has been deterritorialized by emigration, enslavement, or exile—and we can add exploration, though that usually is accompanied by a quest for territory and colonial control. Cultural creolization is especially helpful in understanding those New World societies where Native American, European, and African populations have been in continuous contact, conflict, and transformation since the colonial period. Creolized societies conjoin two or more formerly discrete cultures in a new setting to create a social order in which heterogeneous styles, structures, and contents are differentially preserved while becoming wholly constituted in and adapted to new circumstances, with new and multi-faceted meanings. Yet in all this, earlier cultural traditions, practices, symbols, and sensibilities are often maintained, revered, and even highlighted—though often with transformed shades and subtleties of meaning. The coexistence of, and tension between, traditional and transformed elements, processes, and structures of culture in a creole society—and I believe all societies are creole to some degree—may seem like a paradox. However, it is precisely in the creation of creole expressive culture that such apparent inconsistencies can live side by side and even thrive in new socially embracing forms of traditional art.

A creole cultural perspective on American society suggests examining relations between and within diverse groups rather than the assumed singular evolution of one group's culture in the "hyphenated-American" image of the "melting pot" metaphor—an assumption which persists even in many of the increasingly divergent multicultural descriptions of America, especially in group-centric or unilinear explanations of origin. A creole approach to American society sees it as constantly forming new cultural wholes, while accounting for the continuity of elements that remain distinct in local communities. It suggests that questions of "authenticity" and "heritage" are contingent upon the ongoing process of culture formation. In French Louisiana this sort of concern is played out for Creoles in a social order where they are not considered culturally and socially "French enough" by certain Francophile groups among Cajuns (with race as a socially significant boundary), such as Cajuns, or not "Black enough" to be African American (and race or phenotype is significant here as well).

The word *Creole*, in reference to a people, is from the Portuguese *crioulo* (native to a region) by way of Spanish and French and often associated with populations of mixed ancestry in the slave trade and plantation sphere of West Africa and the New World. It is especially significant for folklorists (given our penchant for expressive culture) that the root verb in Latin, *crear*, means "to create." Indeed, Creole peoples are often the makers of memorable and significant new cultural expressions and at minimum find creating their ethnicity as central to a self-conscious world-view. In part this is because purely European control of the word *creole* largely had the "native to the region" initially defined as a White person of European descent born and raised in a tropical colony (Decamp 1971, 15). As was true in Louisiana, where the first Creoles are associated with the *anciene régime* of France and then Spain, this meaning shifted in practice to include people of non-European origin, and especially those perceived as having multiracial, "mixed" ancestry. Today, "Creole" is used in a variety of ways as an ethnic designation in many Caribbean societies where cultural elements of mostly African and Mediterranean origins persist in new arrangements and densities.

In the growing literature of global culture studies, cultural creolization shares aspects of meaning with terms like "hybridity" and "syncretism" (though I and other contributors to this volume have some concerns about the usefulness of the term hybridity). Creolization was first used by scholars to describe the process of language formation that resulted from cultural contact and transmission over generations, such as Gullah (a form of English Creole), spoken in coastal South Carolina and Georgia, or—more relevant to Louisiana—Haitian French Créole. Haitian society, with close to 90 percent French Creole speakers, and the African Catholic religion Vodou—influentially described in terms of "syncretism" between African deities and Catholic Saints by Herskovits (1937b)—grew from many of the same historical, economic, and cultural conditions found in Louisiana. Some Haitians actually fled to Louisiana at the outset of the eighteenth century and influenced the cultural processes described herein as they strongly reinforced southern Louisiana's African Mediter-ranean qualities. Creolization is, likewise, a useful way to describe such disparate cultural processes as the African American and Jewish aesthetic synthesis in New York jazz and vaudeville circles surrounding the growth of klezmer music—itself founded on a merging of styles from Eastern Europe—or the Spanish and Indian interweaving of Yaqui Catholicism in southern Arizona.

The theoretical and descriptive implications of the fluid, emergent qualities of Creole languages, when applied to related aesthetic forms and ethnicities, have been that cultural creolization is a creative, adap-tive process—more complex than acculturation to a singular mainstream or assimilation into a larger social order, national or global. Cultural creolization as a process and concept, if not always a term, has been utilized in América Paredes's interpretations of the Texas-Mexican border culture; John F. Szwed and Roger D. Abrahams's work in African American and Caribbean cultures; folklorist and historian Charles Joyner's creolist approach to the coastal Carolina culture; anthropologists Sidney Mintz and Richard Price's work in the Caribbean; and Virginia Domínguez's work on identity in New Orleans. Domínguez's work *White by Definition: Social Classification in Creole Louisiana* (1986) specifically looks at Creole ethnicity from a view dominated by the dense rhetoric of ethnoscience. She attempts to formally decipher Creole identity both historically and in the present era and come to what appears to be a foregone conclusion: that in such a creole system, identity is manipulated for social ends. Yet Domínguez's approach does not deal centrally with aesthetic aspects of Creole life that are at the heart of creating and defining identity situationally. She tends to deconstruct the shape-shifting meaning of Creole in New Orleans without much of a sense of what this means in people's personal identities and beliefs. Though copious in research and coverage, like many works of anthropological formalism, *White by Definition* is less satisfying than more aesthetically nuanced approaches by folklorists grounded in and supportive of a community's self-representation in all its diversity and complexity.

Early linguistic interest in creole languages grew out of philological inquiry from the nineteenth century and earlier, culminating in Hugo Schuchart's *Kreolische Studien*, published in the 1880s. The question of how to classify and describe the languages that grow from African European colonial contact initially led to answers that viewed such languages as derivative, dialectal, deviant, degenerate, or broken versions of the colonial European "mother tongues." The often-pejorative term is *patois*. Debate over the origins of creole languages covers a wide range of possibilities. There is the "baby-talk" theory of contact and learning, where masters and mercantilists spoke a deliberately mutilated form of standard language to communicate with servants, slaves, and customers. There are universalist claims for parallel language development in situations of contact, accounting for multiple origins of very similar Creole grammars. In contrast is the cultural contiguity-based notion of an underlying pre-Creole grammar probably from Portuguese or a Mediterranean lingua franca called Sabir. Today we have less focus on origins and more upon the ongoing description and interpretation of the linguistic results of a complex array of historic and geographic cultural contacts in "discovery, exploration, trade conquest, slavery, migration, colonialism, [and] nationalism" that have, in Dell Hymes's words (1971, 5), brought the peoples of the world to share a common destiny. The basic conception of creole language scholars long maintained that the initial contact languages for minimal communication purposes are called pidgins. These are trade languages and/or a lingua franca—not a native tongue of either speaker as was often the case with Indian trade languages. When the limited structure and lexical content (essentially vocabulary) of a pidgin is passed on, usually in a situation of continued cultural contact, it may become a creole language, the mother tongue of a speaker.

The process of linguistic creolization entails grammatical and lexical expansion. While many creole grammars in the African European sphere show remarkable similarity, the lexemes or words usually come primarily from the language of the metropole, with additional words from African, Native American (in North and South America), and other European sources. Mutual intelligibility often exists among creole languages with the same lexical base such as Haitian French Creole and Louisiana French Creole, yet the deepest creole forms—the *basilect*, on one end of a language continuum running to *mesolect* and *acrolect*—are usually unintelligible to speakers of the metropolitan language (Decamp 1971, 17). If you are a native English speaker, think, for example, of your (non)comprehension of Jamaican English Creole—not to be confused with dialectal Jamaican English. Today creole languages are perceived by linguists as having an integrity of their own and are characterized by complex, newly constructed grammars that address the needs of the particular speech community in which they operate. Still, recognition by linguists doesn't mean that creole languages are the prestige form of speech in most language communities. Except in some post-independence situations where they are official markers of a new nationalism or overtly linked in ideology to sources of cultural authenticity—such as the Seychelles Islands in the Indian Ocean or St. Lucia in the Caribbean—creole languages have often been associated unfavorably with the non-literate peasantry.

Though creole linguists have had the ability to describe their corpus of materials in a relatively controlled and social scientific manner, the application of creolization to ethnic identity, the social order, and cultural expression is something of a leap by analogy. As structural linguistics once grew to inform a structuralist view of culture embraced by anthropologists and folklorists, so creole linguistics has given some sense of how to look at content, form, and process in heterogeneous cultural expression. A creole metaphor of culture accepts that this is a realm where complexity, instability, ambiguity, semantic elasticity, contingent meaning, creativity, and focus on the processual, combinatory and emergent aspects of culture are paramount. As Lee Drummond, who worked on a creole model for ethnicity in Guyana, has noted, "diversity and divisiveness are fundamental to the system" (1980, 353).

Zydeco et pas salés: The Emergence of a Creole Culture

Here in southern Louisiana, with its merging of culture sources in a semi-tropical, former plantation zone, bounded by interior and exterior waterways, the heterogeneous culture formed in nearly three centuries is as much an extension of the Caribbean as part of the American South. I have described the region as "south of the South" (Spitzer 1982). South Louisiana—and to some extent contiguous areas of the Gulf Coast into Texas, Mississippi, and Alabama—is distinguished from the rest of the South by languages such as French Creole, Cajun French, and Isleño Spanish; folk Catholicism, including Vodou (or, locally, voodoo) home altars, and a ritual/festival complex that includes Toussaint (All Saints Day) and Mardi Gras; foodways such as *gumbo* and *congris* that blend African culinary ideas and ingredients (gumbo is the word for okra in several West African languages and also a term used to name the deeper form of Louisiana Creole French). We also have Spanish, French, and Native American ingredients, seasonings, and cooking methods; and, of course, Creole music genres such as zydeco and New Orleans jazz.

South Louisiana society offers a powerful counter-example to the atomized, "hyphenated-American" image of diverse, bounded ethnic groups that has often been popularly assumed in both the older melting-pot metaphors and even the more recent multicultural descriptions of America. It also offers contrast to the idea that still lingers of a uniformly biracial southern (and United States) society in which African- and European-derived cultures and people are rigidly separate. This is a culturally creolized region in a broader sense than the multivalent ethnicity of people actually called Creoles. However, Creoles as an ethnic group also embody and distill many of these above-noted cultural aspects and processes in their own life histories and expressive culture.

While some Black Creoles have increasingly become interested in African origins and culture—and earlier generations of Creoles of color often asserted their French and Spanish origins—at a practical level south Louisiana is the acknowledged homeland. This is often explicitly or implicitly noted when community talk turns to why some Black south Louisianians speak French Creole, where jazz or zydeco music originated, how migrant Creoles living in Los Angeles feel about where they grew up, or any of a number of common narratives about community and cultural origins.

African French Creoles from rural southwest Louisiana provide complex narratives of their relationships to French ancestors and cultures. These filiations are partly by way of Cajuns descended from the eighteenth-century Acadian immigrants of Maritime Canada. Their ancestry also includes Continental and Caribbean French populations—and African Diaspora peoples (African Americans from the rest of the South and more historically French- and Creole-speaking "People of Color" from the Caribbean) as well as Spanish and Native Americans. For most Creoles, relations to antebellum *gens de couleur libres* (free people of color, historically recognized in French Louisiana and the Caribbean as a discrete class) are especially significant. Most of the Creole communities in which I have worked do not actually speak French Creole as defined by linguists. They live mostly in the Bayou Teche and prairie lands northeast and west of Lafayette. They speak a Creole-inflected Cajun French—though many do call their language "Creole" or just "French."

"Pure" Creole, also known locally as *couri-veni* (for "go" and "come" in the language with obvious association to French), is mostly spoken east of here in a line running from St. Landry through Lafayette, St. Martin, and Iberia parishes, as well as in some of the river parishes near New Orleans and Point Coupée above Baton Rouge on the west bank of the Mississippi. There is not a univocal meaning to Creole ethnicity—though heritage revival movements do sometimes try to make such claims. The shape and situational variation of Creole ethnic identification is influenced by family and settlement history, class orientation, and physical appearance. Race, perceived as a cultural category based on these descriptive and ascriptive processes, is essential to identity. However, race and ethnicity in south Louisiana, like the Caribbean proper, are malleable, interlocked social categories; and an expressive form like zydeco and participation in dances offer ways that southwest Louisiana Creole people show who they are to one another and to outsiders.

Music: "Zydeco et pas salés" (Snap beans, Not Salted)

"Zydeco et pas salés" has Clifton Chenier on accordion and vocal and Cleveland Chenier on *frottoir* (rubbingboard).[2] There is no recorded performance more identified with zydeco as a musical genre in the 1965–1985 period than this blues-inflected two-step from the late piano accordionist, and widely regarded king of zydeco, Clifton Chenier. Like "J'ai fait tout le tour du pays," this is a text with a French antecedent apparently rooted in a horseman's or hunter's song. The "Hyp et Tauid" reference—suggested by some to be the names of mischievous dogs—reinforces the link to the image of the farmer, herder, drover, or huntsman on the land in a sort of bucolic farce situation. Once again the reference to *"les haricots* (zydeco) *et pas salés"* line is present, but this time it dominates the minimal lyrics of the French "story." The singer and his accordion are accompanied by two rhythm instruments, *frottoir* and drums. The African Caribbean rhythm section and blues call-and-response arrangement embrace the French song inextricably. The effect is to create a definitive Creole musical mood statement in which, as the opening repartee says, *"Tout quelque chose c'est correct?* [Everything's alright?]. . . . *Allons zarico* [Let's zydeco]!"

Zydeco music is a creolization of Cajun tunes (waltzes and two-steps), African American blues, and Caribbean rhythms played on accordion and violin with Creole or French vocals and a rhythm section augmented by a hand-scraped *frottoir*. The term zydeco is from *les haricots*, "snap beans" in local etymology. Snap beans, a basic garden food, provide a metaphor in proverbial expression and conversation for how life is going. When two people meet at a country crossroads, at a store, at a bar, one may say *"Tu vas faire zarico*? (Will you have snap beans [to eat]?)" The common response is "Ouais, mais zarico sont pas salés (Yeah, but there's no salt [meat] to flavor those beans.)" It's a way to humorously or ironically say, "I'm going to get by, but barely." There are also a variety of West African words from several ethnic languages that sound and apparently mean something related to the act or event of dancing or partying. In the Yula language spoken north of the Ivory Coast "I dance" is *a zaré*. In other languages *a sa* (Kasm), *me dseré* (Gurma), *merésa* and *meré go* (Ashante) are all used for "I dance" (Köelle 1854, 184). A fuller philological treatment is deserved, but suffice to say here that a pun on these possible source words may underlie the use of *zarico* in the French Creole proverbial expression of rural Louisiana. In current Louisiana Creole parlance, zydecos are also the dance events and parties held at Creole clubs throughout southwest Louisiana, on westward to Houston, Texas, and now in urban California.

These zydeco dances bring together the full range of the Creole community: men and women, young and old, urban and rural, and those who identify themselves as more African American or French in cultural orientation. Zydeco is the premiere symbol of *Créolité* for Creoles to one another, to local non-Creoles, and to larger national and global audiences. Zydecos are performance occasions that intensify and playfully build upon the everyday life of home, family, work, and worship. They provide aesthetic shape and commentary on Creole values and behavior. They encapsulate Creole readings of their fluid ethnic boundaries with Cajuns and African Americans. Zydeco dances—and people's commentary about them—provide eloquent ways to describe and interpret Creole consciousness and identity as both part of and apart from African and European traditions.

Music: "Bon Soir Moreau" (Good Night Moreau) and "Mo Coeur Cassé" (My Broken Heart)

"Bon Soir Moreau," sung by fiddler Canray Fontenot and accompanied by accordionist Alphonse "Bois Sec" Ardoin, is a blues waltz about the farmer who has been dancing and partying all night. He is admonished to get back to hearth and home. The sun is rising, the cow needs milking, and such.[3] "Mo Coeur Cassé," sung by George "Blackie" Derouselle of Sampy and the Bad Habits, is a slow urban blues sung in Creole with accordion and band accompaniment. The text is a fairly straightforward account of a woman who leaves the man all alone, penniless, and with a *mal de tête* (headache).[4] The first represents a European dance form, the waltz, which is creolized in style or texture beyond the typical French waltz by the addition of blues harmonies as well as African Caribbean rhythmic inflections and performance practices. The second is an African American form that is creolized at least in the text (which is in French Creole) and texture or style of performance. Creolization tends to happen most readily in the texture or style of an aesthetic form. When it takes place in the structure, as in the overall organization of the first two musical examples, or in the grammar of a language, as in the French Creole text of "Mo Coeur Cassé" that is a subset of the overall performance, this is a deeper level of transformation.

Louisiana Creole (and Cajun) expressive culture (especially music and food) has gained special attention locally and nationally in recent years, but it wasn't always this way—especially for Creoles. When I first began fieldwork in 1974, most Creoles, including musicians and club owners, felt sure that their music and culture were *apé mort* (about to die). Now over two decades later, all things Creole have become a matter of pride in these communities. Nationally, the commodification of "other" cultures has brought zydeco music into soundtracks on TV commercials for blue jeans, hamburgers, and automobiles. Here we have the conscious use of a creolized aesthetic to appeal to a broad audience.

In the recent growth of a post-modern world-music environment, where performers of all kinds place music from many sources in new contexts, zydeco has also been nostalgically enshrined locally as "heritage," revived, reinvented, commercialized, and transformed in settings from local and national folk festivals to music videos and international tours. Some of these representations—by insiders and outsiders alike—have served Creoles well; others have provoked local discussion as to the future of the culture. In this regard, traditionalists have often expressed concern about language use and music style. Creole elders wonder if young musicians— who don't speak Creole or any form of French—are remaining true to their tradition as they add English lyrics and African American pop music styles, leaving the local community dance hall circuit and community behind to seek a wider marketplace in their nationally heard recordings and related public performances.

Wilbert Guillory, leader of a farm co-op that sponsors the Southwest Louisiana Zydeco Festival—an event that clearly evokes the value of Creole heritage—told me in 1995, "These boys better not forget that culture and agriculture go together." There has also been the concern, expressed officially by the ethnic organization Creole Inc., among others, that Cajuns and the Cajun ethnic pride movement unfairly dominate south Louisiana's public image, politics, and economy—thereby at once eclipsing the distinctiveness of Creole culture and heightening the urgency many Creoles feel about honoring their music as "heritage." As Creole California migrant accordionist Queen Ida dryly told me in 1987, "We're a minority group from a minority area [French], in a state [Louisiana] that people call backward, you know, in the South."

Just as there has been ambivalence about Creole social and cultural ties to local Cajun French communities, so too such relations to English-speaking (mostly Protestant) African Americans are not uniformly understood or accepted in Creole communities. Concern about Black Creole and Black American relations has often been brought to the forefront in times of heightened consciousness of ethnic boundaries from the Civil War to the Civil Rights Movement and beyond. Many Creoles view the binary American system of racial classification as having eroded the Caribbean-like continuum of Creole culture, race, and class in south Louisiana—with its attendant social, economic, and educational privileges, distinctions, cultural creations, and so on. In the post–Civil War transformation of south Louisiana society, acculturation and assimilation as African Americans was considered a loss of social access and advantage by Creoles of color. Some continued to use the designation of FPC (free person of color) in census reports, death announcements, and litigation into the twentieth century, though now technically all people of color, especially Black Americans, were "free" after the Civil War. In the civil rights period, Creoles who found themselves increasingly discriminated against as Blacks often sought to diminish the distinctions between the groups— as the passage of time had already surely done. On this topic of remaining friction between local groups based on racial and/or cultural distinctions, one Creole community leader told me in confidence, "Some Cajuns say we're not real French people. Some Blacks act like we're not all the way African Americans like them. When people ask me what I am I just say 'thoroughbred.' You know, a real mix. Louisiana Creole!"

Music: "Colinda"

The female name in the song "Colinda" appears to have evolved from the word *kalinda*, an African-derived dance form reported in colonial period ritual/festival occasions in West African, the Caribbean, and Louisiana. In the original dance an association with erotic courtship rituals is usually made. In this version that I recorded from a country Creole band in rural St. Landry Parish, Louisiana, in 1976, the depiction in the lyrics of "Colinda" is of a girl who angers the older women by dancing too closely to her beau. The family band, Delton Broussard and the Lawtell Playboys, probably learned this song off a popular Cajun record—or perhaps a country and western version of it from the region. They even play a country melodic figure as a sort of inserted break from the core melody at various points in the performance. The complexities are great in this music. At once it is densely syncopated and in the same moment has a melodic line associated with the French (and later Anglo-American) tradition. The bandleader told me that some people "want 'Colinda' to dance wild to," thereby preserving in his comment a hint of the *kalinda*'s former incarnation as a ritual/festival dance.[5]

Globalization and Today's *Monde Créole*: A Creolizing World

Up to now I've been talking mainly about long-term creation of a "whole" culture with related expressions in music and dance in rural Louisiana out of the mingling of formerly separate cultures. This sort of deep creolization involves a totality of language and/or religion, a newly formed ethnic identity, and creation of expressive culture that is widely shared by an identifiable group of people. In working with Louisiana Creoles I've always felt that I was involved with a whole culture in terms of my own received notions from training in anthropology (which did not always value such creolized New World cultures as areas of research as much as those which appeared less transformed by contact). Ironically, in recent times, scholars may nostalgicize the heterogeneous, diverse, and changing aspects of a culture or culture in general, just as they once vaunted the homogenous, unified, constant aspects of a specific traditional culture. Where contact between cultures was once seen as a diminishing of value in isolation from modernity, now coping with interior ironies, contradictions, and syntheses by members of an identifiable group is often revered by anthropologists and their kin.

I'd compare some of these ideas to the notion of a larger creolized world in the sense that anthropologist Ulf Hannerz has described it and in the sense of post-modern, post-colonial descriptions and interpretations that use a variety of concepts of hybridity in a manner comparable to the idea of formation of a pidgin language—with the pidgin language comparable to the unstable, first-generation beginnings of creolization.

In discussing the systems of global cultural flow between local communities, nations, and metropoles, Hannerz in a series of articles in the late 1980s, and later a book, moved away from an acculturation model that had characterized much anthropology and folklore—the view that the metropole and the forces of Westernization, systems of education, and media within nation-states were relentless in absorbing local culture and ending cultural difference. He was stepping back from a more contained anthropological focus on small-scale social and cultural units. In a parallel sense our own historically bounded view of singular genres or isolated communities was equally limiting. In trying to deal with worldwide cultural complexity and a revised vision of what he calls "center and periphery relations," Hannerz drew specifically upon conversation between cultures as a root metaphor:

> Along the entire creolising spectrum, from First World metropolis
> to third world village, through education and popular culture, by
> way of missionaries, consultants, critical intellectuals and small town
> storytellers, a conversation between cultures goes on. One of the
> advantages of a creolist view of contemporary Third World cultural
> organization, it seems to me, is that it suggested that the different cul-
> tural streams engaging one another in creolisation may all be actively
> involved in shaping the resultant forms. The active handling of mean-
> ings of various local and foreign derivations can allow them to work as
> commentaries on one another. (1987, 555)

Cultural theorist Homi K. Bhabha speaks of the transformative power of what we might call a creole "Third Space" in colonial and post-colonial settings of an "*inter*national culture" (i.e., among or between nationalities/ethnicities) "based not on the exoticism of multiculturalism or the *diversity* of cultures, but on the inscription and articulation of a culture's *hybridity*"(1994a, 38, 39, italics in original).

While much of the globalizing cultural commentary comes broadly from a Marxist perspective that loathes the classic hierarchical control of production and capital in the marketplace, there is increasingly the view that capitalism's fundamentally disorganized and often decentralized nature allows for more diversity, survival, and creativity in culture than was previously acknowledged. Some anthropologists seem to me to be making what sounds essentially like an argument for a hands-on, creolist form of public folklore. Arjun Appadurai, for example, suggests implicit valorizing in the cultural "primordia" of "language or skin color or neighborhood or of kinship" (1990, 306), while noting that diasporas, deterritorialization, indigenization, and other processes affecting people and their culture are less and less displaying a kind of isomorphic linkage of community, place, cultural style, language, economy, and so on.

Partly as a result of both these new global realities and our own tradition of collaborative work within and with communities, these are great times for those folklorists whose practice has been in the representation of aesthetic creolization within and beyond communities. This doesn't mean that we abandon the concern for community-based art or the process of traditionalization, but that we see traditionalization as linked to improvisation and change—as part of an adaptation that both preserves and transforms culture. Our special realm will probably mainly remain the "unintentional" (in Bakhtin's terms) when it comes to the kinds of creolized aesthetics we deal with—as opposed to the use of purposeful syncretism as an avant-garde or popular culture (e.g., world music) artistic strategy. As folklorists, our emphasis perhaps remains more on what has happened in the periphery rather than the metropole. Native American fiddling styles from the northern tier of the United States and across much of Canada come to mind. These are music styles that synthesize Athapascan, Ojibway, Métis, or Micmac aesthetics with those of Anglo, Scottish, French, or Irish populations both during and well after initial contact.

In this light we still are concerned with—but not in a romantic antiquarian way—issues of authority of voice in creating art that audiences find authentic. Were Sun Records producer Sam Phillips's directions to Elvis Presley to sound "more Black" an effort at conscious creolization to please the market as a response to broader shared aesthetics of lowland agrarian southerners, both Black and White? Or in the avant-garde one thinks of the work of Latino performance artists Coco Fusco and Guillermo Gómez-Peña. In Fusco's book *English Is Broken Here: Notes on Cultural Fusion in the Americas* (1995) she lays out a performance art approach based on biculturalism of American/Mexican or, more broadly, English/Spanish border experiences. Gómez-Peña says in one dialogue with Fusco:

> I am very interested in subverting English structures, infecting English with Spanish, and in finding new possibilities of expression within the English-language that English-speaking people don't have. I find myself in kinship with nonwhite English-speaking writers from India and the West Indies, Native Americans, and Chicanos. When I make the choice to work in Spanish, English, Nahuatal, or Caló, I am expressing those transitional zones within my identity that are part of my life as an intellectual and a border citizen. (Fusco 1995, 157)

He also notes what he calls a "vernacular post-modernism" (in Fusco 1995, 155) throughout Latin America with specific references to home altars that contain saints' images and television sets, or festival *conchero* dancers who fuse heavy metal and Aztec images.

Whether we are talking about a kind of avant-garde Latin Catholic art form or if Elvis's musical transformations (some called them transgressions) were market-driven or a personal choice in a time and place where cultural aesthetics crossed social lines, the key question here revolves around mimicry and its intentions. In some colonial settings, attempts at imitation are taken as a form of idealization of or unconscious transformation from the standard—a source of creolization. Or it can take the shape of minstrelsy, which may put down and/or romanticize the non-dominant group. It may equally mock the colonial power. The history of the cakewalk indicates that it has been used both ways—sometimes in the same moment. In the case of Elvis and his rockabilly music, as a hybrid genre, the issues of mimicry, minstrelsy, or genuine creolization remain open to interpretation. Mine is that Elvis's country roots gave him a certain cachet as one of the prime movers in rockabilly. The question of whether his early recorded work is conscious or unconscious creolization may hinge on whether we perceive early rock and roll as a sort of folk avant-garde movement among displaced southern Whites—self-proclaimed "hep cats" involved in putting on the sound and style of the "other" culture.

The Memphis music marketplace with companies like Sun and Stax Records created Black/White commercial creole musics from rhythm and blues to rockabilly and soul that revolutionized the world, something Cornel West has described in part as "the Afro-Americanization of white youth—given the disproportionate black role in popular music and athletics—[that] has put white kids in closer contact with their own bodies and facilitated more human interaction with black people" (1993, 121). West also observes how Detroit's Motown Records and Billboard hits have created a shared space in a part of the popular culture. This is a nice illustration of the classic "folklore as performance" principle that art has the potential to generate social structure. It also shows how popular mass media can further a cultural creolization process that started on the ground in a region-specific locale like the urbanizing riverine Delta and mid-South of the 1950s. Though again, the potential for market control and manipulation and mass production can also act to commodify, homogenize, and alienate—as Elvis's life-and-death arc sadly illustrates.

This tension between heterogeneity and homogeneity in an array of newly market-available world music and the industry genre "world beat" is something that Steven Feld deals with quite well in his article "From Schizo-phonia to Schismogenesis," where he notes: "The opposition or mutual dif-ferentiation scenario of this pattern rhetorically contrasts claims of 'truth, tradition, roots, and authenticity'—under the cover term 'world music' (or, in the lingo of some zealous promoters, 'real world music')—with practices of mixing, syncretic hybridization, fusion, creolization, and collaboration across gulfs, all under the cover term 'world beat'" (1994, 265).

Elvis Presley, I believe, was at least initially just one in a line of many diverse fusionists of cultural style playing in the subversive realm of what Robert Cantwell (1993) has called "ethnomemisis." The conflicted and unstable aspects of this market culture realm can easily be updated from Sun Records in 1950s Memphis to recent Iranian television programs in Los Angeles as described in *The Making of Exile Cultures* (1993) by Hamid Naficy. The author shows how popular Iranian music videos parody West-ern values by portraying Americans and Arabs who are Westernized as Mafia criminals obsessed with sex and wealth. Yet to do this, a female Ira-nian performer must cross dress and appear in evening gowns in the pro-gram—thus actually violating traditional roles regarding women's clothing, public commentaries, and public appearances. The moral message is con-veyed in a manner that uses the clothes of the "other," in this case the West-erner. Naficy calls such video characters and the everyday life roles exiles must play "amphibolic"—they are people no longer comfortable in their homeland, or in exile, who are generating a new cultural identity—what might be considered a move from a pidgin to a creole culture.

Cultural Conservation and Cultural Creolization

I have elsewhere expressed reservations about the analogy to nature underlying cultural *conservation*—although I often pragmatically prac-tice under that rubric (Spitzer 1992, 77–103). I have been concerned about how well cultural conservation dealt with the complexity and diversity of human expression. I posed cultural *conversation* as an alternative anal-ogy and metaphor for our practice. In Louisiana, the expression *gumbo-ya-ya* (also the name of the Federal Writer's Project book published in 1945) proverbially refers to a situation where everybody is talking at the same time. It's a festive social event and moment of group *communitas*. Since gumbo is also taken to mean "Gombo French," actually I've always assumed that the expression *gumbo ya-ya* referenced in part the notion of overlapped speech in African American/Caribbean communities. Everybody in the social order getting the chance to be heard—sometimes even at the same time—it seems to me is a useful way to think about what we can share culturally and what it is that distinguishes us in American and world societies.

Folklore itself is at heart a creole discipline with roots in both the humanities and the social sciences. Public folklore should be particularly creolist since we as practitioners must constantly deal with and find ways to celebrate and explore both the cultural-conserving and the transforming needs of our constituents. Unlike many of the post-modern, post-colonial, transnational and global culture commentators in allied cultural fields, most public folklorists choose to be a part of the cultural flow rather than standing apart from it. Our rigor comes from practice in public before the eyes of individuals, communities, and institutions shaped by forces of both the market and the state—not to mention nature and the cosmos. Our approach to cultural representation has enfolded and even anticipated the theoretical and ethical concerns of post-modern anthropology and cultural studies regarding shared authorial voice and the construction of culture and ethnicity in new contexts. Our cultural conversations with artists and communities have a fluid, improvisatory, unresolved character. In place of deconstruction as an alienated interpretive practice, we focus on restoration of rooted cultural life, social discourse, and aesthetic representation in communities, in our nation, and in the world.

We can hope, as Ulf Hannerz does in his comments on the role of media and popular culture in the "global ecumene," "for continued cultural diversity in the world, with some linkage to local heritage" (1989, 73). It is what he calls "diversity in motion" and "continued coexistence as well as creative interaction between the transnational and the indigenous" (Hannerz 1989, 73). Our own notion of cultural creolization need be neither classic liberal pluralism of bounded mosaic-like diversity and its sometimes-inchoate spin-off into multi-culturalism, nor the assimilationist melting pot of the prior generation. Instead it could be gumbo pots that hold the potential ingredients for creation and remaking of American culture(s). Pots of foreign ingredients—okra from Africa, sassafras from Native America, peppers from the Spanish circum-Caribbean, now all homegrown and stirred with African and French sensibilities—combined in a new domestic, or even virtual, common space, all contributing to the creation of a sauce or roux while retaining essential aspects of their own group primordia.

Music: "Movin' On Up," by Keith Frank

The voicings in this theme song from *The Jeffersons* TV program draw on the style of 1970s soul music but retain a Creole Louisiana quality in the instrumentation (accordion-centered band), the fact that the bandleader is in the role of cultural bragging—such "kings" of the zydeco bands usually portray themselves on stage as figures triumphant in their personal and social lives—and what can't be deduced from a recording: that this song is played in a dance hall, the center of Creole community life, which hardly represents mainstream American or African American style in a context surrounded by far more "traditional" forms of zydeco music in the musician's repertoire.[6]

I began with the juxtaposition of African and European style and content side by side and intertwined in the Lomax *juré* recording of 1934. I'll close with the sounds of a young Creole accordionist, Keith Frank, with his brothers and sister playing the biggest current hit on zydeco radio and in the clubs. The song opens in a traditional African French Creole-style two-step. It switches to an acculturated more African American soul sound and content, yet it is a sound localized to, and controlled by, the Creole community. It speaks to Creole participation in African American and American popular culture as well as cultural dreams back home in the dancehalls and communities of rural French Creole Louisiana. This is to me a primordial *monde créole* that informs my belief in the power of cultural expression to transform social relations, economies, nations, and the world for the better.

Epilogue: Creolization as Cultural Continuity and Creativity in Postdiluvian New Orleans and Beyond

Doing fieldwork, public programs, and scholarly projects on expressive culture in Creole and other cultural settings in urban New Orleans and nearby French Louisiana over the last three decades suggests to me that creolization is part of the cultural continuity of community life and recreation of the social order—especially in the face of social and economic pressures or natural and unnatural catastrophes.[7] In a broader sense this perspective views the relationship between the conservation and transformation of cultures we find symbolized in expressive forms as a potentially universal creative process. The results of continuous co-mingling and adaptation of traditions to one another may produce continuities from past to present and ultimately future cultural arrangements where national or global outcomes may vie with local needs.

The etymological roots of the term "creole" in the Latin *criar* (to beget or create) point to a focus on creativity consistent with the language of cultural creolization. This approach allows us to make explicit the relations of cultural continuity and creativity in ethnographic work that attempts to describe and interpret the conjoining of multiple sources in new cultural identities and expressions, or to describe the mediation of complex identities through participation in unified creole processes and symbols of performance.

The natural and unnatural 2005 catastrophe of Hurricane Katrina and its post-storm flooding caused by engineering malfeasance in New Orleans offers a practical and compelling illustration of the role of cultural creolization as a framework in materially and socially rebuilding the city and affected areas of the region. It's an area that includes communities identified as Creole, but, perhaps more importantly, it is a place where recovery in cultural terms can be described in the creative, transformative, and sometimes improvisatory terms of cultural creolization that extend beyond particular Creole communities.

Hurricane Katrina caused over 1.2 million people to flee greater New Orleans, where levees failed to protect both urban and outlying areas. I have elsewhere described the cultural catastrophe that ensued as people evacuated their densely settled neighborhoods, many of which were covered by floodwaters (Spitzer 2006, 305–328). Among these evacuees were the very musicians, traditional chefs, building artisans, ritual-festival celebrants of Carnival, and members of social aid and pleasure clubs who contribute to the core public cultural expressions for which New Orleans is famous. In the months and years that have followed the storm, flooding, and evacuation, much attention has gone to how these carriers of intangible culture in family and neighborhood networks made such an impact on the shared citywide vernacular culture. These consist of a series of overlapped cultural layers that include creolized forms such as traditional and brass band jazz played at second lines and clubs; Carnival celebrations such as the Mardi Gras Indians, African American and Creole Bone Men, and Baby Doll parade societies, the Zulu parade, White working-class walking societies, and Uptown elite float parades; Creole cottages and shotgun houses with their French, West African, and Caribbean sources; and neighborhood restaurants and family cooks such as Lil Dizzy's (Creole and soul food) or Mandina's (soul, Italian, Cajun mixed menu and recipes) that prepare local Creole and creolized traditional food, respectively.

Creole culture and creolized forms of culture have served as agents of return and recovery in New Orleans. In the face of federal, state, and local government indifference and/or incompetence in responses to the disaster, local expressive forms, creative new uses of them, and realigned lateral relationships between African Americans, Afro Creoles and Whites in varied downtown and uptown neighborhoods all testify to the primacy of non-institutional forces at work in the recovery. On All Saints Day 2005, a jazz funeral was held for all those lost in the floods citywide. The sacred second line parade, which revealed what bands or portions thereof had returned to the city, made use of a form that conjoins the Catholic and broadly Christian funeral tradition of suggesting hope in a triumphant passage to the "gloryland" with West African ritual/festival processions. These generally include a somber procession to the cemetery by a "first line" of mourners and funeral officials, followed by an uproarious "second line" of neighborhood celebrants. The second line is broadly understood as having Senegambian sources for celebratory processions and is not unlike forms across the Caribbean that combine European formalities with African Diaspora improvisations. Roger D. Abrahams, for example, describes the elegant speakers at a "tea meeting" and the rough, mocking commentary on them by the "rude boys" (1983). This carefree and sometimes unruly bunch is related to those who dance and drink behind the jazz funeral band after the body is "cut loose" at a New Orleans cemetery (though the entire procession, like the tea meeting, retains some formalized and "respectable" behavior).

The jazz funeral—normally a family and smaller neighborhood-specific creolized ritual-celebratory form—was expanded to stand for the mourning and hope, seriousness, and performative play associated with the present and future of the entire city/region. The return of particular family funerals around this time was also taken as a sign of "life" in the neighborhoods of New Orleans. As time passed and more people returned, such sacred second lines could again "walk through the streets of the city," in the words of a locally popular hymn. In so assembling, participants could see who had returned and what the condition was of churches, clubs, stores, homes, public housing, and the neighborhoods in which the marches took place. They could assess the "health" of the beloved music scene based on what brass band might be available in whole or part to musically lead the jazz funeral and its second line.

This symbolic expansion of returning performers also occurred with weekly secular second-line processions sponsored by a wide network of local social aid and pleasure clubs. For example, the return of specific parades such as the Tremé Sidewalk Steppers in spring 2007, two years after the deluge, was taken as a sign of recovery for the city as a whole (Spitzer 2008). Leaders of other clubs joining in with the Tremé second line took pains to suggest that they were marching not only for themselves but for the city as a whole—a place where new social configurations were already in play, which was brought out in my interview with a leader of a social club:

BUCKNER: I'm Edward Buckner and I'm president of the Original Big 7 Social Aid and Pleasure Club. The crowd has changed. It's very diverse now at the parades in this town, you know. It's white and blacks alike. We all love the parades and we get along together very well. . . . The blacks would be at the parades and the whites would be in the clubs with the bands. So eventually the whites came out the clubs and decided to join the blacks on the street. And now we been havin' this great, you know, intellectual thing that's goin' on with the race, that we really getting along and we find out we all like the same things.

NS: How do you think the parade scene, the second lines, can help the city come back?

BUCKNER: Well we are a strong part of the culture. Actually, you look at the Indians and the second lines and we are the culture that go all year round. We are the culture that don't stop. We don't want to take nothin' from Bourbon St. but, you know, when you talking 'bout partyin' in the street, dancin' in the street . . . this is dancin' in the street. You can't help but enjoy this. (Spitzer 2008)[8]

At the same time, Rebirth Brass Band leader and tuba player Philip Frazier sang the praises of the second line and its bands as instruments of the recovery, he also expressed concern about how many people were back participating in the clubs:

Last year there wasn't that many parades. They only had a couple. This year more clubs done came back and you know we got people travelin' all the way back from who be in Houston, and Arkansas, and Atlanta comin' back down just to parade, 'cause they love it so much. The only problem, the only thing I worry about, we have the bands growin', but the social aid and pleasure clubs, I haven't really been seein' any young people. That's the scary thing. You know we gotta get young people back involved with the social aid and pleasure clubs. 'Cause this been goin' on for years, years and years. We can't let that culture die, no matter what. (Spitzer 2008)[9]

The social aide and pleasure club model of mutual assistance, public entertainment, and cultural celebration has been invoked by a wide range of organizations from non-governmental organizations (NGOs) like the resettlement agency Sweet Home New Orleans and the anti-crime group Silence Is Violence to nightclubs such as the Mother-in-Law Lounge and Tipitina's, all of which have encouraged the return of the population and improvement of quality of life in the city by enlisting musicians, music, and traditional creolized festival forms to do so.

No cyclical festive event defines New Orleans' expressive culture more completely both locally and globally than Carnival or Mardi Gras. There was great concern that the annual celebration prior to Ash Wednesday and the forty days of Lent would not be enacted in 2006, the initial year after the deluge. Beyond the pragmatic realities that Mardi Gras in a badly wounded city would add to local economy and tax revenue even in a scaled-back form, the social and cultural counter-argument was made that Carnival was an essential rehearsal of return necessary for New Orleans civic life (Abrahams et al. 2006). As a powerful and often satirical mingling of classes and cultures in public feasting, float parades, walking societies, krewe balls, and more, Fat Tuesday offered the first chance for a large public of those who had fled to Atlanta or Dallas, Baton Rouge, or Birmingham the chance to come back, view the conditions in the city, and participate in the event that is a primary part of natives' sense of place through public performance and spectacle.

The smaller traditional groups in Carnival, such as the Mardi Gras Indians, especially found themselves given greater local and national press attention than ever before as they appeared on the front page of both the *New York Times* and the *New Orleans Times-Picayune* on and after Mardi Gras day 2006. In so doing, the "Indians," one of Carnival's most creolized groups—uniting European, African Caribbean, and Native American structures, aesthetics, performances, costumes, and images—became a kind of report on the health of the city as a whole via their widening recognition both in the press and in the streets. In so doing, the status of Mardi Gras Indian tribes was temporarily elevated in a social order that increasingly was looking to such creolized cultural symbols and performances as evidence of recovery—a return to festive normalcy.

New Orleans music, especially traditional jazz, brass bands, and all manner of rhythm and blues, soul, and funk music, also stands for the city as a year-round signifier to America and the world of the city's cultural sources and resources. In addressing the role that musicians have played, I have opined that after Katrina the players often became "model citizens," in so far as they were viewed as heroic carriers of the endangered intangible culture. They had become workers (at play) on behalf of the neighborhoods, nightclubs, and second-line parades in need of performers and performance to again become vibrant symbols of the community (Spitzer 2006, 305–328).

I interviewed the Creole pianist, producer, and songwriter Allen Toussaint—nationally known for his rhythm and blues and soul recordings. He had early on become a major spokesperson for the cultural recovery during the dark days of September 2005, during his evacuation to New York City. The locally revered musician noted that the "spirit didn't drown," as he enumerated the loss of his Gentilly neighborhood home and its contents, then under eight feet of water: a Steinway grand piano, all his sheet music, and personal recording archives. The logical extension of his thinking, we agreed, was that there was no water line on music, or the soul. He could still perform, record, and produce music. It was a simple but profound realization about how intangible culture can survive, even thrive, under adversity and be re-created to great effect under new, heightened conditions—a kind of vernacular humanities that creolized Catholic teachings with experience and phenomenological knowledge of music.

Allen Toussaint's repertoire blossomed as he remade his upbeat social anthem from the 1970s, "Yes We Can Can" (originally written for local body shop man and singer Lee Dorsey of "Sittin' in Ya-Ya" fame, and later made a hit by the Pointer Sisters in 1973). Toussaint sang with the most muscular and funky voicing he had mustered in over twenty years. "Yes We Can Can" was the first track on the *Our New Orleans 2005: Benefit Album* CD (Spitzer 2005b) that raised over a million dollars for Habitat for Humanity's efforts to create new housing—a "Musicians Village" in the city. It instantly became the soundtrack of recovery, blaring from radios as hammers rang, saws cut, and backhoes cleared throughout the city. At the same time, Toussaint's minor key and slow tempo on another song on the CD, "Tipitina and Me"—a variation on his mentor Professor Longhair's jaunty "Tipitina"—presented a darkly luminous mood that carried the listener from funereal to hopeful thoughts about the city's "resurrection," as Toussaint called it in 2005. Toussaint as a piano professor nouveau of the next generation demonstrated his authority in the role with a repertoire diversity that showed cultural creolization in the Afro-urban pop music with a 1970s-era message of inclusiveness and tolerance that prefigured the then soon-to-be President Obama's message of hope ("Yes We Can"). Was Toussaint's use of "Can Can" the kind of intensifier often used in creole languages? He also invoked the nineteenth-century New Orleans Creole classicist, French Jewish composer/performer Louis Moreau Gottschalk, in his haunting rendition of "Tipitina and Me." If "Can Can" was uplifting for recovery workers, then "Tipitina and Me" captured the night mood with candles burning before the power and the neon lights and club life had returned.

Toussaint then joined forces with Elvis Costello, the eclectic British rocker and lover of New Orleans music, on the CD *River in Reverse*, one of the first recordings made in New Orleans after Katrina in December 2005—the studio session of thematic songs about the disaster was emblematic of the nascent return of musical infrastructure. In 2009, Toussaint continued his solo efforts with a new recording of old New Orleans jazz modernist classics under the title of Thelonious Monk's *The Bright Mississippi*. In his commentary on the recording, Toussaint returned to Christian metaphors for the city's triumph over misfortune, but he replaced "resurrection" with a sense of the birth of new creative possibilities: "Spiritually Katrina was a baptism as far as I'm concerned. Many wonderful things came out of Katrina and are still going on and will be going on forever. That is quite a jolt in life to have to flex new muscles in every way, physically and spiritually. So I find Katrina to be much more of a blessing than a curse. Not only for myself, but for many that may not recognize it that way" (quoted in Spitzer 2009).[10]

Beyond the recovery and revaluation of artists, the question was raised whether New Orleans jazz as a whole would again be heard regularly in the recently submerged city. Traditional jazz emerged at the end of the nineteenth century—a period of huge repression for people of color. It was a brutal social transition for Creoles and African Americans—who were jazz's primary early creators and players—as the hope of post–Civil War Reconstruction faded into the Jim Crow era. Writer Ralph Ellison later suggested that jazz's birth and growth was a "freedom statement," "Constitution," and "Bill of Rights" for African Americans. In New Orleans, Creoles, African Americans, and some Euro-Americans (especially Italians) have long played the music.[11] Early jazz had mostly European instrumentation (excepting the African-descended banjo and in some sense the use of drums even in manufactured kit configurations), a musical and social connection to American military and Catholic saints' day parades, and African/Caribbean/American-inflected performance practices, rhythms, scales, harmonies, and associated street dance forms. Early New Orleans jazz has long been distinguished more by style (heterophony and group improvisation) rather than repertoire—the latter may include parlor and popular songs, hymns, blues, and marches.

Over a century after its emergence, the post-deluge question was, Will New Orleans traditional jazz—with all its creolized aspects and neighborhood base of performance—survive in a depopulated city of destroyed neighborhoods? One answer in the affirmative was from clarinetist and musical activist Dr. Michael White. White famously lost to the floodwaters an important personal collection: thousands of books and rare recordings, original sheet music and correspondence from now deceased musicians, historic photographs and antique instruments that belonged to legendary artists such as King Oliver and Sidney Bechet. In an intensely creative several years after the catastrophe, the mild-mannered humanities professor composed nearly forty new tunes in traditional jazz style![12] It was an unprecedented act in the recent history of the music. Michael White also returned to a vigorous schedule of teaching at Xavier University (the only black Catholic university in North America), playing locally with the new brass band stylists he had previously eschewed as not traditional enough, and touring nationally and globally. All of which—along with other notable musicians—brought new attention in national and international press to New Orleans' cultural revival as a sign of larger material, social, and economic recovery.

The same report of a huge new creativity and musical output would include a spectrum of players and institutions. The New Orleans Jazz and Heritage Festival—its racetrack grounds badly damaged—was, like Mardi Gras itself, able to mount an event in 2006. It was produced with huge support from the public, musicians, and politicians who felt that the sprawling—sometimes chaotic, sometimes controversial—commercial celebration of the culture could not be allowed to cease for the sake of the economic, public relations, and, ultimately, emotional and spiritual needs of the citizenry.

Soul queen Irma Thomas made a new choice: to sing the blues (previously not appropriate to her image as an urbane progressive soul singer) and to update classic blues woman Bessie Smith's own tale of flooding, "Backwater Blues," from the 1927 inundations. Likewise, Creole pianist and sometime carpenter Eddie Bo (Edwin Bocage), in his late seventies, reawakened his building skills to repair homes of family and friends while working on new recordings such as his improvised, creolized version of "When the Saints Go Marching In," taking the old familiar, sometimes clichéd song to another level by creating it anew in improvised words and music. At the end of the session recorded in October 2005, Eddie Bo addressed his own and the broader New Orleans public's need to return, live in, and rebuild the cityscape by memorably concluding, "I want to *be* in that number" (quoted in Spitzer 2005b).

A sixth-generation Creole craftsman from Algiers Point, Bo also readily suggested that his work as a carpenter was as creative as making music:

BOCAGE: We, as Bocage youngsters, had to learn to do, the craftsman, when he was five. All the males had to learn how to start off and build. . . . And I think we also had the shipbuilders and . . . engineers in the family. So they taught us what might be of interest to us, and what might help us out as far as having another skill other than what you choose. If you tend to choose something else, you would always be able to fall back on that.

NS: And what skills did you learn as a builder?

BOCAGE: Bricklaying and carpentry was basically what my dad did, so I had to learn to do it too.

NS: Did you like that work when you did it?

BOCAGE: Oh yes. I love it as much as the music.

NS: Really?

BOCAGE: Yes, indeed. I love to stand back and look at what I put together. And you know, because I know it is constructed properly. I know that and then there is always new techniques and try to learn around everybody I go around.[13]

In a city famed for its music and (now partly destroyed) built environment, the linkage of creativity between work and play among Creole craftsmen—many of whom had been part of multiple-generation families of building artisans since the antebellum times of their *gens de couleur libres* ancestors—was a powerful addition to the discourse of recovery and rebuilding. Music could temporarily reassemble the artist families and their audiences of natives and visitors alike; however, the question of rebuilding the old infrastructure of nineteenth- and early twentieth-century wood and masonry houses as well as dealing with shattered brick subdivisions and moldy sheet-rocked (not old Creole plaster) interiors remains to this day. Still, in a city recognized for a *bon vivant* attitude, the efforts of Creole and other building artisans revealed a work ethic that could aid the recovery of New Orleans.

The late Earl Barthé was a renowned sixth-generation, self-identified Creole of color plasterer from the Seventh Ward Gentilly neighborhood. A leader in the Creole Fiesta and later a National Heritage Fellow recipient in 2005, Barthé's ornamental plaster was created with a sense of musicality. Earl compared the work to his favorite performances, noting that he was just as happy listening to his sister Débria (now deceased), an opera singer performing *Carmen*, as playing the records of Muddy Waters or Ray Charles on the job. Barthé said that *Carmen* had the "plastering beat" (quoted in Spitzer 2002, 123) and went a step further in the analogy of musical style to, particularly, the Creole plasterer's craft: "You run the mold and then you place the dentils, those little square things that are cast and placed in the mold. It all has to be in tune. When you run your arch, you gotta put your corbel on the bottom. That's like the big bass. It looks like a bass. So the musicians as I spoke about like Milford Dolliole and Tio with Chocolate Milk, which is a funk band—and there were many others that were good plasterers and musicians—they had that musical touch. They'd be singing the songs of Muddy Waters . . . and be placing dentils and ornaments into this cornice" (123).

Earl Barthé was dubbed the "Jelly Roll Morton of plastering," owing to his similar features, loquacious style, and love of music as a metaphor for his work. His "articular" plaster medallions were featured in the museum exhibit and catalog *"Raised to the Trade": Creole Building Arts of New Orleans* (Hankins and Maklansky 2002). Barthé and family took refuge from Katrina in Cypress, Texas, and returned months later to repair their heavily damaged home, their workshop, and the homes of their many clients. In a 2007 interview (Ellis, Smith and Spitzer 2007) Barthé expressed longing for the cooperative social order of Creole workers he knew as a youth, in hopes that such reciprocal labor could be applied to the recovery:

"The Creoles would build each other's houses. So they would have the cement masons to do the foundation. Bricklayers, carpenters to do the framing, roofers, and plasterers and painters would come in and finish up. And they would say, 'We're going to start your house this week'—so they would lay the foundation and frame it."

The late Earl Barthé's social dream and work aesthetics, along with the late Eddie Bo's approach as Creole craftsman, are slowly being put into practice across the cityscape by a wide array of non-profit organizations and private developers, following the collaborative model to varying degrees and through a renewed focus on continuity in the building arts as taught informally in family businesses and institutionally at specialty elementary schools and community colleges. The cooperative labor ideal has been enacted through college, church, and community assistance networks nationwide that sponsor "voluntourism" for visitors who work on building or repairing homes. Outside artists, scholars, students, and professionals have also contributed to the collective rebuilding effort as part of the city's "brain gain" in a fulfillment of the traditional "social aid" side of the original social aide and pleasure clubs. The "pleasure" aspect of a culturally based lifestyle imbued with music, food, Carnival, and *joie de vivre* is, of course, also available. Owing in part to the West African/Mediterranean/Caribbean aspects of New Orleans society, these enjoyments and entertainments—like the historic linkage of music and the building arts—are seen as related to concerns for the future of the social order. The hope of many New Orleans craftsmen and others is to more fully enact a collaborative rebuilding, at a WPA (Works Progress Administration) level not seen since the 1930s, wherein young apprentice builders learn the trades while building sweat equity and gaining knowledge of finance and entrepreneurship so that learning the skills and assisting others can translate into a livelihood that repopulates the city with skilled homeowners in the neighborhoods they helped rebuild and will ultimately stabilize by their presence.

In the difficult days that followed the floods of 2005, there were many calls to move New Orleans upriver (cf. Giegengack and Foster 2006, among others) by earth scientists, social scientists, politicians, and others. There may have been good science behind urging historic city dwellers to leave problematic natural environs for a rural location one hundred miles north in Morganza, Louisiana, but it was amateur social policy that ignored the deep symbolic associations of place, culture, and community in peoples' lives. There was also the dilemma, faced by governments, NGOs, foundations, and private investors, that the material infrastructure of New Orleans was already in terrible shape *prior* to the deluge—with collapsing and abandoned buildings, poor roads, dilapidated public schools, and, of course, a haphazard and permeable levee system surrounding a partly below sea level "bowl" of a city, located on a rapidly eroding coast line. The focus of much disaster recovery anywhere is on infrastructure, but in New Orleans the case was made that as a kind of Venice of the vernacular with a whole lot less water in it than that other great city of the arts, a focus had to be as much on restoring the intangible culture by encouraging the return of the citizenry—the carriers of the culture.

Humorously, some said that intangible culture was anything *without* a waterline on it. To this I would add that it was always hard to find a native New Orleanian, a new settler, or a tourist to the Crescent City who stayed or moved here because he or she thought the infrastructure was especially attractive.[14] The comedian Harry Shearer added, in multiple media appearances, that after Katrina, "New Orleans broken is far better than other places fixed."

What made the city worth enduring chronically broken infrastructure, often retrograde policing, weak and illicit governance, and subpar public schools was the creative and "easy" lifestyle associated with enduring creolized cultural vernaculars of the cityscape—a legacy of a dominantly French/Spanish West African society, later leavened with immigrants from the American South, Germany, Ireland, and Italy, among many other sources. New Orleans, as a cultural and social order created from these diversities in a provincial location of geographic and climatic difficulty, of religious difference from the rest of America, in a former slave society with all its post-colonial problems, was now more than ever relying on the power of the expressive cultural continuities that set the city apart from the South and that made it more kindred to the Caribbean. The advantage of looking at the city this way geographically has recently been reaffirmed by archaeologist Shannon Dawdy's anthropological history, *Building the Devil's Empire: French Colonial New Orleans* (2009). Dawdy shows the emergent eighteenth-century polyglot port city that developed its own "rogue colonialism" as part of a kind of organic and creative economic and cultural creolization process. Rogue colonialism reconfigures and conjoins the many cultural streams into the urban social landscape in a manner more adaptive and appropriate than conventionally understood metropole-periphery relationships of governance, economy, and society based in formal institutions of colonial powers (here, France, then Spain, and, I add, America and the Confederacy) usually allow for. I have referred to New Orleans as being "south of the South" (Spitzer 1982). The relative worldliness of the city is noted in terms of its location on the northern rim of the Caribbean culture area. Andrés Duany, the new urbanist architect and planner, confronted the city's infamous disorder and corruption: "And then I realized . . . that New Orleans was not an American city. It was a Caribbean city. Once you recalibrate, it becomes the best governed, cleanest, most efficient, and best-educated city in the Caribbean. New Orleans is actually the Geneva of the Caribbean" (quoted in Curtis 2009, 64).

New Orleans' community-centric Creole and creolized cultural expressions have moved increasingly to the center of local public discourse in the years after the floods. Partly this was possible because much deeply traditional life had long remained in the city, and also because the tradition writ large has been one of explicit improvisation—be it musical, in cuisine, in the built environs, or in Carnival aesthetics. An initial recovery suggestion was that the city—with its largely intact and distinctive eighteenth- and nineteenth-century high-ground landscape and its continuing Latinate laissez-faire attitudes—was well pre-adapted to further develop a gaming economy as a kind of historic competitor to Las Vegas. Public ridicule and social awareness in a far less complacent post-catastrophe city quickly deflated such speculation. Beyond the previously dominant focus on preserving the past in material terms, the question of the cultural future had become central in New Orleans' public discourse.

Although concerns for authenticity are not fashionable in some academic circles, the new civic discussion often asked how the city could remain "authentic," meaning historic and connected to its cultural legacies, compared to the rest of the United States. The focus, however, was on linking the cultural past to an "authentic future" (Spitzer 2006, 308). At its most realized, the idea is that cultural expression in the streets and clubs would remain on an intimate local scale defined as the creative zone where creolized culture met a need for continuity, neighborhood-based culture, the arts, and economic sustainability—all founded on local diversity and new economic approaches to creative "industries," cultural tourism, environmental services, public education, and urban planning alongside more traditional areas such as shipping, petrochemical industries, finance, and medicine.

Culture as the primary agent of return to and recovery of New Orleans has been central to the mission of NGOs like Sweet Home New Orleans that early on emphasized the resettlement of the musicians, ritual/festival participants, chefs, and building artisans who made the city distinctive and attractive. While infrastructure in the form of schools, housing, medical facilities, highways, and drainage is essential, a public narrative emerged, claiming that, without cultural continuity linking the past to the future, there is little point in developing infrastructure for its own sake. There had to be a sense of possibility for a cultural future to justify the efforts to rebuild and reinvest.

While a social justice perspective argues for careful planning and infrastructure development to improve the quality of life for the population, in New Orleans it is arguably the laterally connected, intimate, creative, and creolized "way of life,"[15] in the words of jazz saxophonist and Mardi Gras Indian Donald Harrison, that has kept the city afloat through this perilous passage. This way of thinking liberates the notion of infrastructure to serve as a human need in society that supports a way of life, but it does not embody or create that society. Rather, it is mainly the agency of creative tension between continuity and transformation of culture that generates the livable future on the terms I have outlined.

In this way, New Orleans has begun to emerge as a national model in recessionary times for cities that build on the instrumental and expressive aspects of their vernacular culture to move beyond devalued landscapes and neighborhoods, high unemployment, and a general distrust of national economic institutions based in Wall Street or Washington. While few urban centers have the Creole cultural inheritance of New Orleans, many cities with historic cultural influences and new immigrants are creolized at the community level in certain ways. Some are just beginning to look deeply at the resources and applications that are available in this way of thinking. New Orleans' civic and cultural leaders increasingly sense the role that the city could play in shaping a national discourse about cultures that are distinct and shared at the local level via expressive forms, with their artistic proponents leading the way.

However, New Orleans has not historically been a place for resident intellectuals bent on describing how the rest of America could learn from the city's creole cultural processes of tradition and improvisation as a way to better understand the potential for viewing creative freedom in terms that reconcile the *pluribus* and *unum* in localities nationwide. The New Orleans tendency instead has been to simply perform the culture's traditions of creativity here or on the road, and so draws adherents, be they tourists and music fans, architects and foodies, scholars and policy wonks, or globalization theorists and chairpersons of federal agencies devoted to the arts and humanities.

One attempt to nationally present the idea of New Orleans Creoles—specifically, a jazz banjo player from New Orleans named Don Vappie as an ultimate, socially adaptable, yet culturally grounded American—was a PBS film called *American Creole* (Vappie, Pitre, and Benoit 2006). The documentary was planned in antediluvian days to show Vappie and his large kin network functioning effectively in an array of occupations (including professional musicians in New York and Los Angeles) and communities nationwide. Post-Katrina flood waves redirected the project toward how a creative Creole like Vappie could use the cultural expression of jazz and his family ties to help people return to and rebuild New Orleans from the musician community outward.

On the larger question of re-understanding American vernacular culture, other artists, like the well-known blues singer Taj Mahal and the rising young Louisiana Creole fiddler Cedric Watson, have independently suggested that the United States might best be understood as a "Creole nation" (Spitzer 2003, 2010). In a Creole nation one imagines that culture is viewed as a creative creolizing process where group identities show both continuity, synthesis, and differential change, rather than the more linear culturally centric or islanded multicultural conceptions of diverse social orders. These particular artists that gave a voice to such observations are from backgrounds that reflect Creole cultural contact and transformation: Taj Mahal is of African American and British West Indian parentage; Cedric Watson claims Louisiana Creole, Mexican Spanish, Native American, and African American cultural forebears. They are connected to Creole societies of the Caribbean and the Gulf of Mexico, and both are aware of the creolization in their personal identities and musical expressions.

From a more critical point of view some scholars, especially anthropologists (Munasinghe et al. 2006), have debated the utility and appropriateness of even using "creolization" as a way to universally describe and interpret the processes of continuity and creativity in cultural identities, expressions, ecologies, economies, and related realms. A key concern raised in the discussion is that specific Creole societies often recreate either the insular and intolerant hierarchies of the former colonial metropole in the provincial setting or, as they evolve into settled ethnic communities, find ways to exclude those who do not fit into the reified mix of genealogy and cultural markers used to maintain those ethnic boundaries.

Examples from New Orleans and other Louisiana Creole communities are not uncommon (cf. F. Smith 2003, 113–128), and Viranjini Munasinghe (2006) describes the plight of marginalized East Indians in the colonially-derived West Indies Creole communities.

Still, we are bound by our comparative and ethnographic traditions to find ways to describe and interpret how cultural communities in the present maintain links to varied pasts—often multiple Old Worlds—and creatively address the present and future in transformations that allow for recognizable linkages between times and places. In this light, cultural creolization is a useful way to address traditional creativity in many forms, variations, and places in the world. The people called Creoles who have made that process explicit in their identity and aesthetic expressions of their culture will continue to discuss, argue, and sometimes disagree about group boundaries; and those feeling excluded from Creole groups may add to the discontent.

The question of "Who is a Creole?" will likely remain, but what has emerged as more broadly significant is that cultural creolization as a means of describing tradition, creativity, and continuity from past and present into the future of human communities is a hopeful and engaged human discourse when compared to the alternative: global monoculture and assimilation within nation-states.

New Orleans is distinctive within America with its Carnival, music, cuisine, and building artisanship, but shares these expressions broadly with Creole societies of the Caribbean through parallel development in the New World, African European plantation colonial sphere as well as long-term intraregional migrations. The city has long been a kind of Creole hearth of creativity and symbolic soul for America and anywhere in the world where creolization as a vernacular process creatively connecting the past to the future of community-based culture has not been made explicit. As Rebirth Brass Band leader Philip Frazier says, "Without New Orleans, there is no America" (quoted in Spitzer 2006, 326).

Notes

This essay was originally an invited plenary address for the 1995 meetings of the American Folklore Society in Lafayette, Louisiana. I am indebted to Robert Baron and Ana C. Cara for their assistance in transforming this presentation for inclusion in this volume. Thanks also to my colleagues at the School of American Research in

Santa Fe for their intellectual and institutional support in the 1995–96 academic year, when this address was initially prepared. I also appreciate the long-term scholarly input on the topic by Roger D. Abrahams, Richard Bauman, Ian Hancock, the late Américo Paredes, the late Ulysses S. Ricard, and all the Creole community leaders and musicians who have assisted me, especially the late Alphonse "Bois Sec" and Marceline Ardoin, the late Delton Broussard, BéBé and the late Eraste Carrière, the late Wilson "Boozoo" Chavis, Jo Ann and the late John Delafose, the late Slim and Irene Gradney, Ida Guillory Lewis, and the late Wilbert Guillory, and their families. Musical selections may be heard at by searching "Deep Routes."

1. *Louisiana Cajun and Creole Music, 1934: The Lomax Recordings*, 1987, notes by Barry Jean Ancelet, Swallow Records, LP-8003-2.

2. *Clifton Chenier: Louisiana Blues and Zydeco*, (1964) 1990, produced by Chris Strachwitz, Arhoolie Records, CD 329.

3. *Canray Fontenot: Louisiana Hot Sauce, Creole Style*, 1993, produced by Chris Strachwitz, Arhoolie Records, CD 381.

4. *Zodico: Louisiana Créole Music*, 1978, field recording and notes by Nicholas R. Spitzer, Rounder Records, LP 6009.

5. Ibid.

6. Keith Frank, *Movin' On Up!*, 1995, Maison de Soul, CD 1055-2.

7. Creole expressive culture in French Louisiana—the rural parishes south and east of New Orleans to the Texas border—was the jumping-off point for discussion of the local and global aspects of cultural creolization in the original 1997 *"Monde Créole"* presentation to the meetings of the American Folklore Society in Lafayette, Louisiana, and now reprinted in this volume. This epilogue offers the counterpoint and complement of post-Katrina New Orleans, its own urban Creole communities, and, more broadly writ, the impact of creolized tradition and creativity on the general populace of the city/region.

8. Interview with Edward Buckner was broadcast August 22, 2007, on *American Routes*.

9. Audio clip of Philip Frazier courtesy Matt Sakakeeny, who edited the Tremé second-line segment for *American Routes*, broadcast August 22, 2007, on *American Routes*.

10. Allen Toussaint interview was broadcast August 22, 2007, on *American Routes*.

11. Personal communication, Robert O'Meally, 2004.

12. The CD containing some of these is the 2008 *Blue Crescent* on Basin Street Records: New Orleans. White had previously made much of this connection to elder jazz musicians whom he had learned from (on records or in person), been advised by, or played with, musicians such as George Lewis, Danny Barker, and Doc Paulin. He referred to these and other players of traditional jazz as now "dancing in the sky" and made a recording of the same name also on Basin Street Records prior to the floods of 2005.

13. Interview was broadcast November 2, 2005, on *American Routes*.

14. I must admit, though, that we probably will never know exactly how many people left New Orleans before Katrina or never returned after it because of the city's weak infrastructure, limited economic opportunities, or racial and class barriers.

15. Harrison's remark was made at the Penn Institute for Urban Research Seminar, Arts in the City: Can the Arts Revive Our City and the Nation's Economy? Philadelphia, March 2, 2010. I distinguish "way of life," as an organic cultural attribute, from "quality of life," which more often is a kind of add-on or enumerative set of features favored by advocates of economic development based in "creative economy"—most prominently Richard Florida, who ironically has New Orleans low on his quality-of-life rankings compared to many cities with far less organic "way of life" depth.

Creolization, *Nam*, Absent Loved Ones, Watchers, and Serious Play with "Toys"

—GREY GUNDAKER

Introduction: What You See Is What You Get

This essay points up the multiple theoretical trajectories associated with the term "creolization" over the past forty years. In light of this history, I argue that the term has outlived its usefulness as a unitary theoretical rubric. However, as an open-ended synonym for "mixture" it can still usefully draw attention to cultural processes that remodel ancestral precedents, selectively synthesize multiple cultural resources, and pointedly reject the notion of mixture to foreground moments of irreducible seriousness.

The essay weaves together three threads. First, it engages, though by no means resolves, problems in theorizing the complex interactions of diverse peoples who historically and culturally comprise the African Diaspora(s), paying particular attention to the rubric creolization and its history. It then proceeds to explore a classic anthropological moment, when a received classification or category associated with a dominant cultural history obscures other possibilities and explanations, which were voiced by the field consultants whom I interviewed. I call this situation "toy blindness" because the third thread of this essay concerns themes of loss and figural substitution, exemplified by figure 1. This object—mislabeled and trivialized as a "toy" by outside observers—is composed at the intersection where one small loss opens onto many bigger ones in the diasporic experience. Finally, it turns to Kamau Brathwaite's concept of negative creolization, arguing that it sheds light on the theme of loss and the issue of essentialism.

1. Stuffed Snoopy on garage roof. Ruby Gilmore, Hattiesburg, Mississippi, 1990. Photo: Grey Gundaker.

In certain African American settings in the United States, figural proxies—like this stuffed Snoopy—retain their surface associations but add another layer as stand-ins for the bodies of absent loved ones who have died, been forcibly taken away, or remain unborn. Other forms like dressed trees and ensembles of memorabilia also serve this purpose, commemorating these loved ones, preserving a physical place for them, and reminding others to respect those in the other world of spiritual beings.[1] Parallel arrangements serve similar purposes in West and Central Africa, Cuba, Brazil, Trinidad, and other parts of the African Diaspora.[2] However, as sometimes happens when a dominant classification holds sway, such figures can be mistakenly labeled as *merely* and *only* "toys." Although play is also serious business, when it is applied to the doings of peoples who in the past were routinely labeled "childlike," a term like "toy" that lacks the serious connotations of, say, "sculpture," "statuary," or "effigy" also hints that infantilization as a mode of othering may still linger in the politics of race and class.

The threads of theory, classification, and figuration in my essay come together through a pair of insights about creolization. One is the warning that *in contexts of cultural mixture what seems obvious to outsiders probably isn't* because word and eye play, code and style switching, command of multiple registers, indirection, and rapid shifts in frame of reference abound.[3] The other is Kamau Brathwaite's *nam*, a purposeful rejection of creolizing mixture in favor of actions with the affective armor of undiluted ancestral precedent. According to Brathwaite, *nam* comes into play in creole societies at moments of the highest importance. Loss of loved ones is certainly such a moment.

Over the past twenty-odd years, Brathwaite's writings on creolization have been critiqued from many directions. *Nam* in particular has been called an essentialist assertion of connections to Africa that do not exist.[4] So, let me be clear from the outset. When I argue that *nam* can help us understand figuration that represents absent loved ones and that it can usefully counter toy blindness, my aim is not to authenticate some ultimate, generalized "Africanness" for these figures as a patronizing way to assert "agency" for agents who do not need my intervention. Rather, I aim to foreground practices that have been rendered largely invisible, or worse trivial, by differences in the epistemological premises that inform participants' and outsiders' ways of seeing.

While anti-essentialism is, well, essential in the sense that we must be wary of reification, I would also argue that certain important dimensions of the African side of American cultural history have been dismissed too quickly, especially in anthropology of the United States. In a recent paper that cautiously argues for African origins to resolve a narrowly focused debate about creolization in Haiti, Andrew Apter sums up current attitudes in cultural anthropology.

> Unless critically deconstructed, the idea of African origins is decidedly out of favor. On methodological grounds alone, criteria for establishing African provenance have remained controversial since the [Melville] Herskovits–[E. Franklin] Frazier debate, demanding strict functional correspondences that can never realistically be found ([M. G.] Smith 1957), involving essentialized tribal designations that should be abandoned (Mintz and Price 1992), or invoking a play of tropes within a historically situated discursive field that can never be transcended (Scott 1991, 1997). According to these methodological strictures, African cultural practices may well exist in the Americas, but they cannot be known with any specificity. They lie beyond the limits of anthropological reason.[5]

This line of argument remains entangled in continuing debates about the pioneer anthropologist Melville Herskovits and his legacy. Working, as I do, across the street from Colonial Williamsburg, it seems clear that a different perspective is needed. Although the population of Williamsburg was more than half black during the period the site celebrates, a visitor would have to read or be told this fact; nowhere is it apparent. Further, since the model village was created in part by stealthily eradicating the black heart of the town, the need to write Africans and African descendants into the foreground of American history and culture(s) seems aggressively apparent.[6] What's needed is not the flip-side—essentialism—but theoretical, historical, and cultural *parity*, for without parity the default continues to be the application of European American categories where they don't necessarily fit or where they might mask a more complex story. Toys that are more than toys, like the Snoopy, are a case in point.

The need for more research close to home—most anthropologists of the Diaspora work outside the United States[7]—and for parity across the board become clearer when we compare the state of the art for research on the material world to other domains like African American music and performance. The latter have been richly studied. Yet, emerging from generations of detailed descriptions and nuanced debates, we still do not have a definitive account of transatlantic African contributions to various genres. Nor, perhaps, should we want one. But at least there is overall agreement that contributions exist and that scholars can focus on them or not, depending on their predilections. This is not the case, yet, for material expressions where it is reasonable to assume that African contributions are just as important as any other.

Some material expressions, like the special African American yards I study, have qualities that are well described for other performance genres, including music and carnival. (I say *other* performance genres, for I have come to see some of these yards as slow-moving masquerades.) But unlike more ephemeral performances, material forms persist. So, it is one thing to experience a carnival once a year, but quite another to have the floats around for a decade next door. As Mary Douglas famously said, "Dirt is matter out of place."[8] Thus, for those who wish to present a clean, cultivated image to the world through their yards and neighborhoods, a Snoopy in a plastic bag on the roof is an affront.

Although the Snoopy doesn't qualify, some yards also contain handmade items and Duchamp-like constructions that attract art dealers and collectors. When these objects enter galleries and museums, they usually do so under rubrics like "visionary" or "vernacular" or "folk" or "outsider": the work of Nellie Mae Rowe, discussed below, is an example. For such work, much interpretive writing follows the same profile that Johannes Fabian and Ilona Szombati-Fabian laid out for Zairois painting: the work is either "aestheticized," stripping it of social and historical context (see the review of a Rowe exhibition below), or "sociologized," reducing it to an inevitable outcome within whatever account of context is proffered.[9] Furthermore, both strategies, obviously, apply only to work that is collectable in the first place.

Much isn't. One has only to read the chapter "Non-institutional Aspects of Negro Life" in Gunnar Myrdal's *An American Dilemma* to be reminded of a list of "lags" in acculturation, ranging from a love of loud colors to preferring expensive cars and even wearing a tweed suit, which supposedly diminished the wearer as a failed "imitator" of whites. Such failure is inescapable because the wearer is not and will never be white, but also because formality and decorum have been appropriated entirely by the European descendent population of North America to their own history.[10] Follow up Myrdal with a brief review of elaborate Wolof or Yoruba greetings to dispatch that notion. Or peruse contemporary rebuttals like Herbert Aptheker's *The Negro People* (1946), St. Clair Drake and Horace Cayton's massive *Black Metropolis* (1945), or Drake's subsequent programmatic tomes, *Black Folk Here and There*.

Thus, while I agree with the calls of Paul Lovejoy, James Lorand Matory, and others for historical specificity in African Diaspora research, it is also true that many human encounters take place before we know what we should in order to understand each other. Much learning depends on giving each other the benefit of the doubt, at least at the outset. This certainly seems warranted when the contexts—death, absence or loss of loved ones, illness, and the need for protection—argue for high stakes.

The discussion that follows explores these issues by first examining theories of the African Diaspora, especially creolization. The first thread leads us to *nam*, the second thread takes us to an analysis and reflection on toys and absent loved ones, and the final section presents a brief reconsideration of essentialism.

Creolization?

Is it possible to theorize in some overarching way how peoples, languages, histories, and cultures interact in the African Diaspora? Surely not, for even the choice of label, African Diaspora, implies a politics that could be otherwise. Charting some of the major contenders—assimilation, acculturation, Pan-Africanism, creolization (to which I return below), hegemony and power, transnationalism, and hybridity, among others—in a rough timeline from the late nineteenth century to the present, it becomes clear that all address timely issues that other approaches seem to neglect at their peril, and that the perils for those whose lives they strive to explain seem to diminish as the timeline approaches our day.

But who knows what pitfalls will seem obvious in thirty or fifty years? While all these theories have academic aspects, they also figure in the social movements of the day, as do critiques that expose their limitations. Having started out believing that better thinking replaces worse, as the *callaloo* metaphor replaced the *salad* that replaced the *melting pot*, I look at them now in awe of the struggles the list glosses. I refer here to both historical struggles and ways that people of African descent have turned the constraining projections of theory back on the designers. For example, in the early twentieth century, the uplift movement's displays of black accomplishment turned the assimilationist rhetoric of European American superiority on its head, even as racial prejudice made assimilation impossible. African American acculturationists like E. Franklin Frazier set the master's tools of sociology to work dismantling the master's house of inequality, while others as different as Marcus Garvey and W. E. B. Du Bois were arguing that this was impossible from within U.S. borders alone: only Pan-African solidarity applying global pressure could bring about economic and social justice. Working from opposite poles of diasporic rupture, both Frazier and the pioneer white anthropologist Melville Herskovits followed the social science convention of the 1920s through 1950s of using an ideal type to measure progress or loss: for the former, a composite of African American success; for the latter, a picture of the cultural riches of Africa that the Middle Passage supposedly stripped away. Although Frazier rejected the notion of constitutive African influence in African American culture, as one of my colleagues succinctly put it, "He didn't have time for 'Africanisms' when he was dealing with dead babies in Chicago." And Herskovits, for his part, didn't live with the stereotypes of Africans that his work may have helped to mitigate in the long run, but which at the time on every hand associated African Americans with cartoon cannibals stewing missionaries in pots: African Americans whom the stereotypers also claimed were rescued from their pagan ways by white people's Christianity and, yes, even by slavery. So, in context of their times, one could say that Frazier and Herskovits virtually had to be essentialists.

The call-and-response list could go on. Viewed within the politics of theorizing in their own times, all these efforts to make sense of diasporic experience have fallen short, perhaps because whenever the stigmatized open a door, racism finds a way to close it in what seems to be increasingly subtle ways. Nevertheless, all these theories-as-strategies have much to teach about overcoming loss and oppression within specific historical circumstances.

For some, creolization as an approach to sociocultural change offered a path out of the acculturationists' bind by rejecting ideal types and addressing problems that earlier frameworks could not encompass: rapid cultural emergence; mixed histories, languages, and cultures; coexistent, multiple timelines of change, to name a few. But thinking of creolization as one theory is misleading. There is no single theory of creolization. There never has been. Differences in theoretical orientation arose because circumstances, including power relations, differed according to context, but also because *any* version involves claims about mixture, history, and culture that cannot possibly encompass all stakeholders' perspectives. This has meant that debate about creolization tends to be contentious.[11]

It was surely no accident that creolization and creole linguistics gained currency in the 1960s and '70s, decades that saw heated debates in the social sciences about the limitations of linear, reductionist models borrowed from the natural sciences, the centrality of formerly excluded groups, and the politics of research practices. During the same decades former colonies in Africa and the Caribbean were gaining independence and striving to fashion unified citizenries out of diverse ethnic and class groups. The label Creole made a history of racial and ethnic mixture into a basis for shared contemporary identities. But, as scholars especially from Trinidad and Tobago have pointed out, the terms creolization and creole/Creole can also come to refer primarily to people of African descent, to the exclusion of South Asians, Chinese, Lebanese, and other contributors to the formation of Caribbean nationalities.[12] Thus, simultaneous with talk of inclusive mixture, creole and creolization became terms of exclusion.

During the late 1960s and early '70s, around the time of publication of two influential books, Dell Hymes's collection *Pidginization and Creolization of Languages*,[13] and Kamau Brathwaite's *The Development of Creole Society in Jamaica*,[14] three different approaches converged under the creolization rubric: (A) studies of populations who self-identify as Creole or as members of creole societies; (B) a focus on mixture, emergence, performance, and flexibility; and (C) the birth of a new Afro-American culture in the Americas, with the example of the rapid development of new creole languages as a loose model. My consolidation of theorizing into three camps is a heuristic move; in practice there was overlap among them and, more important for readers/users, little meta-clarification of the differences. As a result, recently, as creolization is experiencing something of a revival (if it/they ever went away), several thorough critical analyses advocating the authors' own stances are available to readers who want to delve more deeply into these confusing waters.[15] Further, Creolization A is generating enormous literatures, often centered on specific regions, like the French *creolité* movement moving out from Martinique and Guadaloupe. Discussion of these I leave to the better informed.

My exposure to what I'm calling Creolization B came through a remarkable course, called "The Creolization of Literatures," that John Szwed taught first at the University of Pennsylvania beginning in the early 1970s and later at Yale. Several other contributors to this volume took this course. It was innovative in its focus on authors writing in languages not their own, and languages like creoles and regional Englishes whose grammars and lexicons revealed legacies of cultural mixture, more often than not, forced: literatures that advocates of the canon dismissed as marginal and impure.[16] (Not incidentally, M. M. Bakhtin's writings on monologic versus polyvocalic utterance and Umberto Eco's expansions on Peircean semiotics were gaining prominence at the same time.)[17] Whatever John Szwed intended, my impression was that creolization wasn't an overarching theory that "explained" the Diaspora (or anything else); it was a toolkit from linguistics, expanding beyond words into performance studies, that could draw attention to then-neglected phenomena of mixture in the writings and other practices of migrants, the displaced, and the colonized. For research on material expression, for example, the notions of loan translations and calques seemed especially promising. These operate by investing a newer lexicon with words, phrases, and definitions imported from an older one: "day spring" for dawn in Gullah, for example. From this perspective, an arrangement like the one in figure 4 (see below) is a calque, using locally found objects for a memorial that might in the past have comprised grave offerings or those on an ancestral altar.

What Lee Drummond called a theory of intersystems came closest to formalizing Creolization B into big T theory. The guiding premise of Drummond's stance is "that internal variation and change, rather than uniformity and synchronicity," are key features of languages and cultures (and, one might add retrospectively, of definitions of creolization); "cultures are neither structures nor plural amalgams, but a . . . set of intersystems" that shape lived experience as participants reconfigure relationships among intersecting, interfering, and often hierarchical cultural systems to fit changing circumstances (Drummond 1980, 354).[18] A major weakness of Drummond's formulation is its lack of attention to power relations, crucial factors in how intersystems mesh and differentiate in participants' lives.[19] When Africans from different regions and societies encountered each other and Europeans in Africa and later in the Americas, they often made the most of cognate forms in order to communicate. But at the same time they selectively loosened objects and activities from their previous moorings, treating them as resources to draw on as new situations warranted. As a result, intersystemic creolization is less concerned with origins than with how continual innovation combines with highly patterned behavior, varying from moment to moment.[20] This, too, can be seen as a weakness. Origins can be traced more often than scholars realized in the 1970s. Further, different disciplines have different priorities, so assertions of radically co-mingled patterns by an anthropologist have little appeal for those seeking parity in U.S. history, or for historians whose narrative strategies emphasize chronology. Again, for a focus on the material world, however, Drummond offered a way to talk about how African diasporic religious practice, art, performance, and music mix past precedents with the latest technology and consumer goods, continually updating how things *should* be done to make a just, livable world, without making the claim (as Creolization C does) that the "new" has eclipsed the "old."

Of the three approaches, Creolization C, which focuses on the rapid birth of a new culture, has been most influential among historians and some anthropologists in the United States. Unfortunately, until recently it has been so dominant that for all practical purposes it "is" creolization in some circles. Yet this approach presents serious limitations. Because it can lead to misunderstandings about what I am trying to say, I now avoid the general term "creolization," focusing instead on a mixture of specific elements and repertoires. The toolkit of Creolization B remains useful in conjunction with vernacular epistemologies and any other theory that raises good questions about the problems at hand. The proponents who gave birth to Creolization C, Sidney Mintz and Richard Price (1976, 1992), claimed that Africans enslaved on plantations were too diverse to reestablish significant institutions in the Americas and that in any case planters would not permit the challenge such institutions would represent. Taking a page from Talcott Parsons (1985),[21] Mintz and Price saw social institutions as the carriers of culture. If African institutions could not cross the Atlantic intact, then new institutions and new cultures had to be formed within the plantation economic unit, the most salient institution in Afro-American cultural development for Mintz and Price.[22] To account for the many similarities with African rituals, behavior, and aesthetics that Herskovits and others had described, they argued for a cultural version of Chomskian generative grammar, a deep structure that organized cultural productions so that the new resembled the old.[23] To the politics of diasporic definitions, Creolization C offered respect for the "creativity" of the enslaved and their descendants. For Americanist scholars there was a practical advantage also: no need to learn specifics about African history, let alone do transatlantic research, for the Middle Passage broke meaningful threads of connection and deep structure took care of the rest.

In the last decade, historian critics have pointed out that Creolization C's construction of the "old" as African and the "new" as characteristic of the Americas has reified Africa and obscured its local engagements with European and North and South American societies. As Africanist historians Paul Lovejoy, Robin Law, and John Thornton have shown, given the 350-year history of the Atlantic trade, the vastness of the African continent, the vastly different relationships among various African and European polities, and the internal migrations and other historical changes within African societies, there cannot be one but must be many African Diasporas.[24] However, as Thornton has also argued, this does not mean that enslaved Africans were too diverse to communicate with each other or find common ground. Rather (excluding the East African trade), the West and Central African regions devolved into three major cultural and linguistic areas: Senegambia and the Upper Guinea Coast, the Gold Coast around the Bight of Benin to the Bight of Biafra, and the Bantu cognate zone extending from what is now Cameroon southward.[25] While populations within—and, for some practices, across—these areas do not have everything in common, *under duress* they could certainly find much to recognize as familiar. For African Americanist historians, especially a younger generation whose work moves us closer to parity, there is simply too much documented evidence for contributions from specific African populations and regions to ignore.[26] Newly available slave trade information is aiding the case. All the newer work discussed above yields a more complex picture of relations between old and new than seemed possible in the 1960s and 1970s, when some still assumed few documents existed for researchers to use.

Kamau Brathwaite is claimed as an ancestor of Creolization B and C, though for different reasons. His foundational study of creole society in Jamaica laid groundwork for the new. But Brathwaite also paid attention to religion, folklore, and non-institutional practices, finding much in the mix that was old.

Nam

Alert to the politics inherent in creolization, Kamau Braithwaite's writings in the 1970s and 1980s insisted on the continuing importance of *nam*, resources from the past that oppressed people of African descent purposefully withheld from erasure through mixing. He also calls this move *negative creolization*.

> The idea of creolization as an ac/culturative, even interculturative process between "black" and "white," with the (subordinate) black absorbing "progressive" ideas and technology from the white, has to be modified into a more complex vision in which appears the notion of *negative or regressive creolization*: a self-conscious refusal to borrow or be influenced by the Other, and a coincident desire to fall back upon, unearth, recognize elements in the maroon or ancestral culture that will preserve or apparently preserve the unique identity of the group. This quality of consciousness is recognized in all modern societies as one of the roots of nationalism.[27]

Brathwaite's term for ancestral culture, *nam*, eye and ear plays around the Jamaican word transliterated as *nyam*, "to eat" and, more broadly, "to be sustained," creating a both/and formation that makes the most of what Karl Reisman has called the "linguistic ambiguity."[28] The contrast between the more theoretical-sounding "negative or regressive creolization" and the vernacular ("Nation Language")[29] *nam* encapsulates Braithwaite's unusual range as both a historian and poet. From either perspective the phenomena in question are ideological. Their "authenticity" derives from experiential depth and emotional attachment, over and against origins alone. As a vernacular term, *nam* builds in echoes of past uses that pile redundancies of association onto usage in the present. This same layering, as habitual creolizing practice, allows the Snoopy on the roof to retain the affect of a cuddly toy while concurrently joining a long trajectory of figurative memorialization.

The essence Brathwaite invokes with *nam* is race based, not biologically but in the sense that race classification is integral to the entire development of the African Diaspora as well as its politics. This also comes through in Brathwaite's definition of *nam:* that combination of "(1) *lore* (direct conscious teaching), (2) *behavior* (energy patterns of expression, speech, movement and sociointellectual praxis), and (3) *ideological myth* . . . which have somehow kept Afro-Caribbean cultural expression 'African' and/or 'black,' especially at moments of crisis or in the so-called margins of the society, despite the obvious material and social advantages of Afro-Saxonism, for instance."[30]

While *nam* may be obscured by mixed forms on a superficial level—the substitution of a modern-day object for its historical predecessor, for example[31]—its role in cultural processes also complements other paradigms like Du Bois's vision of a Pan-Africanism. In this vision, diasporic Africans of the Americas draw strength to overcome racial injustice from both a shared heritage and a future relationship with the homeland.

One might also find some overlap between *nam* and Herskovits's notion of "cultural focus," the idea that the more important a practice is to participants, the more likely it will involve African retentions. Herskovits thus found the strongest cultural focus in religious ritual, especially pertaining to protection of the human body and living space and to birth, death, burial, and the afterlife.[32] Because Herskovits used retentions as one pole of a continuum of culture change from largely African to Euro-oriented norms, his cultural focus is relative. Braithwaite's *nam*, however, has an irreducible quality: as long as invoking the past holds out potential to thwart racism in the struggle for justice, the move will be *part* of living culture.

Nam also involves what Gregory Bateson (who wanted to understand how Balinese trance dancers could inflict deep knife wounds without bleeding) called the *self-evident*, an irreducible premise that marks a bottom line for anthropological analysis.[33] Using the vocabulary of logic along with E. F. Evans-Pritchard's study of Azande witchcraft, Hugh Mehan and Houston Wood called such premises *incorrigible propositions*.[34] Note that in both instances the limits of anthropological reason have been reached. But rather than ruling out what lies beyond them a priori, these scholars tried to tackle the problem and came to similar conclusions: just because anthropology reaches its limits does not mean that participants have reached theirs. Research does not skid to a halt at this point, but the ground rules change. From this point forward, what Knut Myhre calls "vernacular epistemology" must take over.[35]

Whatever one's views on the self-evident, these scholars also agree that foundational premises are extremely resistant to anthropologists and to the flux of intercultural exchange. Further, because they inform a continual round of observable, habitual practices, they do not require a conceptual loophole like "deep structure" to explain their durability. In the Diaspora, these premises and practices are precisely those most likely to ground enslaved Africans' efforts to make a bearable, recognizable world under unbearable conditions of rupture and forced separation.

Such matters, therefore, are utterly serious: death, loss, and life under constant threat to the well-being of self and family, a point that must be stressed in light of toy blindness. The context of Brathwaite's definition of *nam* is a discussion of slave revolts and developing Caribbean and Black nationalisms. However, this essay finds *nam* and negative creolization useful for interpreting smaller scale, more intimate moments where the stakes for persons involved are arguably of comparable magnitude: threats to person and property and the death, loss, or absence of particular loved ones in unjust, ethically bereft circumstances. If emergent nationalism is the macro-politics that Brathwaite sees occasioning *nam*, the absent loved ones in this essay concern a micro-politics of interpersonal encounters and affects. For these, it is the poetics of *nam*, a semantic reach into the realms of irreducible premises, that makes it aptly fit expressive practices that use figural forms as place markers in contexts of what R. P. McDermott, following Harvey Sacks, has called "accountable absences": contexts in which something missing, unsaid, or unsayable nevertheless plays a constitutive part.[36]

Toy Blindness

Strangely enough—or, sadly, logically enough—even researchers who would strenuously agree that life has been filled with danger and loss for Africans and their descendents in the Americas seem more than willing to forget that fact when confronted with a "toy." Consider these three examples.

First, in the spring of 1988, my colleague Judith McWillie took me to visit the artist Thornton Dial at his home in Bessemer, Alabama. Iron, wood, and painted works-in-progress were scattered around his yard. Mr. Dial was in the process of striping black, red, and white paint on a sculpture composed of several small human figures, a duck, a snake, one or more fish, and a Coke bottle, all rising into the air along the vertical bend of a gnarled driftwood root. The legs of the human figures were splayed and one had an open mouth, as if crying out while leaping into the air. To my eternal embarrassment, I said something like this to Mr. Dial: "It looks like they are having a lot of fun and you seem to be having a lot of fun making them. What is happening, exactly?" Mr. Dial's patient reply was caught on tape: "Two people went fishing on the river, but started eating what they had caught, covering it with ketchup. Before they had gone home, while they were still out there they looked and saw things rising against them, and they got real scared, so they tried to jump in the ketchup bottle they brought."[37] With heaps of schooling and not much education to guide me, and despite the serious play of Mr. Dial's explication, two little people trying to jump in a bottle that was smaller than they were still struck me as comic—and nothing more. I was living proof of the venerable pieces of Black and biblical wisdom other artists sent my way pointedly over the next decade: *You knew it was a snake when you picked it up. If you can't see it on your own, you don't need to know it. It's a waste to throw pearls before swine. People only see what they have a mind to see. It is impossible to impart wisdom to the spiritually unprepared.*

Later, in an exhibition catalog essay based on a telephone interview with the artist, Robert Farris Thompson wrote about the piece I saw: "In one of his most intense compositions . . . Thornton Dial 'signified' against men who waste nature, who fish in a river when they aren't even hungry. Dial shows *'the river sending its stuff against the spoilers, scaring them so much they jump into a ketchup bottle.'*[38] He thus criticizes waste with humorous citation of one of the tenets of the bottle tree tradition, the coaxing of all evil into a container. In the process of releasing extraordinary narrative richness, Dial weaves themes of spiritual entrapment into a moralizing observation of the world as it is."[39]

The second instance, an exhibition entitled "The Art of Nellie Mae Rowe," curated by Lee Kogan at the Museum of American Folk Art in New York, included a film of the artist in her elaborately decorated home and yard. Rowe was famous not only for paintings and drawings but also for adorning her surroundings with found objects, including store-bought and homemade dolls. In her catalog essay on Rowe's art, Kogan states, "Artistically expressive in several media, Rowe made dolls among her earliest works. Rowe said that dolls—those she made, found, received—kept her company and were playmates in the 'playhouse' (her term for the special place she created): they substituted for the children she never had."[40] An exhibition reviewer in the *Journal of American Folklore* took exception to this claim. The author argued that Kogan's statement about Rowe's child-lessness—which the reviewer rephrased even more judgmentally as "bar-renness" —was included in the catalog only as one of many markers of Rowe's "outsider" status and was not relevant to her art. Therefore, the exhibition's effort to place Rowe in an artistic tradition of using figuration for such purposes was "superfluous" and demeaning. Instead, Rowe's work should be approached on wholly aesthetic grounds, like the work of Jack-son Pollock, Pablo Picasso, and Vincent Van Gogh on display in other New York museums at the same time.[41]

For me the premises of the review are suspect from the outset, given that the bracketing of "aesthetics" off from everyday life is a key element of European/American modernism, a worldview that might fit Pollock, Pica-sso, and maybe Van Gogh, but one which Mrs. Rowe does not appear to have shared—though many academic art experts still seem to regard art-for-art's-sake as universal, at least among "civilized" peoples.

Third is the photograph from my fieldwork of a stuffed Snoopy posi-tioned beside a "Keep Out" sign on the roof of the garage of Mrs. Ruby Gilmore in Hattiesburg, Mississippi (fig. 1). On seeing this image in the manuscript of my book *Signs of Diaspora* along with Mrs. Gilmore's quoted explanation that the Snoopy was her "watchdog," a noted historian of North American slavery wrote that this is one of the most (of many) untenable claims in the book: the Snoopy was a "toy," and as such it could be nothing other than an icon of American popular culture.[42] Although I responded with photographs of other Snoopies in guardian and memorial contexts, the historian replied that he was sorry I was upset that he didn't like the book, but, yes, a Snoopy is an icon of American popular culture. Period. More on this Snoopy later.

As my encounter with Mr. Dial shows, when I began fieldwork I held preconceptions similar to the historian's. Arriving at the home of Mrs. Gilmore on November 1, 1988, I noticed a Frankenstein mask hanging on a side window of her house and an orange plastic jack-o-lantern and a life-sized skeleton windsock positioned in front of the main entrance. (I have discussed these "decorations" elsewhere.)[43] What stands out now as I write is a vivid memory of the pitying look Mrs. Gilmore gave me when I pointed to these items and said, "I see you have your Halloween decorations up."

But the jack-o-lantern, skeleton, and mask were not Halloween decorations; they were not "toys."[44]

A goal of this essay is to refocus the ascription of childishness off the user of ostensible toys and onto the outsider/learner by tracing part of the education prompted by that look—the look a wise adult directs at a child who does not know better. In the examples that follow, Creolization B could theorize the re-used materials selected, but only *nam* or some idea like it can account for the basic premise, the incorrigible proposition, at the heart of the process. What words could sum up this premise? Perhaps the hope of restoring balance when loss destabilizes links among the dead, the living, and the yet-to-be-born.

Absent Children, Embodied Souls, Spirit Guides, Little People, and Toys

In diasporic North America no theft was more poignant than that of children and spouses. A white Northern schoolteacher in Reconstruction Virginia recalled in her memoir:

> Dear old Aunt Esther and Tom could talk together of spiritual things with a keen appreciation. . . . Aunt Esther bore the "mark in the forehead," if ever any of God's children did. . . . [She] lived alone in a house on the old Tucker plantation. . . . Very little of her early history was known, but . . . her children were all born there—yes, and sold from there, all of them. It was said that they were sold in a financial panic, and . . . [her] mind lost its balance for a time.
>
> After two or three years she apparently regained her mental powers entirely, but she seemed to have no realization that her children had gone from her. They lived in an invisible world about her, played in her cabin while she worked and sang, sat down with her at the table when she ate, and were reproved or caressed by her as they merited.
>
> And they never grew old. A blessed infatuation, one might say, for they seemed to be given back to her in perpetual youth. . . .
>
> In every other respect Aunt Esther seemed fully possessed of her reason. . . . She was shrewd, intelligent, and capable. . . . Her faithful and skillful care was considered invaluable in serious illness. She always went to nurse the sick, when sent for. But after she became weary with nights of watching, she grew restless about the children

at home. Whenever she began . . . saying that they had no supper
because their old mammy was gone, then the friends of the sick whom
she was nursing knew it would be impossible to keep her longer. . . .
People did not talk about [the invisible children]; it was something
sacred in their eyes.[45]

These children were not given material substitutes but remained real
presences for their mother. The fragility of infants also warranted special
treatment. Frances Anne Kimble recalled that babies were wrapped in red
flannel, the color of vitality, on the coastal Georgia plantation where she
resided.[46] Planter Archibald Rutledge from South Carolina wrote:

> There is a strange belief among the Negroes of the old plantation
> regions, which by the sensitive and truly discerning will hardly be
> called superstition. It suggests too much spiritual insight for that.
> They believe that a baby's spirit is inclined to wander away from its
> new domicile in the body, especially if the child is taken outdoors.
> Therefore, when a baby is carried out of a house, some responsible
> member of the family keeps calling to the spirit in the most tender
> and endearing way, appealing to it not to take flight back into the
> vast regions whence it has so lately come.
>   Whatever may be its real name, a frail child is called "Come See"
> —the implication being that the soul is but a casual visitor in such a
> body; it has just come to look about for a little while. . . . These two
> beliefs indicate clearly the Negro's recognition of the soul as an entity
> in itself, a heavenly visitor.[47]

Many visitors or entities that separated from the body at death or guided
the soul to heaven are recorded in African American folklore and conversion narratives. For example:

> We had an open fireplace. . . . My grandmother had a chair and that
> was hers only. She was named Sonia and was about 80 years old. We
> burned nothing but pine knots in the hearth. . . . We were all in bed
> and been for an hour or two. There were others sleeping in the same
> room. There came a peculiar knocking on grandmother's chair. It's
> hard to describe it. It was something like the beating of a distant drum.
> Grandmother was dead, of course. The boys got up and ran out and

brought in some of the hands. When they came in a little thing about 3½ feet high with legs about 6 or 8 inches long ran out of the room.[48]

During the 1940s Harry Middleton Hyatt recorded a description of an object used for divination: a little man in a bottle called a "bodyguard." "At times he be jes' as bright as de mawnin' star."[49] Interestingly, in KiKongo, the word for star, *nduzi*, puns on the word for the place the soul is located in the body.[50] "Since the soul (ndunzi) is thought to be located in the head, more particularly in the forehead (ndunzi), it is sometimes represented on statues as a circular or rectangular metopic spot. . . . Such shapes are also sometimes called "stars" and the soul is said to be like a shining star."[51]

As here, soul beings are also little,[52] an attribute that Elijah Muhammad, whose family name was Little, and who was small in stature, developed in his writings: "I call myself a 'Little Fellow' because the Bible makes Him little. . . . I know am Little. It is up to you to read, and as you read, remember. God says in the Bible: 'Before that dreadful day shall come I will send you Elijah.'"[53]

Often, soul beings and soul guides are also white, the color of spirit (as opposed to Caucasians, whom African American and African artists usually represent as pink). In a passage that resonates with Elijah Muhammad's words, Zora Neale Hurston recounted a conversion vision narrative that she described as traditional: "They found themselves walking over hell on a foot-log so narrow that they had to put one foot right in front of the other. . . . Lord! They saw no way of rescue. But they looked on the other side and saw a *little white man* and he told them to come there. So they called the name of Jesus and suddenly they were on the other side" (my italics).[54]

The Fisk University collection of conversion vision narratives, recorded during the 1930s, contains numerous mentions of the little man or little white man guide at the threshold of Heaven. These have been discussed in detail by Mechal Sobel (1979) in her *Trablin' On: The Slave Journey to an Afro-Baptist Faith*. She relates the guides to the "little me" inside the "big me," that part of the soul, or the one of two or three souls, that quests for conversion and returns to Heaven after death.[55] Also during the 1930s, while researching calls to preach and religious experience in the Sea Islands, Samuel Miller Lawton reported recurring accounts of the little white man guide.[56] Thompson relates such guide figures to BaKongo *bitumba* grave guardian statuary.[57]

2. Grave figure. Snow Hill, Maryland, 1989.
Photo: Grey Gundaker.

Combining the creolizing use of new materials with a *nam* affect that
seeks to do right by those who have passed, the photograph in figure 2
shows a handmade "toy doll," this one the female of a pair, one male, one
female, placed alongside a statue of Jesus on graves in Snow Hill, Maryland, as if to guide the deceased to the next world. In an African American
cemetery in Collegedale, Tennessee, the white concrete statue of a small
cherub stands beside the larger figure of Jesus, presiding over the cemetery, a guide for all who are buried there, as well as a reminder that their
souls have already arrived at their heavenly destination.

Small guide figures also offer a different perspective on what may—or
may not—be another case of toy blindness: two plaster figures of Old Black
Slave spirit guides photographed in two different botánicas in California,
discussed in a recent Internet posting. One squats among other religious
statuary. The author states that the figure looks old and wise. The other figure is also placed alongside other religious statuary on the top corner of a
glass case. Shown from a three-fourth's view, it is much like the first except
that in the crook of one arm it carries a small stuffed Winnie the Pooh bear.
The contrast between statues led the author to conclude that sometimes

this spirit is treated as old and wise, but at other times is shown as "infantilized" because it carries a toy.[58] However, given that the Old Black Slave statue represents an important spirit who advises participants in healing rituals, a serious matter, one cannot help wondering if the small bear, like the unprepossessing-looking old man depicted in the statues, is layered, like Snoopy, to be something else, something more as well.[59] One thing is certain: if this little bear were in Brazil, not Los Angeles, he would give viewers fair warning that Exu/Eshu, the diety of the crossroads and unpredictability, was "playing" nearby.

Commemorations and Watchers

Memorials to the named and unnamed dead have also been characterized as "playful," and their contents as toys. Effie Graham, a white, early twentieth-century dialect writer from Kansas, described the yard of an African American woman in one of her novels with such detail that she must have based her account on observation. This yard resembles a number of actual yards others and I have documented.[60]

The first impression on viewing [the yard] was that of a half-pleasing, half-offending jumble of greenery and gleaming color; of bush and vine; of vegetable and blooming flower; of kitchen ware, crockery, and defunct household furniture. A marvelous mixture it was, of African jungle, city park, and town dump. . . .

One noted . . . the unique receptacles for growing plants. Modern florists trust their treasures to the tender bosom of Mother Earth; not so Aunt June. She elevated her darlings in every conceivable manner. Marigolds bloomed in butter kits, and geraniums in punctured "deeshpans." Easter lilies were upheld by insolent punch-bowls, and johnny jump-ups were ensconced in baby buggies. . . .

"Seem lak dem li'l jum'-pups suah do enjoy demselves crowdin' each other 'roun' in dat ole baby carriage," Aunt June would say. "Dem blue-eyed flowers make me reco-mem-ber Mis' Judge Cartwright's chillun I use to push 'roun' in dat ole baby buggy. . . .

"Whose dat other baby carriage dar wif de white flowers hangin' over de sides? Dat's ole Mis' Preachah Newton's onliest li'l gal's, what's daid. . . . I plant dem white posies in it. Just budded good when Mis' Newton come heah, Memorial Day. She lookin' hawd at dem li'l buds an' she say, "Don't pull dem po' things yet, Aunt June. Dey would be scairt out'en de cemete'y, all alone. Keep 'em twell dey bloom out full. . . ."

"Lan' sake! dat nex' onliest kid o' hern, dat Ralph Newton. . . . Brekin' in heah an' tearin' up Jack, trompin' down flowers, only"— dropping her voice—"he—nevah—teched—dat—*littles' baby buggy*— where dem white flowers is. . . ."

Easily the most conspicuous thing in the yard, and one highly prized by Aunt June, was a mound near the gate. Here, on a rounded pile of earth, was displayed such a collection of broken chinaware and glittering, bright colored glass as has not greeted your eyes since you looked last on your old playhouse. . . .

On this mound were crippled cream pitchers, hotel gravy boats, lamp chimneys, whisky bottles, bar-room fixtures, bits of gay glass from a memorial window, crowned by the shattered remains of an old stovepipe, straight, upright, ready for action.[61]

Graham imputes childish behavior to the quasi-fictive "Aunt June." Yet, the littlest baby buggy of two in the yard commemorates a deceased child and is treated with respect even by the child's otherwise rambunctious brother. The flowers in the buggy are white, a color associated with death. The dead child's mother also recognizes the flowers and buggy as a memorial. The upright pipe and broken china nearby resemble a grave.

In figure 3, the maker of the headstone for Joyce Yarborough, a child who died in Chattanooga, Tennessee, took two casts from a plastic baby doll to create a threshold between white twin figures. In 1988, Mrs. Joyce Johnson, a friend of my mother, directed me to this grave. Here, in a row of graves for five children who died together in a house fire, the seriousness of the doll's use was not lost, even on me in this, my first fieldwork. As years passed, I saw many other handmade African American headstones that used paired—twinned—figures and carvings to create thresholds and others with archways made of pipe or wood. Coupled with the space of passage between them, twinned figures evoke an unseen third term of transition or becoming that recurs in African cultures like the Yoruba, where the child born next after twins is honored as part of a triad, and the BaKongo, where twinned forms like roots and liana twisted together are signs of the *simbi* spirits who inhabit woodland pools.[62] The twisted roots and the white clay found in some pools also index the presence of ancestors and the continuing cycle of life and death and rebirth. In Haitian Vodou, the Rada vévé of

3. Headstone of Joyce Yarborough. Chattanooga, Tennessee, 1988. Photo: Grey Gundaker.

the Marassa twins represents them as a threesome, not a pair, while in the Petwo vévé of Simbi, a third form emerges from the twinning of its two parts. The late Vé Vé A. Clark saw an analogy between these forms and the creative, strategic mixture of old and new by African diasporic peoples, terming it "Marassa consciousness," a pervasive drive to make new ways of being that transcend the conflict that Du Bois famously called "that twon-ess," "double consciousness."[63]

In the previous paragraph, I have carefully avoided the word "symbol" because of the Saussurean conceptual baggage it carries. This approach to symbols renders participants' actions and uses of words and materials as tokens of an abstract neo-Platonic ideal (*langue*), independent of individual instantiations (*parole*), fitting all too well with sociocultural ideal types with their contents gained and lost through acculturation. Although proponents have tried to broaden the scope of the symbol to better accommodate observable mixture, Creolization B avoids the necessity of such moves by insisting that people sustain what counts as "abstract" by the work of stabilization they do on the ground: like the example of layered mixture Brathwaite uses to illustrate *nam*, a ship masthead in a Jamaican newspaper in the 1820s, a planned slave revolt that adopts the image for

4. Memorial to Mrs. Packnett.
Gyp Packnett, Centerville, Mississippi,
1993. Photo: Grey Gundaker.

a new project, and, in juxtaposition, an emergent freedom ship pointing toward African regions of a lost past and hoped for future that the newspapers' printers never envisioned. So too, the family members who recruited baby dolls into the process of laying Joyce Yarborough to rest. Sam Sharpe and Aunt June, like the revolt's leader, no doubt had more pressing sorrows and worries than retaining or losing "symbols" from Africa. In events like these, "cultural focus" is not displaying of core cultural traits. It is about using cultural means to pointedly remind us of the seriousness of recurring losses in the cycle of life. *Nam* buffers these moments, as well as events of significance to a larger diasporan group, from oppressive co-optation. As usual, the vernacular makes the point best: *If you've got a lot of lemons, make lemonade; if it's not broke, don't fix it.* And, perhaps, conversely, as Joyce Yarborough's family members broke white china plates on her grave and each of her brothers' and sisters' graves, the following twin ideas were present: that this was *the right way to do things* and that as the children sat at God's table, they and the plates would again be whole.

For Gyp Packnett of Centreville, Mississippi, losses stretched back through his eighty-four years, his age when I met him in 1991, from his wife, most recently, to his father and mother and on back to enslaved grandparents and their African forebears, smuggled into the South illegally at

5. Watcher-Memorial to his father.
Gyp Packnett, Centerville, Mississippi,
1988. Photo: Grey Gundaker.

a landing stage on the Mississippi, about fifteen miles from his home. He created memorials for each generation and viewed doing so as part of his responsibility as the keeper of a home place for his children, grandchildren, and great-grandchildren dispersed around the country. As we talked, he explained that he initially thought the purpose of his efforts would be obvious to everyone, but learned from hard experience that most saw only "junk" and "funny old stuff," like the visual equivalent of being tone deaf. The centerpiece of the yard was an ancient hemlock from which he suspended two huge weights formerly used to counterbalance the scales that weighed the cotton he and his ancestors picked. The present/absent bodies of those who had gone before were evoked through empty chairs, one positioned off the ground as if in flight, others arrayed around the Lord's Table in Heaven—a metal lawn set elevated on tires. Hard-hatted pure white faces made from upended Clorox bottles gazed outward from the fence enclosing the area. He wept as he explained the significance of the weights, tree, and chairs in 1991.

Mr. Packnett also used a baby doll emerging from his late wife's work shoes as the central figure in a memorial he built to her on the side of his carport at a right angle to the easy chair where he spent much of his leisure time (fig. 4). Always at the edge of his peripheral vision, the doll figure and

6. Watcher dolls with gun. Gyp
Packnett, Centerville, Mississippi,
1989. Photo: Grey Gundaker.

a stuffed animal were suspended as if in flight over an empty seat, surrounded by memorial flowers and garlanded with linked pop tops from
soda cans and chains of plastic can holders that the late Mrs. Packnett had
strung together.

He also used a baby doll in one of two memorials to his father, both
also positioned with eyes directed to watch thresholds on the property.
Upon entering his driveway, the first of these was a bull skull with silver
Christmas balls inserted in the eye sockets and red paint accentuating the
gunshot penetrating the forehead of the skull.[64] This signaled Mr. Packnett
senior's role as master butcher for the community, a theme picked up in
the second memorial—and warning to ill-intentioned outsiders—at the
entrance to the carport. In it, a baby doll gazes at all who approach, framed
by the antlers of a buck Mr. Packnett shot and wearing the red cap of an
insecticide can inscribed "Faster killing power" (fig. 5). Like the memorial
to his wife, the doll is accompanied by funereal flowers. An alert figure of
a chicken stands on one side, a wheel on the other.

Outside the back door opening from the carport, Mr. Packnett mounted
two watcher dolls, one with a real handgun (fig. 6). When Robert Farris
Thompson used these in his exhibition *Face of the Gods* (carrying them
to New York in their own airplane seat after some discussion with airport
security about the gun), Mr. Packnett constructed a replacement, again

7. Two stuffed animals on the porch of a vacant house. Victor Melancon, Hammond, Louisiana, 1990. Photo: Grey Gundaker.

8. Incredible Hulk beside the front door. Victor Melancon, Hammond, Louisiana, 1990. Photo: Grey Gundaker.

9. Watcher in ornate skirt-bottle. Victor Melancon, Hammond, Louisiana, 1990. Photo: Grey Gundaker.

10. The Pale Horse of the Book of Revelation. Victor Melancon, Hammond, Louisiana, 1990. Photo: Grey Gundaker.

using a toy, this time including a mirror. Elsewhere, my colleague Judith McWillie and I have discussed watchers as one of the main recurring elements that certain African Americans of a material-expressive bent have used to create a Safety Zone (cf. a gospel song of that name) of protection around their residences.[65]

Not surprisingly, residents most often position watchers when they feel unsafe. For example, Victor Melancon of Hammond, Louisiana, placed stuffed animals in a rocking chair on the porch of the empty house next door that he worried might become a haven for crack cocaine users and a danger to children playing there (fig. 7). He also sat the Incredible Hulk (in fig. 8) in a chair beside his front door and a doll head (watcher) in an ornate skirt-bottle beside his front steps (fig. 9), along with a red-painted root: I have roots here. (All the yards makers mentioned in this essay use this type of word-object translation, pun, or calque.)[66]

Toys can also transition from watcher to memorial. One of the students in my African American material culture course in 1996 told the class that her grandmother, a Virginian of African and Native American descent, became worried about her safety living alone after her husband died. She lined the edge of her front porch with stuffed animals, all looking out at the road. When the grandmother died the family took the stuffed animals to

11. Chip, the late dog of Mrs. Ruby Gilmore, Hattiesburg, Mississippi, 1989. Photo: Grey Gundaker.

12. Mrs. Ruby Gilmore, Hattiesburg, Mississippi, 1990. Photo: Grey Gundaker.

the funeral home and passed them over the casket. When the casket was interred the animals were placed on its lid before the grave was filled.[67]

Laid off from a series of well-paid jobs in the automobile industry, Mr. Melancon lived a precarious existence on welfare when I met him. He made work for himself by collecting refuse around his neighborhood, reading about items like those he found in a large collection of books, and reassembling them in new combinations. Along the left side of the property, he built a "ghost train" presided over by a conductor figure—a pole in a blue, knitted watch cap—invoking the fisherman uncle who raised him. Inside, on a bed in the spare bedroom, his source book was Revelations in the Christian Bible (fig. 10). To the left, a large white (pale) stuffed (toy) horse held a small stuffed tiger (his soul, Mr. Melancon explained) between its soft hooves.[68] To its right, Mr. Melancon arranged the neatly folded clothes in which he would be buried on the seat of a hanging chair "space capsule," ready for the journey, when needed.

The loved ones sorely missed and lovingly commemorated that I have discussed so far have been human. But Mrs. Ruby Gilmore, whose Snoopy could be nothing other than an icon of popular culture for the historian above, mourned her dog Chip (fig. 11). When I first met Mrs. Gilmore, Chip was alive, well, and mistress of Mrs. Gilmore's densely packed yard. After the passing of her husband and the death of a grandson whose medical bills Mrs. Gilmore was trying to pay off, she became a dedicated collector and recycler (fig. 12). Each morning at 5:00 a.m. over a fifteen-year period, Mrs. Gilmore set out to comb curbside garbage for items she could use, sell for scrap, or barter for other goods. Until about 1992 she used a car for her travels, but in later years, when she lacked money to have the car repaired, she adopted a train of supermarket push carts. Around seven, she returned home, sorted the aluminum and other salable metals from her take, and headed for the recycling center.

Mrs. Gilmore's neighborhood, an economically mixed area that ranged from prosperous middle-class city employees to down-and-out corner-hangers, was replete with property protection strategies: bars on windows, fences high and low, old-time material communications with hoodoo undertones like an empty wheel with affixed "no trespassing" sign hanging on a dead tree (come in here and you go through the hole to the Other Side), placards from alarm companies, and alert porch-sitting retirees. Mrs. Gilmore considered her yard especially vulnerable late at night and on Sundays because customers of a bootlegger down the street were known to rifle through her yard for articles they could trade for liquor

13. Memorial to Mrs. Davenport. Elijah Davenport, Georgia, 1988. Photo: Grey Gundaker.

while she was at church. To discourage them, she crafted a barricade of chicken wire, sheet metal, plastic tarps, wood, and clanging chimes. Statues of a duck and a collie watched the street through gaps. To warn her at night, she counted on Chip.

Chip was also good company, the only family member left in the household after her daughter moved to Texas and her nephew entered Morehouse College in Atlanta. The neighbors shunned Mrs. Gilmore, warning me to watch out because she was "a little off." I found no evidence of that but plenty of evidence that Mrs. Gilmore dressed for comfort and convenience, sat on the ground and chopped wood in a manner some might consider un-"uplift"-ed for a matron in her late sixties, and surrounded herself in the "junk" that supplemented her income. Chip, of course, minded none of this, dining well on meat scraps from a nearby butcher's. It was into these scraps, Mrs. Gilmore explained when I returned in 1989, that the bootlegger's customers put rat poison. When she returned from church in her good clothes—the only day of the week she wore a dress—Chip was barely breathing. The yard was splattered with vomit and blood that told the story of poisoning. Mrs. Gilmore had held Chip in her arms until the end.

On my next visit after Chip's death, I noticed one major addition to Mrs. Gilmore's watchers, a large droop-eared stuffed Snoopy dog on the crest of the roof of the carport. Bagged in plastic, it peered over the brink next to a pre-printed Keep Out sign. When I asked Mrs. Gilmore about the Snoopy, she said, "Well, since my real dog is gone, I put up this watch dog." Thus the stuffed dog both commemorated Chip and added its gaze to the china duck and collie watching the approach to the house. As I have already mentioned, she also hung a Halloween mask and skeleton near her door. These faces had no memorial function, as far as I know, and did not stand in for any specific member of the household. Instead, they attested to absence in more general terms, especially the vulnerability of an empty house. Thus, though they may look like playthings, they had the serious purpose of confronting the negative intentions of intruders with a formidable gaze and of letting potential trespassers know Somebody was home, even if the homeowner wasn't.

Like Mrs. Gilmore's Snoopy, though originally marketed for child's play, the broken, tied Snoopy that Elijah Davenport placed on a white column became something altogether more serious. The column stood beside the absent-body-suggesting rocking chair used by his late wife and an overturned Home Comfort cook stove covered with pierced pots, inverted as they would have been on an old-time grave mound (fig. 13).

White commentators have a long history of describing African American memorials comprising broken china, figures, pitchers, and inverted vessels in graveyards and house yards like Aunt June's as childlike, junk-filled, and even comic. The error of these ways has been discussed at great length, and, indeed, grave offerings have been foundational in discussions of transatlantic material continuities. Although some twentieth-century folklorists, like Newbell Niles Puckett, assumed African connections, a point later elaborated by Robert Farris Thompson and others, practitioners themselves never to my knowledge said as much themselves: "It's just something we do" is the gist of most commentary. These days we might quite rightly assume that those queried would hardly "tell all" to a white interrogator with a smirk on his or her face. But the notion that some things are *done*, not *said*, also deserves to be taken seriously. Further, of the more than fifty women and men I have interviewed about memorials, protective signs, and other materials in their yards, only those who came of age after the Civil Rights Movement mentioned Africa in relation to their work. However, several African American elders did refer to such work as part of "the *old way* that's not in the Bible" (my italics).[69]

Giving the benefit of the doubt and putting infantilization back where it belongs means taking these statements seriously also. Even when it is not yet—and may never be—possible to fill in all the specifics necessary to satisfy critics, the vastness of the literature on figuration and masking in West and Central Africa should make clear that these practices are among the many cognate forms that captives from diverse regions and groups would find mutually intelligible, at least in their general parameters. I will list only a few.

Ibeji are Yoruba twin sculptures, one male and one female, honored with ritual offerings and, when one or both of the twins is deceased, carried by mothers of twins in place of live children. In the late twentieth century, commercial dolls and figural wax candles began to be used instead of woodcarvings.[70] Tracing the ritual importance of twins in Africa and the Diaspora, Marilyn Houlberg mentions an African American devotee of Santería who took his *ere ibeji* along while serving on a submarine in the navy and later, when he took his children to Disneyland, he put his *ere ibeji* in his backpack and "let their heads peep out so they could experience Disneyland just like my children were enjoying it."[71] Akua *Ba* are Akan "dolls" that serve as prototypes of beauty for the growing fetuses of pregnant women and focal points of prayers and offerings for women who wish to become pregnant. *Bocio* were Fon figures on which anxieties and personal emotions were projected to resolve problems.[72] Bembe ancestral figures, sometimes clothed and hatted, enclosed relics of the deceased.[73] And certain Kongo *nkisi* were complexes of rituals, medicated embodiments of spiritual power, and coded directives for specific actions.[74]

Thematically, West and Central African figures like these stand in for absent human and animal bodies or instantiate them with new material forms to instruct the young, keep ancestral presences alive for the community, and protect against loss from violence and theft. In addition to anthropomorphic figures, embodiment takes form through containers, roots, flags, material portraits, natural materials, and masks and costumes that under appropriate conditions transform the wearers into ancestral and spiritual personas. Figures signifying specific animal qualities are also widespread in West and Central Africa, serving a variety of purposes.[75] Animal names for dances—jitterbug, buzzard lope, fox trot—flag African American contributions to popular dance.[76] Animal tales—Brer Rabbit, Anancy, Aunt Nancy—reveal the endurance of such characters as the trickster and purvey moral instruction in North America. One, the tar baby, is echoed in a nineteenth-century attestation of African American figural warning and protection, a small black "doll" painted over the door of a blacksmith shop in Sumter, South Carolina.[77] A forceful, handmade iron figure was also discovered in an African American blacksmith shop.[78] In the United States, Cuba, Haiti, Trinidad, and Brazil, dolls and other types of appropriated and handmade figures along with Roman Catholic chromolithographs and religious statuary play numerous roles in such African Diaspora religions as Regla de Ocha, Shango, Vodou, and Candomblé.

In sum, a transatlantic network of figuration links various aspects of the life cycle and important modes of communication with spiritual realms.[79] One needs no notion like an already-underlying grammar to account for patterns because users make material grammars as they go, with each performance, just as speakers make, keep, and change linguistic grammars with each utterance.

Yet, how does figuration reconcile with the emergent nationalism of *nam?* I would argue that an answer lies in Brathwaite's use of the term *nation*, following wider diasporic usage, to mean one's own people.[80] Absent loved ones place-marked with a figure are, indeed, signaled as one's own people—even when they are terriers transmuted as Snoopys.

Essentialism Reconsidered

If creolization entails mixture from formerly divergent cultural sources, and if *nam* pulls back against the resulting mixture in contexts where newness is associated with the ruptures and losses of oppression, what counts as old? What counts as ancestral when the disjunctions of Diaspora leave jagged ends in the fabric of memory? Kamau Brathwaite supplied one answer in a course on Caribbean history. He told the class about writing a poem that required him to describe an African house. However, he did not know what the house should look like because the African past was consciously erased in among members of his childhood community in Barbados.[81] So, he looked African houses up in a book. For Brathwaite, *nam* and emergent nationalism were vested as much or more in the will to search as in any direct link between Barbadian houses and those in Africa. One need not *remember* roots; what mattered was searching for them. Nor did it matter if the house he described was precisely like those of his specific ancestors. For Brathwaite, *nam* resided in the search for workable indexicality, not in the accuracy of the results. Unlike Brathwaite, Mrs. Gilmore did not search books, nor did she set out to select "African" precedents for memorizing Chip. Instead, she searched others' trash for articles that could be used to show she was doing *right* by her dog.

Creolization B and *nam* together encompass the old, the rooted, and the new, the invented, as complementarities within a larger dynamic of keeping and inventing. The absent loved ones and figural proxies that this essay has discussed on one level seem to be textbook instances of visual and material Creolization B. The materials used were usually made initially as consumer products in advanced capitalist contexts, so entrenched in these contexts as to be masked. Like the calques and loan translations of creole languages, they have been lifted from one lexical category, toys, and one grammar of action, play, and inserted into another with a different communicative register, to commemorate, instruct, and protect.

This layered dynamic also suggests that Kamau Brathwaite anticipated and worked past more recent debates about essentialism and anti-essentialism in at least two ways that have not been sufficiently appreciated. First, he did not fall into the lingering acculturationist trap of equating "culture" or group identity with a bucket of traits such that authenticity resides in a fixed corpus of elements a people could retain to a greater or lesser extent. Instead, as a poet he cast *nam*/essence as affective and thus always situated and emergent.[82] Second, Brathwaite bypassed fruitless debates about whether diasporic peoples are more/less "African" or more/less "European," and whether creole Afro-American culture is/is not newly "birthed" on the plantations of the Americas, by theorizing creolization and negative creolization—the experiential truths of mixing and holding back—in relation to each other. For present purposes, this approach is useful because, while in no way ruling out historical specificity as a goal, it does suggest that specific African sources and parallels, specifically situated invocations of an idealized Africa, and specific kinds of blindness about both can figure in the mix.

Notes

1. A companion essay to this one, based on a wider range of sites from my fieldwork, situates figures in certain African American yards in the contexts where makers place them, showing the major modes of figuration that recur and the relationship figures' demeanor to hot and cool affective climates that makers build into the landscape. (Grey Gundaker, "Face Like a Looking Glass: Ritual Figuration and Landscape in Special African American Yards," in, ed. *Materialities, Meanings,*

and *Modernities of Rituals in the Black Atlantic*, ed. Akin Ogundiran and Paula Saunders (Bloomington: Indiana University Press, forthcoming). That essay homes in on material details. Other publications (see note 59) also contain information on these yards, patterns within them, and the individuals who create them.

2. For example, Mikelle Smith Omari, "The Role of the Gods in Afro-Brazilian Ancestral Ritual," *African Arts* 23, no. 1 (1989): 54–61, 103–104; Jean M. Borgatti, "Portraiture in Africa," *African Arts* 23, no. 3 (1990): 34–39, 101–102; Margaret Thompson Drewal, "Portraiture and the Construction of Reality in Yorubaland and Beyond," *African Arts* no. 3 (1990): 40–49.

3. For example, Karl Reisman, "The Island Is Full of Voices": A Study of Creole in the Speech Patterns of Antigua, West Indies" (PhD diss., Harvard University, 1965); Karl Reisman, "Cultural and Linguistic Ambiguity in a West Indian Village," in *Afro-American Anthropology*, ed. Norman E. Whitten and John F. Szwed, 129–144 (New York: Free Press, 1970); Karl Reisman, "Contrapuntal Communication in an Antiguan Village," Working Paper 3, Penn-Texas Working Papers in Sociolinguistics, 1970; Karl Reisman, "Contrapuntal Conversation in an Antiguan Village," in *Explorations in the Ethnography of Speaking*, ed. Richard Bauman and Joel Scherzer (Cambridge: Cambridge University Press, 1974/1989), 110–124.

4. One instance from literary studies is Chris Bongie, *Island and Exiles of Post/Colonial Literature* (Stanford, CA: Stanford University Press, 1998).

5. Andrew Apter, "On African Origins: Creolization and *Connaissance* in Haitian Vodou," *American Ethnologist* 29, no. 2, (2002): 233.

6. Social historians and African American interpreters at Colonial Williamsburg have pressed hard against trends that seem to have as much to do with financial interests in gated golf-course communities for affluent retirees as they do with historical mythologies. See Richard Handler and Eric Gable, *The New History in an Old Museum: Creating the Past at Colonial Williamsburg* (Durham, NC: Duke University Press, 1997).

7. Where, ironically, many of them, following Herskovits, still argue that there are more African influences than within the United States. My research suggests this is an error, both because of parity issues and because it is all too easy for American anthropologists to fall into the trap of assuming they know their own country. The dictums of Mintz and Price are taken seriously in U.S.-based scholarship, for example, although neither they (nor Apter, nor the other anthropologists he cites) have researched the Diaspora within U.S. borders.

8. Mary Douglas, *Purity and Danger: An Analysis of Concepts of Pollution and Taboo* (London: Routledge and Kegan Paul, 1966; reprint, New York: Routledge, 2002).

9. Johannes Fabian and Ilona Szombati-Fabian, "Folk Art from an Anthropological Perspective." In *Folk Art in America*, ed. Scott T. Swank and Ian M. G. Quimby (New York: W. W. Norton, 1980), 247–292.

10. Gunnar Myrdal, *An American Dilemma: The Negro Problem and Modern Democracy* (New York: Harper, 1944). Many thanks to John Szwed for sending me to this book in my first semester of graduate school.

11. See, for example, papers in Charles Stewart, ed., *Creolization: History, Ethnography, Theory* (Walnut Creek, CA: Left Coast Press, 2007); Okwui Enwezor, Carlos Basualdo, Meta Bauer, Suzanne Ghez, Sarat Maharaj, Mark Nash, and Octavio Zaya, eds., *Créolité and Creolization Documanta11_Platform3* (Ostildern-Ruit: Hatje Cantze Publishers, 2002); Prem Misir, ed., *Cultural Identity and Creolization: The Multiethnic Caribbean* (Lanham, MD: University Press of America, 2006).

12. Viranjini Munasighne points out how this accompanies the "upward mobility" of creolization from historical specificity to (ironically) "pure" theory in "Theorizing World Culture through the New World: East Indians and Creolization," *American Ethnologist* 33, no. 4: 549–562.

13. Dell Hymes, ed., *Pidginization and Creolization of Languages* (New York: Cambridge University Press, 1971).

14. Kamau Brathwaite, *The Development of Creole Society in Jamaica* (Oxford: Claredon Press, 1971).

15. Stephan Palmié, "Creolization and Its Discontents," *Annual Review of Anthropology* 35 (2006): 433–456; Richard Price, "The Miracle of Creolization," *New West Indian Guide/Nieuwe West-Indische Gids* 75, no. 1/2 (2001): 35–64.

16. John F. Szwed, lecture notes, October 1988. See John F. Szwed, *Crossovers: Essays on Race, Music, and American Culture* (Philadelphia: University of Pennsylvania Press, 2005), especially chapter 31, "Metaphors of Incommensurability."

17. M. M. Bakhtin, "Discourse in the Novel," in *The Dialogic Imagination*, trans. Caryl Emerson and Michael Holquist (Austin: University of Texas Press, 1981); Umberto Eco, *Semiotics and the Philosophy of Language* (Bloomington: Indiana University Press, 1986); Umberto Eco, *The Open Work* (Cambridge, MA: Harvard University Press, 1989).

18. Lee Drummond, "The Cultural Continuum: A Theory of Intersystems," *Man* (n.s) 15 (1980): 34.

19. Brackette Williams, *Stains on My Name, War in My Veins: Guyana and the Politics of Cultural Struggle* (Durham, NC: Duke University Press, 1991).

20. Cf. Roger D. Abrahams and John F. Szwed, eds., *After Africa* (New Haven: Yale University Press, 1983), 2–42. Performance styles, embodied knowledges, genres (including mixing ones), and habits of attention provide an alternative to the "deep structure" posited by Mintz and Price as an unconscious grammatical basis for cultural similarities between Africa and the Americas.

21. Talcott Parsons, *Institutions and Social Evolution: Selected Writings*, ed. Leon H. Mayhew (Chicago: University of Chicago Press, 1985).

22. Sidney Mintz and Richard Price, *An Anthropological Approach to the Afro-American Past*, ISHI Occasional Papers in Social Change 2 (Philadelphia: Institute for the Study of Human Issues, 1976); Sidney Mintz and Richard Price, *Birth of African-American Culture* (Boston: Beacon Press, 1992). Also see collections in note 11 for further discussion.

23. Mintz and Price, *Birth*, 9–10.

24. Paul Lovejoy, "The African Diaspora: Revisionist Interpretations of Ethnicity, Culture, and Religion under Slavery," *Studies in the World History of Abolition and Emancipation* 2, no. 1 (1997).

25. John Thornton, *Africa and Africans in the Making of the Atlantic World, 1400–1680* (Cambridge: Cambridge University Press, 1992).

26. See, for example, the excellent introduction in Jason R. Young's *Rituals of Resistance: African Atlantic Religion in Kongo and the Lowcountry of South Carolina in the Era of Slavery* (Baton Rouge: Louisiana State University Press, 2007), 1–23; and at the forefront of this trend, Sterling Stuckey, *Slave Culture: Nationalist Theory and the Foundations of Black America* (New York: Oxford University Press, 1987); Michael Gomez, *Exchanging Our Country Marks: The Transformation of African Identities in the Colonial and Antebellum South* (Chapel Hill: University of North Carolina Press, 1998).

27. Kamau Brathwaite, "Caliban, Ariel, and Unprospro in the Conflict of Creolization: A Study of the Slave Revolt in Jamaica in 1831–32," in *Comparative Perspectives on Slavery in New World Plantation Societies*, ed. V. Rubin and A. Tuden (New York: Annals of the New York Academy of Sciences, 1977), 55.

28. See Kamau Brathwaite, *The History of the Voice: The Development of Nation Language in Anglophone Caribbean Poetry* (London: New Beacon Books, 1984); Reisman, "Cultural and Linguistic Ambiguity," 129.

29. Brathwaite, *The History of the Voice*.

30. Brathwaite, "Caliban," 41.

31. Brathwaite gives the example of the ship-pictured masthead of a newspaper in Jamaica coming to represent a Freedom Ship for participants in the Sam Sharpe rebellion. Brathwaite, "Caliban," 77.

32. Melville Herskovits, *The Myth of the Negro Past* (Harpers, 1941; repr., Boston, MA: Beacon Press, 1958).

33. Gregory Bateson, "Some Components of Socialization for Trance," *Ethos* 3, no. 2 (Summer 1975): 148.

34. Hugh Mehan and Houston Wood, *The Reality of Ethnomethodology* (New York: John Wiley & Sons, 1975).

35. Knut Christian Myhre, "The Truth of Anthropology," *Anthropology Today* 22, no. 6 (2006): 16–19; Knut Christian Myhre, "Divination and Experience of a Chagga Epistemology," *Journal of the Royal Anthropological Institute* (n.s) 12 (2006): 313–330. Returning to the Ndembu after the death of her husband, Edith Turner took this (unpopular) position; see Edith Turner, with William Blogett, Singleton Kahona, and Fideli Benwa, *Experiencing Ritual: A New Experience of African Healing* (Philadelphia: University of Pennsylvania Press, 1992).

36. Sacks's research is presented in Emanuel Schegloff and Harvey Sacks, "Opening Up Closings," *Semiotica* 8 (1973): 289–327; R. P. McDermott, "Inarticulateness," in *Linguistic in Context*, ed. Deborah Tannen (Norwood, NJ: Ablex, 1988), 37–68.

37. Tape recording by Judith McWillie, February or March 1988. This sculpture was subsequently exhibited in the exhibition *Another Face of the Diamond: Pathways through the Black Atlantic South*, curated by Judith McWillie for INTAR Latin American Gallery, New York City, in 1989. Its photograph and quotations used here appear on page 39 of the catalog of the same name in Robert Farris Thompson's essay, "The Circle and the Branch: Renascent Kongo-American Art."

38. Robert Farris Thompson telephone interview, September 1988; Thompson, "Circle," 58.

39. Thompson, "Circle," 58.

40. Lee Kogan, *The Art of Nellie Mae Rowe: Ninety-nine and a Half Won't Do* (New York: University Press of Mississippi in association with the Museum of American Folk Art, 1998), 27.

41. Pravina Shukla, Exhibition review of *The Art of Nellie Mae Rowe: Ninety-Nine and a Half Won't Do*, Museum of American Folk Art, *Journal of American Folklore* 113, no. 447 (Winter 2000): 90–92. (However, at the time of the Picasso, Van Gogh, and Pollock exhibitions, several biographies and numerous critical essays were in print for readers to consult about their lives if they wished. The same cannot be said of Rowe.)

42. It seems uncharitable to identify the historian by name. The statements mentioned occurred in a readers report and subsequent correspondence in 1994.

43. Grey Gundaker, "Halloween Imagery in Two Southern Settings," in *Halloween and Other Festivals of Life and Death*, ed. Jack Santino (Knoxville: University of Tennessee Press, 1994b), 247–266.

44. Ludwig Wittgenstein, *Philosophical Investigations*, 3rd English edition (New York: Prentice-Hall, 1973).

45. Henrietta Matson, *The Mississippi Schoolmaster* (Boston: Congregational Sunday-School & Publishing Company, 1893), 137–139.

46. Frances Anne Kemble, *Journal of a Residence on a Georgia Plantation in 1838–1839* (Athens: University of Georgia Press, 1984).

47. Archibald Rutledge, *It Will Be Daybreak Soon* (New York: Fleming Revell, 1938), 44.

48. George P. Rawick, ed., *The American Slave: A Composite Autobiography* (Westport, CT: Greenwood Press, 1972), vol. 10: *Arkansas Narratives*, pt. 5.

49.Harry Middleton Hyatt, *Hoodoo—Conjuration—Witchcraft—Root Work*, 5 vols. (Hannibal, MO: Western Publishing, 1970–1978), vol. 2:1295.

50. Wyatt MacGaffey, *Religion and Society in Central Africa* (Chicago: University of Chicago Press, 1986), 124.

51. MacGaffey, *Religion and Society*, 124.

52. Also see Julius Lester, *The Knee High Man and Other Tales* (New York: Penguin, 1972); Ruth Bass, "Death Is a Little Man," originally in *Scribners' Magazine* 97 (1935): 120–123, reprinted in *Mother Wit from the Laughing Barrel*, ed. Alan Dundes (Jackson: University of Mississippi Press, 1990), 388–396.

53. Thanks to John Szwed for pointing out this passage. Abass Rassoul, ed., *The Theology of Time by the Honorable Elijah Muhammad* (Hampton, VA: U.B. & U.S. Communications, 1992), 2.

54. Zora Neale Hurston, *Dust Tracks on a Road* (1942; repr., Harper Perennial Classics edition, New York: Harper & Brothers, 2003), 220.

55. Mechal Sobel, *Trablin' On: The Slave Journey to an Afro-Baptist Faith* (Westport, CT: Greenwood, 1979; repr. Princeton: Princeton University Press, 1988).

56. Samuel Miller Lawton, "The Religious Life of South Carolina Coastal and Sea Island Negroes" (PhD diss., George Peabody College for Teachers, Nashville, TN, 1939).

57. Robert Farris Thompson and Fr. Joseph Cornet, *The Four Moments of the Sun: Kongo Art in Two Worlds* (Washington, DC: National Gallery of Art, 1981), 184, 210n.

58. This photo by Patrick Polk was posted online along with a summary of a talk presented on November 2, 2005, Día de los Muertos (Day of the Dead/All Souls Day), "The Lives of the Dead: Botánicas, Spiritism, and the Ghosts of Slavery" as part of the Institute of Signifying Scriptures Brown Bag Lunch Discussion. Also see Patrick Polk's book, *Botánica Los Angeles: Latino Popular Religious Art in the City of Angels* (Los Angeles: UCLA Fowler, 2005).

59. Following from uses of smaller figures alongside larger ones that I have documented, the bear's "toy" qualities signal vulnerability, compared to the strength of the guide. Thus the bear would stand in for the seeker of spiritual advice who has placed himself or herself in the Old Black Slave (Preto Vejho's) care. See figure 12 and the comments of Victor Melancon.

60. I conducted fieldwork on assembled objects in African American yards in eleven states between 1987 and 2002. On African American yards, see, for example, Richard Westmacott, "Pattern and Practice in Traditional African-American Gardens in Rural Georgia," *Landscape Journal* 10, no. 2 (1991): 87–104; Richard Westmacott, *African-American Gardens and Yards in the Rural South* (Knoxville: University of Tennessee Press, 1992). On yard shows, see Robert Farris Thompson, *Face of the Gods: Art and Altars of Africa and the African Americas* (New York: Museum for African Art, 1993), 76–95; Grey Gundaker, "Tradition and Innovation in African American Yards," *African Arts* 26, no. 2 (1993): 58–71, 94–96; Lizetta LeFalle-Collins, *Home and Yard: Black Folk Life Expressions in Los Angeles* (Los Angeles: California Afro-American Museum, 1987); Robert Farris Thompson and Joseph Cornet, *The Four Moments of the Sun: Kongo Art from Two Worlds* (Washington, DC: National Gallery of Art, 1981); Robert Farris Thompson, *Flash of the Spirit: African and Afro-American Art and Philosophy* (New York: Random House, 1983); Robert Farris Thompson, "The Circle and the Branch: Renascent Kongo-American Art," in *Another Face of the Diamond*, ed. Judith McWillie and Inverna Lockpez (New York: INTAR Latin American Gallery, 1988); Robert Farris Thompson, "The Song that Names the Land: The Visionary Presence of African American Art," in *Black Art: Ancestral Legacy*, ed. Robert V. Roselle, Alvia Wardlaw, and Maureen A. McKenna (Dallas, TX: Dallas

Museum of Art, 1989); also Grey Gundaker, "African American History, Cosmology, and the Moral Universe of Edward Houston's Yard," *Journal of Garden History* 14, no. 3 (1994): 179–205; Grey Gundaker, *Keep Your Head to the Sky: Interpreting African American Home Ground* (Charlottesville: University Press of Virginia, 1998); Judith McWillie, "Art, Healing, and Power in African American Yards," in *Keep Your Head to the Sky*, ed. Gundaker; Grey Gundaker and Judith McWillie, *No Space Hidden: The Spirit of African American Yards* (Knoxville: University of Tennessee Press, 2006).

61. Effie Graham, *The "Passin' On" Party* (Chicago: A. C. McClurg, 1912).

62. Marilyn Houlberg, "Magique Marasa: The Ritual Cosmos of Twins and Other Sacred Children," in *Fragments of Bone: Neo-African Religions in a New World*, ed. Patrick Bellegarde-Smith (Urbana: University of Illinois Press, 2005), 16–18; Robert Farris Thompson, "Bighearted Power: Kongo Presence in the Landscape and Art of Black America," in *Keep Your Head to the Sky*, ed. Gundaker, 61; Ras Michael Brown, "Walk in the Feenda: West-Central Africans and the Forest in the South Carolina–Georgia Lowcountry," in *Central Africans and Cultural Transformations in the American Diaspora*, ed. Linda M. Heywood (Cambridge: Cambridge University Press, 2002).

63. Vé Vé A. Clark, "Diaspora Literature and Marasa Consciousness," in *Comparative American Identities: Race, Sex, and Nationality in the Modern Text*, ed. Hortense J. Spillers (New York: Routledge, 1991), 40–61; W. E. B. Du Bois, *The Souls of Black Folk* (New York: McClurg, 1938).

64. Photograph in Thompson, *Face of the Gods*, 95.

65. Gundaker and McWillie, *No Space Hidden*, 130–139; Gundaker, "Face Like a Looking Glass," forthcoming.

66. Many more examples in Gundaker, "Face Like a Looking Glass," forthcoming.

67. Personal communication, Crystal Montague, February 14, 1996. This seems similar to the well-known custom in coastal South Carolina and Georgia of passing an infant child over the grave of an elder during the funeral (see Nichols 1989).

68. Interview, Victor Melancon, Hammond, Louisiana, March 1992.

69. See Gundaker and McWillie, *No Space Hidden*, 19.

70. The literature on Ere Ibeji is large. Robert Farris Thompson, *Black Gods and King: Yoruba Art at UCLA* (Bloomington: Indiana University Press, 1976); Henry John Drewal, John Pemberton III, and Rowland Abiodun, *Yoruba: Nine Centuries of African Art and Thought* (New York: Center for African Art in Association with H. N. Abrams, 1989); photographs of contemporary doll and candle Ibeji appear in Susan Vogel, ed., *Africa Explores: Twentieth-Century African Art* (New York: Center for African Art in Association with Munich: Prestel, 1991).

71. Marilyn Houlberg, "Magique Marasa: The Ritual Cosmos of Twins and Other Sacred Children," in *Fragments of Bone: Neo-African Religions in a New World*, ed. Patrick Bellegarde-Smith (Urbana: University of Illinois Press, 2005), 30–31.

72. On Bocio, see Suzanne Preston Blier, *African Vodun* (Chicago: University of Chicago Press, 1996).

73. Mary H. Nooter, "Secrecy: Art that Conceals and Reveals," *African Arts* 26, no. 1 (January 1993): 59.

74. Wyatt MacGaffey, Michael Harris, and David Driskell, *Astonishment and Power: The Eyes of Understanding: Kongo Minkisi* (Washington, DC: Smithsonian Institution Press, 1993); Robert Farris Thompson and Joseph Cornet, *The Four Moments of the Sun: Kongo Art in Two Worlds* (Washington, DC: National Gallery of Art, 1981); and numerous other sources.

75. Allen Roberts and James Fernandez, *Animals in African Art: From the Familiar to the Marvelous* (New York: Museum for African Art in association with Munich: Prestel, 1995).

76. For example, Dena Epstein, *Sinful Tunes and Spirituals: Black Music to the Civil War*, Silver Anniversary Ed. (Urbana: University of Illinois Press, 2003), 44; Sterling Stuckey, *Slave Culture: Nationalist Theory and the Founding of Black America* (New York: Oxford University Press, 1987), 66; Samuel A. Floyd Jr., *The Power of Black Music: Interpreting Its History from Africa to the United States* (New York: Oxford University Press, 1996), 53–55.

77. Newbell Niles Puckett, *Folk Beliefs of the Southern Negro* (Chapel Hill: University of North Carolina Press, 1926), 41, citing H. C. Davis, *Journal of American Folklore* 27: 245.

78. Photograph and discussion in Sharon Patton, *African-American Art* (New York: Oxford University Press, 1998), 37–38.

79. Robert Farris Thompson, "The Song that Named the Land," in *Black Art: Ancestral Legacy*, ed. Robert V. Roselle, Alvia Wardlow, and Maureen A. McKenna (Dallas: Dallas Museum of Art, 1989), 124. Thompson lists figuration as a foundational principle of African American yard shows.

80. As Palmié has pointed out, "nation" does not mean unmixed, though its ideology may characterize it as such, nor are nation names—Kongo, Calabar, Nago—reliable markers of an unbroken historical trajectory back to a homeland. Stephan Palmié, *Wizards and Scientists: Explorations in Afro-Cuban Modernity and Tradition* (Durham, NC: Duke University Press, 2002).

81. This erasure must have been contextual then, as it continues to be to the present. For example, on a research trip to Barbados in 1991, I was repeatedly told that Barbados was "very British" with nothing significant of the African heritage remaining. Yet driving within five miles of Brathwaite's birthplace, a friend and I documented a cemetery with pierced and overturned vessels, imagery of the sun, whiteness, pipes, and other traditional burial offerings in abundance. It is located on a clearly marked road with a signpost at the corner inscribed "Congo Road."

82. Compare to John Jackson's brilliant *Real Black: Adventures in Racial Sincerity* (Chicago: University of Chicago Press, 2005).

Ritual Piracy

Or Creolization with an Attitude

—RAQUEL ROMBERG

It is a view that implicitly understands that folding of the underworld of the conquering society into the culture of the conquered not as an organic synthesis or "syncretism" of the three great streams of New World History—African, Christian, Indian—but as a chamber of mirrors reflecting each stream's perception of the other. . . . [T]his chamber of mirrors was, from the colonizer's point of view, a chamber conflating sorcery with sedition, if not in reality at least as a metaphor.

— MICHAEL TAUSSIG
Shamanism and Colonialism and the Wild Man

The first thing that attracted my attention when visiting the altar room of a Puerto Rican *bruja* (witch-healer) was the bizarre mishmash of Catholic saints and Afro-Caribbean and Amerindian deities, standing in front of a Buddha and the chromolithograph of a blond Jesus, in the midst of all sorts of candles. I also noticed a small packet, hanging from a large bronze cross, a magic work that had been left there to be empowered by the cross.[1] How could the same cross that once persecuted *brujos* (witch-healers) be now empowering their magic works, in partnership with African and Asian deities?

Syncretism and creolization came obviously to mind. Similar uncanny kinds of religious mélange also found in Haitian Vodou, Brazilian Candomblé, and Cuban Santería have been depicted both in scholarly works and lay parlance as syncretic and creole.[2] Indeed, "creole" has been broadly used in scholarly and native discourses as a modifier for language, ethnicity, nation, or culture to suggest some form of "mixture" (Szwed 2003). Thus defined, and unless they are examined as emic terms used as parts of a politics of culture (Aijmer 1995; Allen 2002; Khan 2001; Romberg 1998;

1. Cosmpolitan spirits at a brujería altar and a magic work hanging from the cross.
Photo: Raquel Romberg.

Stewart 1995, 2007; Stewart and Shaw 1994; Trouillot 1992), "syncretic" and
"creole" are more suggestive of *end products* and less of the *production* (the
very processes and power relations) that shaped these so-called fusions in
the first place.[3] For even in their most sophisticated rendition, "mixture"
and "fusion" reflect only the materialization of extremely witty, complex
yet painful earlier processes of intercultural contact, involving unequally
situated groups brought together in specific geopolitical contexts.

In reassessing the kinds of religious mélange I address here, I thus limit
my discussion to the historically specific circumstances of late nineteenth-
century Hispanic and Luso-tropic colonial societies, centered on urban
slave and highland peasant-maroon societies under Catholic colonial rule
(societies that were overall intensely linked to European settlers and their
mores).[4] For, within this particular set of historical circumstances, more
than earlier ones elsewhere within the Caribbean, there was a persistent
double bind resulting from the high value placed on the "purity" of metropolitan cultures and the actual "mixing" of uprooted people and cultures
that were relocated in the colonies (cf. Mintz 1985). Rather than being the
essence of "creole" and "syncretic," mixture appears as its problematic referent, entangled in shifting racial, class, and nation-state ideologies.[5] For
example, during various centuries racial and class-based cultural and linguistic mixtures were vilified for trespassing the godly taxonomies of the
natural order (Abrahams 2002a, 2003; Dayan 1995; Hall 1997; Kutzinski
1993; Rhys 1966).[6] Further institutionalized, the vilification of such ungodly

mixture was publicly expressed in social ridicule, if not outright criminal persecution (Burton 1997, Romberg 2005). Once Creole societies entered the process of nation building, however, the tribulations of "creole" mixtures were silenced or at least smoothed to fit new nationalist agendas that portrayed the post-independence national community as the miraculous upshot of the "mixing" of indigenous, European, and African people under colonialism (Abrahams 2003; Bolland 1992; Brathwaite 1971; Burton 1997; Hintzen 2002; Taussig 1987; R. Young 1995). Turned now into a state ideology, "creole" was to signify the idea of creative—non-polluting—mixtures (cf. Bernabé, Chamoiseau, and Confiant 1989; Condé and Cottenet-Hage 1995; Moore 1997).[7]

My reflections on religious creolization processes stem from my work with various Puerto Rican healers, in particular, my close apprenticeship with Haydée, a self-defined *espiritista bruja* (Spiritist witch-healer) who was extremely well versed in Catholic and Protestant worship as well as African-based healing and magic rituals (Romberg 2003b, 2009).[8] They also stem from what the colonial record reveals about the institutionalization of colonial hegemony and the cultural and religious wars of entitlement that it involved. Combining these two research experiences, I propose to conceptualize creolization processes shaping vernacular religions such as Puerto Rican *brujería* (witch-healing) as forms of "ritual piracy" (Romberg 2005), suggesting that they are the result of irreverent appropriations or plunder, not just fusion, of hegemonic religious symbols, gestures, and rituals.[9]

In this light, the Catholic cross and the blond Jesus in the midst of African and Asian deities, mentioned earlier, appear as a tangible manifestation of both past challenges to the exclusivity of the Catholic Church and a current reworking of the illicit takeover of its most cherished symbols and gestures in combination with other African and Asian sources of ritual empowerment.[10] The illicit takeover of Catholic forms of worship and their reworking with African-based rituals found in other creole vernacular Afro-Latin religions such as Haitian Vodou and Brazilian Candomblé offer comparable examples. Recognizing the exclusive power invested in the colonial Catholic state to constitute the idea of civility, the relocation of Catholic worship into Candomblé *terreiros* (temples) may be regarded as ritually significant and intentional. It suggests the symbolic translocation or piracy of the power of Catholicism to the *terreiro* for specific ritual purposes, and not just, as usually portrayed, the unreflexive mixing of African and Catholic beliefs. Similarly, some elements of Catholic worship have been irreverently plundered by the *prèt savann*, a ritual specialist versed in Catholic prayers who opens every ceremony at the *ounfo* (temple) in order to empower the space of the Haitian *ounfo* and by extension to guarantee the effectiveness of its rituals. In both these examples the sacred space and the worship of the Catholic Church have been ritually pirated, in fact, deterritorialized to serve other than their institutional purposes.

Today, Puerto Rican brujería encompasses religious, healing, and magical practices linked not only to popular Medieval Catholicism, popular Kardecean Spiritism (which includes, in addition to belief in the ability of humans to communicate with spirits, East Asian beliefs in reincarnation), Popular Protestantism, and African-based creole religions such as Santería, but also to consumerism and state bureaucratic practices (Romberg 2003b).[11] The experience of healing and magic rituals performed by brujos thereby speak more of historically illicit appropriations of hegemonic symbols of powerful others than just of what has been perhaps too readily called creole "mixtures."

The unique context in which creole religions such as brujería have emerged requires thereby an in-depth (and possibly retrospective) phenomenological examination of the micro-poetics and politics of cultural difference (Taussig 1987; R. Young 1995). How else can we begin to make sense of the slight of hand that transformed "polluting" mixtures into "desired" ones? How else can we explain the shift of status of some groups from being polluting Others to being the archetypes of the creole nation? How otherwise explain the drastic shift of attitude that transformed "dangerous superstitions" into tourist attractions?

Far from being a safe, mild metaphor for conceptualizing creolization as mixture, "ritual piracy" implies cultural and religious transgression, resonating with Stefano Harney's "predatory creolization" (1996, 114–115).[12] Turning the traditional conceptualization of creolization on its head, he argues that far from being the victim of cultural imperialism, creole nations such as Trinidad "*devour* and transform cultures local and alien" (114, my emphasis). Although "piracy" (and "predatory") might add a negative tinge to my revisionist project of creolization (as a colleague otherwise supportive of my thesis suggested), it encapsulates the kind of cultural moves that need to be recovered in discussing creolization processes: cultural plundering as a particular form of cultural production in the context of scarcity and monopoly, not just mixture; and recognition of powerful others and tactical imitation of hegemonic culture, rather than dialogue.[13] Both "mixture" and its more recent reworking by globalization theorist Ulf

Hannerz as "dialogue among difference" (1987, 1990, 1996) imply an imagined equity among social groups and their religious practices that does not seem to have ever existed in the colonial context (nor, for these matters, in the present).

When relocated to broader cultural processes, this predatory dimension of creolization (thus circumscribed) suggests a culture-making process that includes its negation, best characterized as "culture with an attitude" (Fabian 2001) or "in-your-face culture" (Abrahams 2002b). Most importantly to my argument and the particularities of religious practices such as those of brujería, it is crucial to note that ritual piracy presumes a dialectical tension of two seemingly contradictory attitudes, if not a downright paradox. While entailing the recognition of the symbolic power of the Catholic colonial order, brujería practices also defy its exclusivity when they refunnel hegemonic religious symbols to purposes other than those intended by the church.[14] This is what I mean by "creolization with an attitude." As suggested in the vignette, an inherent "rupture of signification" (Taussig 1987, 5) is evident when brujos, historically persecuted as heretics, redirect in their favor the same symbols that had persecuted them. Might this rupture of signification transmute into ritual excess that rechannels the illicit "copying" of Catholic gestures into magic potency? Could this be one of the wicked sides of creolization?

Ritual Piracy

Creole religions in the Americas—considered broadly the cradle of the creole concept—have mostly been discussed in terms of concepts such as "syncretism" (Droogers 1989; Gort et al. 1989; Herskovits 1937) and "acculturation" (Herskovits [1938] 1958), which were later enhanced as "symbiosis" (Desmangles 1992), "parallelism" (López Valdés 1995), "interpenetration" (Bastide 1960), "inter-system" (Drummond 1980), and "transculturation" (Ortiz [1947] 1995). This is far from being an exhaustive list, but it points to a range of scholarly attempts at theorizing visible cultural and religious change and "creative mixtures" in situations of intense (problematic) contact (see Baron this volume).

For nearly four centuries of Spanish colonial rule (1510–1898) Catholicism was not merely the official religion but also the civil government in Puerto Rico. Until the nineteenth century the island was severely underpopulated and marked by both a weak slave-plantation system and a strong military-bastion, outpost structure. Unlike other Caribbean islands, the *"sociedad cimarrona"* that developed in Puerto Rico was composed of unorganized, isolated, semi-nomadic family units engaged in a slash-and-burn subsistence economy combined with some forms of contraband (Quintero Rivera 1995, 1998a, 230–231). Characterized "by isolation, not active opposition," the military colonial government did not conceive of this population as a threat but dismissed it for being composed of "indolent primitives" (Quintero Rivera 1998a, 230).[15]

Of interest to me is the emergence of such an isolated maroon society in the mountains, outside of the control of the colonial center. Within these sociocultural spaces at the margins of centers of colonial government— "interstitial spaces" (Mintz 1974, 146) or "systemic fissures" (Trouillot 1998, 23)—groups of runaway slaves, shipwrecked sailors, and landless peasants operated in economic and cultural parasitic relations with, yet outside of, the colonial order.[16]

Due to the island's chronic colonial under-funding (funds were purposely diverted instead to South America, where gold and silver were extracted) and the consequent endemic lack of priests, the church authorized and promoted Catholic worship in provisional spaces such as *ermitas* (small country chapels), where services were conducted by devotees (*rezadoras*) who had proven in some way their devotion and/or spiritual qualities (J. Vidal 1994, 21, 213 n. 36). Also lay fraternities, or *cofradías*, were sponsored by the church in order to instill in the peasantry Catholic forms of worship and liturgy as part of their everyday life activities, as a way of life.

Scarcity partially explains this and other sponsored creole processes (Abrahams 2002b). From its very colonial inception, the Caribbean had been marked at various times by economic and in some ways sociocultural scarcity as a result of civil and religious colonial under-funding, highly fluctuating populations, and the unreliability of transportation and communication between the colonies and metropolitan centers—just a few of the causes. Following the conquest and decimation of its indigenous populations, and the nature of colonial settlements and urban and plantation slave cultures, one can argue that creolization entailed the transmutation of the cultures of the original groups into new ones—a process that for Michel-Rolph Trouillot is still "a miracle begging for analysis" (1998, 8). Assuming scarcity as formative of later creolization processes and Caribbean cultural histories, various writers have imagined the world of creolization as characterized by "chaos" and the productivity of the unknown

(Benítez Rojo 1992, Glissant [1990] 1997). As noted earlier, plantation societies were not the only hubs of creolization processes; urban colonial centers as well as isolated rural areas, marked as they were by existential conditions of scarcity, gave rise to the development of intricate informal markets operating on their margins, becoming fertile grounds for religious and cultural creolization processes (Abrahams 2002a, 2002b, 2003).

But, of course, scarcity had different outcomes for Europeans, Creoles, and Africans of distinct social positions. Various interstitial groups— pirates, buccaneers, and maroon societies (especially Catholic folk healers among the latter)—structured their tactics of survival on the margins, yet also in parasitically close, if adaptive, relations to local and metropolitan centers of power. Indeed, very much like the Cuban *cabildos* (Brandon 1993; López Valdés 1985), the Catholic Church's sponsoring of *ermitas* and *cofradías*, following what is often referred to as "sponsored syncretism," allowed for the eventual development of anti-institutional forms of worship and celebrations under the auspices of the very church.[17] Who could really control what was going on in these services?

The metaphor of ritual piracy I am suggesting here for creole religions has been inspired by these kinds of Caribbean histories, which show the intricate dependency of the margins on centers of power, on their demands, desires, and symbols. The creation of maroon societies and maroon cultures and the pirating and privateering that persisted in the New World attest to the paradox arising from the simultaneous acceptance and rejection of metropolitan powers on the fringes of the social order.

These tactics resonate with native trickster modes of economic as well as cultural survival, such as *jaibería* (astuteness), a folk term that denotes a wide range of popular practices of resistance to, and negotiation with, colonialism, "of taking dominant discourse literally in order to subvert it for one's purpose, of doing whatever one sees fit not as a head-on collision . . . but a bit under the table" (Grosfoguel, Negrón-Muntaner, and Georas 1997, 30–31; cf. Browne 2004).

Indeed, piracy encapsulates a typically Caribbean pioneering force. Initially a local Caribbean response to monopoly mercantilism, piracy subsequently transformed into forms of clandestine political and military support of Creole uprisings. Privateering, the legitimate plundering of enemy ships, was once approved and even sponsored by seventeenth-century metropolitan powers (French, Dutch, and English), but turned illegitimate and was then prosecuted as "piracy" when European interests shifted from mercantilism to a capitalist plantation economy. Undoubtedly, these were not the sole examples of "artful" forms of partnership between centers of hegemonic power and their margins, for mutual dependency and ambiguity have inspired other parasitic relationships in the Caribbean since colonization, such as those between piracy and imperial commerce; privateering and metropolitan interventions in Latin American independence wars; maroon economies and plantation systems; and, currently, between informal economies and global markets.

Although vernacular religions operate at the margins of society, their practices—like those of contraband above—are paradoxically both dependent on and opposed to power centers (whether religious, political, or economic) (cf. Cantwell 1993; R. Williams 1980). Notwithstanding similarities in practice, vernacular religions end up threatening the very centers of power that inspired them.

This paradox is best illustrated in Puerto Rico when church-sponsored practices such as the establishment of the above-mentioned *ermitas, rezadoras,* and *cofradías* end up contesting the very hegemonic intentions that have inspired them. Such anti-ecclesiastical practices remain alive among the folk even when the official reasons for their creation cease to be relevant. Even after the legitimacy for their creation ceases to be viable, vernacular religions manage to stubbornly survive on the margins of officialdom. "[When] some experiences, meanings and values, which cannot be verified or cannot be expressed in terms of the dominant culture, are nevertheless lived and practiced on the basis of the residue—cultural as well as social—of some previous social formation," they tend to linger on as forms of "residual" culture (R. Williams 1980, 40). In the long run, residual forms of Catholic religious practices were established on the margins of society, away from the gate-keeping practices of the church. These included the mushrooming of home chapels and altars where devotees were able to develop their own particular forms of Catholic worship, their own miracles, and offerings in combination with African-based religions and *espiritismo* (from the nineteenth century on). The impotence of the church in preventing these irreverent acts of appropriation (persecuted and punished as heresy) is a constant obsession of the church, inscribed in numerous ecclesiastical edicts (see below).

One can argue, following Stuart Hall's (2003a, 31–32) characterization of creole societies as translation societies, that what these edicts aimed at achieving was the curtailment of unauthorized "translations" of its liturgy and worship. Hall suggests that translation always bears traces of the original, but in such a way that the original is impossible to restore.

Imagine what this could have meant for the continuing hegemony of Spanish Catholic rule. Further, since translation always retains the trace of those elements that resist translation, which remain leftover, so to speak, in lack or excess, they constantly return to trouble any effort to achieve total cultural closure. No translation achieves total equivalence, without trace or remainder. That is, even when they suddenly become unauthorized and persecuted, residual cultures or translation societies (that had been inspired by hegemonic systems) tend to persist on the margins as "noise" or "excesses" (often misread by intellectuals as "Baroque" [Cara 2002]). Perhaps this is one of the ways—albeit unexpected and clashing—in which marginalized local cultures and communities were able to hook up with global forces they had no control of, and which had encompassed them during major historical transformations such as those of colonialism or nation-state building.

When residual excesses resulting from the imposition of Catholicism reappear in popular ritual practices, they are perceived and labeled by outsiders as "magic." Indeed, after centuries of being persecuted by the church, Puerto Rican brujos today pursue an essentially anti-ecclesiastical attitude toward religiosity that many Catholic devotees find quite familiar. They continue to appropriate the church's symbols and recognize their power (following the colonial experience of imposed religion and civility), smuggling their own agendas into their healing and magic rituals while refusing, however, the institutional exclusivity of the church.

At noon one day, when I am visiting Tonio—a ninety-year-old brujo—at his home in Loíza, the phone rings. In a flicker, he crosses himself before picking up the receiver—over his chest and over the ear against which he will press the receiver. It is a client from Manhattan. He gives her precise and detailed instructions, suggesting that she pray before going to work, buy some herbs, oils, and prayers at a nearby *botánica* (store that sells religious paraphernalia) on 117th Street, and wait until he mails her a package with a special magic work. Puzzled, I ask him why he crossed himself before picking up the phone and murmured the Rosary after hanging up. "My enemies might still be trying to bewitch me using every possible means, such as a phone, especially at noon, when magic works most effectively. [Reminding me he's a powerful witch:] I'm a *brujo malo!*"[18]

Oblivious of any scholarly, rationalist separation between religion and magic, Tonio (a faithful follower of the Gospels and their reinterpretation by *espiritistas*) constantly invokes the powers of Catholic symbolism without revering its institutions.[19] Paradoxically, Jesus, represented on the cross, had protected priests and Spaniards in Spain and its colonies from brujos like Tonio and all other sorts of evil since the Inquisition. But now the same cross—once the symbol of European hegemony and the spiritual shield used against brujos and other "dangerous" beings—is being invoked by a brujo as protection against other brujos in Puerto Rico. By what kind of mimetic cunning has the spiritual power that was once monopolized by priests been seized by brujos? Why have those considered the repositories of evil appropriated the very power that was meant to destroy them?

The magical power of imitation or sacred mimesis was essential in European medieval popular forms of Catholicism. The idea that spiritual power can be attained by mimesis, or imitation, of God follows a long tradition initiated in the Gospels and codified in *De Imitatione Christi* (The Imitation of Christ), the set of fifteenth-century Christian devotional books attributed to Thomas à Kempis (1380–1471). Influential ever since, and reinterpreted within the ethos of nineteenth-century Spiritism as the Law of Love, sacred mimesis entails the emulation of the life of Jesus—and all other enlightened spirits, according to Spiritism—as a way to achieve a personal, direct spiritual unity with God.

After Catholicism was imposed by force by the threat of annihilation, indigenous and marginal creole populations crossed themselves and prayed (in innumerable instances, probably) for protection not only against a host of newly imported evils anathema to Catholicism, but also for protection against the evils of colonial oppression itself. Since the cross was intimately associated with colonial rule, it was most likely seen not only as a religious symbol but also as a symbol of power—a power that was as much coveted and ritually appropriated as it was feared: the power invested in the cross "pirated" by those who were meant to fear it.

Accessing chains of similarities at cosmic crossroads between this and other worlds, at the intersection of the four cardinal points, the ritual symbolic gestures of crossing oneself might have been unexpectedly familiar for some. After all, the European cross might have elicited—via infinite chains of resemblances—safe memories of other crosses, those that used to summon the Congo gods unwillingly left across the ocean.[20] The ability to tap into and intervene in chains of similarity—using all sorts of magical rites that concretize displaced images of desired referents—might have informed this unforeseen fascination with the colonial cross and its symbolic power.

The civilizing power of the colonial state, which for centuries, and under many guises, had aimed at taming the unruly, wild sphere of African and Indian healing and magic through Catholicism (and, later, through Modernity) was transformed by brujos and reflected back on the civilized world in an uncanny way: fascinated by the symbols of colonial power that were meant to subdue them, brujos rechanneled these symbols into actual magic power.

What is the role of the imaginary in all this? How does it influence visionary and spiritual experiences? The religious imagination of the colonized was perhaps one of the most powerful albeit less conspicuous arenas of creolization processes. Think of the power of icons in the proselytizing of colonial Latin America and its effect in shaping the collective imagination of the colonized. As Marc Augé notes, the colonization of Mexico, for instance, took place "through the image," as two powerful imaginations— Amerindian and Catholic—"confront one another and come together" (1999, 21) in the realm of practice. Also in the realm of practice is where these confrontations of the imaginary are iconically resolved. As if bracketing centuries of exclusion and oppression, these confrontations and the layers of embodied counter-hegemonic "habit memories" (Connerton 1989; Lipsitz 1990; Stoller 1995) that they created find ways to reappear in the enactment of rituals, dreams, visions, and magic in order to answer the immediate problems of practitioners.

Like the bush priests of Haitian Vodou and the priests of Brazilian Candomblé, Puerto Rican brujos invoke the power of God when asserting their spiritual gifts, spiritual mission, and healing abilities. In line with the Catholic genre of miraculous apparitions, brujos recount their miraculous beginnings as healers in reference to an uncanny encounter they had with God or the saints, portraying and framing their "godly gifts" and "mission" as healers following the teachings of Jesus and his parables. Haydée, the bruja with whom I worked as an apprentice in Puerto Rico, made sure she situated her *obra espiritual* (spiritual work) in relation to God: "God gave me the blessings and the abilities [*dones*] to heal, and in abundance! . . . Without God, I don't do anything. God is the one [who heals]" (Romberg 2003b, 111).

The improvised prayers performed by Haydée for opening and closing the *altar* (altar-room) before and after the consultations of the day are good examples of the confrontation in practice between the various religious imaginaries mentioned above. The following closing prayer was conducted by Haydée after a whole morning of consultations in the altar-room and before she, a group of clients, her assistant, and myself would head to the cemetery and El Yunque (the rain forest). There, they would deposit a few magic works that had been prepared earlier for further empowerment by the spirits dwelling in these places.

> My God and celestial Father, at this moment I close this humble altar-room, which has been opened for the good and closed for the evil. If something has remained or been said that was not of your pleasing, my God, I plead for your forgiveness.
>
> . . . Now I ask you to take me safely where I'm heading with Raquel, my reporter, and Reina, and return me safely to my home. Remember that while you walk with me, you're the driver of the car that takes us. Remember, my Caridad, that I leave, but you stay in my home; I leave my enemies, those who are entangled with me, in your arms and hands, and at your feet, so you can deal with them, not me. I plead that no hate will be sown in my heart; because in order to work this clean and pure *cuadro* [spiritual gifts] as it should, I cannot harbor any hatred towards people. . . . I beg you to give me strength to continue my *obra espiritual*, to help me to help others.

After centuries of Catholic rule, it is not coincidental that brujos today derive their spiritual legitimacy directly from Jesus or Papá Dios, who appears to them in dreams or visions to announce to them their godly gifts and mission as healers. During my fieldwork I heard about many such visions. Haydée, for example, not only narrated the vision to me but also asked me to record her vision in the exact place where God appeared to her as the Sacred Heart of Jesus. It was at the seashore of Loíza, seven years before she started working as a healer. Papá Dios commanded her to work *la obra espiritual*, saying, "I want you seated." After replying, "But I am already seated. You know that I work seated as an administrative secretary, working at the computer," Papá Dios repeated the same command, which for Haydée was a sign that he had meant "seated in your own altar-room, working, helping people, doing *la obra espiritual.*"

The life and deeds of Jesus as a healer and the many parables that they had inspired are constantly reworked in specific healing and magic rituals performed by brujos today, following the notion of sacred mimesis. By virtue of the very system of sacred mimesis that had been in place and imported to the colonies in accordance with the medieval Church's own devotional teachings, the gates to the realm of miraculous occurrences had been opened wide to an eagerly devout public ever since the earliest days

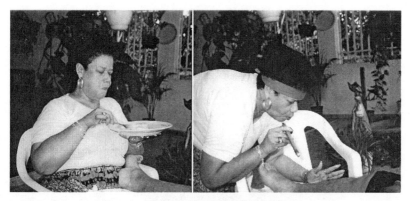

2. "I eat while I heal, like Papá Dios." Photo: Raquel Romberg.

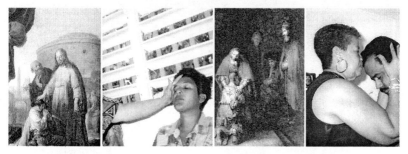

3. Brujos performing the healing gestures of Jesus. Photo: Raquel Romberg.

of colonization, forging popular devotions outside the confines (and control) of the church.

Once at noon, Manuel, a heavy man in his forties, came to see Haydée after he had visited several doctors who tried in vain to cure his recurrently infected leg. Following a divination session, it was revealed that his was a combined physical and spiritual problem, and thus the treatment should combine both types of healing. Haydée had Manuel sit in the waiting room with his leg stretched out in front of her and placed on her lap in order to first spiritually cleanse it with the sacred smoke of the Indio and then dress it with a special mixture of healing, sacred herbs. Lunchtime came, but Haydée was still curing Manuel. Nina (her housekeeper) brought her a plate of food, and while applying herbal compresses to the ulcerated leg, Haydée began eating her lunch of fried eggs and said, "I eat while I heal, like Papá Dios did with the lepers. He lifted up San Lázaro from misery. I live happy: *yo doy y recibo* [I give and receive]" (Romberg 2003b, 121).

4. Consecrating or baptizing *collares*. Photo: Raquel Romberg.

In addition to emulating the life and teachings of Jesus, brujos summon his power in performing healing and magic rituals by means of mimicking the hegemonic gestures of the Catholic Church. Conjuring their assumed transcendental powers, they redirect them to their own rituals and *trabajos* (magic works). A kind of transmutation or relocation of the power embodied in these gestures is thus activated. It is as if these ritually staged gestures connect *this* healing ritual in the present with *that* performed by Jesus in a distant past.

During my fieldwork, I participated in various exorcisms performed by brujos in order to *levantar causas* (lift bewitchments), that is, to free clients from evil spirits (of *muertos*, the "dead") that are pestering them. When brujos *cogen causas*, or manifest in their bodies these evil spirits (as a diagnostic device), Our Fathers and Hail Marys and even the crucifix are incorporated to protect brujos from falling prey to them. In addition, a novena might be prayed in litany by those present at an unbewitchment ritual to assure that the muerto that had been causing all sorts of misfortunes to a client leaves the world of the living and departs in peace to the world of the dead. Elements of Catholic worship are also included in the making or consecrating of a *trabajo* or an amulet. To assure its efficacy, a few drops of water from a baptismal fountain (taken conveniently and placed in a small bottle ahead of time) might be used, illustrating once again what I mean by ritual piracy. On one occasion Haydée decided to give Lauro, a young man recently married, a beaded necklace for protection against the dangers he might be encountering as a result—the spirits had revealed—of the malign gossip his mother-in-law was spreading against him. For this purpose she consecrated the necklace he had bought earlier at a nearby botánica by dipping it in the *fuente*, a transparent bowl she always kept filled with water in her altar—the fuente becoming the proxy for the less available baptismal fountain at the church.

The appeal of the Catholic imaginary, its signs, gestures, visions, and miracles, to brujos—considered "heretics" since colonial times by the church—will be further elucidated once the technologies of magic and the power of negativity are considered in tandem. This is where the power of negativity (Fabian 2001) transmutes into "creolization with an attitude," refracting sacred mimesis within not-so-neighborly contact spaces back into magic.

Contact and Mimesis

Cultural contact and transmission have occurred in the Americas in not-so-neighborly contexts (Mintz 1971b; Mintz and Price 1976). These "contact zones" were marked by "conditions of coercion, radical inequality, and intractable conflict . . . [and] the spatial and temporal copresence of subjects previously separated by geographical and historical disjunctures, and whose trajectories now intersect" (Pratt 1992, 6–7). The historical record shows that such contact zones in many cases produced real and imaginary nightmares of pollution and cannibalization as well as perhaps an unfounded fascination with the assumed magic power of exotic others (Dayan 1995; Pratt 1992; Taussig 1987, 1993; R. Young 1995). What kinds of cultural alchemy are involved in such contact zones? Specifically to religious practices, how can illicit copying transmute in such contact zones into magic potency?

In situations of problematic contact, the form and meaning of dominant religious symbols and gestures have been transformed on the margins via processes of change that resemble those that linguists of language-contact have identified as occurring at both formal (phonemic) and semantic levels, and which they have conceptualized as "remodeling" (Taylor 1964) and "transvaluation" (Reisman 1970), respectively. Brujería, like other such creole religions, has emerged in no small measure as the result of the *illegitimate* "remodeling" of hegemonic Catholic worship, gestures, and symbols and the "transvaluation" of their meanings.[21] The persecution of these vernacular practices further points to the "rupture and revenge of signification" (Taussig 1987, 5).[22] In the Caribbean, such rupture and revenge of signification have yielded several innovative forms of political, economic, and cultural subsistence predicated on mimicry, parody, and irony—explored by some folklorists represented in this volume—which resonate with the idea of "creolization with an attitude."

Mimicry and, more broadly, the production of similes and other tropes are integral to creole religions, their rituals, and, as such, to "ritual piracy." During Spanish colonial rule, Catholic symbols were forced upon the colonies and called on to legitimize Spain's colonial order as a whole. Jean and John Comaroff (1993) remind us that the signs and techniques that are incorporated in ritual often come to be potent precisely because of the historical circumstances in which they acquire their meanings. One needs only to follow some of the colonial accounts that trace the elaborate religious/state rituals that were performed every time a plantation was inaugurated, a city founded, or a chapel consecrated. These usually involved a priest who, together with colonial officials, publicly asserted the colonial social order through the power of religious symbols or through the symbols of religious and state power. These kinds of state rituals explain why certain symbols and gestures acquired such transcendental potency within vernacular religious practices. The emulation of these symbols outside of the church was severely opposed and punished in order to protect their exclusive use within the church. In fact, the imposition of religious symbols, the recognition of their transcendental power, and their subsequent appropriation were essential to the dynamics of ritual change under colonialism (cf. Stoller 1995; Taussig 1987, 1993, 1997).

In this light, the Catholicism found in Vodou, Candomblé, and Santería was not just an ecumenical screen meant to hide the worship of African deities from official persecution, as some syncretism scholars have suggested. Rather, it was the religion of the colonizers, revised, transformed, and appropriated by the oppressed in order to harness its power within their own universes of meaning. In this way, argues Andrew Apter, slaves took possession of Catholicism, thereby repossessing themselves as active spiritual subjects in the process (1991, 254).

Miraculous appearances—first institutionalized by the Catholic Church and forming the basis for the creation of colonial chapels and towns—were soon freed from its dominion, mushrooming in the countryside and popular imagination and worship. Religious images, originally meant to be worshiped within chapels, were adopted, changed and worshipped in private altars (and later brought together with Spiritist entities and African deities) away from the centers of religious power (Romberg 2003b). In a similar vein, Roger Bastide (1978, 278) interprets the effect of popular Catholicism among slaves, who were exposed to "the *ex votos* testifying to miracles performed by the Virgin or the saints in response to desperate prayers and promises, making them recognize that the whites were masters of benign or formidable powers." Bastide suggests that "some connection may have formed in [their] unconscious mind[s] between the stronger *mana* of the Catholic religion and the whites' higher place on the social ladder. This explains why [they] grafted the Catholic tradition onto [their] own."[23]

When Catholic symbols were used illicitly by brujos outside the confines of the church, they were seized on opportunistically, without changing or claiming to change the existing power relations in the colony. This ambiguity that subverts from within the imposition of one culture on another, noted by Homi Bhabha (1994), explains why creolization processes can be best characterized as a tactic, not a complete strategy, of resistance. Here I follow Michel De Certeau's distinction between strategies and tactics of contestation, arguing that the latter does not imply a plan for total social change, but rather points to taking advantage of occasional opportunities seized for momentary maneuvers of empowerment: It is "knowing how to get away with things" (De Certeau 1984, xix).[24]

Brujos do not embody Catholic sacred narratives of apparitions and miracles in their dreams and visions only in order to legitimate their power as popular creole healers. They also do this by directly taking over the role of priests. Contesting the monopoly of the institutional church, brujos may pray novenas at wakes and occasionally while making magic works, may perform special "baptisms" when clients need to be cleansed or amulets consecrated, and may conduct "spiritual" weddings when the bond between couples needs to be restored (Romberg 2003b). The challenge to the very spatial exclusivity and religious hegemony of the church appears to be double: not only do brujos seize its most central symbols outside its control (as occurs with many other popular Catholic practices), they also combine them and make them speak to Spiritist and African-based spiritual traditions, which were obstinately fought against by the church. Think of the innumerable occasions in which hegemonic Catholic gestures were performed by brujos, drawing their ritual power and then re-channeling them to fit their "heretical" magic purposes—the potency of the original official gestures stolen with a vengeance, if you will.

Problematic contact zones create situations in which mimicry becomes a way of life, an adaptation strategy, and sometimes a form of empowerment. Scholars, writers, and poets have critically discussed mimicry in relation to the production of alterity and cultural change in colonial situations (Bhabha 1994; Fanon 1967; Memmi 1965; Naipaul 1967; Taussig 1993). But, as many critics have noted, mimicry in the context of nation-building ideologies becomes highly problematic. How can mimicry, envisioned by some critics as the result of submissive reliance on colonial culture and language, be acknowledged as the formative basis of cultural creolization and the triumph over colonialism?

Some postcolonial writers have explored the particular culture-making aspects of mimicry and its predicaments, which I would like to draw from in addressing the magic potency of copies, even imperfect ones, found in brujería and similar creole religions. The inherent internal ambiguity recognized by W. E. B. Du Bois concerning the "double consciousness" of African Americans under conditions of modernity can also be applied to earlier colonial displays of mimicry and aping, as well as their social costs. Resonating with Du Bois's notion of double consciousness, Mervyn Alleyne (1985) and others suggest that beyond the devaluation of the language of the colonized, the internalization of the colonizers' values created a colonial syndrome, which made the colonized see themselves though the eyes of the colonizers, thereby self-deprecating and negatively evaluating themselves and their own behavior. Similarly, a number of postcolonial Caribbean intellectuals (such as V. S. Naipaul) talk of mimicry signals and the impossibility of colonial subjects ever engaging in a real transformative action from a place that has not been already colonized.[25] For example, in Naipaul's *The Mimic Men* (1967), the main character, Ralph Singh, expresses an inappropriate fascination with traits that he always finds in English women, such as the innate imperial predatory greed that scares him and makes him feel inadequate and ashamed (Galloway 1996). Acknowledging this, Ralph reflects: "It seemed to me that to attach myself to her was to acquire that protection which she offered, to share some of her quality of being marked, a quality which once was mine but which I had lost" (Naipaul 1967, 47).[26]

Left at the moment of fascination and terror with the culture of oppressors, mimicry or rather imperfect copies appear as tragic outcomes of colonization, forever entangling any possible authentic expression of identity and real transformation. Always falling short for producing inevitably imperfect copies, the colonized "can never succeed in becoming identified with the colonizer, nor even in copying his role correctly" (Memmi 1965, 124). But this ambiguity and impossibility acquire a different meaning within magic, where this imperfection is constitutive of its technologies and excesses. I take this to be one of the "wicked" sides of the mimicry and magic of imperfect copies.

Magic, Sir James Frazer ([1901] 1960) noted more than a century ago, is about producing copies or taking significant parts to stand for the whole—following the sympathetic (similarity) and homeopathic (contact or contagion) principles. Following the law of similarity in magic practice, the copy affects the original to such a degree that the representation shares or acquires the properties of the represented (Taussig 1997, 48–49). Magical mimesis on the colonial frontier (Taussig 1993, 59) points to a basic empowering effect of the imitation function—either through the production of similes by mimicry or by contiguity and contact—by which a copy partakes in the power of the original.[27] The technologies of magic illustrate that copies, even if imperfect, enable a transmutation of meanings; similes draw on the power of the original and transmute it to the copy. Here the link between the mimetic faculty of magic and ritual piracy becomes evident, since, by means of the unauthorized, strategic albeit imperfect copying of symbols of power (religious or civil), they become empowering within rituals *against* their initial purpose.

When brujos and their clients pray Hail Marys and Our Fathers in litany during the performance of a "black" magic work (itself an assembly of various African-based creole practices) meant to symbolically punish (i.e., neutralize) wrongdoers, they are transmuting the original significance of these prayers to their illicit copies. Like the offerings of novenas for an evil spirit that has been exorcised after "lodging" in the body of an unfortunate victim, these liturgical copies pirate their original purpose and meaning. On one occasion, Haydée fashioned—out of a cardboard box emptied of its bar of soap—a "coffin" (complete with cotton balls padding its interior) in which to "bury" her client's enemy (a small lizard serving as the surrogate corpse, in this case). This powerful *trabajo* was performed in order to heal Haydée's indigent client, who had been suffering all kinds of serious misfortunes, ending in a stroke that had left her half-paralyzed. This was the imperfect copy of a "real" wake, performed in the presence of an imperfect copy of a funerary coffin, which was intended—just as in an actual wake—to help the soul of the wicked enemy depart peacefully to the "celestial mansions" by means of the power invested in Hail Marys and Our Fathers. Is this not an uncanny use of such prayers?

Mimicry, Pollution, and the Threat of Imperfect Copies

More than likely, it was this recurrent and uncontrollable creation of copies—of Catholic worship and elite speech, dress, and leisure—that opened the cultural Pandora's box of gate-keeping nightmares and irreverent usurpations at different periods of Puerto Rican history. The numerous regulations that were created in Caribbean colonial and post-emancipation societies to prevent such unauthorized acts of mirroring from happening point to crucial, yet often subtle, wars of entitlements over gestures, dress, and language (Brereton and Yelvington 1999; Burton 1997; Nettleford 1970; Olwig 1993). These wars were not so subtle between European and African creoles and became even more draconian after the Haitian Revolution. What the civil and religious authorities feared, especially on plantations, were the kinds of "licentious behavior" that under the pretext of religious worship could lead to a bloody end of the slave system as well as the colonial order.

The menace of mimicry in colonial contexts, according to Bhabha (1994, 88), is its "double vision," which in disclosing the ambivalence of colonial discourse also disrupts its authority—mimicry easily turning into mockery. Authoritative discourses must be singular and hegemonic—their "very nature incapable of being double-voiced, [they] cannot enter into hybrid constructions" (Bakhtin 1981, 344). Taking the symbols of Catholicism away from the cathedrals and making them speak in *ermitas* was indeed a threat to the exclusivity imposed by the colonial religious and civil authorities (Romberg 2003b, 29–53). Even when unwilling slaves and peasants were made to mimetically follow Catholic rituals by force, the result of their compliance was never regarded within the colonial context as quite the right gesture but rather the result of inappropriate, submissive, ignorant aping.

Here is an added component to the "game of mirroring" (Bhabha 1994, 85–92). What may have looked from the outside like successive acts of submission or incompetent mimicry may well have been tropes of cannibalization or consumption through the imitation of symbols of powerful others, or contact with parts that stand for them, not at all foreign to the technologies of magic, as noted earlier. Maybe it was against the fear of being cannibalized (at least symbolically) that the colonial ruling elites reacted so defensively by ridiculing those free-colored Creoles whom they saw "aping" them (for Saint-Domingue, see Dayan 1995; for Brazil, see Bastide 1978). This menace of mirroring is evident also in Richard Price's report on the folklore surrounding the imprisonment of Médard: "That enigmatic, silent sculptor who died a decade ago, was sent to the French Guiana prison camps for having made a perfect *'photo'* (a sculpture in wood) of Colonel de Coppens. . . . [Absolutely everyone] knows that Médard once saw Coppens, that he fashioned his image in wood with every detail, from facial expression to military medals, exactly in place, and that he was condemned to the prison camps for this act of gross impertinence" (1998, 171–172).

Those who persecuted witches in colonial times evidently "knew" that magic worked through copies, even imperfect ones. Catholic worship was all about the spiritual power emanating from the transmutation of the physical into the spiritual realm. Thus it was imperative for the church to keep the transcendental realm in official hands as a matter of survival for the whole colonial order. Several edicts in Puerto Rico prohibited the invocation of Catholic saints, and any material embellishments added to them, outside the church. For roughly three centuries, the Inquisition and numerous ecclesiastical and government decrees sought to restrict the practices of individuals ("heretics") who had "illegally" mimicked the gestures of the church and thus were accused of appropriating the management of "the sacred" outside the church by means of establishing illegitimate forms of contact with its power.

The Catholic Church allowed only priests to perform and supervise healing procedures leading to spiritual cures, circumscribing these procedures carefully in a series of laws. Specific techniques and rituals that involved the invocation of supernatural powers were described in Constitution CXV (1645), in accordance with the Council of Trent (1545–1563). Constitution CXV prohibited the exhibition of *nóminas* (amulets listing the names of saints), the use of *ensalmos* (magic spells), and the use of objects of superstition (e.g., "unknown characters," "divination systems") unless first seen and approved by the church (Huerga 1989, 132). Since church officials performed *ensalmos* and *nóminas* as part of their regular practices, Constitution CLVII gave full authority to local church officials to police the performance of these among non-ecclesiastical practitioners, asking the authorities to determine ad hoc which instances were to be punished as superstition, sorcery, bewitchment, divination, or spell-induced enchantment (Murga and Huerga 1989, 480).

Ironically, by virtue of the very system of imitation or sacred mimesis that had been in place in accordance with the Catholic Church's own devotional teachings, the gates to the realm of miraculous occurrences had been opened wide to an eagerly devout public ever since the earliest days of colonization. Indeed, the possibilities of vernacular reworkings of the ideology of sacred mimesis—which promoted the imitation of the life of Jesus—had become unlimited. Many of the faithful, following the official stories heard in their churches, claimed to have had miraculous experiences—some in the form of apparitions, others in the form of wondrous encounters with sacred artifacts, which then often became the objects of popular devotion, outside the confines and control of the church. With the aim of restricting the creation and propagation of unauthorized religious images and artifacts, Constitution CIX reserved to the church alone the right to certify miracles and to incorporate into its liturgy new holy relics (Murga and Huerga 1989, 437).

Despite the prohibitions of the church, individuals who believed strongly in the stories of the church persisted in claiming to have experienced their own private miracles, wrought by prayer before the statue or picture of a saint, which then would eventually become the subject of public veneration. Such was the case of Francisca Lares, a woman from the village of Moca. On July 4, 1865, she was accused by the parish priest of claiming that her carved-stone image of Nuestra Señora del Rosario had "grown and developed miraculously" through time. Amazingly, her case instigated a huge revolt, fueling the exchange of official letters (through the rest of July and August of that year) between the mayor, the parish priest of La Moca, the bishop, and the civil governor of the island, at the end of which her miraculous image was confiscated (no more details were recorded) by the parish priest (Archivo General de Puerto Rico 1865).[28]

Harsher consequences followed at different conjunctures in Puerto Rican history, when vernacular healers who incorporated hegemonic religious symbols in their practices were persecuted as heretics during the first three centuries of Catholic colonial rule and as charlatans during the state-building process of the first half of the twentieth century (Romberg 2003a).[29] However, theirs was not an open subversion. In fact, vernacular religious practitioners challenged the exclusivity of religious experiences imposed by the church "not by rejecting or altering them, but by using them with respect to ends and references foreign to the system they had no choice but to accept" (De Certeau 1984, xiii).[30] These "weak" forms of subversion correspond to Nigel Bolland's characterization of creolization as the infiltration of metropolitan culture by Creole innovations (1997, 20). Puerto Rican brujos have been doing just that: smuggling their own agendas with a twist into hegemonic religious symbols.

Creolization with an Attitude

Imitating the symbols and gestures of powerful others "with an attitude" is probably the closest characterization of the phenomenology of creolization, as specified here. It certainly does not exude heroism. In my research on Puerto Rican brujería, I have found that at different historical circumstances brujos have appropriated religious, intellectual, bureaucratic, and commercial symbols of power. It was in light of colonial religious and cultural hegemonic gate-keeping practices that the "irreverent" appropriations of Catholic signs and gestures by Creole brujos acquired their transcendental empowerment. These techniques of adaptation and relative empowerment—representing the tactics or "the art of the weak" (De Certeau 1984, 37)—ethereal as they might seem, draw their particular sociological significance from the specific configurations of power that gave rise to them in the first place. In this sense, they provide a "diagnostic of power" rather than a romantic view of resistance (Abu-Lughod 1990, 42). In fact, ritual piracy was undoubtedly not the sole example of "wicked" forms of partnership between centers of hegemonic power and their margins. Mutual dependency and ambiguity have inspired other parasitic relationships in the Caribbean since colonization, which, in the context of an inherent phenomenology of scarcity, made the recognition of powerful others and the imitation of their symbols essential to the dynamics of ritual change under colonialism (cf. Lionnet 1992; Stoller 1995; Taussig 1993, 1997). After all, "the space of a tactic is the space of the other" (De Certeau 1984, 37).

Especially intriguing is the social price paid by metropolitan whites living in the Caribbean and colored Creoles alike for being like "but not quite" (Bhabha 1994, 86). In colonial situations of cultural contact under conditions of scarcity, this social price needed to be kept as a public secret. What kinds of power might be derived, and released, from this form of "defacement" (Taussig 1999)? From the parody and tragedy that result when open discussion of a "public secret" (known to all) is precluded? The power released from refracting mirrors, in which the object of desire gets further blurred as it is reflected back through a host of images in a chamber of mirrors, is presented here as an alternative to various meta-phors of mixture suggested for creolization, such as dialogue, negotiation, and hybridity.

In postcolonial contexts, the power unleashed from these chambers of mirrors was interpreted and enacted in various, often contradictory forms. Caribbean poet and playwright Derek Walcott, for example, reflects in his overture to *Dream of Monkey Mountain* (1970) on the ambiguities the actors of his plays must contend with in a post-slavery context. "If I see these as heroes it is because they have kept the shared urge of actors everywhere: to record the anguish of the race. To do this, they must return through a darkness whose terminus is amnesia. The darkness that yawns before them is terrifying. *It is the journey back from man to ape.* Every actor should make this journey to articulate his origins, *but for these who have been called not men but mimics, the darkness must be total*" (Walcott 1970, 5, my emphasis). However, this darkness, Walcott further suggests, carries an unprecedented culture-making, political force. Paul Gilroy, on the other hand, recognizes that the psychological ambivalences result-ing from "double consciousness" or "double vision" are "neither simply a disability nor a constant privilege" (1993, 61), whereas Henry Louis Gates (1988) highlights their performative, culture-making aspects as "double-voicing." I find the latter to be analogous to what I have formulated here as creolization with an attitude or, more specifically, ritual piracy. Broadly, ritual piracy—far from being a "relatively safe counterhegemonic revision of the way we understand culture, power, and culture change" (Khan 2001, 272)—suggests the plundering of cultures as *itself* a form of cultural pro-duction. And yet, cultural pirating has been offered here as an unquestion-ably non-heroic but nonetheless empowering form of tactically "wicked" partnership between centers of hegemonic power and their margins. Hence, the goal of this partnership has been more a "partaking of" rather than "resistance to" dominant culture. Pragmatically drawing upon the advantages of its coterminous networks of power, "ritual piracy" paradoxi-cally begets, if unintentionally, its incorporation at the margins rather than its erasure.

Notes

Many commented on earlier versions of the ideas developed here, which were initially presented at "Rogerfest," the Voice/Over symposium held at the University of Pennsylvania in 2002 in honor of the lifetime achievements of Roger D. Abrahams in folklore. My appreciation goes to Roger Abrahams, Aisha Khan, Georges Fouron, Richard Price, Paul Garrett, the editors of this volume, and the anonymous reader for their comments.

1. Unless specified otherwise, all ethnographic references to Puerto Rican *brujos* (witch-healers) are based on my eighteen-month fieldwork in 1995–1996, which I conducted particularly but not solely in the metropolitan areas of Loíza and Canóvanas around San Juan, on the northeast side of the island. I worked intensely and intimately with healers and their clients during consultations, in particular, with Haydée, a *bruja* who adopted me as her apprentice and allowed me to tape-record and photograph every aspect of her work. For a reflexive account of my relationship with the healers I worked with and the ways this shaped my ethnographic style, see Romberg 2003b and 2009. All translations from sources in Spanish are mine. Conscious that the negative stereotypes of *brujería* (witchcraft, here translated as witch-healing) stem from a long history of persecution (paralleling that of European witchcraft), *brujos* today deliberately call themselves, among insiders, "*brujos*" and what they do "*brujería*" to index not only their ability to heal and solve spiritual problems, but also their pride—even arrogance—in their trade, a far cry from the dread and shame of the past.

2. Elsewhere (Romberg 1998) I argue that "syncretic" is not a neutral, etic term, but rather is part of a local, emic discourse of spiritual authenticity. For instance, Scientific Spiritist centers label the practices of popular Spiritists as "syncretic," de-legitimizing them as inauthentic, uninformed mixtures of various unrelated beliefs.

3. The distinction between product and production is developed in William Roseberry's (1989) critique of Clifford Geertz's textual model of culture.

4. Initial (first- and second-generation) creolization processes, of the kind described by the Prices in Suriname and Trouillot in Haiti, for example, took place in socioeconomic and cultural circumstances very different from those I describe here, with much less input from Europeans and their cultures (cf. Price 1973).

5. Creolization has been addressed in anthropology, linguistics, and literary criticism to speak broadly of cultural transformation (Balutansky and Sourieau 1998; Chaudenson 2001; Fernández Olmos and Paravisini-Gebert 2003; Shepherd and Richards 2002). But the nature of this transformation and its agents, motives, and products are by no means agreed upon, being often entangled in controversial portrayals of the past (Brown 2003; Matory 2005; Price 2001, 2009; Stewart 2007). Elsewhere (Romberg 2005) I discuss the conundrum of "creolization" as process, ideology, and theory. "Creole," things creole, and "creolization" have become contested terrains not only in academic circles but also within native contexts, reflecting the often contradictory sociopolitical local meanings (e.g., racist, developmental, modernist, or conciliatory) they have gathered during colonization, nation-building, and postcolonial processes (see Condé 1999; Enwezor et al, 2003; Hall 2003b; Price and Price 1997; Schwartz and Ray 2000; Yelvington 2001).

6. "Uncontrollable concubinage and licentiousness"—Dayan notes in reference to the writings of white nature-scientists of the eighteenth century on racial degeneration—were considered by some as producing "unholy mixtures" or, in the words of a colonial administrator in 1722, "'a criminal conjunction of men and women of a different species, giving birth to 'a fruit that is a monster of nature'" (Dayan 1995, 238).

7. It is striking to see how these initial emic notions of creolization, signifying broader notions of contagion, deviancy, and abomination (Abrahams 2003), were transformed after emancipation within the new ideology of nation building into an index of a wholesome homogeneity of heterogeneous, historically constituted multilingual, multiethnic, and multiracial societies and the epitome of modernity (Brathwaite 1971; Bolland 1992). Furthermore, the reinsertion of creolization or creolité aesthetics by Caribbean Francophone writers as a trope with revolutionary potentials in postcolonial cultural politics (see Condé 1999; Schwartz and Ray 2000; Yelvington 2001) points to the relevance of revisiting the historical conditions under which distinct emic notions of creolization were constituted (Bolland 1992; Trouillot 1998).

8. She was born into a Catholic family; her father was an *espiritista;* her mother converted to Protestantism after the American invasion, as did many Puerto Ricans.

9. My revisionist project has been inspired by recent discussions within folklore, anthropology, religious studies, and literary criticism about creolization processes and theories. See, for example, the volume of *Plantation Society* (1998) edited by James Arnold, the special double issue of *Caribbean Quarterly* (1998) edited by Rex Nettleford and dedicated to Edward Kamau Brathwaite, and the volume of the *Journal of American Folklore* (2003) edited by Robert Baron and Ana C. Cara.

10. Similar forms of ritual takeover are reported (though not characterized as "ritual piracy") in previous scholarship of African-based creole religions in the Americas, for example, in Bastide (1978), Brandon (1993), Cabrera (1954), and Desmangles (1992).

11. See also Quintero Rivera 1998b; Duany 1998; and Román 2000.

12. I thank Aisha Khan for suggesting this connection.

13. A parallel interpretation of creole economics as oppositional and subversive is developed by Katherine Browne (2004). I thank Richard Price for drawing my attention to her work.

14. I limit my discussion here to Catholic hegemonic symbols, but elsewhere (Romberg 2003b) I discuss how *brujos* took over other spiritual and bureaucratic symbols of power pertaining to nation- and state-building periods in Puerto Rican history and added them to their healing and magic rituals.

15. The early colonists, most of whom came from Andalusia and later the Canary Islands, were from the lower and marginalized classes. These colonists settled in isolated areas and engaged in subsistence agriculture and trading in contraband with nearby islands and passing pirate vessels (see Caro Costas 1983). They practiced a

popular form of medieval Mediterranean Catholicism common to various sixteenth-century European societies. In Puerto Rico, however, this form of popular Catholicism continued to flourish with little control by the official church (Vidal 1994, 13). Some aspects of the history of Puerto Rican popular devotions in the eighteenth century are well documented in López Cantos (1992) and Vidal (1986, 1989). For a current representation of these popular devotions, see the catalog of the exhibition on popular religion in Puerto Rico curated by Alegría-Pons (1988) and the volume edited by Quintero Rivera (1998b).

16. See Duany (1985) for the development of Puerto Rican ethnicity and folk culture, centered on the feudal, patriarchal system of the coffee hacienda.

17. Similarly, David Brown (2003) and Lorand Matory (2005) trace the emergence of Cuban Santería and Brazilian Candomblé, respectively, to urban contexts.

18. Literally, it means "mean witch" and refers to those who are powerful enough to deal with evil spirits and perform "black magic."

19. As do many Puerto Rican *brujos*, he follows Allan Kardec's *The Gospel According to Spiritism*.

20. Robert Farris Thompson (1984, 1993, 2005) has traced and recorded how the memories of the various cultures of Africa had been materialized in the adornment of yards, homes, and bodies as well as in the gestures of dance and worship in different parts of the Americas. See also Gundaker (1993).

21. Also Szwed (2003, 11) notes that the concept of transvaluation is useful in addressing "the duality of cultural identities, a theme elaborated by Black writers in the Caribbean and the United States (the theme of *masking* and *doubleness* in W.E.B. Du Bois, Ralph Ellison, and George Lamming) as well as by folklorists (Roger D. Abrahams [1983] on tea meeting in the Anglophonic West Indies, and John Szwed and Morton Marks [1988] on set dances)."

22. The notions of cultural "borrowing" or "conversation" among cultures suggested by Hannerz (1987, 1990, 1996) for conceptualizing creolization (as part of his theorization of globalization) are utterly foreign to the processes I am addressing here.

23. I purposely omitted the end of this quote, where Bastide reiterates the sociological categorical differentiation he makes throughout this work between (Catholic) *religion* and (African) *magic* (my emphasis), not because it is meaningless but because such a discussion exceeds the purpose of this essay.

24. Parallel maneuvers in discursive terms are brilliantly illustrated in Cara's (2003, see also this volume) work on the intricacies and poetics of Argentinean *criollo* talk.

25. This dilemma has been discussed extensively by Lionnet (1992) and Spivak (1990), among others. See Livingston (1992) for a psychological/literary interpretation of mimesis.

26. A similarly inappropriate, demeaning fascination with symbols and gestures of power is vividly expressed in the completely different world of Jerzy Kosinski's *The Painted Bird* (London: Bantam Books, 1965) by the young protagonist, a Jewish boy who looks like a Gypsy and manages to escape the Holocaust by hiding in farms.

Encountering a German SS officer dressed in full military garb, the boy describes his fascination:

> He seemed an example of neat perfection that could not be sullied: the smooth polished skin of his face, the bright golden hair showing under his peaked cap, his pure metal eyes. Every movement of his body seemed propelled by some tremendous internal force. The granite sound of his language was ideally suited to order the death of inferior, forlorn creatures. I was stung by a twinge of envy I had never experienced before, and I admired the glittering death's–head and crossbones that embellished his tall cap. I thought how good it would be to have such a gleaming and hairless skull instead of my Gypsy face which was feared and disliked by decent people. (119)

27. Grey Gundaker (1998) identifies the imitation of signs of African divination systems as an alternative mode of literacy in the African Diaspora.

28. This became a silenced miracle, since it was (like many others) dismissed by the Catholic Church, unlike apparitions such as those of La Virgen de Guadalupe and La Virgen de la Caridad del Cobre, which not only were authorized by the church but also recognized as the patron saints of the Mexican and Cuban nations, respectively.

29. After roughly the 1980s, state-sponsored persecution and vilification of popular healers ended as a result of an overall "spiritual laissez-faire" context that developed under the ideology of multiculturalism and the practices of consumerism in Puerto Rico (Romberg 1998, 2003a, 2003b).

30. Followers of the Afro-Brazilian Candomblé still celebrate their *orisha* Oxalá at the Brazilian Church of Bomfim in Bahia during the yearly "washing of the steps" festival (Silverstein 1995). This ritual commemorates the promise a Portuguese soldier made to Jesus before he went off to war during colonial times. He pledged that if he came back unhurt he would wash the atrium of the church. For Candomblé practitioners it is "a doublet of the ritual for purifying the divine stones" representing the *orishas* (deities) with "the water of Oxalá" (Oxalá being the Candomblé counterpart of Jesus), a yearly ritual that is meant to renew their *ashé* or "power" (Bastide 1978, 276).

Africa's Creole Drum

The Gumbe as Vector and Signifier
of Trans-African Creolization

—KENNETH BILBY

The story told here—a transatlantic story of displacement, cultural reinvention, and creolization—begins well over two centuries ago, in 1800.
Almost precisely at midnight, on the first of October in that year, several
hundred black people completed a long and grueling transatlantic voyage.
According to oral traditions that have survived to the present, the ordeal of
capture, incarceration on European ships, and forced removal from their
country of origin had taken place not, as one might expect, on the shores
of Africa (Bilby 2005, 378–410). In fact, Africa was where the long journey
ended—not, as one might expect, where it had begun. The original point of
departure (and country of origin) had actually been the Caribbean island
of Jamaica, on the other side of the Atlantic Ocean.

The captives on this "reverse" transatlantic voyage were Jamaican
Maroons—descendants of enslaved Africans who had escaped from plantations and fought their enslavers to a standstill, forcing the British government in 1739 to sign a treaty recognizing their freedom and their right
to a semi-autonomous territory of their own in the interior of the colony.
Nearly six decades after this, a newly arrived colonial governor, Lord Bal-
carres, had provoked these Maroons into a second war. Unable to defeat
them through force of arms, the corrupt governor had resorted to trickery
and had used false promises and duplicitous diplomacy to entrap them and
deport them en masse from the island.[1] In 1796 they had been sent against
their wishes to Nova Scotia in Canada. After four trying years in this harsh
climate, they finally arrived in the fledgling colony of Sierra Leone on the
coast of West Africa.

The story of these Jamaican Maroons who ended up in Sierra Leone
points to an important but often neglected dimension of the African

Diasporic experience that has begun to receive increasing attention in recent years: the "return" of Africans and their descendants from the Americas to their continent of origin.[2] The Maroons who were exiled from Jamaica at the end of the eighteenth century were among the earliest of these "returnees"—and certainly among the first to make this reverse voyage in large numbers, as a group. Nearly six hundred strong, they were able to bring much of the robust Afro-creole culture their ancestors had forged in Jamaica across the ocean with them. Among the things they carried with them was the knowledge of a distinctive type of musical instrument— an unusual square frame drum with four legs, known as *gumbe.*

This study follows the transatlantic trajectory of this Caribbean drum, examining a number of questions raised by its transplantation from American to African soil. Even more remarkable than the journey of the gumbe drum from Jamaica to Africa is the fact that, once there, this Afro-Caribbean instrument became the basis for a series of important new musical and social developments. After becoming firmly established in Freetown, Sierra Leone, during the first half of the nineteenth century, the gumbe drum diffused across much of West and Central Africa; and certain musical and social practices, characteristics, and tendencies appear to have spread along with it.[3]

The questions raised by this complex story of transoceanic and transcontinental musical and cultural transmission have as much to do with change, adaptation, and shifts in identity as with cultural continuities and shared values and aesthetics. How did the gumbe lose its specific ethnic association with its original Jamaican Maroon "owners" in Sierra Leone? How did it come to be attached to other groups and identities? What are some of the factors that help to explain its spread from Maroons not only to other populations in Sierra Leone, but also, subsequently, over a period of more than a century, to a wide range of peoples in several different parts of the African continent? Why would this particular drum and the kinds of music played on it, and dances danced to it, be so appealing to people from widely varying cultural backgrounds dispersed across such a vast geographic area? And why would this particular drum be more likely than any other to be seized upon and used for the kinds of performance events in Africa associated with rapid cultural change? In short, why did the gumbe become "Africa's creole drum"?[4]

As this epithet suggests, the gumbe presents us with unique opportunities for the study and analysis of creolization, both as a fluid social process occurring over time and as a cultural phenomenon that, in order to be meaningful, always entails some degree of continuity with multiple pasts. After following the trail of the gumbe over more than a century and a half, stopping along the way to consider a few specific ethnographic sites, I will return to these broader themes, concluding with a discussion of some of the theoretical insights to be gained from this particular example of ongoing musical creolization.

A Caribbean Drum Lands on African Shores

How far back in time can we trace the gumbe, and what grounds do we have for styling it a "creole" drum? So far as I have been able to determine, the earliest written references to a square or rectangular frame drum bearing this name come from Jamaica, and they go back no further than the late eighteenth century.[5] Variants of this instrument continue to occur in later historical writings on the Anglophone Caribbean. During the early nineteenth century, the gumbe was associated with a variety of social contexts on Jamaican slave plantations. By the middle of the century, the instrument begins to crop up in descriptions from other parts of the Caribbean and North America as well. A handful of scholars noted the continuing existence of the gumbe in rural parts of Jamaica during the twentieth century. By that time, it had come to be identified specifically with the Maroon community of Accompong, in the western part of the island; but its existence was also reported in conjunction with a particular variant of the masked dance known as "John Canoe" (also known as Jonkonnu or Jankunu) that was practiced in non-Maroon areas (Beckwith 1929; Roberts 1924).[6]

Not surprisingly, when confronted with this unusual drum, scholars generally assumed an African origin. And when they turned to the African continent for confirmation, they indeed found square or rectangular frame drums there with cognate names that could reasonably be thought of as precursors.[7] But the evidence now available suggests that these African gumbe drums are actually derived from the *Caribbean* gumbe rather than the other way around.[8] It is not possible in the amount of space available here to examine in any detail the growing body of evidence pointing in this direction, but the line of reasoning that leads to this conclusion will emerge in the course of the discussion that follows. Lending additional strength to this conclusion is the fact that neither I nor others have been able to locate any mentions of an instrument fitting this description, whether called by

1. *Band of the Jaw-Bone, or John-Canoe*, 1837, by Isaac Mendes Belisario. Illustration showing a non-Maroon version of the Jamaican gumbe drum witnessed by the artist in Kingston, Jamaica, during the mid-nineteenth century. Lithograph with watercolor. From I. M. Belisario, *Sketches of Character, An Illustration of the Habits, Occupation, and Costume of the Negro Population, in the Island of Jamaica* (Kingston: J. R. De Cordova, 1837).

2. Non-Maroon Jamaican gumbe drummer. Lacovia, St. Elizabeth, Jamaica, 1991. Photo: Kenneth Bilby.

3. Close-up of non-Maroon Jamaican gumbe drum, showing tuning mechanism consisting of wedges that produce tension by driving an inner frame against the skin attached to the outer frame. Lacovia, St. Elizabeth, Jamaica. 1991. Photo: Kenneth Bilby.

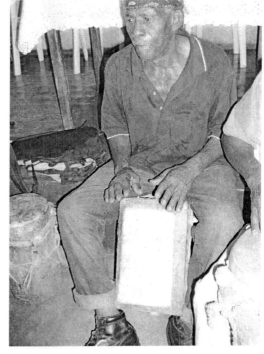

4. Maroon from the Windward (eastern Maroon) community of Scot's Hall playing the gumbe drum used in the traditional ceremonial music of that community. Moore Town, Portland, Jamaica, 2008. Photo: Kenneth Bilby.

this or another name, from anywhere on the African continent before 1800. Indeed, I know of no unambiguous descriptions of such an instrument in Africa even during the nineteenth century (although there are good reasons to believe that the occasional references to a musical genre called "goombay" in the nineteenth-century literature on Sierra Leone are tied to this specific drum, as we shall see). By the mid-twentieth century, in contrast, mentions of square or rectangular frame drums known as gumbe, or sometimes by other names, were common in Africa. Remarkably, these descriptions come from several widely separated parts of the continent—a matter to which we shall return shortly.

Let me sketch out a plausible scenario that will help to illustrate how this likely occurred. We have no direct evidence that the Maroons who left Jamaica in May 1796 brought any drums on the ship with them, or that they used drums during their four-year stay in Nova Scotia. Not suprisingly, the sparse written documentation that has so far been brought to light reveals very little about the Maroons' expressive culture, which was viewed by the colonial officials entrusted with their care as a hindrance to their "civilization." But historian Allistair Hinds points out that in Nova Scotia "the Maroons were settled in a manner which made it easy for them to retain the sociopolitical structures and attitudes which they brought with them from Jamaica. As the Report of the Maroon Committee put it, they were kept together in 'a body forming a distinct colony, and preserving all the habits and prejudices of Maroons [in Jamaica]'" (2001, 213).

In 1798, some two years into their stay in Canada, the Maroons, disillusioned with the harsh climate, bound themselves to a collective oath intended to ensure their removal to another country. According to Benjamin Gray, the clergyman who had been assigned to them, the oath-taking was "attended with a dreadful religious ceremony" (in Hinds 2001, 215).[9] Gray also reported that "Christianity failed to make an impact because even though they attended church 'a great many of the Maroons were so far unacquainted with our own language, as not to comprehend fully what was addressed to them from the pulpit'" (218). To make matters worse, "the Maroons objected to Gray's involvement in their marriage and burial ceremonies," and as a result, according to the missionary, their interments were generally "the occasion of festive excess" (218).

As "Governor Wentworth [of Nova Scotia] attempted to cleanse the Jamaicans of their 'dirty habits'" (Picart 1996, 175), the Maroons apparently stayed true to their oath, practicing the culture they had brought with them while biding their time and continuing to agitate for relocation to a country with a more suitable climate. During this period, according to one source,

> The Trelawny's [i.e., Maroons'] burials were never performed by a chaplain of the established church. While they lived on Preston estate [near Halifax], they continued to conduct their burials in the Coromantee rituals. The deceased was simply taken to a place of rest where he/she would then be buried under a heap of stones. Various articles that were deemed necessary to help the individual on the voyage to the other world were buried as well. The usual articles included such things as a bottle of rum, a pipe and tobacco, and two days' food rations. Singing, which perplexed some Nova Scotians, was part of the service. Since singing at funerals was not unusual in Nova Scotia, it might have been ancient African burial songs the Maroons were chanting during their funerals, which would explain why Nova Scotians found them perplexing. One member of the House of Assembly was bewildered after learning that the singing he heard was actually accompanying a Maroon burial. (Picart 1996, 175)

Clearly, throughout their exile in Nova Scotia, the Maroons had maintained a high degree of social solidarity and cultural integrity, and there can be no doubt that their traditional religion, from which their music and dance were inseparable, had played a large part in this. The attempts of the local authorities to convert and acculturate them had been, in Hinds's words, "a dismal failure" (Hinds 2001, 218). Indeed, it was partly because of this failure that the idea of permanent settlement in Nova Scotia was abandoned by the authorities, and a decision was finally made, less than four years after their arrival, to send them to the new colony of Sierra Leone on the West African coast.[10]

Once again, the written documentation is silent on whether there were any drums on board the ship that carried the Maroons to Sierra Leone, or whether they engaged in any performances of music or dance while en route to Africa. But given what we know of their time in Nova Scotia, it is safe to assume that a substantial portion of their religious (and thus musical) culture crossed the ocean along with them. This is suggested, for instance, by a report made almost two years after their arrival in Sierra Leone, which stated that they still "believed in Accompang, whom they called the God of Heaven" (Archibald 1889–91, 153).[11]

5. Martin-Luther Wright, colonel (leader) of the Jamaican Maroon community of Accompong (whose close relatives from Trelawny Town were shipped en masse to Nova Scotia in 1796 and to Sierra Leone in 1800), demonstrating playing of the gumbe drum used in the traditional ceremonial music of that community. Accompong, St. Elizabeth, 1978. Photo: Kenneth Bilby.

6. Colonel Martin-Luther Wright displaying side view of the Maroon gumbe drum. Accompong, St. Elizabeth, 1978. Photo: Kenneth Bilby.

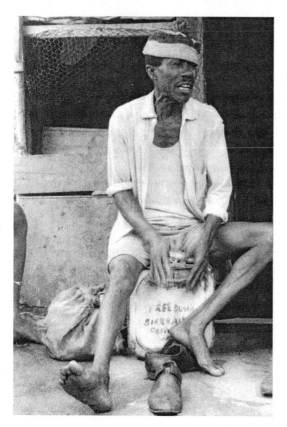

7. Arthur Pinkney (of the Krio gumbe band Freetown Goombay No. 1) playing the Sierra Leonean gumbe drum. Freetown, Sierra Leone, 1977. Photo: Kenneth Bilby.

8. Morlai Kamara (of the Krio gumbe band Freetown Gumbay No. 1) displaying side view of the Sierra Leonean gumbe drum. Freetown, Sierra Leone, 1977. Photo: Kenneth Bilby.

In fact, we have very good evidence to support the idea that the Maroons brought their traditional ceremonial music and dance with them to Sierra Leone. George Ross, the British employee of the Sierra Leone Company who accompanied the Maroons on their voyage from Nova Scotia to Sierra Leone, kept a journal recording certain parts of this journey, as well as a number of events that occurred during the first few months after their arrival in Sierra Leone. In his entry for October 23, 1800, roughly three weeks after he and the Maroons had disembarked in Africa, Ross attends a Maroon funeral in the vicinity of Freetown, at which one of the Maroons "chant[ed] over the corpse before burial." Ross goes on to comment on "some of the Maroon songs sung this evening." He also mentions that the night before, the Maroons' elderly leader, Montague James, had sung "a koromantyn song with great earnestness," and that this had "electrified all the Maroons who heard it" (in Campbell 1993, 28). In a couple of other journal entries written over the following days, Ross makes a few ambiguous references to drums and drumming among the Maroons (though he does not offer any actual descriptions of drums and never mentions the word *gumbe*).

The Maroon community of Accompong, which still exists in the hills of western Jamaica, can help us to interpret this fragmentary information. The Accompong Maroons were originally part of the same larger group of Maroons to which those who were deported to Sierra Leone—the Trelawny Town Maroons—had belonged. (The people of Accompong Town and those of Trelawny Town in fact constituted a single Maroon ethnic group and polity, known to the British as the Leeward Maroons.) When war broke out in 1795, the Maroons of Accompong had refused to join their sister Leeward community of Trelawny Town in the rebellion (Bilby 2005, 379). Because of this, the Accompong Maroons were allowed to remain on the island, while their brothers and sisters from Trelawny Town were deported to Nova Scotia and then Sierra Leone. Today, in the Jamaican community of Accompong, Kromanti ("koromantyn," in Ross's 1800 rendering) songs are still sung at Maroon funerals and certain other kinds of ceremonies; and these songs, along with various others, are sometimes backed with the Maroon drum called gumbe—the same square frame drum with which we are concerned here.[12] There can be little doubt that the Maroon Kromanti musical tradition briefly glimpsed by Ross in Sierra Leone in 1800 and the Maroon Kromanti musical tradition still practiced by Accompong Maroons in Jamaica today are cognate. Given the central role of the gumbe drum in the Accompong tradition, it seems virtually certain—especially when all the other evidence is considered—that the very closely related Trelawny Maroons who were deported to Sierra Leone brought the gumbe drum, or the knowledge of how to make it, with them.

Indeed, the Accompong Maroon gumbe drum I photographed in Jamaica in 1978 (see figs. 5–6) and the West African Krio (Creole) gumbe drum I photographed in Freetown, Sierra Leone, a few months earlier, in 1977 (see figs. 7–8), are so similar and share such a distinctive design that it is difficult to avoid the conclusion that the latter is derived from the former. Both are square frame drums that resemble a stool with four legs, and they feature the same unusual tuning mechanism, consisting of an inner frame driven by wedges against a skin stretched over an outer frame.[13]

From Maroon Drum to Krio (Creole) Drum

What changes did the Jamaican Maroon gumbe undergo in Sierra Leone as the nineteenth century unfolded? In short, it became the basis of a new popular dance music identified with the mixed Afro-American and African population that came to be known as Creoles; this new genre eventually took the name of the drum itself, becoming known as *gumbe.*

Creole society in Sierra Leone emerged from an amazingly complex coming together of diverse peoples. The cultural process involved was strangely reminiscent of what had already transpired a thousand times over on the other side of the ocean, beginning some three centuries earlier, when African people of multiple origins were thrown together on the slave plantations and in the towns of the Caribbean. In the earliest years of the Sierra Leone experiment, the key players among the subalterns newly introduced into the colony were the Jamaican Maroons, together with the so-called Settler population that had preceded them, composed of a few thousand black Nova Scotians with origins in Virginia and South Carolina. But in the following decades, the situation changed drastically as the capital of Freetown became one of the main destinations for thousands of "Recaptives" or Liberated Africans—people who had been captured and enslaved along the coast of West Africa, only to be intercepted by British patrols before the ships in which they had been imprisoned could reach the Americas. These individuals, who came from a great many different regions and were culturally extremely heterogeneous, constituted the bulk of the population that was rapidly to evolve into a new people known as Creoles.

In the early years, each of these distinct groups—the Settlers (African Americans who had come via Nova Scotia), the Maroons from Jamaica, and the Liberated Africans—was internally differentiated. According to Claude George, "the Settlers [i.e., Nova Scotians] belong to a variety of African tribes whom the accident of slavery had brought together, but had by no means lost their original languages, which were not as various as those of the Liberated Africans" (1904, 198). To judge by present-day oral evidence (Bilby 2005, 79–87), the Maroons too—though they had already evolved a distinctive Afro-creole society and culture of their own by this time—probably still displayed internal cultural differences that reflected their diverse African ethnic origins. But the group that was by far the most heterogeneous (as well as the largest) was the Liberated Africans.[14] Indeed, this group may well have represented the most diverse population on the entire continent of Africa at that time. According to George, "the term *Liberated Africans* [in Sierra Leone] comprises by far the most varied and multifarious elements found to exist on the West Coast of Africa, from the Gold Coast down to Nigritia, viz. the Cromanties, the Popos, the Yorubas, including Egbas, Ijebus, Kankajas, Gbomnas, the inhabitants of the Niger territories, Congo, Fernandopo, Cameroons, etc." (1904, 198). Gary Stewart and John Amman provide us with a particularly effective indication of the sheer diversity of the emerging Creole society of Sierra Leone. "By the early 1850s," they state, "a German missionary named Sigismund Koelle had documented 160 languages and 40 dialects among Freetown citizens who had come to the colony from up and down the West African coast and as far east as Malawi and Mozambique. Names of areas within the colony like Congo Town and Kroo Town reflected this astonishing diversity. The mix of people produced Freetown's Creole community—now called Krio—whose European-influenced culture and language—also called Krio—came to dominate the region" (Stewart and Amman 2007, 20).[15] According to Akintola Wyse (and a number of earlier authors he cites), "this motley collection of Africans 'represented about as heterogeneous an assemblage, in language, custom and belief as can be imagined'" (Wyse 1989, 2).

Although the absorption of the Maroons into the larger population occurred gradually, the first stages of this process had already been set in motion within a few years of their arrival in Sierra Leone. Nemata Amelia Blyden argues that "though the [M]aroons initially kept their separate community and retained their identity, eventually they began to interact more with other settler groups. By the time the Crown took over the colony in 1808, some semblance of unity existed between the different groups of settlers in Freetown" (2000, 31). According to a number of historians, the Maroons played a particularly prominent role in gradually bringing about this "semblance of unity," making fundamental contributions to the emerging Creole culture as the new society evolved over time. "By mid-nineteenth century," says Mavis Campbell, "the Maroons and the settlers were to grow together through marriage, business and religious affiliations and to become the cornerstone of the Creole society of Sierra Leone" (1992, 101).

We have little information on exactly how and when the gumbe lost its specific association with Maroons and became identified with the broader Creole population. Describing the situation in 1834, a British observer asserted, "the nationality of the Maroons in Sierra Leone is distinctly maintained" (Rankin 1836, 116).[16] The same writer mentioned a dance known by the Maroons as "Tallala," which he characterized as "the all-ravishing dance of the Freetown maidens" (Rankin 1836, 283).[17] This wording would seem to suggest that although this dance was understood to have Maroon origins, it was now danced by "Freetown maidens" from various groups, not just Maroons. Some three decades later, in 1868, another British writer, relying partly on Rankin's previous account, gives the name of this dance as "Talla"—adding, very importantly, that this dance was "the mother of Goombay" (Sibthorpe 1868, 28). One might infer from this statement that by this time music and dance styles once associated exclusively or primarily with Maroons had produced new "offspring" that were still identified with the gumbe drum (having taken on its name), though no longer necessarily specifically with Maroons.[18]

One thing we do know is that in the crucible of creolizing culture that was Freetown during the first half of the nineteenth century, music and dance performances were privileged sites for the negotiation of interethnic sociality, cultural difference, and identity. According to one observer writing in the 1830s, "there are numerous . . . dances amongst the mixed population of Freetown and the neighbouring villages. Nothing is easier than to make one; nothing more is required than to give a man money to strike a tomtom, and numbers of either sex will rapidly collect together, without further invitation, and set themselves in motion" (Rankin 1836, 307). It is safe to assume that the drum ("tomtom") of choice on such occasions was often the gumbe. A few years later, in a passage in which the "Creoles," the "Settlers," and the "liberated Africans" are all mentioned in the same breath, Clarke points out that "all classes of the Africans are very fond of dancing" (1843, 57–58). His description of these dances that draw Africans of all sorts is worth quoting at length:

A circle is generally formed, from which two of the group of opposite sexes step out, waving the arms, clapping the hands and singing,
whilst they move towards each other, the man bending the body in
no very decent way as he approaches his partner, who jerks the hip
from side to side. One by one, others join the dancers, till the excitement becomes general, whilst the drums are fast and furiously beaten,
and continual accessions pour in on all sides, wherever the music is
heard, in order to participate in the joyous festivity. The young Creole
girls attend the dance with the hair generally neatly plaited, whilst
staid matrons stand looking on, with their piccaninnies, either in their
hands or swathed to their backs, their head-dress being the general
one, consisting of a kerchief gracefully arranged. (Clarke 1843, 57)

"The song and dance," observes Clarke, "are often kept up with the
utmost vivacity till dawn, and for several successive nights, the excitement
being sustained, and fanned into an almost maddening intensity by deep
potations" (1843, 58). As the nineteenth century moved on, these danced
interethnic encounters must have been one of the main theaters in which
ethnic identities were performed and renegotiated, and there can be little
doubt that gumbe drummers continued to be enlisted for many such gatherings. In any case, by the last few decades of the century, the gumbe had
become the drum of the Freetown masses, identified with the lower-class
Creole population in general.

It is easy to imagine why this drum and some of the elements of style
associated with it might be selected more readily than others in such polyethnic contexts. In a sense, the gumbe had arrived in Africa ready-made for
the bridging of inter-African cultural difference. Its design and the Afro-
creole music originally associated with it had evolved in a distant Caribbean land and represented a new synthesis that had no association with
a specific indigenous African ethnic identity or language. It was not seen
as belonging to people from Yoruba, Asante, Mandinka, Kongo, or any of
the dozens of other provincial ethnic categories (or sub-categories) that
had been thrown into the mix in Freetown; it excluded no one. It did not
carry the divisive potential of the music and dance genres closely identified
with these specific ethnolinguistic groups, which could easily be used to
maintain ethnic boundaries by highlighting linguistic and musical differences. Yet, at the same time, the gumbe and its rhythms remained identifi-
ably and palpably "African" in a broad aesthetic sense. People from all the
African ethnic groups named above would have heard and felt things in

this Afro-creole music that were more familiar to them at first—and more similar to their own musical practices—than the sounds encountered, for instance, in Christian churches or other European-dominated contexts. This no doubt contributed to its wide (and almost immediate) appeal in a social setting defined by the presence of an uprooted, displaced African population, bewildering ethnic and linguistic diversity, and an imposed European colonial culture that was both alien and alienating.

The Sierra Leonean Diaspora: The Spread of Africa's Creole Drum

The emerging Creole population of Freetown soon became one of the most mobile in Africa. As the historian A. P. Kup notes, "Freetown Creoles were [from the 1830s on] likely to be drawn along the coast. Many young men got clerkships and by [the middle of the nineteenth century] Creoles were to be found from the Gambia to Fernando Po" (1975, 157). Soon after this, the advent of the steamship led to rapid expansion of the Krio diaspora all along the West African coast, opening the way for a whole new outpouring of "country traders"—small-scale hawkers for whom long-distance maritime travel had previously been unaffordable. As a result, by the 1860s, substantial communities of Freetown Creoles—made up of both wealthier merchants and more humble traders—could be found in Fernando Po, Liberia, Gambia, Bonny, Calabar, the Cameroons, and beyond. Indeed, it has been estimated that around this time fully 20 percent of the population of Lagos consisted of Sierra Leoneans (Lynn 1992).[19]

Simultaneous with the development of this traveling culture was the emergence in Freetown of a new generation with a strong sense of local Creole identity. Leo Spitzer tells us that "by the 1870s the lines separating the Nova Scotians, Maroons, and Recaptives had virtually disappeared. The last of the original settlers from the United States and the West Indies were dying out. The importation of new Liberated Africans ceased completely during the 1840s and the Creoles—the children of the settlers and recaptives who had been born in Sierra Leone—began to outnumber their parents and grandparents" (1974, 12). These travelers belonging to a new generation (and others belonging to subsequent ones) no doubt brought the gumbe drum and its rhythms with them as they fanned out along the coast of West Africa.[20] And from here the story becomes too vast and complicated to relate in any but the most cursory way in the amount of space available here. By the first few decades of the twentieth century, the gumbe drum and its varied offspring had spread out across an enormous swath of coastal West Africa and had moved inland as well, having been adopted, refashioned, and, in some cases, "re-indigenized" in numerous local contexts. By mid-century, cognate traditions using the same or similar drums, sometimes known as gumbe, sometimes by other names, had been documented in—among other West African locations—Senegal, Gambia, Mali, Guinea Bissau, Ivory Coast, Gold Coast, Dahomey, Nigeria, as well as in several parts of Central Africa.[21] In virtually all these cases, these cognate traditions were associated with migration stories; in many cases, they were tied to polyethnic, often urban, social contexts. As André Schaeffner noted in the early 1960s, "the term *gumbe* is applied today to musical performances in urban environments, not so different from those provided by our [Parisian] cellar clubs, music parties, or cabarets" (1964, 248, my translation). Even where variants of gumbe-based music had been thoroughly indigenized, now forming part of ethnically specific repertories and used to back songs in local languages, they were still recognized as something relatively new, something that had been introduced from elsewhere relatively recently.[22]

One of the first to recognize and suggest some of the broader implications of what I am pointing out here—certainly one of the first to put this recognition in writing—is the art historian Judith Bettelheim. In her 1979 dissertation on the Jonkonnu festival of Jamaica, she included an appendix on the gumbe (or gumbay) drum, in which—after a brief survey showing its wide distribution in both the Caribbean and Africa—she anticipated the thrust of the argument I am making here, in the following passage:

It seems reasonable to assume, from all the above data, that the frame drum of West Africa, sometimes called gumbay, might owe its origin to a Caribbean source. The use of the word gumbay in the above West African examples is usually associated with non-traditional musical groups. These groups demonstrate either multi-ethnic composition or include influences from non-indigenous sources. Is it not possible that Caribbean Blacks introduced both the frame drum and the word gumbay to West Africa? Beginning with the Maroon immigrants of 1800, and then taking into account other returning Blacks, there certainly has been ample communication between West Africa and the Caribbean. (Bettelheim 1979, 318)[23]

As Bettelheim recognized, there would seem to be some connection between the probable Caribbean origins of the gumbe and its association in several parts of Africa with groups that "demonstrate either multi-ethnic composition or include influences from non-indigenous sources." Indeed, one might conjecture that as the gumbe left Sierra Leone and traveled from one point to another, social, economic, and cultural factors similar to those that had operated in Freetown in the first decades of the nineteenth century combined in comparable ways to produce similar outcomes elsewhere on the continent. If this Afro-creole drum had proven to be particularly well suited to the bridging of ethnic and cultural differences and the fashioning of new identities in the polyethnic cauldron of Freetown shortly after 1800, why could the same not have held true of later versions of this drum as they were introduced into new polyethnic environments in other parts of Africa during the later nineteenth and twentieth centuries?

The rapid expansion of world capitalism during the twentieth century helped to produce an explosion of such new environments. During this period, much of Africa was radically reshaped by massive labor migration and rapid urbanization. Like Freetown in its early years, the new cities that sprang up across the continent were characterized by tremendous ethnic heterogeneity. Urban peripheries in particular were typically made up of displaced people who came from disparate cultural zones and spoke several different languages. These new town dwellers, living side by side on the margins, were faced with the necessity of adapting to difficult and shifting economic circumstances. Just as importantly, they found themselves in nascent and somewhat chaotic social environments lacking the kinship-based structures and relative cultural stability of the rural communities from which they or their parents had migrated. Like the gumbe drum rhythms first brought to Freetown by the Jamaican Maroons in 1800, the music and dance styles associated with later generations of this Afro-creole instrument no doubt retained recognizable features of a generalized "African" musical aesthetic; at the same time these gumbe-based expressions would have remained largely free of musical and linguistic features perceived as narrowly ethnic or "tribal." For this reason, the gumbe drum had a special appeal and could easily be adapted to the needs of these emergent polyethnic communities. As a part of this process of adaptation, the gumbe also became an emblem of "modernity"—an expression of the new condition in which these polyethnic migrants, many of them young, found themselves—and, in keeping with these symbolic associations, came to

9. West African *cumbé* player. Equatorial Guinea, 2007. Photo: Isabela de Aranzadi.

10. West African *cumbé* drum, showing modified (lengthened) version of original Caribbean tuning mechanism consisting of wedges that produce tension by driving an inner frame against the skin attached to the outer frame. Equatorial Guinea, 2007. Photo: Isabela de Aranzadi.

act as a kind of magnet and container for "non-indigenous" musical influences, whether European, Afro-American, or other. The gumbe was now on the way to becoming not just Sierra Leone's but Africa's creole drum.

African Gumbe Variations

Let us briefly examine three well-documented and particularly revealing examples of the gumbe drum in West Africa. The Ga people of coastal Ghana have an important musical genre known as Gome (sometimes pronounced "Gombe" or "Gumbe"). Using a modified version of the same four-legged, rectangular frame drum brought to Sierra Leone by Jamaican Maroons, it is a vital and still-growing tradition encompassing several sub-genres. Today, Gome is closely associated with Ga ethnic identity, and Gome songs are typically sung in the Ga language, or in a mixture of Ga and English.[24] As late as the 1960s, however, many of these songs were sung in West African Pidgin English.[25] The ethnomusicologist who has worked most extensively with this Ga tradition, Barbara Hampton, tells us how this came to be. "Gome," she points out, "is a musical system that was introduced into Kpehe [a heterogeneous neighborhood in northwest Accra, whose residents come from the Ga, Akan, Ewe, Dagomba, and other ethnic groups from northern Ghana and Togo] by Ga labor migrants when they returned from Fernando Po, an island of Equatorial Guinea, where they say that they learned it from Sierra Leonean artisans after 1947" (Hampton 1979–1980, 5).[26] She goes on to state that "Gome is an urban musical ensemble because it is supported by a polyethnic, socioeconomically diverse patron group; is distinctly of the city; serves the musical needs of city dwellers; and is, itself, linked to the urban-industrial complex through direct interactions with it" (Hampton 1979–1980, 5).

A closer look reveals that one of the most distinctive things about Gome is the open attitude of those who practice it. Hampton makes the important point that the very way that the tradition evolved in Ghana (and perhaps even before that, in Fernando Po) suggests "a perception of Gome as a potentially appropriate music for the needs of a diverse population" (1983, 222). Ethnic heterogeneity was a fundamental "social fact" from the very beginning. In Fernando Po during the late 1940s, where Ga migrants originally learned the rudiments of gumbe drumming while playing alongside fellow laborers from Sierra Leone, the new music "served as a bridge across ethnic boundaries among colonial subjects for the limited objective of recreation" (226). Although the version that was introduced to Ghana by returning migrants in the early 1950s was played at first by groups made up exclusively of Ga individuals, Gome was soon adapted to changing political and economic conditions in Accra (and in the new nation of which it was a part) that created a rapid "influx of people into the community from all regions of Ghana" (218). As Hampton observes, "this situation contributed to the acceptance of friendship [rather than kinship or ethnicity] as an alternative associative relationship by Gome musicians and ultimately the use of friendship as a basis for recruitment" (218). Because of this, "in 1957, the Gome ensemble, just as Kpehe and Accra were, became polyethnic in composition" (218).

Hampton sees the historical circumstances that led to the birth of this still-young tradition as having continuing significance in the present, arguing, "The precedent for this shift from an emphasis on kinship to friendship in recruitment as well as from monethnicity to polyethnicity in the composition of the musical ensemble was established in Fernando Po" (1983, 218). This would suggest that the process of musical and cultural "recreolization" of this relocated and incipiently indigenized offshoot of the gumbe tradition, which had been set in motion by the sudden appearance in the mid-1950s of tremendous ethnic heterogeneity (accompanied by social fragmentation) in this neighborhood of Accra, was supported by cultural values that had become intertwined with earlier versions of the tradition in Fernando Po. What we see in this particular case of transplanted gumbe, then, are signs of a developing "tradition" of adaptive openness supported by an ethic of inclusiveness. This is reflected, for example, in "the lack of boundaries between positions within the age cycle, as reflected in the dance arena" (223). (In keeping with this, "members of Kpehe society say that young people and children are attracted to Gome because it allows them unrestricted participation" [223]). It is also reflected in the "relaxation of sexual boundaries [that] was extended to the Gome dance arena, resulting in male and female duet or couple dancing and in the portrayal of romantic love in mimetic dance variations" (219). The boundaries bridged through this extension of gumbe music and dance, therefore, had to do not only with ethnicity, but also with age and gender.[27]

A rather similar socio-musical configuration, also going by the name gumbe (or Goumbé), was encountered repeatedly by the renowned filmmaker and anthropologist Jean Rouch while he was undertaking his pioneering study of West African labor migration during the 1950s. Rouch described Goumbé to one interviewer as both "the name of a drum" and a "dance of displaced people" (Rouch and Fulchignoni 2003, 167). The inno-vative *ethno-cinéaste* featured the gumbe associations he was in the pro-cess of studying in some of his best-known films, including *Moi, un Noir* (1958), *La pyramide humaine* (1959), and *La Goumbé des jeunes noceurs* (1965). (Center stage was given to one group in particular, based in Treich-ville on the urban periphery of Abidjan in Côte d'Ivoire [Ivory Coast].)

The particular footage Rouch selects to represent these music and dance associations says much about their significance for practitioners. The Goumbé scene in *Moi, un Noir*, for instance, features "a young novice champion, dressed cowboy style," and "bicycle dances (rodeo)," followed by a dance contest in which the winners are proclaimed "King and Queen of the Royal Goumbé" (Rouch 2003, 355)—moments signifying a self-con-scious (and at times ironic) engagement with "modernity." In *La pyramide humaine*, the Goumbé footage is carefully selected to make a statement about the openness and inclusiveness of such dance events and to point to the potential for boundary-crossing and negotiation of new identities with which these urban performing groups are typically associated. The film follows a group of young students, African and European, living in Abidjan, who are groping for ways to develop friendships across the racial line dividing them. In one critical scene, after some of the problems of rac-ism with which they must contend have been exposed, "the Africans take the Europeans to a Goumbé (club for young Abidjan dancers), and for the first time, boys and girls, Africans and Europeans, dance in the streets, led by the 'Goumbé Queen,' Nathalie" (356).

Of the three films mentioned above, the one that is most revealing—and is also one of the best documents we have of West African gumbe performance during the middle years of the twentieth century—is *La Goumbé des jeunes noceurs* (The Goumbé of the Young Revelers). It is in fact a filmic ethnography of a particular voluntary association started by young laborers who had recently migrated several hundred miles from Upper Volta to Abidjan.[28] As Rouch explains, "the young people who come to work in Abidjan often form spontaneous associations for mutual help and entertainment, which are called 'Goumbés' in Ivory Coast, after the name of a square drum that serves as the rhythmic base to their dance" (2003, 360). The members of the association are ethnically and occupa-tionally diverse. What links them together as a single community in this semi-urban agglomeration of displaced people thrown together by chance, according to the filmmaker, is music and dance—"the tambourine player is a tailor, the singer-composer is a button sewer in a clothing-manufacturing business, and the leading lady, Nathalie, is a mother and homemaker" (360). Like the sense of community it helps to generate, this music and dance is actively conceived by its performers as something "new" and "modern"—something that can serve as a suitable expressive medium for a new, still evolving identity. "Every week the dancers practice to invent new dance steps," Rouch tells us. "Once a month, the musicians must compose new songs for the Goumbé." Following this, "every month, a parade of the Goumbé takes place in the streets of Treichville" (360). To address these needs—and to foster other kinds of mutual aid as well—the musicians and dancers have created a formal social structure, replete with "officers" bearing titles such as president, vice president, high commissioner, and secretary, along with a set of "statutes" that are read at regular meetings.

Among Rouch's writings, one finds a beautiful and rather specific description of the actual social circumstances and processes that led to the growth of this and other such gumbe associations on the urban periphery of Abidjan. As we have seen, Rouch was able to observe these processes directly, and even film them, as they unfolded on the ground in the 1950s and 1960s. "Most frequently," reports Rouch,

> the children who are torn between their parents [because of migration and interethnic marriage] settle on the coast, casually brought up by the mother and educated by the father at minimum expense. They are called *dankasa* meaning "born in foreign lands." In both Ghana and the Ivory Coast they form a distinct mixed group held apart by both the indigenous coastal people and the migrants. Belonging to neither the maternal nor the paternal group they have no tradition and attempt to create customs of their own. . . . Rejected by all, they have formed themselves into separate groups, finding compensation in creating voluntary societies where loneliness, despair, and dreams are shared. This has led to the creation of *goumbe* societies in the Ivory Coast. Initially similar to the many mutual societies found on the coast, the *goumbes* rapidly become young people's dance societies. . . . This suggests the development of a new type of community, a community of the rejected, but of people who have withstood contempt and are creating a new way of life. (1961, 303–304)

Another major extension of gumbe music and dance—one that has been better documented than most—arose in Mali. One of the earliest accounts from this part of Africa—if not the first—comes from Michel Leiris, who

was told of a tradition called "goumbé" when traveling in the vicinity of
Bamako during the famous 1931–33 Dakar-Djibouti Mission organized by
the Musée de l'Homme. Leiris describes this variant of gumbe as "a new
children's organization," a "gallant association of boys and girls not yet, or
only recently, circumcised." Not only is this clearly a youth-oriented phenomenon—almost all the members are of school age, he notes—but it is
also clear that the performers have a predilection for things perceived as
modern and European. During large gatherings, he tells us, "the *goumbé*
drums of the society are decorated with French flags, and the distinctive
sign of the president [of the gumbe association] is a complete European
khaki suit" (Leiris 1934, 68, my translations).

Some three decades later, Claude Meillassoux (1968, 116–130) under-
took an investigation of three different gumbe groups as part of a larger
ethnographic study of voluntary associations in the city of Bamako. Meillassoux's well-grounded discussion is full of details that are of particular
interest to us here. Like Leiris, Meillassoux notes that this is an activity
associated with youth; many of the members, both male and female, are
in their teens. People generally agree that the tradition "probably came
from Senegal," but "no one knows exactly when" (117).[29] The name *gumbe*
itself (referring to the square frame drum at the center of music and dance
events) is "foreign to any of the languages spoken in Bamako"—in fact, "no
one knows where it came from or what it means" (117). Even more interesting is the fact that, according to Meillassoux, the ethnic background
of participants is "irrelevant" (120). Members include Fulani, Mandinka,
Bamana, Soninke, and people from various other ethnic groups who have
joined together to create new music and dance styles—and to cooperate
in other ways as well—in this polyethnic urban context (120). (Songs "are
inspired by modern music, and phrases of Charleston, *rumba*, samba,
mambo, conga, and cha-cha can be detected"; and dance steps "are even
more directly inspired by Western dances than is the music," with rock and
roll and the twist being among the most recent influences [126].)

The main qualification for joining one of these gumbe groups is what
Meillassoux describes as "a minimum urban standing" (1968, 121). That
is, participation is usually limited to town dwellers whose social ties are
based primarily on locality and friendship (in short, voluntary association)
rather than kinship or ethnic identification. The gumbe groups studied by
Meillassoux, thus, use the principle of inclusiveness—together with the
unifying potential of African-style music and dance—to create solidarity and a sense of community in a fluid and highly heterogeneous social

environment that came into existence only recently as a result of large-scale migration. In sociological terms, these music and dance associations, as Meillassoux succinctly puts it, "were created by groups of friends who wanted to structure their relationships" (119). In creating social structures where none had existed before (in this new, polyethnic urban context), they were forging new forms of culture through what might be seen as a textbook example of creolization.

We know that gumbe groups similar to these were active for many decades not just in Mali, but also over a wide expanse of Mande country. Referencing urban life in the 1950s in places such as Dakar (Senegal), Abidjan (Ivory Coast), Conakry (Guinea), and Bamako (Mali), Manthia Diawara writes of "a style of street party called Goumbé or Bals Poussières, which became extremely popular among the boys and girls of Mande West Africa. The parties brought together in the streets young people who considered themselves urbanized and 'civilized,' but who were not rich enough to afford the cover charge at nightclubs. The Goumbé had the reputation of bringing together elegant young men, or *zazaou*, and beautiful young ladies who were sophisticated enough to dance arm-in-arm with their men" (1998, 114). Diawara adds to this a critical observation, one that clearly ties these groups, as a social phenomenon, to the gumbe associations encountered by Meillassoux in Bamako in the 1960s (and, indeed, to similar groups described in several other parts of Africa): "The young people who organized Goumbé in the cities were usually migrant workers from villages and neighboring countries. The Goumbé brought them together regardless of clan and traditional gender divisions" (114).

Some Final Thoughts on Africa's Creole Drum: Homecoming and Creolization

Certainly, this story of transatlantic "return," neatly encapsulated in the gumbe drum, is significant symbolically, evoking powerful tropes of cultural continuity and reconnection across centuries of exile and separation. One reason the transatlantic voyage of the gumbe makes such an effective symbol of diasporic reconnection is that it is one of the earliest known examples of cultural "diaspora in reverse." As a musical symbol, it can be made to stand for many later examples of transatlantic musical transmission in this reverse direction, including the "return" to Africa, during the twentieth century, of popular Afro-American musical genres such as jazz, rumba, calypso, salsa, reggae, and hip-hop/rap (which, in turn, as we have seen, themselves often influenced new developments in gumbe music and dance in various parts of the continent). Such cases of diasporic musical "feedback" may be imagined as a kind of "coming home." Paraphrasing this larger story of musical reunion in a way that suggests its truly epic proportions, John Collins argues for the special significance, both symbolic and substantive, of the gumbe as the very first in a long line of "returnees":

The earliest "homecoming" is a Jamaican frame-drum dance music known as Goombay . . . introduced by freed Maroon slaves [sic] to Freetown, Sierra Leone, on October 1, 1800, where it is still played and laid the basis of that country's first popular music (c. 1900), known as Asiko (Ashiko). . . . Goombay and Ashiko subsequently spread from Sierra Leone to many West and Central African countries (Mali, Côte d'Ivoire, Ghana, Nigeria, Gabon, Congo, Cameruns, and Fernando Po), creating an important musical building block for various 20th century African popular and neo-traditional music styles: such [as] Maringa, Milo Jazz, Highlife, Juju music, Gube, Gome, Le Goumbe, Simpa, and Gahu. (Collins 1998, cited in Horton 1999, 231)[30]

As appropriate as this figurative notion of "musical repatriation" may be in this context, I would argue that the gumbe serves just as effectively as an emblem of what has aptly been called "the miracle of creolization" (Trouillot 1998; Price 2001, 2006). As a Caribbeanist, I am in sympathy with those of my colleagues who have expressed reservations about the increasingly broad and uncritical use of a term ("creolization") whose somewhat murky origins and complex (and often contradictory) prior meanings are bound up with historical circumstances specific to the circum-Caribbean region and a number of other American locations that share certain features with it. Not surprisingly, as the term is applied with increasing alacrity across disciplines to a range of vastly differing contexts and phenomena, criticisms of creolization as a theoretical construct have begun to multiply (Mintz 1996, 1998; Khan 2001, 2007a; Palmié 2006, 2007a, 2007b; Stewart 2007).

Among the risks brought by this proliferation of unanchored "creolization discourse" are loss of theoretical coherence and trivialization (through facile contemporary "multiculturalist" analogies) of social and cultural processes that have often involved tremendous human costs—particularly in the paradigmatic Caribbean setting, where such processes cannot be viewed apart from histories of decimation, colonial domination, forced migration and repopulation, slavery, and ongoing economic exploitation and marginalization, as well as the continuous struggles waged against all of these (Trouillot 1998). To give too little weight to these specific histories in attempting to imagine (and, in doing so, theorize) the "miracle of creolization" that issued from these histories is to lose sight of what arguably makes "creole" cultural formations distinctive to begin with—that is, the social conditions that favor (if not force) the relatively rapid combination (and recombination) of cultural forms that once seemed disparate and their creative use in reconstituting a shattered sense of community or society. In the Caribbean (and, clearly, in some other parts of the world), these formative social conditions, past and present, are most often reflexes of large-scale political and economic forces. If static, autonomous, or overly mechanical models of culture fail to do justice to the contingent complexities of social reality in general, they are particularly unhelpful in this context. The uncritical use of linguistic models (themselves currently under attack) in theorizing cultural creolization has also come under fire, partly because creole linguistics has of necessity relied as much on speculation about unknown (and perhaps unknowable) historical sociolinguistic factors as on the collection of empirical data (Palmié 2006, 2007b).

Such criticisms notwithstanding, the case at hand almost unavoidably invites analysis in "creolist" terms. How else might one make sociological sense of the growing mass of empirical data that confronts the persistent researcher of the gumbe drum? An instrument that appears to have been born in the Caribbean as an Afro-creole invention, once transplanted to Africa, becomes the initial basis for an astonishing array of new forms of music and dance across much of the continent, all of them (at least at first) self-consciously "non-indigenous." Although the driving economic motor in the African contexts where the gumbe took root is not slavery, these varied African environments nonetheless display certain unmistakable similarities with many Caribbean (and other American) slave plantations—most notably, culturally and linguistically heterogeneous groups of Africans thrown together in new, economically precarious settings devoid of a preexisting sense of "community" and lacking overarching older social institutions and relatively coherent "traditional" cultures into which these displaced individuals might readily be integrated. And although the conditions facing these uprooted and displaced migrants in Africa may not have been as harsh or traumatic as those under which enslaved Africans lived and labored in the Americas, they involved severities and challenges of their own. (One is reminded here of Rouch's portrayal of the marginalized gumbe adherents on whom he focused as "a community of the rejected," a joining together of "people who have withstood contempt" even while "creating a new way of life" [Rouch 1961, 304].)

The case of the transatlantic, pan-African gumbe suggests that cultural creolization, for all its problematic aspects (especially when divorced from "the historical conditions of cultural production" [Trouillot 1998, 8]), remains an avenue of inquiry into social and cultural change well worth exploring further.[31] Whether or not we wish to apply the label "creole" to the various manifestations of the far-flung gumbe drum and the genres of music and dance associated with it, it is difficult to avoid the conclusion that there is something about this "gumbe complex"—something distinctly "cultural"—that has led to its repeated selection for similar social and aesthetic purposes over such a long period of time and across such a broad expanse of space. (Of course, gumbe is but one of many different Western-influenced music and dance traditions that have spread over large portions of Africa, some of which have been used in similar ways; but, aside from being one of the most widespread, it stands out as the one with the longest history.[32]) One thing this particular example of cultural creolization seems to demonstrate (and, for some of us, to reconfirm) is that, for all their newness, creolized forms of culture—in this case, music and dance—can contain substantial amounts of "history"; that is, they can easily retain enough from a cultural past (or pasts) to make them readily (and appealingly) recognizable to persons raised in cognate cultural traditions associated, in contrast, with more narrowly defined ethnic identities. Such creolized forms can speak to a broad range of people who can sense a kind of kinship (even if a somewhat distant one) with their own specific cultural traditions.

Because of this—and this is part of their creoleness—such creolized traditions, as long as they retain enough of this history and at the same time do not become too thoroughly indigenized and narrowly identified with a specific ethnic group, can continue to be used to bridge ethnic differences and can serve as an effective basis for the creation and expression of new social formations and identities in situations of rapid change, upheaval, and accelerated intercultural contact. In this particular case, as we attempt to account for the repeated selection of the gumbe in African polyethnic contexts over time, we find ourselves falling back on the notion of a shared, generalized West African cultural substratum that was theorized by Melville Herskovits and was further developed by Sidney Mintz and Richard Price (1976)—an idea that has at times been criticized as too vague, or too difficult to pin down empirically (Palmié 2007b, 182–187), but which remains powerfully persuasive when applied to cases such as the present one.

The spread of the gumbe in Africa clearly has to do with the continuing operation of underlying cultural principles and predispositions—shared values, aesthetics, and the like. Indeed, arguments for the existence of a shared African cultural substratum may perhaps be made more clearly and persuasively with regard to music and dance than any other cultural sphere. It is no doubt partly for this reason that musicians and dancers have played such a prominent role in the on-the-ground negotiation of new forms of belonging and identity (as well as the mass-mediated versions of such negotiations) throughout sub-Saharan Africa. The ethnomusicologist David Coplan, who has looked closely at such processes not just in South Africa, but in Ghana (Coplan 1978) and other parts of the continent, makes a strong case for the privileged position of urban musicians as cultural brokers who are able to help dislocated people recreate order in rapidly shifting, anomic social environments throughout Africa:

> Urban performers have been centrally involved in the processes of cultural communication and collective reinterpretation, transforming expressive materials to reflect social forms and objectify new meanings. Musicians function as cultural brokers partly because they are able to provide social commentary in musical terms as well as in verbal expression associated with performance. In urban South Africa, musicians and musical occasions have been important in re-establishing bases of social communication and order in situations of extreme disorganization, segregation, oppression and change. (Coplan 1982, 120)

If the specific reference to South Africa were removed, this passage might just as well serve as a description of the creative, community-building activities of gumbe musicians and dancers from one emergent polyethnic zone to the next, beginning shortly after this Afro-creole Caribbean instrument first found its way to African shores at the beginning of the nineteenth century.

When Jean Rouch was undertaking his seminal study of labor migration in West Africa in the 1950s, the vogue for what has come to be known as "creolization" was still many years off. But, as I earlier suggested, many of the concomitants of the creolization concept are already there in the

11. Ghanaian guitar band Bokoor in Ofankor, Ghana, circa 1980. *At the far right* (with the player seated upon it) is the Ga gome drum, derived from the Sierra Leonean and Jamaica Maroon gumbe. *On the left*, a musician plays the handheld tamalen, a related frame drum that uses a variant of the same distinctive turning mechanism. Photo: John Collins/BAPMAF Archives, Accra.

description of his that I quoted above: the uprooting and sudden throwing together of people with diverse cultural pasts and their need, under these unusually fluid and challenging circumstances, to—in Rouch's words— "create customs of their own" and bring into being "a new type of community" by "creating a new way of life" (Rouch 1961, 303–304). Despite the current popularity of critiques dwelling on the essentializing sins of the past (and present), and the constant (and necessary) reminders that representations of "traditional" societies and cultures as static and clearly bounded were never anything more than Western anthropological fictions, it would be pointless to argue that the rapidly forming, unusually heterogeneous social environments observed by Rouch did not contrast in very significant ways with the more homogeneous and culturally stable (though not "static") communities from which the individuals who made up these settlements on the urban periphery (or their parents) had recently migrated. And this is partly what made them such hotbeds of cultural (and especially musical) creolization.

This particular story is far from over. For echoes of "Africa's creole drum," the gumbe, are still quite audible in some of the continent's most vibrant contemporary musical expressions.[33] These range from Ghanaian highlife, which is traceable in part to gumbe and ashiko music (Collins 1989) and was later influenced by (and itself influenced) a neo-traditional gumbe-related genre known as kpanlogo (Salm and Falola 2002, 178–179; Rentink 2004, 34–37), to the currently reigning electric pop style of Guinea-Bissau—known, not coincidentally, as *gumbe* (sometimes spelled *goumbe*)—which has recently been making incursions in world music markets (Duran 1992).[34] According to Manthia Diawara (1998, 115), "the current wave of Mande jazz and blues performances by such artists as Oumou Sangaré, Morfinla Kante, Zani Diabaté, Ali Farka Touré, and Toumani Diabaté is indebted to the Goumbé songs."[35] Other African bands that have recently become popular among world music consumers in the West, such as Orchestra Baobab of Senegal, cite gumbe drumming and dance as among their formative influences. Almost predictably, one of the latest confections to arise and have some international impact is known (and marketed) as *reggae goumbé*.[36] In this new urban sound from Côte d'Ivoire, which marries the rhythms of the West African gumbe drum with the reggae "beat"—born in the 1960s on the other side of the ocean in the gumbe's original homeland of Jamaica—the remarkable trajectory of this Afro-creole drum has symbolically come full circle.

Among other things, these still-resounding echoes of transatlantic movements that can be traced back more than two centuries ought to remind us that the African continent, like the Caribbean cradle of creolization to which it made vast contributions, has long been a privileged site for the interlinked kinds of cultural confrontation, radical recombination, and identity creation that garner so much attention in the academy these days. In this sense, at least, Africa has long been—like several other supposedly far-removed "outposts" in the Atlantic world of which it has long been a part—in the vanguard, rather than the wake, of what we know today as "modernity."[37]

Notes

1. For detailed accounts of the Second Maroon War and the treachery of the British governor that led to the deportation of an entire community of Maroons from Jamaica in 1796, told primarily from a Maroon perspective, see Bilby (1984, 2005, 378–382).

2. As Michael Gomez points out, "Africa itself would be profoundly impacted by these returnees [from the Americas], especially in Liberia, Sierra Leone, and

Nigeria, so that while an understanding of the Americas is unattainable without an appreciation of the African background, Africa itself cannot be understood without recourse not only to the transatlantic slave trade, but also to the consequences of the reversal of that trade, consequences that continue to reverberate" (2006, 11). Recent studies focusing on particular manifestations of this diasporic "return" include Blyden (2000) and Campbell (2006). The implications of such "return" migration for anthropological theory, and the need to conceive of it as part of a larger Afro-Atlantic "dialogue" rather than a one-way reverse movement, are discussed notably in the work of J. Lorand Matory (2005, 2006). Scholarship on musical "return" or "feedback" from the Americas to Africa includes many works by John Collins and a recent study by Richard Shain (2002), showing how Cuban popular music has spurred many new creative developments in Senegal during the twentieth century.

    3. I am not the first to propose that the gumbe drum originally came to Africa along with the Jamaican Maroons who arrived in Sierra Leone in 1800. That distinction goes to Maud Cuney-Hare; so far as I know, she was the first to suggest this derivation in print, in an article in which she states, "the Gumbia is the name of the drum of the Maroons of Sierra Leone—it is also known in Jamaica" (Cuney-Hare 1918, 50). She reiterated this idea of a Jamaican Maroon origin particularly clearly in a list of African instruments she published in 1936, in which she again mentions a drum called "gumbia." She defines this as "the drum of the Maroons of Sierra Leone," adding that "it is also known in Jamaica from which Maroons were taken to Nova Scotia and thence to Sierra Leone" (Cuney-Hare 1936, 393). My own "discovery" of this path of transmission dates back to 1977, when, immediately after spending a summer in Sierra Leone (where I recorded a group of Krio gumbe musicians in Freetown), I headed to Jamaica to begin ethnographic fieldwork with Jamaican Maroons. Shortly after arriving in Jamaica for this fieldwork, I encountered the Maroon gumbe drum of Accompong (which I had earlier read about in writings by Katherine Dunham [1946] and others). Not long after this—with help from John Rudel, a drummer then studying for a degree at Wesleyan University, and Joe Galeota, another drummer at Wesleyan who had previously studied in Ghana, where he had built a Ga-style gome drum of his own—I began to gather additional information on the gumbe drum, with a view to establishing the details of its passage from Jamaica to Africa. Around 1979 I gave a number of classes at Wesleyan University in which I sketched out and discussed this story of likely "transatlantic return." In fact, as I later discovered, I was but one among a number of researchers—including Judith Bettelheim, John Collins, Barbara Hampton, and Flemming Harrev—who had independently begun to investigate this question around the same time and had come to more or less the same conclusions. Since learning of their shared interests in the 1980s and early 1990s, I have exchanged considerable information about variants of the gumbe drum with each of these scholars. John Collins and Flemming Harrev, in particular, deserve to be singled out for special mention. Collins has carried out the most extensive research on new genres of African popular music to date, including gumbe-based styles, and has been untiring

in his attempts to increase public awareness of the story of the gumbe's return from the Caribbean to Africa (see Lusk 1999); his contribution, which also includes a good deal of scholarship on other examples of "musical feedback" from the Americas to Africa, has been tremendous (see Collins 1985a, 1985b, 1987, 1989, 1994, 311–331, 2004, 2007). Harrev has undertaken the most extensive survey so far of the gumbe in Africa, unearthing many sources that have helped create a clearer picture of the instrument's spread (and its role in the emergence of new forms of popular music) across much of the continent. With considerable justification, Harrev has argued that the story of the gumbe requires us to push the history of urban popular music in Africa much farther back in time than is usually done—all the way back, in fact, to the beginning of the nineteenth century. His three important papers on the topic, unfortunately, remain unpublished (see Harrev [1987] 1998, [1993] 1997, 2001). I would like to thank all of the above-named colleagues for their help and their generosity in sharing information. I am grateful as well to the late Jean Rouch, Ian Hancock, Richard Graham, Robert Nicholls, John Chernoff, Isabela de Aranzadi, and Ivor Miller for providing helpful materials and exchanging ideas with me about the origins of the gumbe.

4. In choosing this phrase as the title for the present essay, I intentionally pay homage to the book *Creole Drum* (Voorhoeve and Lichtveld 1975), a path-breaking study of literature and verbal arts in Sranan Tongo, the creole lingua franca of Suriname. Much can be gleaned from that book about processes of creolization—linguistic, musical, and cultural, more broadly—but the book's connection with some of the points I intend to make here is perhaps best illustrated by the authors' description of "creole drum" (krioro dron in Sranan Tongo) as the part in a particular Afro-Surinamese dance and music cycle "in which everyone [without distinction] gets the opportunity to venture his [or her] criticism in songs of his [or her] own making" (Voorhoeve and Lichtveld 1975, 19). Of course, the title I have chosen is also appropriate in the more obvious sense that the emergent "neo-African" ethnic group in Freetown, Sierra Leone, that originally adopted the gumbe drum as its own eventually became known (and still is today)—for reasons very germane to this study—as Creoles (spelled Krio in more recent times). Finally, the title also suggests the drum's ongoing association with "creolization" processes as it became detached from this specific Sierra Leonean Creole (Krio) ethnic group and spread across West and Central Africa.

5. The first clear reference to a square or rectangular gumbe drum appears to be in Long (1774, 425), where it is reported in conjunction with "John Canoe" (Jankunu) festivities held by slaves in Jamaica. Square frame drums do occasionally appear in historical accounts from other parts of the Caribbean as well as nineteenth-century North Carolina in conjunction with the related "John Kuner" festival (where the name "gumba box" is noted [Warren 1885, 201]). There is also a well-known written account (as well as drawing) from nineteenth-century New Orleans of "a square drum, looking like a stool" that appears to have been yet another variant of the gumbe, although no name is given for the drum (Latrobe [1818–1920] 1951, 49–51). A square frame

drum known as *gumbé* has also been documented in eastern Cuba, probably brought there by Jamaican migrant laborers in the late nineteenth or early twentieth century (Ortiz 1952, 417); this drum might have contributed to the development of the various box-like percussion instruments in Cuba known as cajón, used in early rumba and a number of other Cuban genres. (The oldest report of a square frame drum that I know of from a Caribbean location other than Jamaica comes [indirectly, via the Virgin Islands] from Antigua and was published in 1777, although the name of the drum is not mentioned; in this account of a slave funeral, it is stated that "the drums consisted of small square boxes over which skins had been stretched" [Oldendorp (1777) 1987, 264]. My thanks to Robert Nicholls for this reference.) For several other eighteenth- and nineteenth-century accounts of drums called gumbe (spelled a number of ways) in Jamaica and other parts of the Caribbean, see Abrahams and Szwed (1983). In any case, judging from the number and frequency of reports from Jamaica, and the continuing existence of the instrument there in several different areas even today (see Bilby 1999, 2007), Jamaica appears to be the particular Caribbean location in which a square frame drum known as gumbe first emerged and had the most significant impact and the widest local distribution. Richard Graham (personal communication, March 1997), who has carried out extensive organological research on a number of Caribbean instruments, suggests quite plausibly that the gumbe might have developed as an Afro-creole innovation (whether in Jamaica or another Caribbean location) by slaves or free blacks skilled in carpentry, perhaps using old chairs or tables as frames or as partial models for frames. (The presence of functionless "legs" on the Jamaican gumbe, as well as the Sierra Leone gumbe and some of those in other parts of Africa derived from it, lends support to this idea.)

6. Variants of the square or rectangular frame drum known as gumbe continue to be found in Jamaica today not only in Accompong, but in the Windward Maroon communities of Charles Town and Scot's Hall on the other side of the island as well as in a number of non-Maroon communities; in the latter, it is still associated with Jankunu (Jonkonnu) masquerading and dancing, as well as spirit possession and healing (see Bilby 1992, 1999, 2007). Its occurrence in these widely separated present-day contexts suggests that this drum had a broad distribution in Jamaica during the slavery period and that it might actually have developed over time into a kind of pan-African (Afro-creole) drum used by slaves (as well as Maroons), regardless of ethnic background, across the island.

7. Lacking the evidence regarding migration from Jamaica to Sierra Leone that I provide in the present study, both André Schaeffner and Jean Rouch concluded that the gumbe drum originated in Africa, though neither was able to specify exactly where. Schaeffner guessed that "its existence in Africa is ancient or relatively ancient" (1964, 231, my translation)—based on the fact that there were reports of its use among Africans in the Americas going back to the eighteenth century, and also because drums of this exact design were not documented anywhere in the world except in Africa and parts of the Americas with African populations. Rouch, in contrast,

believed that the gumbe was "no doubt of Mandingo origin" (Rouch and Fulchignoni 2003, 167); but he never presented any evidence to support this assertion. (He may have been relying on Ortiz, who speculated, on the basis of scant evidence, that the Jamaican gumbe might have been "of Mandinga origin" [1952, 417].)

8. The thesis of a Jamaican Maroon origin for the African gumbe, first developed by Bettelheim, Collins, Hampton, Harrev, and myself (though earlier suggested by Cuney-Hare), has yet to gain wide acceptance, though it has been acknowledged in a handful of scholarly publications. (In his comparative discussion of frame drums, N. Scott Robinson, while describing the gome [or gombe] drum of Ghana, notes that "similar drums are played by the Maroon people of Jamaica" [2003, 364] but leaves it at that.) Among those who have explicitly come around to the idea of Jamaican origins is John Storm Roberts, who, citing myself and John Collins, states that "there is evidence the goombay or gumbe drum—a distinctive Jamaican neo-African instrument—had been brought to the West African coast by the 1820s" (1998, 259). He also writes that the gumbe was "developed in Jamaica on African principles and re-exported to Africa in the early nineteenth century" (Roberts 1998, 35). Similarly, Impey, citing John Collins (1989), states that "the first popular music of West Africa is believed to have developed in Freetown, Sierra Leone. Its style became known as gome or gombay, and it is believed to have derived from the gumbay, a frame drum brought to Freetown by freed Jamaican slaves [sic] in the early 1900s [sic]" (Impey 1998, 419). Likewise, Horton, clearly relying on the work of Collins, writes that "the name gumbe must have been brought from Jamaica to Sierra Leone by various groups who returned to Africa around the late eighteenth and early nineteenth centuries . . . [including] a number of Maroons from Jamaica [who] arrived in 1800" (1999, 230). Also apparently on the basis of Collins's work, Salm and Falola state of the closely related Ghanaian gome drum that "it is believed that it was brought from Jamaica via Fernando Po" (2002, 173).

9. For a detailed discussion of African-derived oath-taking practices, both historical and contemporary, among Maroons in both Jamaica and the Guianas, see Bilby (1997).

10. For further information on the stay of the Jamaican Maroons in Nova Scotia, see Winks (1971, 78–95), Campbell (1990), Lockett (1999), Hinds (2001), and Grant (2002).

11. "Acompang" in this passage is probably a distortion of a West African Akan word for the Supreme Being, such as Asante-Twi "Onyankopong" (in the Kromanti ritual language of the Windward Maroons of Jamaica, a cognate term, "Yankipong," still carries this sense [Bilby 2005, 483]). Much confusion has been caused by the similarity of "Accompong" (the name of the surviving Leeward Maroon community in western Jamaica) and "Onyankopong," and the assertion that the former is derived from the latter is repeated and uncritically accepted in a wide variety of sources. It is more likely, however, that "Accompong" (since the town was named after a prominent Maroon under-officer said to have been the brother of Cudjoe, the eighteenth-century leader of the Leeward Maroons) is derived from "Akyeampong," a personal name common among speakers of a number of Akan languages.

12. For discussions of Accompong Maroon musical traditions, see Roberts (1926), Dunham (1946), Bilby (1981b, 1992) and DjeDje (1998). All four authors provide background on the important role played by the gumbe drum in Maroon ceremonial contexts. DjeDje (1998, 115) provides a transcription of one Accompong Kromanti song. Bilby (1992) includes an audio example of a version of the same song (performed a cappella). For more on the Kromanti tradition of the Jamaican Maroons and its relationship to cultural traditions of the Akan-speaking peoples of present-day Ghana and Côte d'Ivoire, see Bilby (1981a, 2005).

13. The famous musicologist and organologist André Schaeffner was particularly intrigued by the gumbe, partly because of its unusual, highly distinctive design and partly because it was found so widely in Africa (sometimes appearing under other names). This led him to undertake the first comparative study of square frame drums. Pointing out that no instrument of this type was attested anywhere in Brazil or Europe, and that drums with a square shape were rare outside of Africa, he went on to assert that "the tuning system is absolutely unusual and derived from no other" (Schaeffner 1964, 239–240). (Ortiz [1952, 415–419] encountered a drum of more or less the same design in Santiago de Cuba but concluded that it was derived from the Jamaican gumbe drum; in all likelihood, this drum reached eastern Cuba via the migration of Jamaican laborers there during the late nineteenth and early twentieth centuries.) Because of its rareness, Schaeffner concludes that this peculiar instrument is in all likelihood "an African invention" (1964, 239–240, my translation). Apparently, he was unaware of the mass migration of Jamaican Maroons to Sierra Leone in 1800 or of the important role played by a square frame drum called gumbe (incorporating the exact same rare tuning mechanism) among contemporary Jamaican Maroons.

14. Wyse (1989, 2) puts the number of Liberated Africans brought to Sierra Leone between 1808 and 1864 at eighty-four thousand.

15. The work to which Stewart and Amman are referring was published in a book called *Polyglatta Africana* (Köelle 1854). Using present-day linguistic classifications, the number of languages documented by Köelle would actually be about 120.

16. Another passage by a roughly contemporaneous writer points to the same conclusion: "A young friend of mine, about 1825, was in a vessel which touched at Sierra Leone; and on my asking what had become of the Maroons, told me that several were then alive, and that some of advanced age still delighted to speak of Trelawney, and the mountains [in Jamaica] they had left with so much regret" (Vernon 1848, 49).

17. Less than ten years later, another writer mentions a type of music (and presumably dance) of the Maroons in Sierra Leone known as "Fullulah" (Clarke 1843, 57–58). Although I have carried out extensive ethnomusicological and ethnographic research among Jamaican Maroons (see Bilby 1981a, 1981b, 1992, 2005), I know of no music or dance terms used in any of the present-day Maroon communities that bear a resemblance to either "Tallala," "Talla," or "Fullulah."

18. Apparently relying on the same 1868 source, Wyse writes of "the talla dance of the Maroons—which became the goombay of their Krio descendants" (1989, 1).

19. For a detailed discussion of "Saro" people (Sierra Leonean Creole immigrants) in Nigeria during the late nineteenth and early twentieth centuries, see Dixon-Fyle (2006).

20. The island of Fernando Po (now known as Bioko), located in the Gulf of Guinea off the coast of Cameroon and Old Calabar, seems to have played a particularly important role in the spread of the gumbe, partly because of its close connections with Sierra Leone. As Lynn states, "Fernando Po 'Creole' society was very similar to that of Sierra Leone—it had a similar history and was in some ways an outgrowth of Sierra Leone" (1984, 258). Although in the early years "Sierra Leonians formed the core of the town [of Clarence, the main British settlement] and gave it its early Creole character," it soon became a "true melting-pot" (Lynn 1984, 258). According to Lynn, "a missionary survey of the 873 inhabitants of Clarence in 1841 noted thirty-six different ethnic groups in the town, with a spread across Africa from Senegal to the Congo" (1984, 260–262). When introduced (or re-introduced) to this environment by Freetown Creoles at various points, the gumbe must have once again found fertile ground. As we will see below, we know of at least a few documented cases of the diffusion of the gumbe drum directly from Fernando Po to mainland Africa, including to both the Gold Coast (Ghana) and the Belgian Congo. A version of the gumbe drum (the same basic design, with four legs), known as *cumbé*, is still played in the present-day Republic of Equatorial Guinea (Aranzadi 2009, 131–146, 175, 202–203). (Bioko [Fernando Po] now forms part of Equatorial Guinea; the nation's capital, Malabo, is actually located on Bioko.)

21. Most of these cognate traditions appear to belong to one or another of three somewhat distinct musical streams, known (sometimes interchangeably) as gumbe, *assiko*, and *maringa* (Harrev 2001). Over time instrument designs have undergone certain changes, as have the names applied to them. One of the most common transformations is the loss of the four "legs" or "feet" characteristic of Jamaican and Sierra Leonean gumbe drums (though these are still found, for instance, in Ghanaian gome, as well as the *cumbé* tradition of Equatorial Guinea [Aranzadi 2009, 134–135, 202–203]). Other than the disappearance of these more or less functionless appendages, and considerable variation in size, the design of the drums in question remains more or less constant (all are square or rectangular frame drums with basically the same unusual tuning mechanism). All of the West African drums that have retained the four legs appear to have kept the name gumbe (or names that are very close cognates) as well. Many of those that no longer have legs are now known by different names, such as *tamalen* (from English tambourine) in Ghana, *tambalí* in Equatorial Guinea (also from tambourine) (Aranzadi 2009, 204–205), and *samba* in Nigeria. (Other legless versions, however, are still known as gumbe; see Schaeffner [1964, 240–241] for several drawings of one such legless "gumbe" drum from Benin [then known as Dahomey]; interestingly, some of Schaeffner's informants in northern Dahomey told him the name of this drum, gumbe, was of Fon origin [242].) These changes in both the design and the names used for these drums render the historical

connections between these related instruments less apparent, and for this reason most scholars have remained unaware of these connections. (Robinson [2003, 364], for instance, focusing on size and playing techniques and ignoring the almost identical tuning mechanisms that characterize them, discusses the gome [or gombe] and tamalin [or tamalen] of Ghana and the samba of Nigeria alongside a number of other, unrelated frame drums, yet fails to note any connection between these three clearly cognate drums.) But in many cases, the connections remain traceable. Take, for instance, the legless, rectangular frame drum known in Lagos and other parts of Nigeria as samba. Drums of this kind and the styles associated with them played an important role in the development of *asiko* music as well as juju music and other popular Nigerian genres (Alaja-Browne 1989, 233; Waterman 1990, 39–40, 46, 49). For a detailed drawing of a Yoruba samba drum clearly showing that the tuning mechanism of this legless, square frame drum is—or originally was—exactly the same as that of the Jamaican gumbe, see Thieme (1969, 274); for a photo of an Edo (Bini) samba drum from Nigeria with the same features, see Dagan (1993, 116); see also Schaeffner (1964, 242) on the presence of square frame drums of the exact same design in Lagos. Several sources suggest that Nigerian asiko music and the samba drums on which it was played were originally associated with "Saro" people (a Nigerian name for people of Sierra Leonean origin residing in Nigeria) (Waterman 1990, 39–40). Thomas, for instance, writes of asiko (played on rectangular samba drums) that "this music was common with the Christians and the Saros" (1992, 73). Another source suggests strongly that drums of this kind (or earlier versions of them) were once known as gumbe in Yoruba-speaking parts of Nigeria, and that these were recognized as being of Sierra Leonean origin: discussing Yorubas who converted to Christianity and became preachers in the early twentieth century, Toyin Falola mentions that "a powerful sermon was written [in the Yoruba language] in 1909 by A. W. Howells to criticize the goombay dancing style, alleged to have been imported from Sierra Leone" (Falola 1999, 18; see also Howells 1909). For additional photographs, drawings, and discussions of gumbe drums (or related frame drums) from various parts of Africa, including Sierra Leone, Ghana, Côte d'Ivoire, Niger, Benin, Gabon, and Congo, see Dagan (1993, 96, 116, 127) and Meyer (1997, 224–231).

22. An interesting description of one such heavily indigenized urban gumbe tradition is provided by Bohumil Holas (1953). The particular gumbe (*goumbé*) group studied by Holas in Abidjan, Côte d'Ivoire, founded in 1936, was by the 1950s ethnically homogeneous, made up entirely of young Dyula (Dioula) people, all of whom were Muslims. (Its music and dance, however, continued to be based on an ensemble of gumbe drums—square frame drums of non-Dyula origin—sometimes supplemented with an imported "jazz" drum kit [Holas 1953, 129].) Even in this ethnically homogeneous case, Holas stresses "the theoretical absence of ethnoreligious criteria" of membership, the weakening of traditional gender divisions, and the overall "theoretically open character" of this particular gumbe group (120–122).

23. In a later article, in which she updates her work on the gumbe drum and adds a number of new references, Bettelheim maintains her position on the Caribbean origins of the drum, pointing out once again its association in many parts of Africa with polyethnic contexts and "non-indigenous" forms of music (1999, 10).

24. Rentink writes of Gome that "nowadays it finds its place in the traditional music of the Ga and is usually danced by elder people or by cultural groups" (2004, 35). An interesting example of how Gome had already been indigenized and given new local meanings by the 1970s is provided by Barbara Hampton, whose Ga teachers were able to offer an inventive folk etymology, telling her that "Gome is derived from the Ga word for 'caterpillar,'" and that "the musical system is so-called because the associated dance movements, in the perception of the musicians and patrons, depict those of the caterpillar" (Hampton 1983, 227 n12).

25. For an example of a Ga Gome song ("Mr. Jacobson") in pidgin English, recorded in the early 1960s, see Annan (1964). Working in the 1970s, Hampton found that "Gome texts are bilingual, using both pidgin English and Ga" (1983, 222).

26. See also Hampton (1977). Based on interviews with elderly Ga musicians, the ethnomusicologist John Collins believes that at least some variants of Gome were introduced by Ga carpenters and blacksmiths returning from the Cameroon and Belgian Congo areas much earlier than this, around 1900 (Collins 1985, 103, 2004, 9; Rentink 2004, 34). These Ga laborers, Collins notes, had been "working alongside Sierra Leone artisans, as these two groups of skilled West African workers were employed between 1885 to 1908 in building the docks and infrastructure of the then Congo Free State" (2004, 9). Adding another piece to the puzzle, Coplan notes that "carpenters from the Gold Coast returned from the Cameroons with a type of syncretic singing in pidgin English called gombe" (1978, 102).

27. Given this boundary-bridging aspect of gome, it is not surprising that this instrument (and certain musical characteristics associated with it) became an important component of one of the most popular Ghanaian bands of the mid-1970s, Wulomei, whose music, though played by musicians who were mostly Ga, represented a self-conscious blend of elements from diverse Ghanaian ethnic genres—a "multi-ethnic symbolic complex" intended to appeal to young people from Ga, Akan, Ewe, and other ethnic backgrounds while at the same time remaining "indigenous" in a more general way (Coplan 1978, 111–112). According to Collins, the music of Wulomei "crossed all boundaries in Ghana" (1985, 47).

28. La Goumbé des jeunes noceurs has pertinently been described as a "film about a goumbé society formed by migrants in Treichville as a focus for social activity amongst people living away from their homes and the traditional kinship structure" (Eaton 1979, 19).

29. Interestingly enough, in Senegal, the local gumbe tradition (as well as the related style known as assiko or ashiko, "played on a wooden square instrument covered with goat skin") is said by some to have originated on Gorée Island (Benga 2002, 78 n2). Since this island is known above all for the important role it played

in the French slave trade, the idea that the gumbe drum and its rhythms originated there suggests that it is seen as non-indigenous, and perhaps as something tied to the European slave trade and the circulation of creolized forms of culture with which that trade was closely associated. In another article, Thioub and Benga suggest that the Senegalese gumbe is sometimes seen as "Afro-Brazilian" and note that its ostensible origins on Gorée Island are "difficult to date" (1999, 216, 221).

30. This passage is part of a personal communication from John Collins to Jacqueline DjeDje of December 28, 1998, reproduced by Horton in his article. A similar representation of the "Pan African Goombay drum-dance" as the embodiment of a process of "homecoming" can be found in Collins (2007, 179–182).

31. Among the more sustained and serious attempts to grapple with cultural creolization (in the broadest sense) to date—though from rather different perspectives—are writings by Chaudenson and Mufwene (2001) (which is of particular interest in connection with the present study, since it includes an entire chapter specifically on musical creolization [198–224]) and Haring (2004b). See also Baron and Cara's introduction in the present volume.

32. See, for instance, Schmidt (1998) on the spread of "palm wine" guitar styles from Freetown to Fernando Po and beyond as part of the "Kru diaspora" along the West African coast.

33. Gumbe music has continuously exerted a powerful influence on the popular music of Sierra Leone, ranging from the early efforts of Ebenezer Calender in the 1950s (Bender 1989, 45, 52–54, 64, 1991, 112) to the *mailo* (or *milo*) jazz style (based partly on gumbe rhythms) that took over as one of the most popular musics of Freetown in the 1980s (Nunley 1987, 160–173; Ashcroft and Trillo 1999, 634–635). This is hardly surprising, given that neo-traditional groups and popular electric bands would often share the same performing spaces. According to Naomi Ware, "rhythm bands" known ("after the principal drum") as "goombay" or "gombay" were very much a part of this equation in Freetown during the 1960s. As she was able to observe in 1968 through 1970, "goombay groups and a similar type of rhythm music called 'milo jazz' frequently appear as alternate entertainment with popular bands at outdoor dances only" (Ware 1978, 304). Writing more recently, Tom Spencer-Walters states that "today, goombay music has captured the interest of the younger generations with a much broader appeal in the Western Area of Sierra Leone, if not beyond. It owes a great deal of this acclaim to a goombay musical genius, Dr. Ohloh" (Spencer Walters 2006, 249). Reuben Koroma, leader of the internationally known, reggae- oriented Sierra Leonean band the Refugee All Stars, told interviewer Banning Eyre in 2006, "Gumbe comes from the Kriol people, the returned slaves. . . . In fact, most of our music, this African music, is gumbe. We just transfer it onto the Western instrumentations. What we used to play on the drums, we just transfer it to the bass and the guitars. But it is purely gumbe" (Afropop Worldwide Web site, http://www.afropop.org/multi/interview/ ID/105/Reuben+Koroma-Refugee+Alls+Stars-2006 [accessed July 10, 2007]). See also Cummings (2006, 39).

34. Among the better known Guinea-Bissau gumbe/*goumbe* performers who have released recordings are Cobiana Djazz, Gumbezarte, Ramiro Naka (and his band, N'kassa Cobra), Tabanka Djaz, Justino Delgado, Eneida Marta, and Manecas Costa. In this setting, too, gumbe music, despite varying degrees of indigenization, appears to have retained many of its general "creole" characteristics. According to Guus de Klein, gumbe in Guinea-Bissau "combines a contemporary sound with the ten or more musical traditions that survive in the area. . . . The lyrics of gumbe are in Kriolu, a creole synthesis of African languages and the colonial Portuguese . . . [and] Kriolu is an integral part of gumbe music" (1999, 499).

35. In addition to urban popular music, gumbe has also influenced the growth of other "neo-traditional" musics in various parts of Africa that fulfill similar functions. One example is Ghanaian *kpanlogo* (Rentink 2004), mentioned above. Another is *simpa*, played in the polyethnic (though primarily Dagomba) town of Tamale in northern Ghana. Much like gumbe associations of the 1950s, simpa groups, according to Chernoff, "are like clubs for the young people of various neighborhoods," and they "practice for their competitions, singing songs with flute or harmonica and drum accompaniment to Highlife, Rumba, Cha-cha, Kalakala, Meringue, Soul, and Agbadza rhythms," backed by a variety of "different instruments, from dondons to sets of square-frame drums to sets of conga and jazz drums" (1979, 129). Elsewhere, Chernoff notes that "a style of music and dancing called Gumbe" once existed in northern Ghana, but that "Gumbe has evolved into the Simpa music of today;" he adds that "Gumbe groups originally used square-frame drums with bells, rattles and occasionally a squeeze drum" (Chernoff 1985a, 163). An audio example from northern Ghana of gumbe-style drumming played by Dagbamba drummers can be found in Chernoff (1985b). Some gumbe-related neo-traditional styles have even made their way to cities in the United States, such as New York, where a gome drummer, Kimati Dinizulu, and his group, the Kotoko Society, regularly performed a rather creole-sounding mix of West African genres during the 1980s. Using the gome, "a square drum laid on its side," Dinizulu and his group would launch into "a variety of different traditional rhythms including Kpanlogo and Asafa from Ghana and Temine from Sierra Leone" (Strmel and Wachtel 1988, 25). According to two observers, "the admixture of these elements becomes an Esperanto for all who are conversant in the language of the drum" (Strmel and Wachtel 1988, 25). For more on the contributions of gumbe drumming and dancing to the development of neo-traditional music and dance genres in Ghana (including *gome, simpa, gahu,* and *konkoma*), see Collins (2007).

36. Although the best-known exponents of *reggae goumbé*, Les Frères de la Rue, are now based in Paris, they hail from Abidjan, Côte d'Ivoire, and their style, which represents a new fusion of Jamaican reggae with local Ivorian "traditional" genres, is inspired partly by the rhythms of the same square frame drum documented by Rouch in Abidjan (and elsewhere in West Africa) in the 1950s. In any case, the members of Les Frères de la Rue are not the first reggae artists from Côte d'Ivoire to have been influenced by gumbe. International Ivorian reggae star Alpha Blondy had a gumbe

singer in his family while growing up in Abidjan (Konaté 1987, 107, 126 n4). In one interview, when asked about his earliest memory of music, Blondy mentioned "gumbe, which is a kind of popular dance, . . . a very popular African folklore kind of style"; and he added—perhaps the most interesting observation in this interview, from the perspective of the present study—"and strange, I found gumbe in Jamaica!" (Davis 1988, 34).

37. In invoking "modernity" in this context and in this way, I clearly owe a debt to Sidney Mintz's writings (e.g., Mintz 1966) that point to the Caribbean as the site of one of the earliest—if not the first—manifestations of certain key social and economic features generally associated today with the onset of modernity.

Techniques of Creolization

—LEE HARING

Creolization, presented in detail by authors in this volume, is gaining currency around the world under various names. Its realities, in the socially situated interaction of human beings, deserve attention. As an example of flattening the concept through uncomprehending use, Ulf Hannerz mistakenly simplifies creole cultures into "those which draw in some way on two or more historical sources, often originally widely different. They have some time to develop and integrate and to become elaborate and pervasive. There is that sense of a continuous spectrum of interacting forms, in which the various contributing sources of the culture are differentially visible" (1987, 552).

The Celtic and Saxon sources of English culture have developed and integrated nicely; readers of the *Times* (London) still find the differential sources of their culture visible enough to comment on; but the merging of different sources in England is not creolization. Something has dropped out of the concept. Theorists like Hannerz, James C. Scott, or the influential Benedict Anderson "seem to base their arguments on local cultural situations," says Roger D. Abrahams (personal communication), but they fail to demand that their readers look closely at the forces determining those situations: the historical burdens of creole societies, the socioeconomic or politico-cultural conditions that are the matrix of creole artistic communications, or even the history of words like *creole, hybrid,* or *contamination* (Abrahams, this volume). Something called creolization has even been proclaimed as a basis for a quite improbable political solidarity between the Southwest Indian Ocean and the Caribbean. The compositional processes and techniques of creole narrators, under examination, restore the notion of intertextuality to an existing sociocultural setting. There, it turns out, oft-used literary devices and techniques take on special force.

Creolization emerged from the discovery that certain new languages develop more rapidly than they "should," according to received linguistic theory. The notion posed broad implications for language change and also for the societies using creole languages. In particular, the sudden unpredictable pidginization and creolization of languages (the title of a groundbreaking book) is observed to occur in situations of forced inequality. Linguists called for criteria:

> If, then, we want to assume creolization processes as the source of language change in the past, a number of conditions need to be met: (a) there must be clear evidence of a break in continuity in language development; (b) there must be linguistic features characteristic of *creolization* (successive phases of simplification [by reduction and fossilization of the preserved material] and restructuration); (c) there must be adequate evidence of the socioeconomic or politico-cultural conditions by which the deculturation/acculturation processes of outsiders acquiring the language can be documented. (Polomé 1982, 276–277)

A break in continuity is a euphemistic way of describing the history of Haitians, Fijians, and other peoples speaking creole languages. But the point about socioeconomic or politico-cultural conditions must not be ignored. As a linguistic or cultural process, change will occur wherever cultures meet in expressive interaction, but creolizing meetings occur in oppressive moments like the slave trade, which undergirded the world capitalist order of the modern period. In the Southwest Indian Ocean, slavery, settlement from abroad, and exploitation of the soil for foreign export have given the five island groups some common history. Where societies come into a colonized, multiracial existence for the benefit of a European minority, the normal reaction of the constituent groups is to renegotiate both language and culture. So were born the creole languages of Mauritius, Réunion, Seychelles, and the Comoros. Even in Madagascar, which displays a linguistic unity astonishing in an island 587,000 km², there are pidginized and creolized forms. Moreover, when Islam invaded Madagascar in the twelfth century, the Great Red Island underwent a kind of creolization that can be called cultural. All the islands have known this renegotiation; each has its own story.

Resettlement from East Africa to Madagascar obliged Africans to shift from subsistence agriculture into the plantation economy; it did not destroy their capacity for cultural remodeling. The Makoa of Madagascar's west coast, for example, descend from slaves of Mozambican origin, who were freed in 1877. They created coastal villages; they remembered millet cultivation and the use of the hoe in African soil; they kept their language. Tales collected a century later in the Makoa language (*emakhuwa*) "speak to us of traditions from beyond the sea: the tale of the pheasant brings onstage a fowl unknown in Madagascar. Doubtless too it speaks of the forgetting of the old country by new generations" (Gueunier 1990a, 5). But real-life multilingualism obliges Makoa people to practice "heteroglossia" (M. M. Bakhtin's term for the variety of voices), speaking Malagasy and Kiswahili. In the Comoros, another example, islands lying between Africa and Madagascar, the ethnic mix of the Islamized African population of 476,678 resulted early on from the convergence of peoples—the Arabo-Persian Shirazi, the Swahili, and the Malagasy, among others. From the tenth century on, these peoples renegotiated their older models into an Islamic environment. Forever neglected as a colony, now a resentful, conflict-ridden client state of France, continually aspiring to the dependency already achieved by its rebel island of Mayotte, the poverty-stricken Comoros continually undergo coups d'état. In the Seychelles, north-northeast of Madagascar, ethnic groups—African, French, Chinese, Indian—began mixing with each other in the twelfth century. Today, recognizing no internal ethnic divisions, many of the 72,000 Seychellois gain their livelihood from European tourism. The island of Mauritius (once Isle de France, 900 km east of Madagascar) was long uninhabited. Destined for multiculturalism, Isle de France imported slaves from Portuguese East Africa and Madagascar to work its French-owned sugar estates. After emancipation, Indian indentured laborers added the decisive ingredient to the ethnic mix, which today numbers over a million in an island 2,040 km². In the same period, Frenchmen, East Africans, Malagasy, and Indians produced a similar mix in Ile Bourbon, the other Mascarene island, renamed Réunion during the French Revolution. An overseas department of France since 1946, Réunion saw its moves toward independence bought off by goods and television from the metropole. The five islands represent different stages of becoming creole societies (a label none of them would claim for itself).

What effect has this history of slavery and exploitation had on artistic traditions? Against this background of cultural clash, the arts of the word have become as creolized as the varying languages of the islands. Obviously the "unlimited and unbounded generating process" of language continued under oppression; there could be no cessation of "this unceasing operation of the drives toward, in, and through language; toward, in, and through the exchange system and its protagonists—the subject and his institutions" (Kristeva 1980, 17). But the history forced a material realization of intertextuality, "the transposition of one or more *systems* of signs into another, accompanied by a new articulation of the enunciative and denotative position" (Kristeva 1984, 59–60). Not to mention the position of the speakers managing the signs. Consequently, as creole languages are unpredictable from their parent traditions, creole folktales are likely to be new products, pieces of *bricolage* using materials from everywhere. Some stories were remembered, all were remodeled, yet Madagascar, Mauritius, Réunion, Seychelles, and the Comoros share a common stock of traditional folktales. A few came from France; more came from East Africa by way of Madagascar. There are trickster tales like the deceptive tug-of-war, the tar baby and the rabbit, the deceptive agreement to sell or kill mothers, and the hare inside the elephant (Haring 2007, 83–90, 124–125, 102–106). One typical example of creole remodeling combines the East African swallowing monster with an Indonesian seven-headed snake. Most popular of all is the African tale in which a disobedient daughter refuses husbands in favor of an animal in disguise (Görög-Karady and Seydou 2001; Haring 2007, 147–167). The regional sharing of cultural products has not been a prominent feature of cultural policy in these newly independent nations.

Another effect of the history has been an empowerment of women, quite unexpected by liberal Westerners. In these creole societies, women are cultural mediators. "The sex or gender system is a primary dimension of the history of these islands. . . . By adding newer cultural patterns to older ones, Southwest Indian Ocean women have acted as agents of creolization, as gatekeepers for the new multiplicity of cultural identities on which survival has depended" (Haring 2004, 169–170). *Contra* the assumption of European critics, the tale repertoire of every island contains pieces definitely marked as speaking for women or belonging to a particular performer. Women have developed skills, recognized by their local audiences, at manipulating multiple linguistic codes, registers, and channels (Haring 2004, 177). The blindness to oral literature, which feminist critics share with their fellow comparatists, prevents them from recognizing women's power and artistry in creole societies.

Performing these creole tales, the female or male storytellers of the Southwest Indian Ocean employ techniques known to every novelist: shortening, lengthening, mixing in other languages, quoting, and parody, among others. Such universal techniques are not created by the high temperature of creole society, but the violence and oppression of creolization gives them a special energy.

Framing

One prominent technique of creolization is to frame one story in another. Long before writing, it was a favorite device of Indian and Arab story-tellers and is universally recognized in the *Arabian Nights*. In Mauritius, where Indian and Islamic traditions merge with African and European influences, Sydney Joseph, of Grand Bel Air, recorded in 1990 a forty-min-ute performance he calls "The Siren-Girl," in which he frames one story, "The Grateful Animals" (Type 554 in the standard catalog), inside another, "The Man on a Quest for His Lost Wife" (Type 400 [Uther 2004, 323–325, 231–233]). His hero, unlike nearly every other folktale hero, is poised for a long time between two women; at the end he goes back to the first one he met. "The Siren-Girl" is a rich assemblage of plots, characters, and inci-dents from other storytelling performances, which have been recorded in India, Africa, and Madagascar. Sydney Joseph's suspenseful framed story, unpredictable, if not disapproved by the mainstream of folktale scholar-ship, is the narrative counterpart to the new and unpredictable products that creole linguists discover (Haring 2007, 178–199). As to framing, "what is this device, so familiar in writing, so beloved of European readers of the *[Arabian] Nights*, but a formal stylization of people's habit of interrupting their oral discourses and going to another level? It is a human habit; it is probably a cultural universal, preferred in certain story traditions, losing visibility in others. . . . Conceived so diversely, visible in so many more settings of performance than Shahrazâd's demonstration that story can subdue aggression . . . , framing requires multiple modes of interpretation" (Haring 2007, 136). In a creole society, the political interpretation takes precedence: one's life has often been interrupted by outside forces.

On the plantations of a small island like Ile Bourbon (now Réunion) or Isle de France (now Mauritius), where peoples from Portuguese East Africa, Madagascar, and India faced those of Brittany and Normandy, what techniques other than framing did creolization develop for storytelling? Which themes were peculiar to the creole situation? The worldwide tale of "The Animal Languages," for example, is all about multilingualism: a man learns animal languages but is enjoined not to reveal the secret. The story was bound to be told in Seychelles (Haring 2007, 352–354). When the hero, locally named Ti Zan, rescues a snake, he gains power: knowl-edge of a new language. The motif is international; the meaning is strongly local in islands where your overseer or your new neighbors may well speak an unknown language. Thus a cultural emphasis renders an imported tale especially appropriate. Some adaptations were inevitable. They show what creolization consists of.

Referential Content

A story relies on the referential function of language; it holds up and arranges certain actors, objects, or incidents from the world of experience. When African tales are transported to Mayotte or Réunion, they are re-rooted in the new place by localization, which narrators rely on to "re-con-textualize" the story. Several narrators in Mayotte use local place names to locate the action (Gueunier 1990, 311). One places her story's character in an abandoned house "like in Mirereni" (Gueunier 1990, 288–289). Another points to a tree like one in her story and compares a magical light to a Petromax pressure lamp (Gueunier 1990, 322–333). Localization through the imaginary has covered the island of Réunion, which the French have insistently made their own since 1638, in Malagasy place names. There too, localization of song lyrics happens quite deliberately (La Selve 1984, 150–151). Such localization is a defensive device, a means of hiding what is strange under a cloak of familiarity.

Then there is the scene of performance, which always shifts when cultures come into contact. The forced migrations of Makoa and Makonde to Madagascar, the subsequent exportation of Malagasy to Ile Bourbon, and the importation of Indians to Mauritius obliged storytellers to perform in new times and places. In Madagascar and the Comoros today, economic forces continue to affect the storytelling event. The custom, shared with East Africa, of telling stories at evening to entertain adolescents and children is endangered by work schedules. In Mayotte, the rice harvest, a basic part of Comoran life for many centuries, is still the main occasion of storytelling. "On those days, to encourage the workers," writes Noël Gueunier, "an old grandmother tells them stories from her repertoire. Tales must succeed one another," and telling them must "last as long as the work of harvesting." In the Comoros, where oral history is as vital as the verses of the Koran, government schools threaten the Islamic habits of memorization, which have sustained folklore performance. In Mauritius, where agricultural land is being sacrificed to cyber-development, the scenes of performance must change. Formerly, creole artists like Nelzir Ventre in Mauritius, whom I recorded in 1990, were expected to perform after a death, when family and friends watched over the corpse for *wi zour* (eight days). "The women," his friend John Brasse told me in an interview, "were on the inside and the men outside. So if there were no stories, nobody sang outside. Sometimes they invited Nelzir inside to tell stories. They'd invite someone who could tell stories. Well, often it was Nelzir who was there."

Now, no narrator has taken Ton Nelzir's place in his village of Poudre d'Or; one is told that the *wi zour* ceremony isn't done any more. In fact, it is flourishing, but no observer is recording its performances. Among Réunionnais poor whites too, a wake was formerly the scene for storytelling; more recently card playing and mass culture have threatened performance (Carayol 1980, 10). In Seychelles, where literacy is constantly encouraged, what is known about folktales comes in the form of printed texts dictated for recording, and not much is known about scenes of performance.

Under the impact of forced coexistence, in the face of a change in audience or setting, a storyteller of the Southwest Indian Ocean can still rely on conventional rhetorical devices. Three such devices, not caused by forced immigration, are intensified by the coexistence of European, African, and Indian cultures. One is *reduction* of the length of a tale, which may well have been necessary for creoles of Réunion (then Ile Bourbon) or indentured laborers of Mauritius (then Isle de France). Nowadays, reducing a story may reflect no more than a sense of distance from it. "*Pa plis k-sa minm, koné pa plis,* There's no more of that, I don't know any more," says Marie-Rose d'Ambelle, a *petite blanche* (poor white) of Plaine des Cafres, Réunion, at the end of a curtailed version of Cinderella (in Haring 2007, 270–271). In Mayotte, one of Noël Gueunier's informants, after telling him about the songs that figure in the tale she will tell, launches right into the story without her usual opening formula. "The whole tale is quite elliptical," Gueunier remarks; "the tale is known to the audience and the teller does not take the trouble to give each episode in detail" (1990, 218 n4). Full performance is optional, not inevitable.

If an audience can be relied on to understand the references, the storyteller can combine reduction with a second device, allusion. Trickster tales, told in clusters, invariably allude to other trickster tales. Any performance of (for instance) "The Tarbaby and the Rabbit," which Joel Chandler Harris made into the best known of all African-derived tales for readers of English, depends on allusion: the depredations of trickster were narrated in other tales, and now the other animals seek revenge. More broadly, it is always useful, when there are eavesdroppers, for storytellers to define the knowers against the ignorant by alluding to what only certain listeners know.

Augmentation is no less important than reduction. Gérose Barivoitse, in Réunion, continually lengthened his performances with opinions, memories, and reflections, raising the question of what constitutes a digression and who would call it that. His compatriot Daniel Fontaine augmented his version of "The Three Stolen Princesses" differently, through characterizing his hero as loquacious. The character begins his long speeches shortly after birth; near the end of the tale, he manifests it by reproving his antagonists and recapitulating what has happened. "Guys," he says,

> you'll have your heads cut off, I declare, once I'm married. One week after my marriage, the sentence will be carried out. You ought not to have tricked me like that. When I saved these three girls, you ought to have said that one of the four of us, me, would marry one, and two of my friends would have married the others. I would have had two brothers-in-law, and one could have been my witness or minister or something. But now, no minister, nothing, you'll be condemned, condemned to death by me. Right, I'm going to get married. A week after my marriage, when I've had a nice rest, you'll pay me so. (Decros 1978, 178–213)

When, like Mr. Fontaine, you are economically deprived and politically powerless, a loquacious hero personifies the residual kind of power you, the performer, still retain. Throughout Southwest Indian Ocean history, the powerless have asserted and defined their identity through the arts of the word. Verbal eloquence in the islands has been enhanced from the beginning by pre-existing African and Malagasy cultural preferences. Anyway, reduction, allusion, and augmentation are worldwide rhetorical devices, catalogued by classical rhetoricians. But like the motif of multilingualism, or like some other techniques I turn to now, they take on special force in creolized situations.

Language-Mixing

Where people speaking different languages meet, their languages mix, even to the point where certain sounds seem to have no meaning any more. The *séga* artist Nelzir Ventre made this obvious in several narratives he recorded for me in 1990. Obscure words, for instance the name of his title character, "Dyendyengulu," he called *langaz*. The plots of narratives, he said, had to be explained to the audience first (rather like the dumb show in *Hamlet*). Ton (Uncle) Nelzir called that practice translation: "I had to have finished presenting [*tradwir*] the story—to present all the words before the people listening. Do you understand me? Drum players and musicians accompany me. There is no dancing at that point. *Tradwir* means to tell the whole story beforehand, while singing. No dancing, just drumming. Everybody sits down and listens" (Ventre interview).

I wonder how many other Southwest Indian Ocean storytellers have been as expert translators as Nelzir Ventre. Unknown foreign languages are heard repeatedly in the many tales Noël Gueunier has collected in Mayotte, where one village speaks *shimaore* and the next Malagasy. In one tale, because the ogre's wife does not understand Comoran, her position is much weakened, but his song has already revealed the menace of his identity to the multilingual audience (Gueunier 1990, 80). Incomprehension is no novelty.

Lexical Mixes

With their mixing and translating, storytellers also insert lexical items from one language into another. For Westerners, complaints about *franglais* and, for instance, the increasing prominence of Spanglish indicate that many Europeans and Americans have now begun to experience that creolization of languages which is ordinary discourse in a place like Mauritius. A joke in the Bhojpuri language, which is spoken by many thousand Indo-Mauritians, was collected in 1984 by an American anthropologist in Mauritius; it requires comprehension of two languages to be funny. The narrator and the central character are Bhojpuri speakers.

> Once an old lady was in the bus station waiting for a bus. The bus was gone already, the old lady didn't know. She asked a Creole man, "What time is it, son?" "Seven o'clock." So she says, "Has the bus gone?" The Creole says, "Maybe [*peut-être*]." But the old lady didn't understand. She went over to two or three men playing cards and said, "Has the bus gone?" They said, "Didn't that Creole you were with tell you?" She said, "He says '*petet, petet*,' I don't know what it means." They say, "Oh,

grandmother, *petet, petet*, you know what it is [fart]. He cursed at you."
The old lady went and hit the Creole man. (Haring 2007, 94)

Such ethnic parody from Indo-Mauritians—the dominant group in Mauritius numerically and politically—points to the self-consciousness that multiculturalism brings. Even more pointed is another joke collected at the same time, when the Mauritian government was encouraging emigration. A father bilingual in Kreol and Hindi has sent his son to study medicine in the United Kingdom. He returns wearing spectacles, and at the airport he greets his father in English, "Hello, Daddy!" The father answers in Creole, "I sent you to become a doctor, now you come back, you wear spectacles, you don't recognize your father, you are calling me your grandmother" [*dadi* in Hindi] (Haring 2007, 325–326). Not only are the words in the foreign language thought to be insults, but also the voice of the homeland declares that foreign influence corrupts family relations. Thus creolization in language is both performance and critique; what is metalinguistic becomes metanarrative. Here Mauritius is the model for the rest of the world (Haring 2004).

Mixing the Narrative Lexicon

Analogous to language-mixing, but more conscious and deliberate, is the mixing of narrative lexicon that occurs when storytellers insert or rearrange story elements. A set of rules governing the insertions or rearrangements in creole stories—if such rules could be formulated—would constitute a creole narrative grammar. A large-scale instance of insertion (or is it digression?) happens in the earliest recorded text of *Ibonia*. This Malagasy tale of a hero's quest for a wife is still current in performance (Noiret 2008). The early text, combining an 1830 manuscript with an oral dictation, is epic in manner, by virtue of several episodes of praise poetry depicting the hero's petty victories before his final triumph. Other versions, recorded later, are more linear (Haring 2007, 50–56). Other Malagasy instances of mixing the narrative lexicon were recorded from master Sakalava narrators, whose confident invention and rearranging of episodes show their skill in the power of words to represent relations of power (Dandouau 1922, 188–208; Lombard 1976). The anthropologist Philippe Beaujard says that storytelling performances in Madagascar today are ideological thrusts (1991, 421). Doubtless they always were.

Mixing Channels

Another effect of cultural convergence, rather in the spirit of T. W. Ador-no's search for the ways in which social struggle and class conflict imprint themselves on works of verbal art, is the technique of throwing together the various channels through which storytelling can happen: speech, song, and writing. Probably, however, channel-mixing, in Madagascar and the Comoros, is not a result of creolization, but a persistent substratum of African performance style. "In all Malagasy folktales and myths," writes Beaujard, "song . . . represents the 'normal' mode of communication in the beyond, whether that means Heaven or the world of the dead, or between the beyond and the world of the living" (1991, 493). Even when a Mahorais narrator, relying on her audience's knowledge, launches into her story without an opening formula and summarizes it instead of dramatizing, she will give the songs in full (Gueunier 1990, 218). Nelzir Ventre in Mauritius, like his African ancestors, regarded songs as the essence of his narrative. He called them *séga*, a word whose various meanings bespeak the variability effected by creolization. Sometimes it is a traditional dance song; formerly it was a piece of island dance music played on a European instrument, the piano; now it's a costumed touristic dance for European hotel guests. In Seychelles too, where few songs have been recorded except through the annual Festival Kreol, song has ever been a privileged channel for revealing truth in tales. For instance, trickster sings a song he has learned at a donkey's funeral. When one of the donkeys wants to know where he learned the song, he fastens the blame on tortoise, his dupe (Abel 1981, 22–26). Another Seychellois trickster teaches his dupe to confess trickster's own crime in song, at the king's ball (Carayol, Chaudenson, and Doomun 1978, 122–129). Elsewhere, channel-mixing looks like part of creolization. Music in Réunion shows the mixing of European and African styles, the adoption of African styles by the *malbars* (Indian indentured laborers), the influence of the diatonic accordion on chromatic tunes, and the growing influence in the 1930s of recordings by Georges Fourcade, the *barde créole* (La Selve 1984).

Parody

Awareness of different cultures leads storytellers in the Southwest Indian Ocean, as everywhere else, to make fun of them. Parody flourishes in

creole societies, as the example of the "Mighty Sparrow" shows. The dislocation of cultural clash puts an artist's attention on the form or shape of
a narrative; other forces do too. The Malagasy narratives collected under
colonial domination again and again are parodies of myth. One useful tool
for reflexivity is the frame in which friendship is made and then broken
(Dundes 1971; Haring 1972). At the beginning of such a tale, two characters obviously mismatched—say, cat and rat—make friends. Already the
pre-contact days are being mocked, through the fantastic remoteness of
mythic time. By the end, the friendship has been broken by a trickster's
violation of appropriate behavior, cat and rat are bitter enemies, and we are
in the real, modern world, where ethnic conflict rules. Dozens of examples
of this frame, which derived originally from Africa and is found throughout the African Diaspora, have been collected in Madagascar (Haring 1982,
295–346). The parodic frame that surrounds the numerous stories about
enmity between species of animals points to human enmities between,
for example, the Sakalava and Merina two centuries ago, or between the
Merina and the southern Antandroy. While parodying myth, the frame
also reverses the power relations known to a colonized audience. Long
ago, it says, interdependency had more force than it has today. Parody
remains one of the chief "games of the powerless" (Holbek 1977).

It yields a new and unpredictable artwork in one Seychelles tale. Its editors call it "Queen of the Sea"; it is a cognate of three Réunionnais tales. A
poor man, after fishing for a week without avail, finally catches the Queen
of the Sea, who says she will give him a goat. "You'll never have to come
to the sea again," she says. "You'll say, 'By the virtue of the goat the Queen
of the Sea gave me, I want to see everything I need!'" But his *komer* (god-
mother of the child whose godfather he is) invites him to her house and
exchanges goats while he's asleep. When he tries the formula at home,
the goat defecates in the children's bed. In a second, similar episode, the
komer intervenes and the children are stung by bees. In the third episode,
the queen offers him a club with the same formula. This time the club
strikes the *komer*, and her mother along with her, until she confesses and
gives back the magic gifts. Thenceforward he lives rich with his family. The
storyteller ended with a closing formula characteristic of the region: "The
other day, I met this guy and said to him, '*Konper*, do something for me.'
Zot! he socked me and right then I up and left" (Carayol and Chaudenson
1978, 132–141). This piece frames a plot known all round the world, "The
Table, the Ass, and the Stick" (Grimm no. 36), into a parody of the best
known of all legends from Madagascar, told as true. In the legend, a water-

spirit takes pity on a poor fisherman, marries him, and gives him gifts and children; he loses these only when he violates a taboo on mentioning their origin (Haring 2007, 17–18). Surely the folktale is parodying the more serious genre, which Malagasy know as *tantara*.

The parodic story exemplifies the new kind of narrative that arises from the interplay of Malagasy and European traditions under certain circumstances. It illustrates Julia Kristeva's intertextuality operating on the ground, so to speak, in the situated social interactions of tale performance. So often, the "folk," in this region as elsewhere, have invented something concrete, which critics discover and formulate more abstractly.

"Signifying"

The frame of making and breaking friendship was brought to the islands from Africa, as people were forced to become aware of other traditions. The chief stylistic effect of that awareness was a greater capacity for coding covert messages. In African American folklore this technique is called "signifying"; the covert message conveys social criticism, which is meant to be decoded by the target (Mitchell-Kernan 1973). Similar ambiguities are heard in the Southwest Indian Ocean, Madagascar, for example. Before World War I, Jean Paulhan showed signifying to have reached a peak of development in the proverbs and oral poetry (*hainteny*) of the highland Merina (Haring 1992, 98–151). A concept of "beautiful language," the same ambiguous style, has been extensively documented as a collective property of the Betsileo of the highlands, neighbors to the Merina. In a counting game called *kanisa*, children count from one to ten, using parodic number words (rather like Cockney rhyming slang [Ashley 1977]). *Kanisa*, like riddles, requires a child to know the answer. Thus the game teaches not counting but signifying (Michel-Andrianarahinjaka 1986, 227–228). Farther south in the Great Red Island, Philippe Beaujard finds the same kind of humorous, playful allusion in the Tanala adaptation of a well-known folktale motif, the recognition of a disguised princess by a bee that lights on her. Beaujard notices how frequently the motif turns up in Malagasy and other regional stories; he explains its popularity out of the double meaning of *voto*: stinger of a bee or wasp, but also penis (Beaujard 1991, 429). Interpretations of ambiguity are part of Tanala thinking. On the same principle, many Tanala tales point to and remind people of political conceptions and historical events. Then on the east coast, Father

Maurice Schrive confirms this deliberate ambiguity for the Betsimis-araka. The humor of folktale, he says, aids people to put aside hatreds, murders, and disorder. The boy who performs is learning "how to express himself in public, learning his language and the forge at the same time" (Schrive 1989, 21). The east coast is the region most closely connected to the Comoros and other islands, geographically and culturally; it shares cultural habits with them (Bavoux 1994).

When British missionaries had been living in Madagascar for a couple of generations, collecting tales about tricksters and other characters, they could have observed that performance is a mode of signifying and critique. It is ironic that one of the earliest publications in Malagasy folklore (in Malagasy language, indeed) was the forty-two-page collection of trickster tales (1875) by Rabezandrina, who under another name later became governor of the port of Tamatave. In these tales, the inseparable Merina tricksters Ikotofetsy and Imahaka (Wiley and Cheatam) enter into partnership after they trade a worthless spade for a cock, which is really a crow that flies away. Recognizing each other's guileful nature, they become sworn brothers and commence a string of deceptions against each other and their neighbors. What was being signified to British missionaries and French emissaries, if not that deviousness and treachery were approved forms of behavior? To colonials like Georges-Sully Chapus, the tales showed the high place Malagasy accorded to trickery and guile. A subtler interpretation of what is signified, of its multidimensionality and density, would have required a closer reading than the colonialist could provide.

One African habit of performance may have been especially useful to island storytellers. The great Africanist Denise Paulme called it a law in African trickster tales: an improvement will be followed, sooner or later, by some deterioration. A successful hero will become ungrateful or boastful; a disadvantaged character will rise to a more stable position (Paulme 1975, 576). This device, which aids the signifying habit and often governs the sequencing of trickster tales in performance, shows up in a Comoran tale of spurious friendship between cock and hare. Their contract is that each will plant a field. When cock has a good harvest and hare a bad one, hare violates their contract by proposing they exchange. When cock finds he got nothing in the deal and begins counteracting, the downward movement reverses direction. Cock, to get revenge, hides his head and reddens his neck. Once Hare sees him, he goes home, takes a sharp knife, and cuts off his own head. Thus the second episode answers the first, and the dupe gets revenge on the trickster (Fontoynont and Raomandahy 1937, 76–77). In so African a culture as the Comoros, an African substratum is no surprise. Under French domination, the sequence of trickster's victory and come-uppance could have special force, casting the trickster as a rebel against cultural hegemony. Another example is a century-old Mauritian piece that remodels the Indian tale of "The Jackal Trapped in the Animal Hide." The initial situation is Elephant's great age. Ridiculously old and decrepit, dis-regarding the drought and famine around him, the king of the animals sits around with his mouth open all the time. The hare jumps inside the elephant and begins eating his organs. When he starts on the heart, the elephant dies. Hare vainly tries to get out. As the other animals mourn loudly, the monkey suggests to the young elephant that the corpse be embalmed in Malagasy style. The young elephant agrees; monkey has the dead elephant's entrails removed and thrown away; hare escapes, in a victory for the clever over the strong. At the cemetery, hare practices the slave's power over verbal ambiguity: first he excuses himself by saying he was visiting a sick relative; then he declares, "No one knows as I do what a good heart, what an excel-lent heart our king had" (Baissac 1887, 338–345). These Indian and African tales, in their remodeled versions, were tools of an enhanced capacity for reflexivity or self-reflection on the part of performers and audience.

The nature of creolization in such stories gets confused by Eurocentric interpreters. Antoine Abel, writing from and about Seychelles, declines to interpret the African Seychellois trickster as a local symbol. For him as for some universalizing Westerners, Sungula is a mythical character between human and animal, embodying all the defects and vices of humanity, showing us ruse and intelligence triumphing over brute force and stupid-ity (Abel 1981). One can say that about any trickster anywhere. The histori-cal reality in these islands is that the use of trickster tales to celebrate the superiority of wit attests to African influence and that the trickster vicari-ously enacts the need for rebellion. For groups such as the Bhojpuri nar-rators of Mauritius, who show no African influence, creolization is either incomplete or unobserved (Auleear and Haring 2006).

Reported Speech

Dialogue, the reported speech of characters, is an essential of folktale style, affording opportunity to mock the other speaker's discourse. James Joyce, himself a creole creator, erected quotation into the central device of all cre-olization. From his perspective, as from that of Indian indentured laborers in Mauritius or Malagasy in Réunion, the other's language is always foreign. At an oft-quoted point in Joyce's *Portrait of the Artist as a Young Man*, the Irish hero Stephen Dedalus comes to a sudden, keen consciousness of his status as a creole in language: "His language, so familiar and so foreign, will always be for me an acquired speech" (Joyce 1976, 453). Stephen acquires English to quote it; later, in *Finnegans Wake*, the Irish Joyce weaves a tissue of continual semi-quotation, framing, reduction, augmentation, and allusion, in countless languages. Against the background of multilingualism, quotation is indistinguishable from recontextualization. It is what folklore collectors do, as much as traditional artists.

Storytellers all over the Southwest Indian Ocean prefer to quote the dialogue of their characters rather than summarize it. When I translate (report the speech of) Southwest Indian Ocean folktales, I feel bound to remind my reader, by a literalness doubtless tiresome on paper, of the large number of times an artist reminds his audience that a character is speaking. Daniel Fontaine of Salazie, Réunion, says *la di* and *i di*, he says, incessantly; Sydney Joseph of Grand Bel Air, Mauritius, invariably labels his characters' dialogue; the anonymous writer of the Ibonia epic repeats *hono*, "they say," almost as many times as the oral narrators of Dahle's other texts. The device continually reminds the silent, solitary reader of the distance between writing and hearing. Translators often omit it. In live performance, these narrators send a triple message, simultaneously establishing their own reality, the identity of their character, and a separation between narration and dialogue, often through the vocal manipulation so beloved of African narrators.

This fondness for dialogue gives special force to the verbal arts of Madagascar, which has given the region's narrators a base on which to build multilingual quotation. In Madagascar and Zanzibar, audiences have usually recognized quotation through a speaker's proverbs or aphorisms (Haring 1992, 141–145; Steere 1870, 113–137). In Mauritius in the 1880s, a Creole narrator, who may well have been of Malagasy origin, dictated a personal experience story that depends for its effect on dialogue between himself and the turkey he steals: "Sir, you know what that turkey said to me? 'Chongor, eat me, eat me, eat me!'" (Baissac 1976, 105–108). Generous quantities of dialogue appear in Comoran tales; in texts recorded in La Digue and Praslin, Seychelles, in 1980; and in the performances of Daniel Fontaine, Germain Elizabeth, Gérose Barivoitse, and other skilled Réunionnais narrators (Barat, Carayol, and Vogel 1977). The editors report the reporting by narrators of the speeches by the characters.

Sometimes, in another variety of quotation, they make their performances into dialogues by opening formulas. Throughout this region, performers bridge ordinary talk and performance by their formulaic dialogues with the audience. The Mauritian storyteller says, *"Sirandann!"* His audience must answer, *"Sanpek!"* Because *sirandann* is the word for riddle, the formula connects storytelling and riddling in Mauritius, Rodrigues, and Réunion (Carayol 1980, 30–36). Gérose Barivoitse of Réunion would say, *"Kriké!"* In order to continue recording him, Christian Barat had to answer, *"Kraké mesyé! Kraké, sir!"* When Daniel Fontaine, another Réunionnais performer, encounters helpful birds, he asks his audience, "What did he say to the birds?" (Decros 1978, 202). Opening and closing formulas are oral quotation marks.

For two Réunionnais narrators, dialogue with the video camera of a university collecting team evokes contrastive behaviors. Ebullient, irrepressible, rightly known as the "King," Gérose Barivoitse of Sainte-Suzanne (Réunion) gets up from his chair, moves around, and sits back down, obviously enjoying his own performance. His upper body, hands, and head are active enough for collectors to systematize his paralinguistic codes (Barat Carayol, and Vogel 1977, 103–109). Germain Elizabeth of Dos d'Ane, older and more restrained at the time of recording, sits in a chair outside his house, politely cooperating with the camera. In their different styles, both, of course, are reporting the speech of their predecessors, and it would be hard to choose which is the greater artist.

Folklore Collectors as Creolizers

So too with collectors: to report the speech of storytellers, they too have their techniques and their "metadiscursive practices"—a phrase designating how people's expressions are identified and made available to a new audience. In the hands of Jakob and Wilhelm Grimm, for example, one such practice was to invent dialogue for characters in folktales, as if the narrator had been reporting a character's speech (Briggs 1993, 393–394). The Grimms and other folktale collectors employ the very devices of quotation visible in Southwest Indian Ocean tales. Whether they invent dialogue or translate it, they advance their narrative of folk storytelling by quoting, or at least seeming to quote, what has been said to them. Having first made a story into a "text," they award it a new context; "decontextualization" must be followed by "recontextualization," in a particular variety of what the Russian critic

V. N. Volosinov (1971), in a celebrated essay, calls "reported speech." In the editorial practices of collectors as much as in the performing of storytellers, we again see the renegotiation of cultures. In Seychelles, for instance, the publication program of the Institi Kreol (a division of the Ministry of Culture and Education) is itself a creolizing influence. By transferring Kreol folktales from oral performance to print, the Institi Kreol asks contributors to integrate their older model of artistic production into the new sociocultural environment that tourism has engendered. At the same time, as much as any folktale collector, the Institi Kreol is engaged in reporting speech. Four metadiscursive practices or techniques related to creolization come into play in this region, as they do in so much folktale study: replication, elaboration, invention, and simulation (Dorson 1972).

Videotape and audiotape gave the collecting team that recorded Mm. Barivoitse and Elizabeth a modern technology not yet available to the storytellers. They could reproduce a recorded performance verbatim on tape, as now the Internet offers multifarious means of distributing performances. Efforts in this direction began with Charles Baissac's study of Mauritian Kreol (his native language) in 1880 and gained strength with the influence of scientific linguistics in Madagascar and the other islands (Baissac 1976; Faublée 1947; Barat, Carayol, and Vogel 1977). In the archives of the Centre National de Documentation et de Recherche Scientifique in the Comoros, and in unpublished theses and dissertations, when collectors do their best to replicate oral texts, they produce a written counterpart of the phonetic mixing that characterizes creolization everywhere. The pioneer among practitioners of phonetic mixing in this region is Robert Drury, the cockney sailor shipwrecked in Madagascar from 1703 to 1716, whose collaboration with Daniel Defoe bequeathed a vocabulary of southern Malagasy words in cockney (I should really call it cockeyed) spelling (Defoe 1750). In modern times, virtually unknown till now is a manuscript of Seychellois creole tales, written for production on national radio. The pieces were transcribed before orthography was standardized and accommodate many French spellings, whose variousness is a written analogue to the linguistic variety of the region. Literature and folkloristics rely on such "metadiscursive practices": they mix languages and decide how to render dialect. Mauritian literary history displays another sort of creolization when Mauritian Kreol discourse has been translated into standard French with no attempt at replication (Joubert, Osman, and Ramarasoa 1993). All translation could be seen as a mode of creolization, but few translators would agree to call it that.

Print culture demands renegotiation of oral style. Since the René government in Seychelles began encouraging a Kreol publication program, the Ministry has encouraged writers to elaborate and revise oral tales, which are published annually by the Institi Kreol. In the same revising spirit, Antoine Abel produces a smooth Seychellois version of a well-known African trickster tale, in which a dupe is persuaded to take Sungula's place in a sack (Abel 1977, 19–20). Similar elaborations and revisions are the rule in storybooks addressed to young Malagasy reading French (Vally-Samat 1962). From Mauritius, J. M. G. Le Clézio, of an old Franco-Mauritian family, who was awarded the Nobel Prize for Literature in 2008, has published a collection of riddles only slightly revised (Le Clézio and Le Clézio 1990). Recontextualization for print seems to necessitate revising, if not elaborating.

Inventing tales based on oral folklore was the great vocation of Samuel Accouche, who wrote and broadcast his engaging stories on Radio Seychelles between 1966 and 1973 (Accouche 1976). The diversity of his sources shows him to have been an expert creolizer. In Mauritius, Ramesh Ramdoyal's two collections of tales (1979, 1981) announce themselves as a "supplementary reader" to extend the English language experience and vocabulary of schoolchildren. In Réunion, such inventions have been central to the writings of J. F. Sam-Long, such as his lurid, sensational novel *Zoura* (1988), but from the beginning, Réunionnais authors, even the youngest, have usually sought to avoid *le folklorisme* in an attempt to disappear into the culture of the metropole (Vaxelaire 1993).

In Madagascar, written tales based on oral folklore have long been produced. One volume contains several examples by various hands (Mallet 1961, 59–63, 79–101), along with a more believable quasi-ethnographic narration of a funeral with its ensuing ceremonies and feasting (103–112). The same collection contains an artificial or simulated myth, "The Remedy against Death," written by a named author (17–24). And the in-flight magazine of the excellent Air Mauritius can be depended upon to purvey simulated legends to the tourist.

All these techniques of the folklorist are allied to phenomena of creolization, though usually called by other names. Perhaps it is time to reconceive the nature of folkloric change. Creole linguistics teaches that pidgin and creole languages may be something entirely new, that they manifest a break in the continuity of development which traditionally characterized linguistic history. A creole language is a new mixture, only partly explainable through genetic relations. What if creole tales too are

new mixtures? What if their concerns—marriage, kinship, the food sup-
ply, interdependence—and their continual symbolizing of dominance and
oppression demand a new understanding? Human aggressiveness and
defense, slavery, social engineering, colonialism, and integration into the
world economic system have disrupted the lives of creole artists. They have
not choked off their creativity. Folklorists too are creolizers. They remodel
intellectual patterns and insights from neighboring disciplines; they mix
the languages of other disciplines to create their own; they mold borrowed
materials in accordance with their emphasis on art. These are modernist
moves; the collecting of folktales is a modern phenomenon, born in the
industrial age. Postmodern folkloristics, if there is to be such a thing, will
assimilate the discourse of the folk and the discourse of the scholar into
one large realm. Jacques Lacan has remarked on "the unmistakable prestige of legacies: the witness' faithfulness is the wool pulled over the eyes of
those who might criticize his testimony" (2006, 14). The legacies of folklore study continue to accumulate; faithful testimonies continue to come
from modernist observers of Indian Ocean creole storytelling. Mayotte,
for example—now that it moves toward achieving the status of a *dépar-
tement*—is especially favored (Gueunier 1990, 1994; Gueunier et al. 2001;
Blanchy et al. 1993). But in an island like Mauritius, which seeks to inhabit
a world of computers, orientation to consumption, information flow, and
"mediascapes" (Appadurai 1996, 33), postmodern folkloristics will have to
surround itself with analyses of "techno-capitalism." Surrounding the production, consumption, and observation of face-to-face art are forces that
may work to make "folklore" meaningless—or to enhance it through the
Internet. As creole storytellers have interpreted social processes in order
to help people think about questions of kinship, economy, and history, so
critics and scholars will want to interpret artistic processes and the ways
in which the social content of the artwork, as T. W. Adorno said, is mediated through the changing institutional configurations that determine the
where, what, and how of storytelling.

Creole Talk

The Poetics and Politics of Argentine Verbal Art

—ANA C. CARA

Words, and alternative ways of talking, have habitually been the poor man's currency in creole societies; forever, as well, have they served as weapons against oppressive authority, vehicles for solidarity among all manner of disenfranchised peoples, and instruments for extraordinary art.

The man-of-words, as Roger Abrahams (1983) so compellingly demonstrated in his work on the West Indies, plays a critical role in negotiating and celebrating creolization and in achieving meaning in local creole communities. "Talk is never cheap," observes Abrahams, underscoring how the everyday and the extraordinary in verbal expressive behavior are "chained to each other" and how skillful talkers deal in expressive exchange with a "profound notion of their own speech economy" (1983, xix).

Similarly, though in ways unique to the context of the Southern Cone, Argentines also participate in the everyday formulations of a creole politics and poetics through talk. Martín Fierro, the main character of Argentina's national epic poem, for example, underscores the importance of words improvised and rendered in poetry, in "song." He articulates what most Argentines recognize intrinsically: *"El amor como la guerra lo hace el criollo con canciones"* (Love, like war, is waged by criollos through song) (Hernández 1953, 81).

While no creole language per se ever developed in Argentina, the conversational phenomenon that did emerge was nonetheless called *"hablando en criollo"* (not meaning "talking in creole" but "voicing creolity," a more accurate rendering in English introduced here for the native, coded sense of the phrase).[1] Additionally, a whole host of creole verbal art genres flourished, for which I here offer the analytical category "Creole Talk."[2] The two, in tandem, play an important role in the cultural and political negotiations and the artistic expression of everyday verbal exchanges and literary texts. Though distinct, hablando en criollo and Creole Talk are intrinsically interwoven; together they formulate a local, coded, discourse employed by Argentines that references everything "creole."

As a point of entry to the art of Creole Talk in the Argentine setting, I first focus on an exemplary case—the game of *truco*—before examining the more ordinary, everyday discursive matter of "voicing creolity" (*hablando en criollo*). After tracing the cultural and political context of Argentine creolity, I return to the art of Creole Talk and to the phenomenon of an Argentine creole poetics.

Truco: An Introduction to Creole Talk

In his essay about truco, an Argentine creole card game, Jorge Luis Borges brings to life this national pastime: "The game begins; the players, transformed into their *criollo* selves, cast off their daily behavior. A different self, an almost ancestral and vernacular self, takes over the game. In one fell swoop the language changes" (Borges 1984, 109).

Indeed, one could say language or a creole way of speaking is the real contest in truco, the cards only a pretext for the conversation.[3] Talk drives this betting game. "One must accompany each card with sayings," explains Argentine critic and essayist Ezéquiel Martínez Estrada, who (like Borges) turns to truco to explore and characterize Argentine culture and criollo behavior in his celebrated book-length treatise on Buenos Aires. "Truco is a game of talk; conversation, refrains, and even poetry . . . constitute its incentives" (Martínez Estrada [1940] 2001, 191). Borges himself corroborates this with his poetically understated observation that, at the truco table, "more than once, the enthusiasm of the dialogue is excited into verse" (1974, 145). Most players will attest that losing the game is less a failure than failing to be an accomplished talker.[4]

Talk in truco is formulaic, ritualistic, and traditional; but it is also improvised, inventive, startling. Cards have both long-standing and newly minted metaphoric nicknames. As the game advances, players simultaneously repeat time-honored rhyming stanzas or invent new ones as they call out their bets and reveal their hands.[5] Metaphors and allusions, as well as other verbal devices, color their talk: instead of saying *flor* (which indicates a specific combination of cards, but which also translates as "flower"), one might say *olorosa* (scented, fragrant, aromatic) or *jardinera* (flower cart, flower stand, gardener) to announce what one is holding, or simply name this card combination by reciting a rhyming verse:

Alambre de siete hilos   Seven-thread wire
con palos de ñandubay   with posts of *ñandubay*[6]
cigarros marca La Tecla   La Tecla brand cigars
y una *flor* del Paraguay.   and a *flower* from Paraguay.
(Páez 1971, 40, my emphasis)

Strict rules further permit or forbid the use of certain words.[7] Strategic mispronunciations in the midst of conversation devilishly fool one's opponent into playing a losing card. Central to this game, played in pairs, is the constant banter among players trying to distract, provoke, and trick (hence, truco)[8] one another while simultaneously communicating with their partners.

Yet while words are bandied about, talk in truco is never careless or inexact. Language may be veiled, indirect, playful, innovative, provocative, spontaneous, but never false. It is okay to playfully dupe, deceive, or trick one another; it is not acceptable to employ words to actually swindle, betray, or cheat. Players—talkers and listeners alike—walk a witty tightrope of words. Commentary during truco works both to veil and to expose a player's hand and intentions. The good player has learned to talk across the table with his partner and tell him exactly what cards he holds without giving himself away to the opponents sitting next to him. Equally skillfully, he has learned to listen for the truth or the actual facts hidden behind the words of double-talk articulated by both allies and adversaries.

In a move to encapsulate and illuminate the verbal play and personal interactions characteristic of this quintessentially criollo pastime, Borges recounts the brief tale of two peddlers, Mosche and Daniel. By identifying them as Russian and by having them meet in the middle of the Russian steppes (no doubt a mirror of the Argentine *pampa*), the author transports the interaction between the two men away from his native setting in a classic and universalizing Borgesian gesture. As their exchange illustrates clearly the essence of a creole dynamic, it also brings the reader back home to the kind of talk or verbal art emblematic of an Argentine creole poetics:

"Where are you going, Daniel?" said one.
"To Sebastopol," said the other.
At that, Mosche looked hard at him and uttered his judgment:
"You lie, Daniel. You answer that you're going to Sebastopol so I'll think you're going to Nizhni-Novgorod, but the truth is that you really are going to Sebastopol. You lie, Daniel!" (Borges 1974, 146)

Using the game of truco both as model and metaphor for Argentine creole cultural strategies, and the exchange between Mosche and Daniel as an example of this dynamic, Borges demonstrates the kind of lying customary in truco. However, he promptly further reflects that truco "is the action of a lying voice, of a face that feels exposed and is on the defensive, of tricky, unfurled *palabrerío* [*verbiage*]" (Borges 1981, 258, emphasis in original). "Lying," therefore, must not be read literally, for the chatter or silences of truco, as the card game progresses, are more accurately associated with dissimulation and trickery, with indirection, with pretense and masking, with provocation and guile, with cunning and artifice. At play in truco, as Borges notes, is a *lying voice*—a playful, artful voice—rather than an outright lie.

Consequently, in tandem with the mischievous double-talk in truco, the game is also governed, ironically, by certain standards; reputation, respect, and honor hold sway. The *"filigrana de la palabra"* (filigree of words), to use Martínez Estrada's term, must be employed with care. When words are used in a *"deformada, juguetona, perifrástica"* (distorted, playful, round-about) manner, the player must do this only for *"adorno"* (adornment or embellishment). While undoubtedly "the great player is always a master of great style," Martínez Estrada writes, he also cautions that words have to be carefully considered if they are to count. He underscores: "Within truco, which is deceit itself turned into a game, the law exists." One can play with and manipulate words, but one's intentions or actions must not break either the rules of the game or the rules of gamesmanship. Honor is thus honored. Paradoxically, it is *"la trampa"* (actual cheating or fraud) that "turns the game solemn" (Martínez Estrada [1940] 2001, 191).

While explicit rules of play guide the game, truco is nevertheless steered by intuition and wit. Its essence is revealed in the process—in the *act*—of playing. "The magic and the cut-and-thrust of the game—of the playing itself—come out in the action" (Borges 1984, 109). It would be a mistake, however, to conclude that randomness directs the players' actions. As with any traditional cultural performance, truco (and the talk it requires) is a learned and celebrated art form, transmitted from player to player over generations.

Unlike poker players (described by Borges and Martínez Estrada as tac-iturn, serious, categorical, impassive, unresponsive to fluctuation), truco players learn to be expert readers and master second-guessers of a situation, capable of actively distracting and misdirecting their opponents. The game, as Borges sees it, is a "superimposition of masks." He lays it out: a grumbling player who has thrown his cards down on the table might, in fact, be hiding a good hand. That, Borges observes, is elementary cunning. On the other hand, perhaps he is lying by telling the truth (not unlike Mosche and Daniel) so that we disbelieve it. That, he notes, is cunning squared (Borges 1974, 146). The ever-present slyness, astuteness, or what Argentines call *viveza criolla* (creole wit),[9] juxtaposed or interwoven with laid-back dialogue and "innocent" good fun, is all part of truco's strategy—and, as we will see, of Argentine creole culture.

In my own observations of truco in action, the additional use of gestures alongside talk also has a crucial place in the dialogic nature of the game. The accomplished man-of-words is never reduced to a chatterbox in truco. In fact, players tactically draw on a traditional nonverbal repertoire of gestures specifically coded for truco, both to signal a message to their partner across the table and, simultaneously, to fool their rivals: raising one's eyebrows, puckering the lips, winking, tilting one's head, biting the lower lip, and so forth, each performed in less than a second.[10] These gestural tricks are cleverly camouflaged in the midst of the laughter and banter that veil direct speech through the "creole noise" (see Borges, below) that encircles the table as players obliquely communicate among each other. Yet truco never disintegrates into mere brouhaha or ruckus. Conversely, "the truco player who turns somber or chokes on his response is considered boorish" (Martínez Estrada [1940] 2001, 191).

Beyond the mere good fun rendered by truco, the game holds symbolic importance for Argentines.[11] It is no accident that prominent national writers and thinkers like Martínez Estrada and Borges turn their attention to it. Truco's consequential attributes and the magnitude of its significance lie not simply in the complexities of the game, the virtuosity of the verbal art, and the wit of the performers, but, as we will see, on its integral and complex relationship with an Argentine creole ethics and aesthetics. Martínez Estrada, for one, recognizes that "as a game of instinct, premonition, intuition, it is a national game" ([1940] 2001, 192). And Borges more specifically contemplates the parallel criollo universe symbolically evoked by truco: Truco players "seem to be hiding in the criollo noise of the dialogue. . . . [T]he precinct of the card table is another country. . . . The *truqueros* [card players] live this little world of hallucination. They keep it going with unhurried, coarse and witty creole sayings, tending it like fire. . . . It is a narrow world, a phantom of local politics and rogueries; a world invented, after all, by the stockyard sorcerers and neighborhood con men—but not for that any less a substitute for the real world, and no less inventive and diabolical in its ambitions" (1974, 146). In 1930, when Borges published his essay on truco, his reference to "the human sources of the game" alluded back to the 1800s and to the first decades of the past century.[12] He noted the common spirit between truco and the jollity of folks at wakes, the threatening boasts of political bosses, the verbal escapades in the Buenos Aires brothels, and the *milonga* lyrics[13] sung by men around a campfire or in a *pulpería* (saloon, corner bar) on the outskirts of Buenos Aires.

Now, almost a century later, truco and its players operate within the contemporary framework of twenty-first-century Argentine life. Women, men, the young, and older folks (across all social classes) enjoy what in the past was almost an exclusively male game. Players today engage in truco during siesta time or at night after a traditional *asado* (barbeque) with friends or family. Adolescents try out their verbal skills and art of deception among friends after school. Habitual *truqueros* surround the card table away from work on the weekend. Old-timers meet in the back room of neighborhood cafés and recall the past. Exiled Argentines gather around the game to rehearse the criollo rituals of home.

There is something comforting (as with most traditions) in knowing that the game is a repetition of past games and a constant in the nation's vernacular consciousness. "Of course we still play truco—every week," a young man told me on a recent trip to the Argentine interior.[14] Like any other time-honored traditions, truco rehearses and reifies locally held values. If, as Borges writes, "generations of criollos no longer here are buried alive, as it were, in the game," and, in fact, "they *are* the game—and this is no metaphor" (1974, 147; emphasis added), one can argue that truco offers Argentines the opportunity to dialogue with and re-enact past criollo behavior. One could further claim (as scholars have about other folk pastimes or so-called national games)[15] that the truco table is a microcosm of Argentine creole dynamics and that the game's *palabrerío*—a vibrant example of expressive verbal art forms—offers a heightened model, an empirical referent, an analogous counterpart for a more ordinary (though no less powerful) type of creole discourse employed in everyday life, which Argentines natively categorize as *hablando en criollo*.

Hablando en Criollo / "Voicing Creolity"

Outside "the precinct of the card table," when the occasion calls for it in everyday life, Argentines engage in a "way of speaking" (Hymes 1972b, 58) introduced above, known as *hablando en criollo* (voicing creolity). There are countless contexts, both formal and informal, that call for voicing creolity. Contrary to its literal sense, as the examples that follow illustrate, hablando en criollo is, again, *not* speaking in a creole language.[16] Neither is hablando en criollo marked by the kind of manifest artifice in language and verbal dynamics performed, for example, at the truco table. In fact, the only indicator that a speaker is on the verge of, or in the process of, voicing creolity is the person's purposefully explicit (metalinguistic) reference that he or she is now hablando en criollo—thus framing what would otherwise appear to be "ordinary talk" as *voicing creolity* (see Goffman 1974).

The fact that there is no creole language in play makes it clearly inaccurate (even if denotatively the case) to translate "hablando en criollo" as "talking in creole." Such a rendition of the phrase, moreover, misses entirely the specific Argentine cultural signification: a desire not merely to talk *in* creole (even were there such a possibility) but instead to reference— indeed to give *voice* to—an entire creole cultural complex.

So what exactly do Argentines *mean* when they claim to be voicing creolity? What do speakers intend to evoke when they invoke creolity in this way? How does hablando en criollo differ from other talk? What is one actually demanding of someone when insisting, imperatively, "Hablame en criollo" (Voice creolity)? What does playing this card—hablando en criollo—accomplish culturally, politically, aesthetically?

Several examples deliberately selected from different linguistic registers—and from a variety of media, time periods, and contexts—suggest some answers. In the 1934 Spanish-language film *El tango en Broadway* (The Tango on Broadway),[17] Carlos Gardel, the internationally renowned tango singer and the embodiment of creolity in Argentina, plays the role of the dashing Mr. Bazán, an Argentine entrepreneur in New York who runs a talent agency. After a night of women, champagne, and song, he wakes up in his Manhattan apartment and says to his butler, "Che, Juan! Hay novedades?" (Hey, Juan! What's new?), to which the butler, who is trying out his English, tells him there is a telephone message and nothing else. Bazán, annoyed by Juan's response in English, fires back in Argentine Spanish, "Mirá, te he dicho que me hablés en criollo, querés" (Look, I've told you to talk to me in creole, will you). The butler protests (also in Argentine Spanish) stating that it's "más distinguido en inglés" (more distinguished/ sophisticated in English). "En criollo!" the Gardel character insists, once again requiring creolity, threatening to otherwise lower the butler's pay.

"All right, sir," responds the butler again in English, but quickly recovering: "Perdón! Perdón!" (Sorry! Sorry!). No doubt, there is some element of spoof and play in the scene. However, the parody of language and the insistence on celebrating creolity in a film that focuses on down-and-out Argentines trying to seek out a living in New York by performing criollo music and songs on stage for a foreign, elegant New York audience is not accidental. In fact, when a member of the ensemble that is immediately due to go on stage fails to show up, the debonair Bazán (Gardel) takes off his tuxedo, puts on a gaucho costume, and steps onstage to sing and perform in full criollo style.

A second example: on October 16, 2007, Néstor Kirshner, the Argentine president at the time, ended his visit to a Volkswagen plant in the province of Buenos Aires with a speech in which he made the following declaration: "Es muy fácil tener una Argentina dormida o una Argentina con deflación, como hubo en un tiempo con argentinos—discúlpenme la palabra pero me gusta hablar en criollo—excluidos y muertos de hambre como nos pasó en un tiempo donde tenían que rogar la subsistencia diaria" (It is very easy to have an Argentina that is asleep or an Argentina with deflation, as there was once when—pardon me, but I like to voice creolity—Argentines were excluded and starving and had to beg for daily sustenance [my emphasis]).[18] By alluding to hablar en criollo, the president explicitly affirms his already implicit solidarity with his audience.

The next illustration is from an e-mail exchange between two Argentine friends, a man residing in Buenos Aires and his female friend, working abroad in the United States, both of them in their twenties. Frustrated at not hearing from her, he sends her the following message (written in colloquial slang) which reads, in part: "Cómo andás? . . . En criollo, dónde carajo estás? y si se puede ahondar, qué estás haciendo?" (How's it going? . . . In creole: where the hell are you? And, if you don't mind my digging deeper, what's happening? [my emphasis]).[19] In this case, the straightforward familiarity cuts directly to the intimacy of their friendship. He's simply looking for a candid response by voicing creolity.

As a final illustration, several years ago a CD recorded by the well-known Argentine folk singer José Larralde, whose songs are modeled on traditional Argentine improvisational creole genres, had as its title *Hablando en criollo* (Sony BMG, Argentina, 2005). Here, voicing creolity is actually correlated with the traditional verbal art of Creole Talk, illustrated in this case by Larralde's recorded lyrics.

In each of these examples and, more generally, in innumerable other unpredictable (though not random) everyday exchanges (including Internet blogs) the deliberate use of the phrase "hablando en criollo" constitutes a linguistic, social, and cultural marker for voicing creolity. Yet, despite its common usage and its cultural magnitude, the phrase "hablando en criollo" is absent from not only standard, but also folk, colloquial, and other specialized and regional dictionaries. Instead, its significance is preserved and transmitted through oral tradition and vernacular knowledge. When asked, any Argentine can readily explain the use and meaning of the phrase. Fieldwork collaborators, for example, will simply explain that hablar en criollo is *"decir algo sin andar con vueltas"* (to say something without beating around the bush), or, as some say, to express something *"con franqueza"* (frankly).

This native exegesis affords a rather uncomplicated, compressed assessment of hablar en criollo—a phenomenon more easily recognized than defined or analyzed. In fact, not unlike the proverbial tip of the iceberg, this apparently simple phrase hides a far deeper, broader, and invisible (to those not acquainted with it) cultural phenomenon. Typically, as with native speakers everywhere, although they can tell us *how* hablando en criollo is employed, and although their cultural knowledge readily permits them to understand *when* to voice creolity, they (of course) are not likely to be able to offer a sociolinguistic or folkloristic analysis of its significance within the larger Argentine creole context. Lay explanations nevertheless yield perceptions far greater in significance when we recognize hablando en criollo as a ubiquitous rhetorical instrument within the larger Argentine tradition of creole verbal art.

Consequently, while hablando en criollo (simply put) is a marker of candor, it differs qualitatively from other expressions and colloquialisms that also signify straightforward speech, such as, *hablar sin pelos en la lengua* (to speak without hair on one's tongue) and *hablando mal y pronto* (speaking poorly and fast). Yet, *hablar en criollo* is not quite the same in the Argentine context as saying something "without hair on one's tongue" or stating it "down and dirty." Though subtle, the difference is real, concealing the complexities of what it means to voice creolity.

As the phrase itself suggests, hablando en criollo is employed to signify an entire culture's creole poetics without having to actually re-enact traditional creole verbal art or needing to "break into performance" (Hymes 1975). It functions as a cultural shortcut of sorts, recalling creole dynamics and values that transform otherwise ordinary talk into symbolic cultural discourse. By deliberately asserting that they are voicing creolity, speakers do not indicate that they are making a language switch (to a Creole) but that they are enacting a discursive shift. They thus claim, in sum, a creole posture and attitude, performing a cultural repositioning that gestures "creole."

Political Foundations and Emergent Creole Sensibilities

In the Argentine context, what common foundational values and cultural sensibilities, what shared social hierarchies and political factors trigger a shift into a "creole mode"? Some historical perspective on the uses and meanings of the ideologically and affect-laden term *criollo* will help to answer these questions.

Although it is impossible to reproduce here the full complexity of New World colonial creolity (in which Argentina and other nations share a common history), it is nevertheless feasible to outline some prevalent tendencies and critical nuances in the usage—the traditions, implications, and conventions—of criollo in the transitional period from colonial to postcolonial Latin America and, in the Argentine context, since that country's independence in 1810. As with creolization elsewhere, the particularities of Argentine creolity are the unique result of local histories, geographies, demographics, economies, and multiple other factors that engendered and continue to shape the political complexities, values, and dynamics that constitute the country's many cultural intimacies, giving specific meaning, in each case, to the identity "criollo."

With the emergence of newly independent nations in the nineteenth century, "Creoles ceased to be 'new men' of the New World, American all, in order to be transformed into Argentines, Uruguayans, Bolivians and Peruvians, Colombians, Panamanians, Mexicans and Guatemalans, Dominicans, Cubans," the Cuban critic José Arrom observes (1971, 23–24). "And 'criollo,' adjusting itself to the new concept, came to signify not what was essentially American [i.e., of the Americas], but that which was national and particular" (Arrom 1971, 23–24).

First employed in the Americas in the sixteenth century, the term *criollo* had initially been used to differentiate—and discriminate against—those born in the New World of European and African parents from their immigrant parents and ancestors born in the old country.[20] By the 1800s, however, the emergent nation states in Latin America indiscriminately employed the term synonymously with national identity. Although its nuances varied among social classes, criollo was not inherently a class-bound concept.[21] In fact, it was not just human beings who claimed the qualifier; the rubric was also applied to characterize autochthonous flora and fauna as well as local traditions. The eleventh edition (1911) of the *Encyclopedia Britannica*, for example, in underscoring the irrelevance of race in the use of the word *creole*, adds the possible application of the term to at least one four-legged creature: "In itself 'creole' has no distinction of colour; a creole may be a person of European, negro, or mixed extraction—or even a horse" ("creole," 409). Indeed, the horse common to the Plata region in Argentina is referred to as a *caballo criollo* (creole horse)—as opposed to those *caballos* brought from elsewhere—even though horses were not indigenous to the New World. Similarly, a potato native to Cuba—and, certainly, indigenous to the New World—might be characterized as *criolla* to differentiate it from imported ones, such as the Irish potato (Arrom 1971, 25).

As with new criollo citizens, the adjective *criollo* was used to describe the diverse vernacular cultural productions embodying the folk entities and traditions of new nations. For example, the famous *ajiaco criollo* (creole stew), which in Cuba is considered *típico* (typically, traditionally, natively Cuban) and is thereby synonymous with *ajiaco cubano*, also has Peruvian, Colombian, and other versions, each called *ajiaco criollo* and each distinguished by its own native ingredients and local preparation. Like these "national" dishes, other examples of material culture and expressive forms—criollo dances, criollo music, criollo architecture, criollo sayings, criollo weavings, criollo beliefs, and so on—indexed *lo nuestro* (what is ours) in each country, both at a vernacular, everyday level and on a politically valued national plane.

Significant here is the progressively more pointed use of criollo as a cultural and political category capable of embracing people as native sons and regarding local products and customs as *creolized* national patrimony, regardless of origin. Accrued in the qualifier criollo was the sense of someone or something "native" or "native-like" (though not necessarily indigenous) to a place or a culture. Consequently, criollo would eventually characterize not just those individuals actually born in the New World, but anyone whose way of life and sense of self was informed by the criollo values, behavior, and expressions characteristic of the burgeoning creole cultures in the New World. Thus, over time, creolity would indicate in Argentina (as in other nations) not inherent or objective qualities (such as place of birth, family lineage, race, class, or social status) but a *way of life*. Affectively, moreover, identification with creolity evoked a sense of cultural intimacy in emergent nation-states—a sense of place and belonging and a heightened awareness of local tradition as well as a political desire for self-determination and independence from colonizing powers.

This inclination toward what is "ours" and toward creating a unique local culture is famously articulated in José Martí's 1891 essay, "*Nuestra América*" (Our America), where the Cuban poet and essayist underscores the possessive pronoun and makes the case for local practices and native originality, arguing against blindly mimicking Europe or turning exclusively to the Classical canon for models: "Nuestra Grecia," he writes, "es preferible a la Grecia que no es nuestra" (Our Greece is preferable to the Greece that is not ours) ([1891] 1996, 239). Predating Derek Walcott (1974) by close to a century, Martí noted that in the New World "every endeavor is belittled as imitation, from architecture to music," and thus the only "salvation" from such a fate was local (creole) creativity: "El vino, de plátano," Martí insisted, "y si sale agrio, es nuestro vino!" (Let the wine be from plantains; and even if it's bitter, it's our wine!) (239, 241).

But by the first decades of the twentieth century, criollo cultures in Hispanic America were once more contested by more cosmopolitan, avant-garde intellectual, artistic, and cultural ideals, particularly in emerging New World metropolises (such as Buenos Aires and Mexico City), where publishing houses, symphony halls, newspapers, and museums (all modeled on European exemplars) set the new international standards for "culture" in the Americas. Already, by the late 1890s, *Modernismo* had taken hold in the upper echelons of social, artistic, and intellectual circles of the Americas, and although this movement (initiated by the Nicaraguan writer Rubén Darío) embraced both criollo and classical cultures, creolity as a cultural ideal gave way to more Modernist, international currents.

By the 1900s, in the context of the rising metropolitanism of the twentieth century, local criollo cultures were seen as "quaint" and "folkloric"—foreign to the urban life of the Americas. At best, that which was criollo (much like perceptions of folklore in the nineteenth century) was romanticized and idealized (though also decontextualized and "museumized") as relics of "the past" in danger of disappearing. At its worst, it was negatively associated with illiteracy, poverty, and a "backward" rural lifestyle resistant to progress. The term further typified prototypical traditional rural figures, such as the Puerto Rican *jíbaro*, the Venezuelan *llanero*, or the

Argentine *gaucho*, who were stereotypically portrayed as embodying the values and customs of regional criollos.[22]

This reduction and simplification of creolity was not without political motivation or consequences, as the Argentine political trajectory begun in the nineteenth century illustrates. In his polemical book-length essay *Facundo* ([1845] 1961), Domingo Faustino Sarmiento (subsequently president of Argentina) divided the nation into "civilization and barbarism." Within this scheme, the "barbarous" life of the countryside gaucho and rural population needed to be replaced, in the minds of the governing elite, by "civilized" European manners and values. Responding to this vision, the nation opened its doors to immigration guided by the motto "*gobernar es poblar*" (to govern is to populate).[23] Shaped by an elitist ideology and a racist perspective, the aim was to populate the largely deserted Argentina with newcomers (preferably of the Nordic "races") who could "implant" in the new nation the desired "English liberty, French culture, North American and European values" (Alberdi 1984, 60–62, 67). Although this line of thought did not escape contention, the ensuing census figures attest to the outcome of the debate: between 1869 and 1914, the number of *porteños* (residents of Buenos Aires) multiplied nine times (Páez 1970, 12).

Were it not for the fact that most immigrants were fleeing depressed areas in Europe, looking for manual labor and a chance to *hacer la América* (make their fortune in America) rather than aiming to bring elite refinements to Argentina, one might think the nineteenth-century policy had succeeded. Some Argentine intellectuals unabashedly expressed disappointment in the types and classes of newcomers, whose "low cultural level," in their eyes, was no appreciable improvement over the so-called backward native Spanish, mestizo, and mulatto populations. Nevertheless, the onslaught of Italian, Polish, Jewish, Irish, Middle Eastern, and numerous other immigrant groups layered the national population and Argentine culture with a predominantly White, European veneer.

In contrast, during the colonial period Buenos Aires' population had been close to one-third Black (see Andrews 1980, 23).[24] Imported as household servants rather than as plantation workers, African slaves and their descendants lived in close quarters with White families, sharing common spaces and cultural habits both at home and in the city at large. Proximity and cultural intimacy contributed to the creolization of African, Spanish, and indigenous traditions. Indeed, after Blacks "disappeared" from Argentine life (serving as cannon fodder in local territorial wars, intermarrying with Whites, and being vastly outnumbered and thus "erased" by immigration) strong African cultural elements remained intrinsically intertwined in the expressive forms of Argentine criollo vernacular life: musical patterns and performance styles, dance steps, poetic improvisation and verbal contests, culinary arts, storytelling, celebrations, belief systems, and more (see Andrews 1980; Ortiz Oderigo 1974).

Close to half a century of immigration to Argentina (from about 1870 to the outbreak of the First World War) further complicated Argentina's notions of creolity and national identity. Especially threatened by the new arrivals and the ensuing social and cultural changes were the rural and urban non-elite criollo men forced to compete for housing, jobs, women, and social status with the newly arrived (overwhelmingly male) foreign "interlopers." To confound matters even more, one of the largest White slave trade operations was set into motion at this time, with Buenos Aires as its lucrative destination. Both local pimps and organized "professionals" in the business of prostitution furnished women from central Europe, France, and other locations (including the Argentine interior) to the numerous brothels that pockmarked Buenos Aires for several decades.[25] Here, creolization was also in operation. At both fancy and down-and-out whorehouses, lonely men of all ages—both Argentines seeking work in the city and immigrants barely able to speak Spanish as well as *niños bien* (upper-class young men)—gathered not just for sexual but also for social intercourse. In an atmosphere compared by some to that of New Orleans, brothels were a gathering place to hear music improvised by local Black and White musicians and by new arrivals whose clarinets, guitars, flutes, and violins had crossed the ocean with them. Here, also, men and women adapted old and invented new dance steps from European and rural Argentine traditions, thus creating a new creole Argentine dance—the tango. In the countryside barbed-wire fences scarred the open *pampa*, violating the unstructured life of the gaucho as immigrants settled on the prairieland, changing local habits; in the exploding urban context natives confronted, contested, and negotiated cultural differences with one another. Such encounters occurred not only in the local *quilombo, lupanar, queco, lenocinio* (among the countless slang terms for *prostíbulos* or "houses of prostitution") but in the numerous spaces where Argentines and foreigners publicly and intimately interacted with each other: *conventillos* (tenement houses), cafes, factories, street corners, sports arenas, corner stores, public squares, and everywhere during *carnaval*.

Reversing the earlier unequivocal elite support of immigration, a change of heart spread throughout the nation. Around the 1910 Argentine centenary, nationalists began to exalt the gaucho as the paragon of Argentine virtue and national identity. Actual flesh-and-blood gauchos, with all their complications and shortcomings, were recast as a nostalgic symbol of Argentine national virtue and replaced by an idealized gaucho "type" composed of selective truths. Both elite and common criollos invoked gaucho traits and styles in an effort to capture the vanishing Argentine traditions overshadowed or reinterpreted by immigrants. Important among the gaucho criollo traditions valued by Argentines was the art of verbal quickness and clever talk (see Cara-Walker 1987).

Curiously, however, newcomers also realized that they could appropriate the idealized gaucho cultural models to integrate themselves into Argentine culture. Thus the foreigner's antithesis—the gaucho, as icon of Argentine creolity—paradoxically became an important vehicle for the creolization of immigrants. Not only Black gauchos, but Italian, Jewish, Basque and other foreign gauchos worked side by side in the countryside with descendants of the original gaucho culture and celebrated criollo gaucho traditions with them as well. In the city, though their work might be in factories, construction, and numerous other manual labor sites (rather than on horseback, herding cattle), immigrants wanting to become "native" or criollo-like practiced "gaucho sports," played the guitar, and held barbeques, imitating and reinterpreting traditional criollo life.

No longer simply a noun or an adjective, *criollo* now also functioned as a verb and an adverb. The *process* of creolization was made explicit in the common reflexive use of the verb *acriollarse* (to creolize oneself, to become criollo or criollo-like). Immigrants, for example, aimed to creolize themselves by doing things and behaving *a lo criollo* (in a creole way, in a creole mode). Criollo, as an identity, therefore, did not hinge on place of birth, race, class, or ethnicity, but on the cultural participation (of both natives and foreigners) in a "criollo way of being" that indicated a political stance vis-à-vis the (new) *home* culture. The question, then, was not *who* was (inherently) criollo, but rather *when* and *how* one freely opted to engage in creolity.

As with any cultural behavior or attitude, criollo local culture could be called on, incorporated, and performed when needed. Creolity (criollo values and behavior) constituted a transmissible and learnable set of fluid and negotiable beliefs, repertoires, styles, and strategies available to anyone. To acriollarse or become creolized, then, had become an open cultural option. To be criollo was to opt for "homegrown" alternative behaviors (not unlike the homegrown chicks, the *gallinha crioula*, which lent

criollos their name)[26] rather than adhering to external, colonizing, dominant, or official culture. As a result, it was possible to do things *a lo criollo*
all the time or (by easily switching codes) as needed. To be criollo or to
acriollarse, then, was largely a matter of personal choice among cultural
options. Criollo conduct, particularly as manifested in the more open,
expressive forms—dance, music, *carnaval*, dress, food—offered a local,
native, deliberate counter-colonial voice. Moreover, this conscious stance
represented not merely a political posture, but also an aesthetic sensibility that shaped traditional expressive forms. Along the same lines, Creole
Talk reflected criollo attitudes and values, criollo points of view, criollo
humor, criollo art—all things otherwise "unsayable" in standard or official
discourse. Out of this growing constellation of expressive forms emerged,
as well, a new criollo poetics.

Toward a Creole Poetics

As we turn our attention to an Argentine creole poetics, let us first return
to truco and the other cultural spaces and workings of genres (as examples
of Creole Talk), where verbal art moves language from ordinary talk to the
reenactment of the time-honored *tricks* of creolization.

    In a creole social system, the real-life "game" (symbolically relocated to
the card table in truco) lies in the negotiation of sociocultural differences
when two or more interconnected (but not equivalent) value systems confront and contest each other. Plantation cultures have traditionally offered
the most patent examples of this. But similar patterns developed in places
like Argentina, where differences and inequities—between colonizers and
colonized, house slaves and elite society, rural workers and urban dwellers, foreign immigrants and native criollos, male dominance and ram-
pant prostitution—also provoked contestations and precipitated power
negotiations though creole vernacular expressive forms. Covert behaviors
subversively masked dissent and generated resistance to values and social
practices imposed from above.

    Like the exchange between Mosche and Daniel depicted by Borges in
his portrayal of truco, masking in Argentine creole culture is also carefully
calibrated in real life through various forms of Creole Talk. Because audiences, too, are usually insiders in such cases (knowingly participating in the
covert behaviors), the actual trick of most Creole Talk resides in the ironic
and deliberate contrast between apparent and intended meanings. This

masking (camouflage, dissimulation, obfuscation, and the like)—whether real or figurative—assists and assures the transition or shifts between two disparate sociocultural orders.

Yet, while insiders find Creole Talk candid, honest, frank, revelatory, delightfully oblique, and so forth (and therefore employ it as a social cue to elicit solidarity),[27] those "outside" the creole system find such talk circular, perplexing, deceitfully vague, and, as a consequence, unruly, ultimately suspect. To be sure, like resistance fighters who scramble their code to confuse the enemy, Creole Talk is usually intentionally and subversively *designed* to "obscure as it reveals," to actually *be* "noisy" (as in the game of truco). The art of camouflage in creole cultures (as with camouflage in nature) is nothing less than the art of survival.[28]

Analogous to the linguistic shifts into actual Creole languages in other creole societies, Creole Talk (like voicing creolity) in Argentina also signals a change in code. As with the latter, Creole Talk is called on to communicate intimacy, trust, directness, candor—"insider talk." Furthermore, its capacity for frankness also makes it readily subject to the more elemental and vulgar aspects of such communications: the use of gross insults and verbal abuse to tease, swear, boast, or complain about life.[29] Similarly, creole humor—where so many social and cultural tensions are negotiated—is also rife with Creole Talk. So pervasive to certain kinds of joke-telling is Creole Talk that everyone in Argentina acknowledges the existence of a *humor criollo* (creole humor).

Indeed, as at the card table, Argentine criollo culture is everywhere saturated with double discourses and counter discourses expressed dialogically through gestures and talk. What is valued in such instances is not so much which cards one has proverbially been dealt, but what one can do with them through the power of the word. Both in truco and in life, Argentines recognize the significance of *viveza criolla*, which translates not simply as "creole cleverness/wit," but as a native, creole intelligence (cultural knowledge) that "gets" what is going on in the simultaneous use of two or more cultural registers. Like "cunning squared" in truco, creole cultural exchanges don't simply operate on the assumption that "I know you know" or "you know I know," but on squared increments of astuteness that know "you know I know you know I know." This "knowing" further knows that in a creole setting there is always the potential for two-way distrust. As a result, nothing and no one is taken very literally, since all know full well that nothing is ever what it seems. Those who regularly lose in truco, and in life, too often require precision and are "had" or trapped or tricked by Creole Talk.

As participants in Creole Talk simultaneously mediate and differentiate between cultures through conscious artifice, they employ numerous
devices both to bridge differences and to resist cultural crossings: verbal
play, irony, understatement, satire, double-talk, parody, circumlocution,
ambiguity, reversals, puns, and the like. Whether improvising or repeating
set verbal forms, participants in Creole Talk claim power and status (no
matter how insignificant) through their *desafíos* (challenges), insinuations,
and verbal perspicacity. By "recasting" language (and thus defying verbal
and social standards as they "re-script" culture through talk), participants
in Creole Talk sublimate the conflicts of difference and playfully engage in
the recreation of a local creole poetics. The aesthetic pleasure and the cultural bonding generated by this creole poetics is just as central to everyday
life as the social, political, and cultural work Creole Talk accomplishes.

Creole Talk lends itself more readily to oral communication than to
writing since the improvisational quality of Creole Talk is more easily
negotiated orally than on the page. In fact, the written word, particularly
in an "official" guise, runs the risk of appearing too "fixed" and thereby less
likely to be trusted—not because it is *literate*, but because its being ink
on paper makes it *literally* less negotiable. Consequently, a "man's word"
and interactions negotiated face-to-face have traditionally held greater
creole value in Argentina than have written documents. Indeed, despite
all the playful disrespect in Creole Talk, the honor of one's word, and other
"manly" qualities such as self-respect and the courage to speak out, are
celebrated aspects of Argentine creolity.

Nevertheless, despite the directness, immediacy, and flexibility lent by
orality, extraordinary written examples of Creole Talk have been produced,
most notably in Argentina's national epic poem *Martín Fierro*. This book-
length text, written by José Hernández and published in 1872 (as Argentina began looking to Europe for models of "civilization"), offers a literary
version of the oral Creole Talk characteristic of gauchos from the Argentine countryside. The poem follows the traditional oral form of a *payada*
(improvised rhymed verses, recited and sung to the slow strumming of
a guitar). Performed either by a lone singer improvising on topics called
out by the audience or by dueling improvisers competing with each other,
payadas could last hours or even days (see Moya 1959). To be the winner
of a payada was tantamount to becoming a local hero, the attendant status
and respect often earning one an expansive reputation.

The epic is narrated in the first-person voice of the main character (the
gaucho Martín Fierro) with occasional reflections by other characters—and

by the author himself. Sometimes, however, Hernández's voice and Fierro's become (con)fused during the poetic narrative and commentary. Thus the author speaks not only *for* gauchos, but also *as* a gaucho and *like* a gaucho (in a gauchesque language). The very opening stanza could well be the voice of Fierro or Hernández:

Aquí me pongo a cantar	Here I'll sit and sing
Al compás de la vigüela	To the beat of my guitar.
Que el hombre que lo desvela	'Cause a man who's kept awake
Una pena estrordinaria,	By extraordinary sorrow,
Como el ave solitaria	Like a lonely bird
Con el cantar se consuela	Consoles himself with song.

(Hernández [1872] 1953, 5)

Not unlike the cards in truco, the music in *payadas* takes second place to the words. Like truco, but on a grander scale, payada contests truly test each man's cleverness, imagination, ability with words, and worldliness. Martínez Estrada concluded that truco is "a minor version of the payada and a superior version of criollo politics" ([1940] 2001, 192). In any case, the *payador's* quickness and wit, like that of the card player, are essential for improvising verses in response to one's opponent. To linger is to lose the payada, thus compromising one's pride and social standing as a man-of-words. Not coincidentally, José Hernández on more than one occasion compares Fierro's payada to a truco match. The singer says:

Me siento en el plan de un bajo	I'll sit here in this hollow
A cantar un argumento;	To sing my story;
Como si soplara el viento	As if the wind were blowing
Hago tiritar los pastos.	I'll make the grass shiver.
Con oros, copas y bastos	My thoughts play
Juega allí mi pensamiento.	With *oros, copas* and *bastos*
	[truco card suits].

(Hernández [1872] 1953, 68)

Although Fierro's verses in this national epic sing his blues, they are as humorous, insulting, tender, and playful as they are serious and critical of the dominant system in a country where people such as the rural gaucho protagonist (together with his friends and family) were discriminated against and persecuted. The critical truths waged against church and state that Hernández (himself a man of politics elected to Congress as well as a man of letters) expressed in *Martín Fierro* could only have been received with such popularity among readers at the time of its publication (and even today) because of the solidarity elicited by the poem's playful, if frank, Creole Talk. To an outsider, of course, it would be rather curious, indeed, that such a celebrated national epic would be rife with critical comments so boldly disapproving of "the Nation."

Perhaps the best-known example of creole verbal play in *Martín Fierro* is the exchange between the gaucho and the *negra* (the Black woman [as she is referred to in the poem]), who, in a pivitol incident, is the target of the protagonist's insulting criollo humor, which indirectly also serves as a provocation and challenge leveled at her man, the famous *negro* (the Black man) in the poem. The incident occurs one evening when Fierro, having nothing better to do, decides to go to a *milonga*[30] (a gathering, a dance) and proceeds to get drunk. This puts Fierro in a meddling, provocative mood, which leads to his double entendre upon the *negra's* entrance:

Al ver llegar la morena	As she came in I saw
Que no hacía caso a naides	She wasn't lookin' at nobody,
Le dije con la mamúa:	So being drunk I said,
"Va . . . ca . . . yendo gente al baile."	"Cow . . . ming to the dance?"
(Hernández 1974, 50)	

The manipulation of words, which (by stressing and delaying a syllable in Spanish) moves from "*va cayendo gente al baile*" (people are dropping into the dance) to "*vaca . . . yendo*" (literally, "cow [is] going," but better rendered as "cow . . . ming"), leaves no question regarding Fierro's *intención* (a notion akin to signifyin' in African American culture), so common in Creole Talk. Clearly, his is an insult cloaked in a pun, but the woman gets the message:

La negra entendió la cosa	She got the point
Y no tardó en contestarme	And answered me right back,
Mirándome como a perro:	Lookin' me over like I was a dog:
"Más vaca será su madre."	"A bigger cow is your mother."
(Hernández 1974, 50)	

Her insulting comeback referencing Fierro's "mamma" (not unlike "yo momma" in American "Black Talk") also makes *her* intention perfectly plain (see Smitherman 1994).

The *negra's* response sets up Fierro for yet another retort or challenge. Naturally, her man is angered by Fierro's words. So, adding insult to injury, the gaucho tells him: "Por . . . rudo que un hombre sea / nunca se enoja por esto" (No matter how fuzzy-headed a man is / he never gets mad over something like this). Here the pun is on *por rudo* (no matter how crude, how unrefined) and *porrudo* (tangled hair, alluding to the Black man's wooly hair). The verbal duel—perhaps not sufficiently subtle or indirect enough, particularly given Fierro's drunkenness—ends with an actual knife duel that sends the *negro* to his grave. For this crime Martín Fierro is pursued by the police, remaining a fugitive to the end of the poem. A second part, or sequel, was added to *Martín Fierro* by Hernández in 1879, in which the Black man's brother meets up with Fierro to avenge the negro's death. In part 2, however, the challenge—another duel—is carried out not with knives but with guitars: in a *payada* contest or counterpoint (*contrapunto*) between the two. Indeed, these verbal contests were often used to settle scores in Argentine traditional culture, thus avoiding bloodshed while retaining a sense of honor and justice (see Cara-Walker 1986).

The punning, humor, wit, and indirection in Fierro's talk are not random or unique. To be sure, the creole verbal art in the poem is modeled on the traditional Creole Talk that Hernández internalized from hearing the talk by gauchos and *peones* (farm hands) at his family *estancia* (ranch) in the outskirts of Buenos Aires.

Reflecting on his own fieldwork from several decades ago (still relevant today), Ismael Moya offers examples of Creole Talk that parallel the verbal pattern of Fierro's provocation at the milonga. "In many towns of the province of Buenos Aires," he says, it is the custom to "disfigure a word in order to give it a picaresque meaning" (Moya 1972, 80). Usually there is some physical distance between the person who utters the phrase and the receiver. The latter, explains Moya, often "doesn't hear the alternating syllables because the speaker covers them up with a weak stress," so he answers to what "he thought were words said in good faith" (80). Consequently, for example, when "*¡Salud!*" is accompanied by the respective gesture, it is either a greeting, a toast, or a blessing. But by voicing a similar-sounding word—"*¡Coludo!*"—and putting extra stress on the second syllable so the last one is almost inaudible, the speaker appears to be rendering a nicety ("Hello!" or "Greetings!") while actually voicing an insult ("Big-ass(ed)!").[31]

Essentially harmless for the most part, the pleasure in these verbal distortions is the simple exercise of outsmarting or playfully putting down one's target through verbal trickery. If the listener is sharp and catches on, he or she can, of course, "play back." Otherwise, he or she is made to appear the fool in front of others.

Another pattern for these double entendres involves beginning a sentence with a potentially offensive comment but resolving it by "undoing" it with an ending that alters the original intention (*intención*). *"¡Qué tormenta!"* (What a storm!), a person might comment on seeing someone, quickly adding *"la del jueves!"* (we had on Thursday). Similarly, one might call a Black woman *"Negra"* (Black, dark) but readily amend the presumed offense by adding *"suerte la del pobre"* (is the fate of the poor). These provocative wordplays are not limited to racial insults or mockery. The assumption is that anyone can be a target for some reason or other. For example, the speaker might call a short man *"Bajito"* (the equivalent of American English "Shorty" but also, literally, a low bank or gully) and then amend the slight by adding *"que junta agua"* (where water collects) (Moya 1972, 80, 85).

In a similar spirit, playfully insulting nicknames are improvised for the sheer, apparently innocent delight in, and display of, cleverness (*viveza*). These go beyond the common, affectionate, popularly used nicknames in many cultures. In fact, they are often less about the person "named" than a mere pretext for the display of verbal wit. Someone with a limp, for instance, might be referred to as *"Ay, que me undo"* (Oops, I'm sinking). Another, with a defect in vision that causes the person's eyes to look upward, seemingly scanning the sky, might be called *"Busca nidos"* (Nest finder). I've heard, for example, of a dark-skinned womanizer who was called by the name of a local, dark-colored bird, an analogy naturally appropriate for someone dark. The "hidden" reference, however, arises from the bird's being known for laying its eggs in the nests of other birds or occupying the nest outright; hence, the more significant similarity—the behavior of the man, who habitually occupied someone else's bed. We see in this last example a version of "cunning squared." These types of verbal double entendres and intended equivocations also manifest themselves in the Creole Talk of *piropos* (flattery, verbal flirtations) delivered by men when passing women in the street. Also awash with *viveza criolla* is Lunfardo (the urban slang of Buenos Aires), employed in all manner of Creole Talk (see Cara-Walker 1983, 273–297).

Insults, insinuations, mockery, and provocations, however, are not only said about, or directed to, others. Exalting oneself by boasting is a no less common "affront" in Creole Talk. Most frequent are the boasts that center around machismo. An example is the bloated "Donde hay un gaucho hay dos machos" (Where there's a gaucho, there're two machos). The sexual pomposity is clear, as is the *intención* or "intended bravado." By the same token, the statement is (thinly) veiled in the proverbial dimensions that celebrate the ideals and qualities inherent in the "manly" role of being a gaucho in the *criollo* Argentine setting: integrity, courage, and loyal friendship. Echoing these gaucho bravados, their urban counterparts in tango lyrics are also resplendent with such boasts, mockery, *humor criollo*, and Creole Talk (see Cara-Walker 1983, 155–165).

In his essay about horse-cart inscriptions, Borges offers additional examples of this kind. Long before bumper stickers were invented (when horse-drawn carts from the city outskirts made their way through traffic), these vehicles sported written witticisms in classic Creole Talk style. Many of them were simply tongue-in-cheek names, at once boastful and understated: "*El vencedor*" (The conqueror), for example. Others were merely boastful declarations: "*Donde cenizas quedan fuego hubo*" (Where only ashes remain, there was once fire). And back in the days when fruits, vegetables, milk, and the like were sold door-to-door, "*El preferido del barrio*" (The favorite in the 'hood), a boast carefully inscribed in his cart, made patent the driver's claim (Borges 1974, 149).

Such flirtatious, often spicy declarations regarding one's sexual prowess or seductiveness were certainly not limited to men only. In the case of *relaciones* (verses recited during Argentine creole folk dances such as the *chacarera* or *gato*), one might hear a series of rhymed strophes (impossible to translate with the same flair) being recited back and forth—playfully, flirtatiously, provocatively—between men and women. One example suffices:

El: He:
De vicio venís pitando   No use showing off
Florcita de garabato   Little scribbled flower
No por tu bonita cara   Not because of your pretty face
Voy a volver cada rato.   Will I keep coming back.

Ella: She:
Yo no digo que soy linda   I'm not saying that I'm pretty
Ni soy flor de garabato   Nor am I a scribbled flower
Pero tengo una cosita   But I've got a little something
Y has de volver cada rato.   That will keep you coming back.
(Coluccio 1981, 577)

In the case of Martín Fierro, the singer's machismo and his ability with words is clearly stated in the eponymous epic, as his provocation in the following stanza (a literary reworking of an anonymous couplet) demonstrates:

Yo soy toro en mi rodeo	I'm a bull in my corral
Y torazo en rodeo ajeno;	And a bigger one in someone else's;
Siempre me tuve por güeno	I always thought I was pretty good,
Y si me quieren probar	And if others want to try me
Salgan otros a cantar	Let 'em come out and sing
Y veremos quien es menos.	And we'll see who is second best.
(Hernández [1872] 1953, 7)	

The payada's *desafío* (challenge) is a symbolic invitation to combat. Verbal duels, therefore, were serious matters, even when "playful." Sharp, cutting words could lead to all-too-literal knife wounds. Conversely, payadas and other verbal forms (such as the more urban *milongas*) were designed to sublimate violence and thereby achieve the epitome of Creole Talk (Cara-Walker 1986, 283–284).

It makes sense, then, that the poem opens with Fierro/Hernández celebrating the ability to "sing" (to versify) and that many of the stanzas that follow proudly boast about a man's courage and his ability with words—a synonymous pairing in the Argentine creole ethos. Clearly expressing his need (and right) to have his say—to have a voice in society—and expertly flaunting his verbal skills, the epic's protagonist declares about himself:

Mas ande otro criollo pasa	But wherever a criollo walks
Martín Fierro ha de pasar;	Martín Fierro passes too;
Nada lo hace recular,	Nothing makes him back away,
Ni los fantasmas lo espantan,	Nor ghosts scare him off,
Y dende que todos cantan	And since everyone sings
Yo también quiero cantar.	I, too, intend to sing.
(Hernández [1872] 1953, 6)	

Surely, the case has been made that *Martín Fierro* is an accomplished example of Creole Talk. The poem's wide circulation—among illiterate gauchos and educated elites alike—following its publication certifies its success. Jesús María Pereyra, for example, tells of an illiterate criollo who could recite long passages from *Martín Fierro* and who, when asked how and where he had learned them, explained that "back in the day" certain people who knew how to read wandered the countryside with Hernández's book in their pocket, teaching and leading groups in prayer. "After saying the rosary, we would turn to *Martín Fierro* with equal seriousness. The teacher would read it, and would repeat it. It was like another rosary," Pereyra reported, describing the larger lesson as follows: "We had in the prayers a guide for heaven and in *Martín Fierro* a sure guide for living our present life on earth" (Fernández Latour de Botas 1969, 33–34).

Martín Fierro continues to be required reading in Argentine schools today. And though few people can recite the epic at length, most Argentines can produce from memory particular stanzas, memorable lines, and episodes from the book, often quoting from it to make a point. The poem, a model of creole aesthetics and creole values, argues on behalf of a subaltern, disenfranchised portion of the native population and offers a counter-discourse to authority even into the twenty-first century, particularly during moments of Argentine national crises.

Yet, despite the poem's literary prominence, *Martín Fierro* holds a curious place in Latin American letters. On the one hand it is celebrated as Argentina's national epic poem, while on the other it is relegated to (and thus in part marginalized as) a genre of "gauchesque" literature, set apart (as are other so-called folkloric works) from those written in keeping with the Western canon. Consequently, critical readings of *Martín Fierro* (and other gauchesque works by Argentine and Uruguayan writers) have more to gain from insights offered by creolization studies and have yet to be treated in dialogue with the larger dimensions of Creole Talk that permeate Argentine culture and define a creole aesthetics.[32]

In his own search for an Argentine (criollo) voice, Jorge Luis Borges understood the need to move away from the fixed, rather limiting (and paradoxically "foreignizing") conventions of local color. "The Argentine cult of local color," he declared not without irony, "is a recent European cult which the nationalists ought to reject as foreign" (Borges [1932] 1962, 181).

He shrewdly goes on to say in "The Argentine Writer and Tradition" (originally published in 1932) that in the Koran, the Arabian book *par excellence*, there are no camels. Whether apocryphal or not, he employs this notion to eliminate any doubt regarding the authenticity of the Koran. "It was written by Mohammed, and Mohammed, as an Arab, had no reason to know that camels were especially Arabian; for him," Borges explains, "they were a part of reality, he had no reason to emphasize them." In contrast, however, "the first thing a falsifier, a tourist, an Arab nationalist would do is have a surfeit of camels, caravans of camels, on every page." Just as Mohammed "knew he could be an Arab without camels," Borges reasons, "we Argentines . . . can believe in the possibility of being Argentine without abounding in local color" ([1932] 1962, 181).

Borges looked to *Martín Fierro* for inspiration and as a model of criollo writing that twentieth-century writers might emulate, knowing all the while that what Hernández had so brilliantly achieved in the nineteenth century could not be reproduced in the same fashion a century later (any more than the *Quijote* could be written again by Pierre Menard in Borges's short story about this fictive character). Moreover, he understood that an Argentine creole voice did not rest merely on the flavor of local words or the simple mention of gauchos or other native elements. His own experience made this clear when he erred by buying a *Diccionario de argentinismos* and making the "awful mistake" of "working in all the words I found in that dictionary," only to produce a book that no one could be expected to understand or to enjoy (Borges 1964, 9–10). What *Martín Fierro* taught him, instead, was the conceptual importance of Creole Talk for a creole poetics.

At an early age, as his 1926 essay titled "El tamaño de mi esperanza" (The dimensions of my hope) attests, Borges embarked on a quest to find a way of voicing creolity by moving beyond mere nostalgia, beyond static rhetorical and cultural clichés, and by searching for a larger scheme where *criollismo*, instead of being relegated to the margins, would speak to and about the world:

I don't seek *progresismo* [progressivism] or *criollismo* in the usual sense of these words. The former is a subjection to becoming almost North American or almost European, an obstinate wanting to be almost another; the latter, which before had been a word of action . . . is today a word of nostalgia. . . . No great fervor fills either of them and I am sorry for *criollismo*. It is true that to broaden the meaning of that term—today it is often equivalent to a mere *gauchismo*—would be perhaps closest to my enterprise. *Criollismo*, yes, but a *criollismo* that speaks to the world of the individual, of God and of death. Let's see if someone can help me find it. (Borges 1926, 9–10)

His endeavor embraced an ethnographic approach: he took stock of his mother's criollo way of speaking; he sought out famous *payadores* such as Luis García, neighborhood *compadres* like Nicanor Paredes, and early tango composers who wrote lyrics and played music in a creole style; he listened to traditional milonga verses and collected oral stories about criollo life in Buenos Aires and its surroundings (Cara-Walker 1986). Indeed, he examined the art of Creole Talk closely in the noise of truco and the understatements of horse-cart inscriptions. And so, both by allusion—as speakers do when hablando en criollo—and by incorporating devices and dynamics of Creole Talk into his work, Borges achieved a discourse fully integrated with the nuances of Argentine creolity. His creole poetics emerges out of rhizome-like interconnections from Argentine vernacular life, history, politics, and traditional art, permitting him to speak to (and of) the world in a native voice. As he himself observes in the final line of his essay on truco: "And so, from truco's labyrinths of colored pasteboard, we approach metaphysics" (Borges 1984, 112).

Conclusion

Given the nation's European façade, absence of a plantation culture, and lack of a creole language, the exceptionalism of Argentine creole culture offers an interesting case for the study of creolization and the dialogic relationship of language and creolity. It presents scholars with the challenge of locating and (inter)relating the dynamics of creole verbal art, creole discourse, and an Argentine creole poetics. It reveals that rather than inherently residing in an actual creole language or specific genres or in some particular "pocket" of culture, the creole aspects of talk can be constituted and performed across all dimensions of creole culture. To participate in this apparently "invisible" but pervasive sphere, this covert and ever-emergent expressive domain, requires a creole intelligence (cultural knowledge) and an affective (as opposed to sentimental) comprehension of Argentine creole culture that enables participants to improvise a counter-discourse vis-à-vis "standard talk." Whether engaging in the full play and artifice of Creole Talk or simply invoking creolity by hablando en criollo, engaging in creole discourse eschews complacency, enacts selective disrespect of authority, displays courage, elicits solidarity, establishes intimacy, and celebrates the aesthetic pleasures of verbal art. Though other nonverbal expressive forms also comprise Argentine creolity, the art of talk uniquely illustrates the creole paradox inherent in the interplay of appearance, masking, and intention.

Only by learning the codes of local creolity can we accurately access the multivocality of creole discourse and thus profitably read both the folk behavior of everyday life and the masterpieces of international creole authors. Only so may we also gain access to the politics and poetics that engender and perpetuate local creolity.[33]

As Martín Fierro declares, only those "in the know" will perceive the full *intention* of Creole Talk, while others will hear only sounds, hear noise:

Yo que en el campo he nacido,	I who was born in the countryside,
Digo que mis cantos son	Say that my songs [verses] are
Para los unos . . . sonidos,	For some . . . sounds,
Y para los otros . . . intención.	For others . . . *intention.*
(Hernández [1872] 1953, 94–94)	

Notes

1. I wish to thank Bernard F. Stehle for perspicaciously suggesting the semantically apt "voicing creolity" as a quasi idiomatic translation of *hablando en criollo*. This is a revised version of the essay originally published in the *Journal of American Folklore* 116, no. 459 (Winter 2003): 36–56. I wish to express my gratitude to Robert Baron, Phyllis Gorfain, and Diana Grossman Kahn for their generous and constructive comments on drafts of this essay and to thank Bernard F. Stehle for his expert editing. All translations are mine, unless otherwise noted.

2. I distinguish between "native" and "analytical" categories, following Ben-Amos (1976).

3. In truco, each player is dealt three cards, which are played out in tricks; Points are also scored for holding combinations of cards of the same suit. It is possible to bet extra points on who has the best combination or will win the tricks; the bluffing, talking, and joking that go with this are an important part of the game. Truco is usually played by four or more players in paired partnerships.

4. No ethnography has yet been written (to my knowledge) on the game of truco. Martínez Estrada's ([1940] 2001) and Borges's (1974) reflections are two of the very few texts that attempt to describe and characterize the game in light of Argentine culture. My own observations during my fieldwork over the years (begun in the 1970s) and the comments collected from field collaborators coincide in spirit with the remarks cited here.

5. Popular booklets and pamphlets containing traditional truco poems and rhymes that serve as models to be memorized or improvised upon by truco players can be

bought at kiosks and corner bookstores in Buenos Aires. Truco sayings and other verbal art related to the game are also learned from oral tradition.

6. Coded into this little quatrain, the player tells us what he holds: three cards corresponding to the *palo* suit in the Spanish card deck. The literal translation of *palo* is "a stick, wood, log," or (in this case) a "post" for a fence—here, made from wood from the *ñandubay* tree.

7. See the following Website for detailed rules regarding truco: http://www.pagat .com/put/truco.html (accessed February 15, 2010).

8. For a brief history of the game and explanation of its name, see Suárez 1988, 3–5. Apparently, "truco" comes from the Portuguese, meaning "trap," "trick," "cheating."

9. Although a prevalent notion in Argentine culture, *viveza criolla* has not been fully explored. Mafud's 1973 study offers some insight.

10. For a full display of illustrated truco gestures, see Suárez 1988.

11. Proverbial expressions, tango lyrics, and popular culture in general make constant reference to the game.

12. Prior to his essay on truco, Borges had already published his famous poem "El truco" in his collection *Fervor de Buenos Aires*, 1923.

13. For a discussion on *milonga* expressive forms and Borges's interest in this musical style and lyrics, see Cara-Walker 1986. In his essay "La canción del barrio" Borges writes: "The milonga is one of the great conversational genres of Buenos Aires; truco is the other" (1984, 89).

14. My fieldwork over many years in Córdoba and, more recently (2009), in Mendoza, Argentina, reveals that truco continues to be played on a regular basis and remains a popular pastime. Buenos Aires residents also report engaging regularly in truco matches.

15. See, for example, C.L.R. James's study on cricket (1993).

16. No creole language has been charted in Argentina (see Hancock 1971). And although some pidgin-like forms and "hybridized" or "transition" languages have been identified in the region, such as Fragnol (made up of French and Spanish) and more notably Cocoliche (an Italian Spanish mode of speech), no actual creolized language emerged in the Río de la Plata (River Plate) area (see Cara-Walker 1987). "Bozal" (used to portray the talk of Afro-Argentines) and "gauchesque" (a literary version of gaucho speech) have been rendered primarily for literary purposes, neither of them constituting an actual spoken or written creole language in Argentina. No ethnography (to my knowledge) has been done on the practice of *hablar en criollo*.

17. Directed by Louis J. Gasnier, Paramount Films.

18. For the text of the entire speech see http://www.casarosada.gov.ar/index .php?option=com_content&task=view&id=1287 (accessed February 15, 2010).

19. I would like to thank Melisa Wortman (the Argentine woman who received this e-mail in the fall of 2009) for sharing it with me.

20. The Inca Garcilaso (himself a mestizo born of Inca royalty and Spanish nobility) candidly reported in his *Royal Commentaries of Peru (1609–1617)* that the

word *criollo/a* was invented to discriminate against those born in the New World, distinct from those who came from Europe and Africa, since the latter "are held in greater honor and considered to be of higher rank because they were born in their own country, while their children were born in a strange land." Furthermore, the Inca pointed out, "The parents are *offended* if they themselves are called criollos" (in Avalle-Arce 1964, 255–256, my emphasis). Also see Mörner (1967) for charts indicating the social status of criollos vis-à-vis other social and ethnic groups.

21. Criollos belonging to *familias de abolengo* (families of nobility or upper-class descent) naturally enjoyed greater privilege than common criollos. It was not uncommon for descendants of bluebloods to discriminate against lower-ranking criollos. Upper-class criollos constituted much of the New World "aristocracy."

22. Interestingly, the gaucho's woman (partner) is called "criolla" rather than "gaucha" or, more affectionately, "criollita."

23. The statesman Juan Alberdi argued that the country could afford no delay in its "conquest of the desert" and thus advocated a resolution of Argentina's demographic emptiness as well as other political and economic interests by opening the nation's doors to outsiders.

24. Buenos Aires had a higher African and Afro-Argentine population than the rest of the country. Nevertheless, cities like Córdoba and other larger centers had a significant Black population during the colonial period.

25. For a scholarly study of prostitution in Buenos Aires, see Guy (1991). For a more anecdotal account regarding the White slave trade as it operated between Europe and Buenos Aires, see Londres (1928).

26. See Arrom 1971, 15.

27. Compare with Grimshaw 1971, 437.

28. Writer and critic Edouard Glissant notes that in producing creole discourse the storyteller's object is "to obscure as he reveals." He must make language "noisy" and ambiguous (not unlike the language at the truco table). "Noise is essential to speech," writes Glissant; "Din is discourse" (1989, 123) This notion of opacity, obfuscation, encoding, contradiction, camouflage, dissimulation, and masking in recent Caribbean literature and cultural criticism echoes Borges's assessment of creole culture and verbal art in Argentina, articulated in his 1930 essay on truco.

29. Compare with Alleyne 1973, 210.

30. *Milonga* is a multigeneric term that identifies a type of traditional verbal art as well as certain Argentine musical and dance forms. It is also used to refer to gatherings, parties, and celebrations. See Cara-Walker 1986, 281–282.

31. For more examples of this, see Moya 1972, 80, 85.

32. Josefina Ludmer's (1988) excellent book is a step in the right direction.

33. Beyond the Argentine context, the notion of "Creole Talk" might apply to similar phenomena in various Latin American, Caribbean, African American, and possibly other cultural areas. Such may be the case with the Cuban *choteo*, the Mexican *pullas*, the *albur*, and many other examples: *el relajo, la bachata, la joda,* to name a few.

Villes, Poèmes

The Postwar Routes of Caribbean Creolization

—J. MICHAEL DASH

La ville est, au sens fort, 'poétisée' par le sujet: il l'a
fabriquée pour son usage propre . . . il impose a l'ordre
externe de la ville sa loi de consommateur d'espace.
— MICHEL DE CERTEAU, *L'invention du quotidien*

In his 1958 study of Haitian Vodou Alfred Métraux made the following observation: "People are prone to suppose that the purest and richest traditions are to be found in the remotest valleys. The little I was able to see of rural Voodoo convinced me that it was poor in its ritual compared to Voodoo of the capital. Simplicity of rite is not always a guarantee of antiquity. It is often the result of ignorance and neglect" (1972, 61). The conclusion of this celebrated Swiss ethnographer that Haitian popular religion was more dynamic and sophisticated in Port-au-Prince as opposed to the Haitian countryside is a startling one given the fact that Haitian Vodou has always been associated with remote spaces and atavistic impulses. It is equally surprising given that his research was conducted in 1944, a time when a conservative identity politics in Haiti had unproblematically fashioned rural Vodou as the wellspring of authentic Haitianness. Métraux's discreet critique of the mythification of religious authenticity points to the larger issue of the appropriation of rural landscapes as sites of cultural authenticity and national identity. In Haiti and elsewhere, territorializing metaphors of pristine wilderness are at the base of concepts of fixed homelands, dreams of return and the imaginative recovery of stable origins.

Métraux's argument is that urban spaces are more useful sites of enriching cultural encounter than exclusionary locales of containment and homogeneity in the remote and primordial wilderness. From the 1940s he seemed to be suggesting that the margins of urban space are not zones of alienation and exile but ideal creolizing sites of modern transnational contact outside of narrow identitarian politics. Métraux also is making a larger point about how popular ritual is meant to be understood. He argues that it is the "dynamic aspect" of Vodou that should be studied. For him it was "a religious system born fairly recently from a fusion of many different elements" and therefore should not be investigated in terms of cultural survivals and a "search for origins" (Métraux 1972, 61). Métraux is not interested in predetermined meanings and cultural monoliths but in the enriching cultural entanglements of the present.

This observation regarding Haitian popular religion was made at a time when Métraux's friend, the French surrealist writer and ethnographer Michel Leiris, who was also in Haiti, made similar observations regarding the spatial dynamic nature of Caribbean cultural encounter. For Leiris what was remarkable about the Caribbean was that it spawned a culture of intersections and encounters whose predominant sign was that of the urban crossroads. Caribbean "ground" was not located in remote interiors but at the destabilizing intersections of roadways where people and vehicles pass constantly. In his 1948 lecture, "Antilles et poésie des carrefours," he points to what he calls the "poetic" importance of urban contact and collision in Caribbean culture. "What I find seductive first of all in the expression 'crossroads' is that it is taken from the vocabulary of the roadway. Nothing more down to earth, more everyday, than the crossing of roads and streets that we call a crossroads . . . a place which seems to me to be nothing short of the symbol of poetry itself" (Leiris 1992, 71). The crossroads becomes, for Leiris, a transgressive space that allows for the clash of familiar and unfamiliar, which produces the poetry of the unpredictable. The destabilizing of the subject in this zone of convergence exposes him or her to the poetic beauty, the magical potential in the everyday and the previously familiar. Leiris seems to be suggesting a new way not only of looking at travel and cultural contact but of pursuing an ethnography of non-native societies that lack a monolithic essence but are modern, protean, and diverse.

The unsettling space of the crossroads, in which no symbolic order can permanently establish itself, is the zone of risk for the subject forever at the mercy of the assault of unpredictable reality. Culture and space are intimately connected in Leiris's crossroads poetry, which he imagines in terms of the Spanish ritual of the bullfight in which the horns of the unpredictable bull always threaten to catch the traveler/matador by surprise. ". . . The imperturbable posture, on one hand, in which the matador is frozen (all of whose movements must appear duly controlled), the frenzy, on the other hand, which is the nature of the bull with his horns constantly in search of prey" (Leiris 1992, 75). The beauty of this encounter is the disruptive force of the real, which always escapes discursive control. As opposed to his earlier African journey, in which there was no possibility of participation, Leiris is fascinated by the integration of the spectator in his encounter with the Caribbean. It is for this reason that he praises so highly the participatory element in Haitian religious ritual in which the detachment of the spectator is impossible and there are no preordained scripts. The highpoint of such religious drama is the "indispensable participation of the spectator in the action, the necessity for him to experience even the threat of the action" (Leiris 1992, 83). The subject integrated into the ritual and the resulting temporary loss of identity in this journey into a world of cultural fusion has for Leiris a poetic charge. "Beauty cannot be produced in any place other than a crossroads, where there is a convergence, in a surprising unity, of the most contradictory elements, where all that is put into play is presented as a frenzied equilibrium, like a geometric pattern imposed on a sudden violence" (Leiris 1992, 84). The violence of the shock of displacement, the spectator's integration into in the everyday, the unfolding, defamilarizing nature of the real are presented as characteristic of a mobile, composite culture that can be fixed in terms of no monolithic symbolic order. Caribbean cultural diversity offers "the rarest and most dazzling mixture that a European like myself can taste, one who is intensely hungry for a more savory and stimulating kind of nourishment capable of pushing his imagination to its highest potential" (Leiris 1992, 70). Direct, sensual contact is what feeds the imagination, not just surreal games that privilege the gratuitous and the useless. What is striking in Leiris's idiosyncratic ethnography is the way in which he situates the poetry of colliding elements in terms of the lived, the routine, and the everyday. The creolizing process in Caribbean culture is located in terms of the complicating, destabilizing way in which a local community encounters the everyday.

On the streets, vehicles and shop signs are not anonymously utilitarian but emphasize the poetic in the banal. The concrete is never mastered but is always a little opaque, a little unfamiliar in societies in which a new kind of society is emerging, "less strictly utilitarian than Western-type societies, in which all human needs will find satisfaction, not only in terms of the physical but in the need we feel to feed the imagination" (Leiris 1992, 86). The ever renewable, inventive attitude toward reality that Leiris associates with creolizing social forces means that there is no secret code to understanding the real, no originary meaning that fixes the present. While visiting the ruins of Saint Pierre, he sees the statue of a woman that represents the town rising, phoenix-like, from its ashes. But a woman passing by tells him that this is not the case and relates a story of death by fire and water, which completely replaces the official version. For Leiris it is this spontaneously invented reimagining of the real, the sense that absolute meaning is always suspended, in flux, which make the Antilles into a creolizing crossroads. This is not a poetics of authenticity but of reinvention. It certainly brings to mind Métraux's perspective on the Vodou religion not as the enacting of an immutable script but the aesthetic of renewal that makes each performance new.

This idea of dynamic renewal has become the hallmark of a creolizing poetics and can be identified in non-francophone Caribbean writers such as Derek Walcott, who similarly imagines an unpredictable, reversible Creole universe. In the same way that a simple St. Lucian fisherman can become a Homeric character in his poem "Omeros" or Egypt can be transplanted to Tobago, the mythic past of Uttar Pradesh vibrates in the banality of Exchange Village. As he would later explain, "From Ramayana to Anabasis, from Guadeloupe to Trinidad, all the archeology of fragments lying around, from the broken African kingdoms, from the crevasses of Canton, from Syria and Lebanon, vibrating *not under the earth* but in our raucous, demotic streets" (Walcott 1992, 23; italics mine).

The Caribbean's fragments of cultures are not, therefore, preserved "under the earth" but constantly reanimated in an extravagant street theater "in our raucous, demotic streets." As Walcott, somewhat surprisingly for a poet who is deeply associated with the pastoral and an Adamic recovery of Caribbean landscape, states in *The Nobel Lecture*: "A culture, we all know, is made by its cities." Consequently, the "raucous streets" become an exemplary site of cultural recreation in Walcott's Antillean poetics. It is the city that best exemplifies the imaginative excess that he idealizes as a "ferment without a history": "And here they are, all in a single Caribbean city, Port of Spain, the sum of history, Froude's 'non-people.' A downtown babel of shop signs and streets, mongrelized, polyglot, a ferment without a history, like heaven. Because that is what such a city is, in the New World, a writer's heaven" (Walcott 1992, 11). In this city "more exciting than [James] Joyce's Dublin," Walcott privileges the walker as the figure that gives new poetic meaning to a city space that constantly solicits his or her imagination. Mystery is everywhere in the familiar and the everyday. Like Leiris, who appreciates the spontaneous inventiveness of the female passerby in

Saint Pierre, Walcott also sees the creative rapport with urban space as a kind of creolizing crossroads poetry. This perspective can be contrasted with that of Claude Lévi-Strauss's description of New York in 1941. To the latter there was something primordial about New York as a New World city, which was not "ultra modern," "but an immense horizontal and vertical disorder attributable to some spontaneous upheaval of the urban crust" (Lévi-Strauss 1985, 258). He seems to be oblivious to the creolizing forces at work and focuses rather on the process of cultural retention, as in the case of Chinese opera that he observes under the arch of the Brooklyn Bridge, which would "perpetuate the traditions of classical Chinese opera" (Lévi-Strauss 1985, 258).

The creolizing process is about invention and not retention, as Walcott explains in the often-cited passage from his Nobel lecture, where he develops this idea of creolization as an act of recreation producing asymmetric forms made from the gluing together of the fragments of dispersed cultures. "Break a vase, and the love that reassembles the fragments is stronger than the love that took its symmetry for granted when it was whole. The glue that fits the pieces is the sealing of its original shape. It is such a love that reassembles our African and Asiatic fragments, the cracked heirlooms whose restoration shows its white scars. . . . Antillean art is this restoration of our shattered histories, our shards of vocabulary, our archipelago becoming a synonym for pieces broken off from the original continent" (Walcott 1992, 9). What is arguably most important in this process is not the final form of the vase or the origin of the shards but the piecing together. The "white scars" of the reassembling that make the reinvented form richer than the original—this is the central process that creates precarious new wholes in the Caribbean.

Walcott's ideal of the world-weary Adam, who is not an embittered Caliban raging against the injustices of the past, is akin to Leiris's traveler continually negotiating the tensions between familiar and unfamiliar, between the magical and the banal. It is no coincidence that Walcott often uses the performance of sacred ritual as a means of understanding this process. His Nobel lecture begins with a reference to religious ritual and, in particular, to the Hindu religious drama of the *Ramayana* in a fragile New World community tellingly named Felicity. The lecture takes us through the poet's own doubt, his initial impulse to dismiss and trivialize what he is experiencing and not sense the strength of the community's belief, "their delight of conviction," as he puts it. As he self-consciously looks on at this improvised theater, his first reaction is to give a literary reconstruction to the dramatic ritual being played out. He conjures up Percy Bysshe Shelley's "Ozymandias," a "colossal wreck" in the empty countryside of the Caroni plain, in order to make sense of what these improvised gods are doing in the cane fields. He is forced to later confess remorsefully: "I, out of the writer's habit, search for some sense of elegy, of loss, even of degenerative mimicry. . . . I was polluting the afternoon with doubt and with the patronage of admiration. I misread the event through a visual echo of History— the canefields, indenture, the evocation of vanished armies, temples, and trumpeting elephants—when all around me there was quite the opposite: elation . . . not loss. The name Felicity made sense" (Walcott 1992, 6). He becomes a believer and must shake off the doubt and superciliousness that prevents him from feeling this moment of epiphany. Loss, anguish, bewilderment, the petrifying forces of history, all must be transcended in this moment of epiphany. Ultimately, Walcott is attempting to create a fragile sense of order, an imagined Creole community, from a history of privation and displacement. But the poet is careful not to see in these performances of culture the norms of a Creole authenticity. If there is a moment of poetic elation, it is ephemeral and transient. The gods are ultimately consumed by fire. In this regard Walcott rejoins Edouard Glissant in his concept of a fragile and unpredictable Creole community. Glissant's relational errancy is more daring than that of Walcott, his poetics more explosively unpredictable than Walcott's imagined community of reassembled fragments. They both, however, value impermanence, "toppled gods," and the openness of cultures to each other.

Whereas the idea of creolization has become fashionable and even produced a movement in the 1990s, it is important to note that neither Leiris's crossroads poetics nor Walcott's rituals of renewal allow for ideological stabilization. Cultural difference, because it is determined by contact, is never static or preordained but always open to disruption. As Glissant put it in his essay on Leiris,

In the face of the complex reality of the francophone Antilles, Creole and composite societies, what draws his attention is not the meaning (to be stumbled on or understood) of this reality, but primarily their very complexity as meaning. We are faced squarely with an ethnology of interrelating, an ethnography of how one relates to the Other. Studying cultural contact is to already be certain that there is no lesson to be drawn, the nature of such contact being in flux, unpredictable. (Glissant 1997, 131–132)

Glissant was responsible for introducing this idea to Caribbean thought in the 1950s with his travel book *Soleil de la conscience*, which was written in the same year as Claude Lévi- Strauss's *Tristes Tropiques* and Leiris's *Contacts de civilization en Martinique et en Guadeloupe*. Glissant's work differs remarkably from Lévi-Strauss's, who gave the Caribbean short shrift in his travel book and concentrated on the anthropological description of native cultures in the remote Amazon. In 1955 Glissant picks up on Leiris's idea of creole culture as the unpredictable result of the clash of heterogeneous elements. He does so in the context of his stay in Paris, where the contact with the other enables a self-ethnography and a poetics of renewal.

In *Soleil de la conscience* Glissant picks up on Leiris's destabilizing of the idea of insider and outsider and the spatial dimension in cultural *métissage*. The former's text focuses Leiris's ideas in terms of the colonial's relationship with the metropole, which becomes the arena where the latter is both insider and outsider, where there is a constant struggle to defamiliarize the familiar so that a creolizing dialogue becomes possible. As Glissant states, "Outside, it is a French truth which is opposed to mine; through this manifest union of what is contrary with what is other, from which we learn that all truth emerges from a dialectical consummation" (1956, 16). This confrontation is realized in the clash of mental landscapes. Europe's "interminable plain" and "its imprisoning infinity of checkerboard fields," where history seems to have inscribed itself and time seems congealed, are contrasted to his own world, where "landscape remains explosive," making the planted symmetry of Europe unnerving (19). But self-discovery can only come from this juxtaposition of contrasting landscapes. His use of "paysages" as opposed to "pays" indicates the need to deterritorialize space so that it is freed from the hierarchy of center and periphery and able to relate to other spaces. "Thus all knowledge is matter which is freed, turns back on itself, examines itself and takes shape" (19). There can be no "absolute geographies" and exoticism is turned inside out in this concept to cultural transformation. The traveler, through a participatory relationship with a spatial order opposed to his own, can advance toward some kind of luminosity, the hazy sun of consciousness. As he says of the spectacle of snow, "Such is snow: an illumination (I can finally touch winter), an opening (I finally am involved in this spectacle), an expanding, a communication becomes established (snow: as single, durable, definitive as the weight of the sun), the power now to speed up the dialogue, to hold closely on to shared thoughts, as if by a fireside. With it I leave behind my timidity to be swept away to the extreme opposite of my order of things" (18). Out of this acknowledgment of the enriching opacity of the other, the space of writing becomes imaginable—a threatening arena to Leiris's crossroads poetry. "I write far from my house, so that I can safely reenter, regain real flesh again, distance. . . . I can finally write close to the sea, in my burning house, on the volcanic sand" (43). The space for writing is where belonging is precarious, always threatened by the black volcanic sand or the sea's unpredictable surge.

The first part of *Soleil de la conscience* is devoted to the fashioning of a creolizing poetics for a destabilized subject, whose imagination is enriched by the other's opacity. The colonial relationship is not one that can be undone but, on the contrary, dissolves the opposition of self and other, here and elsewhere. Glissant's journey is one that tracks Creole beginnings in the space where colonial relations come to an end. He envisages a world of restless wandering, of commonplaces and crossroads where polarities dissolve and identity can be only relational. The second part of this unusual travel narrative concentrates on the hybridized space of the town, which disrupts the immutable checkerboard of the landscape, bringing heterogeneous elements into constant collision with each other. The final section of his travel book is entitled *"Villes, Poèmes,"* where the two nouns in apposition identify urban space as facilitating the poetry of the unpredictable.

He compares Paris to the cities of Alexandria and Carthage, situated as they were at the geographical intersection of Asia, Africa, and Europe. Urban spaces function as islands of transculturation, which constantly attract and diffract.

These cities come into their own at each moment in history where all falls apart and becomes enflamed. Then, they welcome the casualties, those who come to get lost, leaving the mud of the earth, abandoning the Great Voice that ordains, "and they get lost in the beehive where they are fashioned by solitude. Only then must they reconnect with the earth's impurity, the truth of the tree standing before the house" (Glissant 1956, 67). Indeed, Paris here is separated from the organized space of Europe's continental mass to become an island of explosive space. "Paris therefore, in the heart of our time, receives, uproots, scrambles, then clarifies and reassures. I suddenly know its secret: and it is that Paris is an island, which draws light from everywhere and just as quickly diffracts it" (Glissant 1956, 68). In this new reversible geography, Paris is conceived in terms of relational openness, not as a colonial metropole but as a post-colonial relativizing space where one senses the urgency of a globalizing modernity.

Creolizing urban space becomes for Glissant from the 1950s the "lieu incontournable," the uncircumventable place of cultural contact. In

Faulkner, Mississippi, whose title suggests that southern writer William Faulkner can be visited or frequented as if he were a town on the Mississippi, Glissant contrasts the language of the spaces of the plantation as opposed to that of the town, on one hand, "a writing of the source, the matrix, of slowed time and open space in a closed place (The Plantation)," on the other, "a writing of multiplicity, blinding speed, piling up and undoing (the Town). The landscapes of the pastoral and the slammed together" (Glissant 1996, 334). As in his novel *La Lézarde,* where the colonial town of Lambrianne draws everyone in and scatters them, thereby subjecting them to accelerated, transforming experiences, Glissant sees the Creole town in terms of a crossroads that connects inside and outside, global markets and plantation production. "Creole towns where by their very nature alike and fascinating, whether Havana in Cuba, New Orleans in Louisiana, Port-au-Prince in Haiti, Saint Pierre in Martinique, Kingston in Jamaica or the Brazilian towns in this region, Manaus and Belem. . . . These towns are extensions of the plantation and did not conceive themselves without it: cotton, tobacco, rum and sugar, spices, indigo (gold and rubber in Brazil), invariably bartered for refined products from Europe or manufactured products from the north of The United States" (Glissant 1996, 334–335). Such towns are doomed to extinction with the eventual failure of the plantation system, but their fevered excitement is the unavoidable creolizing "paysage" of a new Caribbean writing. Urban space functions as a kind of delta, a mangrove world that draws in the inhabitants of the plantation from their wide open landscapes into the narrow, twisting fringes of urban shanty towns. It becomes the quintessential relating landscape in Glissant's (1990) *Poétique de la Relation.* "In the Caribbean and Latin America the blossoming urban ghettoes have exerted a magnetic pull on the destitute masses and changed the rhythm of their voices. . . . The space of the Plantation, joined with the ever-expanding surface of the hacienda and the latifundio, eventually broke up into a maze of zinc and concrete where what we are all destined to become takes its chances" (Glissant 1990, 87). As the slowed-down plantation past turns into the twisting frenzy of urban crossroads landscape a new poetics becomes possible.

For instance, Jacques Stephen Alexis's theorizing of the "marvelous" in Haitian popular culture as a transgressive, unpredictable force, a process of "accelerated fusion" and convulsive metamorphosis, was aimed at liberating Haiti from a static post-plantation alterity by invoking its inter-American context of migrant labor and urban ghettoes. His last novel, published in 1959, *L'Espace d'un cillement,* recounts the meeting of two Cubans in the crossroads space of "Carrefour" on the outskirts of Port-au-Prince. Set in a brothel on Holy Week, it is a clear attempt to invoke crossroads poetics in the clash of sacred and profane and sets out to capture the diversity of the patrons of "Sensation Bar," an emergent post-national Caribbean community of marines, gringos, *manolitas, horizontales,* and *chulos* (hookers, streetwalkers, and pimps). Similarly, the largely ignored poetry of the Haitian surrealist Magloire Saint-Aude yields important insights into the space of the subject in which interior and exterior seems interchangeable. A primordial chaos is apparent in his collections *Dialogue des mes lampes* (1941), *Tabou* (1941), and *Déchu* (1956) in which a fragile errancy seems to be the main subject and points to a new poetics of post-plantation space.

This interest in the Creole town has been taken up by Patrick Chamoiseau, who more often than not uses Glissantian terms such as "an urban mangrove" to describe the town. His recent description of the city in the *Livret des villes du deuxième monde* as the landscape of multiple encounters is typical in this regard. "Every town is made up of encounters, contacts and exchanges. Every town is made up of chance and organization, of order and disorder, of chaos and reorganizations in an imperceptible flux of internal mutations. Every town is a living complexity" (Chamoiseau 2002, 24). There is an important difference, however, which is that Chamoiseau's emphasis on the "en-ville" is the space of the urban maroon. In this respect, we are no longer dealing with the risks of crossroads space but have relocated the night of "petit marronage" on the periphery of urban centers, where preserving a culture of opposition seems more important than the kinds of unpredictable metamorphosis envisaged by Glissant. Indeed, the town seems to duplicate the plantation instead of, as Glissant has suggested, replacing it. In so doing, Chamoiseau produces a series of binary oppositions relating to the town, the official world of the written versus the oral expressiveness at the edges, the passive consumerist center as against the improvising creative margins. In *Texaco* the town is legible in terms of the poetics of maroon resistance. "She taught me to reread the Creole city's two spaces: the historical center living on the new demands of consumption; the suburban crowns of grassroots occupations, rich with the depth of our stories. . . . In the center memory subsides in the face of renovation, before the cities which the Occident inspires. Here on the outskirts one survives on memory. In the center all dissolves in the modern world; but here people bring very old roots, not deep and rigid, but diffuse, profuse, spread over time with the lightness of speech" (Chamoiseau 1997, 170). The binary pattern is clear: the destructive spirit of modernization at the center is confronted by the organic, rooted (however precariously) community at the outskirts.

Urban space is therefore saturated by past time in Chamoiseau's novels as it is constructed in terms of plain and hill, in terms of the oppressive world of colonial control as opposed to the restorative, organic zone of the forest.

In *Chronique des sept misères* the "disorder" of the market, the "delirium" of Pipi's vegetable garden, the "ancestral complicity of man and earth" of the Rastas is contrasted with the rationality and regimentation of the municipality which finds its most extreme expression in the sanitizing oppressiveness of the mental hospital at Colson. Consequently, the Creole unpredictability envisaged by Glissant becomes a process of ethnographic salvage in which traditional ways are encroached on by an aggressive modernity. Chamoiseau's novels can be read as chronicles of loss and remembrance, cautionary tales for a threatened community. The creolizing process as envisaged by Chamoiseau is intimately tied to resistance, and his novels lament the fact that what he calls "notre esprit de maintenant" (our current mindset) can no longer fathom the workings of a Creole imaginary. As he laments in his essay tellingly entitled "Les nègres marrons de l'en ville," "The (street) hustler fears becoming too rigid and losing his flexibility. Especially as those around him, the non-hustlers, think only of putting down roots. . . . In town, we must root ourselves in concrete, grow heavy and put behind us the cabin in which we started. We can see today the extent to which concrete is king in our imaginary" (Chamoiseau 1992, 33).

Chamoiseau's idea of creolization and the Créolité movement as a whole is essentially nostalgic, based on the regret that the Antillean population has not better resisted the assimilationist pressure of rapid modernization within the French Overseas Departments. There is little difference between their view of Creole culture and that of Simone Schwarz-Bart (1972) in her homage to "la Guadeloupe profonde" in *Pluie et vent sur Télumée miracle*. Indeed, this novel comes in for high praise in the *creoliste* survey of French Caribbean writing, *Lettres Créoles*, in which we are told that "to read and reread again" the novel is to be "enriched each time" (Chamoiseau and Confiant 1991, 182). On the face of it, such a comment seems as surprising as Schwarz-Bart's vision of pastoral redemption is radically different from the urban space of the creoliste novels. However, the project is the same; Marie Sophie Laborieuse of Texaco is arguably a close kin of Schwarz-Bart's founding mother, Télumée. Their ultimate aim is the recuperation of a creole authenticity from an alienating modernization. As if we needed any further proof of Chamoiseau's (1997) short fable, *L'esclave vieil homme et le molosse* is about a plunge into the redemptive zone of the forest, illustrating the extent to which authentic freedom is tied to an appropriation of remote rural landscapes. If, as Michel De Certeau affirms in the epigraph, the town is poeticized by the subject as a way of escaping institutional control, Chamoiseau has imposed an essentially pastoral order on urban space as he tries to impose maroon clearings on urban jungles.

One is tempted to see in the creoliste championing of Schwarz-Bart's novel the clichéd use of the grandmother figure as a source of traditional knowledge. Such a figure has an honored place even in early exotic literature, where in the stories of Lafcadio Hearn ([1890] 2001) the sentimentalized Black nurse or "da" passed on traditional tales to her young *béké* charges. Women writers can be less sentimental about cultural grandmothers. The ethnographer Ina Césaire (1985), for instance, depicts in her play *Mémoires d'Isles* two old women who relive their memories in a Beckett-like atmosphere of encroaching gloom, which is a far cry from the creoliste rehabilitation of the island matriarch. In a binary structure reminiscent of Glissant, the play, set on a darkened veranda, enacts the lives of an aging light-skinned schoolmistress from the south and an uneducated, Black city-dweller from the north. These are not the reminiscences we associate with a celebratory recuperation of the past. Indeed, in the parallel but diverging symbolic figures, isolated on a shadowy stage, Césaire turns away from the defiant spirit of the underdog epitomized by Schwarz-Bart's protagonist. The static play ends with two immobilized, aging figures who fall silent as the sounds of the Caribbean night invade the verandah.

Maryse Condé may have gone further than anyone else in challenging Creole nationalism. In the same way she earlier called into question the ideal of Black cultural authenticity and stressed the primacy of human fallibility. In her constant desire to privilege lived experience over ideology, she has been openly skeptical of the way in which creolization has been promoted in the French Antilles. In Condé's only novel entirely set in Guadeloupe, *Crossing the Mangrove* (1989), she does not present us with the rich French/Creole continuum or the ethno-cultural mosaic of the typical creoliste novel. Rather we have a mean, parochial, incestuous village whose complexity resists ideological recuperation. The mangrove world of this novel does not produce a richly hybrid culture but challenges literary or ethnographic representation. The standard bearer of cultural resistance, the storyteller, is mocked as a buffoon, and the idea of the *engagé* Antillean writer is parodied in the character of the independence activist Lucien Evariste. The mangrove trope so dear to the creolistes resists legibility in her narrative. If anything, Condé rejects the ideal of a neat Creole hybridity, of regulatory cultural crossroads in favor of a liberating voraciousness, and replaces the island-based vision of creolization with a free-ranging cosmopolitanism. Her interest in Suzanne Césaire's idea of a "littérature cannibale" (Césaire 1942, 50) is telling in this regard. Cultural and literary cannibalization destabilizes the notion of difference that is crucial to the model of interactive binaries of the créolité movement. In this way, Condé may also be provokingly responding to the creoliste filial devotion to Aimé Césaire. By suggesting that his wife, Suzanne, might have provided an even more useful concept for understanding the rapidly changing cultural and social realities of the modern Caribbean, Condé suggests that it is time that the ideal of return to insular plenitude is replaced by one that privileges the risks incurred by ingesting the other.

The ideological positioning of creolization by Martinican nationalists who long for organically whole culture becomes particularly apparent when we read Chamoiseau's tales of urban marronnage alongside a text such as Dany Laferrière's (1996) *Pays sans chapeau* (one is almost tempted to read sans Chamoiseau), in which the Glissantian idea of simultaneously being an insider and outsider in cultures that are being transformed rapidly and unpredictably is revived. Whereas Chamoiseau is always tempted to fix difference, marking it as static and familiar, Laferrière's text feeds on the ironic play of here and elsewhere, the odd and the ordinary. Indeed, Laferrière goes out of his way to mock the process of ethnographic salvage in his satirical portrait of Professor J-B Romain of the faculty of ethnology in Haiti's State University. The author visits Romain in his "cramped office crammed with disparate objects: masks, pre-Columbian statuettes, African sculptures" (Laferrière 1996, 66), indicating his obsession with the origins of Haitian culture. When asked about current happenings in Haiti, he defiantly declares, "In my analysis of Haiti, I am still in Africa. . . . You must go to the root of things" (Laferrière 1996, 66).

As we have seen earlier, this kind of ethnographic comprehension that Métraux rejects in his study of Vodou is now equally mocked by Laferrière, who suggests that even as an "insider" he is faced by a reality of incongruities that defies explanation. Like Métraux, he distrusts profoundly the idea that true Haitian culture exists in the remote parts of the countryside. His satirical portrait of le docteur Legrand Bijou is a hilarious send up of the belief in organic nature and rural remoteness as the site of authentic

Haitianness. "It seems," Bijou declares, "that the Creole of Bombardopolis is the purest in Haiti. . . . The Belgian linguist explained that these folks, the inhabitants of Bombardopolis have become, in a certain way, plants. He explained at length how photosynthesis worked in this case. Through a complete harmony between man and nature" (Laferrière 1996, 163). In order to understand the secret of Haiti's urban culture, the author locates himself in Carrefour with his typewriter. He adopts the position of the writer who returns home and explains his culture to the outside world. In ethnographic style he tries to record objectively the world of chance and spontaneity around him. The text ends up being made of juxtaposed, short, intrusive fragments where events are captured in a fleeting and incomplete way. No complicity between man and nature here, as writing yields to the urban crush of Haiti's overcrowded capital city. Sometimes an insider who understands local customs, sometimes an outsider who forgets, Laferrière lives in the present his relation to a culture that cannot be turned into narrative. Whereas the novel is arranged in alternating sections of "Pays reel" and "Pays rêve," the everyday reality of the first section is ironic, and the incidents relating to zombies and the Vodou gods in the second is deflating. Indeed, the author is incapable of sustaining the orderly sequence of dreamed country and real country, which collapses as two "dreamed country" sections follow each other (Laferrière 1996, 75, 83). Finally he admits, "I am now in the real world, and I see no difference with the dreamed world" (Laferrière 1996, 215).

In *Pays sans chapeau*, not only urban space but the sacred space of the *loas* is overwhelmed by an accumulation of signs, objects, a kind if international kitsch which makes legibility almost impossible. This saturation makes the temptation of ethnographic salvage futile in face of convulsive and unpredictable forces of creolization. Laferrière, unlike Chamoiseau, is not a guide who explains and condemns and cannot construct a system of binarities to explain what is supposed to be his culture. This flies in the face of the conventional autobiography in which the author as protagonist becomes an intermediary between his world and the reader's. In the final section of the work, Laferrière the author comments on the foregoing text. His inspiration is his neighbor, an illiterate painter named Baptiste, who admits that everything in his painting is dreamt and that there was no need to dream the real country. His enigmatic pronouncements make nonsense of the entire structure of the text and the project of interpreting. In this regard Laferrière explicitly recalls Glissant's *Soleil de la conscience*, in which the question is asked at the end, "Who has not dreamt of the book that explains everything" (Glissant 1956, 69). As with the space of Glissant's "Villes, Poèmes," the text becomes a heterogeneous mix of elements that are juxtaposed in a space that is chaotic and unpredictable.

One is tempted to explain the difference between the idea of Creole resistance and cultural salvage in Chamoiseau as opposed to the distrust of all systematic explanation in Laferrière by making a distinction between the "colonial" nature of Fort de France as opposed to the disorder of the Haitian capital. But, Laferrière's return to his native land coincides with the U.S. marine presence in Haiti after the return of President Jean Bertrand Aristide from exile. The fact is that Laferrière, like Glissant, explicitly insists on the cultural over the political. The political configuration of creolization as resistance effectively blocks the process, as envisaged by Glissant, which privileges cultural mobility. Perhaps, it all goes back to the idea of the "poetic" in crossroads space envisaged by Michel Leiris in 1948. The poetry of violent juxtaposition and unpredictable encounter allows the subject to undo the symbolic order of urban space, giving it a new, precarious legibility. The unpredictable nature of urban encounters makes systematic theorizing impossible and avoids the temptation of ideological mystification.

Amalgams and Mosaics, Syncretisms and Reinterpretations

Reading Herskovits and Contemporary Creolists
for Metaphors of Creolization

—ROBERT BARON

Creolization is a slippery concept, powerful in its ability to characterize emergent cultural forms but eluding precision in definition. Perhaps its slipperiness befits a concept so useful for rendering the fluidity of processes build out of the interpenetration of cultures. Ask a creolist what creolization is, and the response may very well include one or more metaphors for combinatorial processes and the forms emerging out of cultural contact. Metaphors in creolization studies, as in any realm of scholarship, fill lexical gaps, drawing from other semantic fields in the absence of adequate existing terminology in a given area of study (see Soskice and Harré 1995). The metaphors of creolists speak to key issues in creolization studies— how (and whether) creolized forms maintain the identities of components derived from source cultures, transformational processes, and the relationships of cultural forms of diverse provenance to one another within the creolization process.

Melville J. Herskovits extensively employed metaphor to similar ends in his circum-Atlantic project examining the retention and transformation of African cultural elements in the Americas. He used metaphors from various semantic domains to render how elements of cultures combine and new forms emerge as a result of cultural contact. While these forms and processes would be viewed today as manifestations of creolization, Herskovits did not describe them as "creole." Seeking to substantiate the presence of a living African heritage in the Americas and analyze its transformations, he utilized both metaphor and schematic, social "scientific" explanations tied to his efforts to create a conceptual framework for the study of acculturation and cultural change.

Contemporary critics of Herskovits contend that he elided transformation as he pursued what Richard and Sally Price characterize as his "genealogical imperative." They view Herskovits as "trait chasing" in his "search for African origins," which Sidney W. Mintz and Richard Price suggest "lead[s] to a somewhat mechanical view of culture and deemphasize[s] processes of change and diversification" (Price and Price 2003, 85; Mintz and Price 1976, 13). While Herskovits did search tenaciously for elements of African culture retained in the Americas, at the same time he was concerned with dynamics of change in Afro-Atlantic cultures, which altered these cultures while maintaining an African heritage. Herskovits could be viewed as a proto-creolist, and like contemporary creolists he employed metaphor as a vehicle for conveying cultural transformation.

Today, scholars and laypersons alike acknowledge the African heritage of peoples of African descent in the Americas. In his own time, Herskovits's views were revolutionary. He argued passionately that African cultural tradition was not lost in the Americas, but retained and transformed in multifarious ways.

Over the course of two decades of intensive research and numerous publications about Afro-Atlantic cultures, Herskovits employed metaphor to represent how African cultural elements were juxtaposed, coexisted with, or combined to varying degrees of completeness with elements of European derivation in the formation of New World Black cultures. His field research in emergent, African-derived cultures of the Americas during the 1920s and 1930s took place in an ideal laboratory for observing creolized processes and products of "acculturation," defined as phenomena resulting from firsthand, continuous interaction between individuals of different cultures. Metaphors drawn from a variety of semantic domains rendered the new cultural patterns brought about by acculturation. Herskovits's use of metaphor diminished in the 1940s as he developed new concepts for the reconciliation of cultural elements and beliefs derived from cultures in contact with one another. *Syncretism*, the best known of these terms, was redefined several times. It was eventually superseded by the concept of *reinterpretation*, which emphasized meaning over form as it referred to processes providing old meanings for new forms and retaining old forms with new meanings.

Why is metaphor of such value for characterizing creolization processes and the forms resulting from cultural contact? Combinatorial processes, and products of creolization, may best be described with terms for other processes and entities created out of two or more components. Herskovits and contemporary creolists use such terms as *amalgam, mixture, compound,* and *convergence.* Their use involves catachresis, the provision of a term where one is lacking in our vocabulary. Janet Martin Soskice and Rom Harré see catachresis as an "activity of filling lexical gaps," such as occurred when the "lower slopes of a mountain were called its foot, or when the support of a wine glass was called its stem, because no satisfactory term was available in the lexicon for this purpose" (1995, 302–303). The sciences use metaphor to describe what is not observable—"properties and relations not available to experience" (297). Metaphor is required as the "only way to say what we mean since the existing semantic fields of the current terminology referentially related to the subject in question are inadequate to our own thought." Think, for example, of the use of fluid imagery to model the nature of electricity, resulting in metaphors like "rate of flow" or "electrical current" (296, 302).[1]

Folklorists have extensively employed biological metaphors, from the discipline's origins in romanticism through much of the twentieth century. Valdimar Tr. Hafstein demonstrates the use of such metaphors to establish a scientific foundation for folkloristics and legitimize it as a discipline. He discusses some of the most important ones, familiar to every folklorist: "life, growth, evolution, death, extinction, natural laws, morphology, 'Märchenbiologie' and tradition ecology" (Hafstein [2001] 2005, 407). Franz Bopp and Jakob Grimm offered a "jungle of organic metaphors, fecund with seeds and sprouts, ripe with fruits and flowers, and one stumbles everywhere across terms like growth, decay, and branching" (Hafstein [2001] 2005, 411). Arnold Van Gennep, Carl von Sydow, and Vladimir Propp all conceived of folklore as a "biological science" and called for folklore to "go directly to biologists for their models and methods" (Hafstein [2001] 2005, 422). While acknowledging the profound influence of these metaphors, Hafstein finds them incompatible with contemporary rejection of essentialist "natural categories," emphasis in folklore theory on "performance as social agency" and a "view of tradition as an achievement rather than a natural fact," and the movement toward reflexivity in folklore and other disciplines concerned with the study of culture (429–430).

As reductive as such use of metaphors may seem for folkloristics, metaphors are nonetheless critically important for every discipline, moving ideas forward through semantic leaps and providing terms where few or none exist from within. While folklorists might view the use of terms borrowed from science disciplines as indicative of the field's academic status, the sciences, as we have seen, also depend on metaphors from other domains. Symbolic anthropologists have noted that figurative language is endemic to discourse about, and within, society and culture (see Fernandez 1986; Sapir and Crocker 1977). This perspective is valid for the theorization of scholars as well as lay discourse examined in ethnographies. Adaptation of the term *creole* itself from its culturally specific meaning within colonial and post-colonial contexts (for cultural identity and language) to new meaning as a broader cultural process of "creolization" involves the fundamental metaphorical mechanism of conceptual displacement, which Elonora Montuschi sees as "the shift of a concept into a new contextual situation" (1995, 317). By tracking metaphors used for creolization and examining their expanded meanings, we can open new pathways to understanding how cultural creolization is theorized.

Like Herskovits, contemporary creolists employ metaphor when characterizing forms and processes resulting from the combination of cultural components of different provenance. Herskovits's large repertoire of metaphors represented patterns of combination of cultural forms and their transmutation into new entities where cultural elements of different provenance may continue to coexist. They also rendered the relationships of creolized forms to their source cultures, a matter also of concern to contemporary creolists. Metaphors of and for creolization are drawn from a variety of realms, especially the sciences, and employed to describe the changes to cultural forms resulting from the interactions of individuals from two or more cultures and the new entities that are formed.

Ian Hancock has probed metaphors drawn from chemistry to support his contention that "compound" is the ideal metaphor for creoles as new languages, in contrast to "mixture." In a workshop presentation at the 1992 Smithsonian Festival of American Folklife (now known as the Smithsonian Folklife Festival), "New Languages Created from Old," he viewed "compound" as a metaphor consistent with the contention of linguists that creole languages are wholly new entities that no longer maintain the separate identities of their component elements. Hancock noted that the constituent substances of mixtures are not chemically united and are not in a fixed relationship to one another while, in a compound, a pure substance is created in which the composition of the constituent substances is constant. The restructuring occurring through creolization results in the formation of a new language, involving the growth of new grammars rather than a mixture of grammars. In contrast to Hancock, other creolists (especially those writing about cultural creolization) often use metaphors consistent with a view of creolized forms as non-fixed and non-compound-like forms that maintain, to at least some extent, the identities of their constituent components.

In *Pidginization and Creolization in Languages*, editor Dell Hymes sees "convergence" as a "creole's most salient property" while noting that processes of linguistic change can result in differential convergence and persistence among phonetics, lexicon, syntax, and semantics. Within the creolization process, there are various possible patterns of convergent change, and Hymes indicates that neither the number of these patterns nor the "sector of such a general field that is to be considered relevant to creolization" has yet been established (1971, 75,76). Creolization in languages is a process of "creativity, entailing the adaptation of means of diverse provenience to new ends," consisting of "convergence, in the context of expansion of use" as well as "expansion in content" (76, 77). The creole language created and developed through this process of convergent change achieves "autonomy as a norm" (65).

Hymes's notion of convergence follows from established use of the term by linguists for "language convergence" processes. In the *Oxford English Dictionary*, convergence is defined as movement directing toward or terminating in the same point, as a coming or drawing together. "Convergence" has been extended as metaphor through its multiple meanings in various fields, and a brief look at some of its uses can help to address its utility and appropriateness as a metaphor for cultural creolization. These definitions speak to the creation of new entities from sources of diverse provenance, with the new entities persistently maintaining—to some extent—the identities of the constituent components. In several fields, convergence refers to comparable processes generating similar results in different species or peoples over the course of time. In ecology, convergence means that similar or identical climax communities develop from widely diversified seral-stage communities, as a diversified habitat evolves into a more uniform habitat. Evolutionist and diffusionist anthropologists viewed convergence as a kind of evolutionary development where cultures evolve toward a similar condition through dissimilar steps. In evolutionary biology, convergence refers to the development of resemblances in the features of organisms of different origins that had evolved independently. "Convergence" has also been used in recent years for new technologies, referring to processes bringing together more than one kind of media for information and entertainment in a single new technology, and for the meeting of voice and data networks within a single infrastructure in such devices as cell phones and personal computers.

As Nelson Goodman indicates, "words often have many different metaphorical as well as many different literal applications" (1979, 176). All of the various meanings for convergence just discussed share, however, a common feature of characterizing—in processual terms—the creation of something new from sources of diverse provenance. This dimension of meaning of convergence has obvious advantages for creolization studies. The product of "convergence," according to some fields, does not necessarily have the "compound-like" quality of an entity where the constituent parts no longer have separate identities. This may serve convergence well as a creolization metaphor, since cultural creolization is widely viewed as an ongoing, emergent process that does not necessarily terminate in an end point and may maintain the identities of components from source cultures. Several of the central concerns of contemporary creolists address the maintenance of identity for source cultures and their interrelationships within the process of cultural creolization. They speak to fundamental questions in creolization studies:

If the identities of cultural forms of diverse provenance are maintained in the creolization process, how are they maintained?
What are their relationships to and/or identifications with one another and to their source cultures?
How can the new products of creolization be characterized?
Are these new products maintained in a relatively fixed form, or are they continuously emergent?

Creolists writing about cultural creolization tend to stress its emergent character, interaction among elements, and ambiguous relationship to source cultures. While, perhaps, a metaphor of "compound" may be appropriate for creole languages, for other dimensions of creolization other metaphors are used that do not suggest a constant, fixed relationship of constituent elements. Edward Kamau Brathwaite contends that creolization can be described "in terms not of a 1:1 give and take of gift or exchange, resulting in a new or altered product, but as a process, resulting in subtle and multiform orientations from or *towards* ancestral originals. In this way, Caribbean culture can be seen in terms of a dialectic of development taking place within a seamless guise" (1974a, 7). Brathwaite calls for a model of creolization that incorporates "blood flow," a rich, multifocal metaphor relating to both physical and cultural interrelationships—and "fluctuations, the half-look, the look both/several ways; which allows for and contains the ambiguous, and rounds the sharp edges off the dichotomy" (1974a, 7)."[2] A poet and historian whose work is infused with figurative language, Brathwaite believes that the definition of creolization "can only derive from a proliferation of images: a multiplication of complex probes: a co-operative effort from us all" (1974b, 6).

"Prismatic" is another metaphor used by Brathwaite, which underscores his view that the creolization process maintains aspects of ancestral traditions while modifying the interacting cultures. This process does not result in a fixed final product. For Brathwaite,

> the prismatic concept . . . conceives of all resident cultures as equal and contiguous, despite the accidents of political history, each developing its own life-style from the spirit of the ancestors, but modified—and increasingly so—through interaction with the environment, and the other cultures of the environment, until residence within the environment—*nativization*—becomes the process (creolization) through which all begin to share a style, even though that style will retain vestiges (with occasional national/cultural revivals back towards particular ancestors) of their original/ancestral heritage" (1977, 42).

Prismatic works well as a metaphor for creolization because of its association with refraction and the multiplicity of colors and shapes seen in a prism. In a Caribbean context, a prismatic conceptualization of creolization counters the "plural society" view of social scientists that stressed social and cultural segmentation (see Smith 1965). In this metaphor, refraction through a prism offers an alternative to a linear approach to the interaction of cultures. The colors refracted through a prism mix in a spectrum in a manner that is not fixed, rigid, or predictable.

Metaphors of and for creolization should allow for continuous interplay and an ever-emerging dynamism that escapes the relative fixedness imputed to more fully formed and seemingly stable cultures. Creolization, as Edouard Glissant indicates, is a "constantly shifting and variable process . . . [of relationships, of variability]" (1989, 15). Françoise Vergès stresses that "creole cultures are not about the mechanics of mixing—the literal analogy of 2+2 is not useful. Creolization is about a *bricolage* drawing freely upon what is available, recreating with new content and in new forms a distinctive culture" (2003, 184). Bricolage as a metaphor speaks to creolization as cultural creativity, bringing together resources at hand to create something new and different.

Creolization is a concept well suited to the transformations wrought by processes of globalization, including those triggered by mercantilism in the Caribbean and Indian Ocean regions where Europeans, Africans, and (in some places) Asians were brought together; or the more universal contemporary phenomena accelerated by electronic media, cyberspace, world trade, and the migrations of peoples. Writing of "the world in creolization," Ulf Hannerz suggests that "the idea of creolization could give cultural studies a fresh start . . . that sees the world as it is in the late twentieth century" (1987, 551). While focusing upon post-colonial Africa, Hannerz also speaks about an "entire creolizing spectrum, from First World metropolis to Third World village," employing "spectrum" as a key metaphor for the relationships of cultural forms of different provenance: "Creole cultures, like creole languages, are those that draw in some way on two or more historical sources, often originally widely different. They have had some time to develop and integrate, and to become elaborate and pervasive. People are formed from birth by these systems of meaning and largely live their lives in contexts shaped by them. There is the sense of a continuous spectrum of interacting forms, in which the various contributing sources of the culture are differentially visible and active" (1987, 552).

Yet, the metaphor of "continuous spectrum" is tangled. The amount and spectral distribution of electromagnetic waves emitted in a continuous spectrum are predictable for particular substances. Each color appears within a set sequence. "Continuous spectrum" conveys the range of cultural "sources" and "forms" in a creole society. However, the notion of "interacting forms" within particular parts of a spectrum represents a questionable metaphoric extension from physics. While metaphor, like ambiguity, has multiple possible meanings, the literal application of the term should be paramount in the use of metaphor. According to Goodman, metaphor differs from ambiguity "because a literal application precedes and influences correlative metaphorical application" (1979, 176). Interpretation of metaphors should not, of course, confuse the full literal meaning of a term with its creative application in metaphor. David Sapir indicates that as metaphors are applied, two terms are placed in juxtaposition that share a bundle of common features but are dissimilar in other ways. Utilizing these common features, "all really apt metaphors . . . stress specificity" and possess "uncanny ability" to "provide a means for making precise statements about their subject" (Sapir 1977, 6, 10). As I track metaphors of creolization, I am looking for these qualities of aptness, specificity, and precision in the juxtaposition of terms from various semantic domains with processes of creolization.

Creole cultures, according to Lee Drummond (1980), contain "intersystems." Grey Gundaker stresses the "variability and adaptability" associated with this perspective. "Participants oscillate within a given set of limits," a view which provides an alternative to a "rigid" notion of a continuum (Gundaker 1998b, 205).[3] In his pioneering account of the creolization process, "Plural and Differential Acculturation in Trinidad," Daniel J. Crowley provides a gorgeous plethora of examples of members of a creole society oscillating in their participation in each other's traditions, as he illustrates how "groups, for all their distinctness, are not functionally exclusive or 'watertight',. . . all the members of any group know something of the other groups, and many members are as proficient in the cultural activities of other groups as their own" (1957, 823). In this quintessentially creole culture, "a Trinidadian feels no inconsistency in being a . . . Negro in appearance, a Spaniard in name, a Roman Catholic at church, an obeah (magic) practitioner in private, a Hindu at lunch, a Chinese at dinner [and a] Portuguese at work" (Crowley 1957, 823).

As members of a creole society interact, they reshape cultural forms that had been associated exclusively with a particular group. Trinidadians continue to provide us with excellent examples of creolization accomplished through social interaction and the creolized forms that result from these interactions. Interactions of Indo- and Afro-Caribbeans through folklore are embodied in a variety of expressive forms. *Tassa* drumming and accompanying dances performed by Indo-Caribbeans are now integrally part of Trinidad carnival. Among Indo-Caribbeans in New York City, most tassa performers are Hindus. The "hands" (sets of distinct ostinatos and meters) of New York City tassa performers include "religious hands" for Hindu deities like Lakshmi and Hanuman, "wedding hands," and "dancing hands," such as the *dingolay*, steel pan, and *soca*. The latter two are of Afro-Caribbean provenance (see Baron 2008). *Chutney soca*, which emerged in the late twentieth century as a variety of Trinidadian calypso performed by Indo-Caribbeans, incorporates elements of Indo-Caribbean folk and popular tradition as well as Trinidadian calypso (see Rohlehr 2004, 181).

Chutney soca is now presented at events alongside Afro-Caribbean soca, itself a contemporary, creolized transformation of calypso, as the name *soca* (for Soul Calypso) implies. Chutney soca, in turn, has had a formal influence upon calypso as performed by Afro-Caribbeans.

Criticizing my discussion of Chutney soca in an earlier version of this essay, Aisha Khan questions whether cultural forms can be exclusively associated with one group "if we [anthropology] no longer claim isomorphic relationships between *a* culture and *a* group or tradition" and states that "we cannot present only selected cultural forms as examples of creolization" (2007, 664). Khan contends that my "claim about creolization speaks more to issues of model building abstracted from cultural practices than to the concrete practices themselves" (2007b, 664). In fact, through concrete, on-the-ground ascriptions of traditional forms with particular groups—and self-identification with traditions by particular groups—cultural forms are associated with one group or another, within communities even if not through anthropological conceptualizations. While these ascriptions and self-identifications may or may not elide exogenous influences and interactions, associations of traditions with specific groups may change in the course of creolization. Chutney soca and tassa warrant recognition as tangible manifestations of creolization processes that shape and reshape cultural forms, with especially intriguing complexity.

Creolists view complexity and multiplicity as constitutive of creolization when they address the relationships of creole forms to their source cultures. "Complexity is the very principle of our identity," according to Jean Bernabé, Patrick Chamoiseau, and Raphaël Confiant (1990, 892). Their discussion of creolization overflows with poetic images—they describe "creoleness" as "our primitive soup . . . our primeval chaos and our mangrove swamp of virtualities" (892). In the Caribbean, where cultural sources are often reduced to Africa and Europe, these three scholars lengthen the list to include "Caribbean, European, African, Asian and Levantine elements, united on the same soil by the yoke of history;" they see "creoleness" as the *"interactional or transactional aggregate"* of these elements (891). As Stuart Hall notes, creolization "could not exist without extensive transculturation" (2003b, 186).

Soup and stew metaphors also appear recurrently in self-characterizations of Creole societies. They are apposite metaphors for creolization, maintaining the identity of individual components while embodying a wholly new character built out of these components. Soups and stews like *zembrocal* contain ingredients with multiple cultural sources, embodying a distinctive taste through the aggregate of these ingredients, yet maintaining the individual flavors of the components. Jean Claude Carpanin Marimoutou indicates that *zembrocal*, viewed as a "culinary metaphor" for the culture of Réunion, has "a new flavor that retains its original flavors at the same time that it surpasses them" (2003, 228), which might be easily said as well for *callaloo*, *sancocho*, and gumbo in the places where they are iconic of creole identity.

If creole cultural processes and forms are viewed as emergent rather than fixed entities, and they are made up of multiple sources that may continue to shape them, then what are their relationships to their historical sources? The specific relationships of cultural elements to their historical sources were a dominant concern for comparative folklore studies prior to the 1960s and diffusionist anthropology during the early twentieth century. As both an anthropologist and folklorist trained in these approaches, Melville J. Herskovits sought to identify African sources for cultural forms of dual and multiple provenance. This project was key to his long-term agenda of establishing continuities with the African past for peoples of African descent in the Americas. He exhaustively searched for "Africanisms," establishing an African provenance for individual cultural components. Herskovits also attempted to sort out the historical sources—from Africa, Europe and elsewhere—of complex cultural forms. In confronting the complexity of these forms and processes, he frequently employed metaphor to render how they were formed and the emergent forms (creolisms, if you will) that resulted from combinations of different cultural components.

Within a few days of arriving in Suriname on his first field trip to a Black New World culture outside of the United States in 1928, undertaken with his wife, Frances S. Herskovits, he confronted the complexity of societies formed out of multiple historical sources. Both European and African sources of complex cultural forms were evident. His field diary noted the "transformations of Dutch caps worn by the Negro women here, which have meanings that are sometimes serious and which constitute as neat an example of cultural diffusion and change as I know of"; and he marveled at other "fascinating" examples of the "intertwining of cultural threads" (Herskovits [SCHP], Personal Diary—Surinam, July 17, 18, 1928).

Much of his subsequent research over the next thirteen years involved sorting out the African threads in New World Black cultures as he formulated other metaphors for their cultural forms. In Suriname, as expected, Herskovits saw Africanisms retained in relative purity among the Maroons, descendants of escaped slaves living in the rain forests. Unexpectedly, Creoles living in the capital, Paramaribo, also maintained an abundance of African cultural elements in their folklore. These elements were combined and juxtaposed in a variety of ways with cultural elements of European provenance.

Field research among the Maroons was the primary objective of this field trip, which was delayed by a fever and rashes experienced by Melville Herskovits, who remained for a longer time in Paramaribo than he initially expected. While fascinated by the cultures in contact swirling around him in Paramaribo, Herskovits was bursting with eagerness to visit the Maroons. His research about the Maroons would form a baseline for his study of African retentions in the New World. In *The Root of Roots: Or, How Afro-American Anthropology Got Its Start*, Richard and Sally Price note that Herskovits viewed his field research with the Saramacas as "pivotal to his career" and indicate that he "developed a comparative vision of Afro-American studies . . . that would fuel his own prodigious work, and that of countless students for years to come" during the voyages to and from Suriname and while he was in the field among the Saramaka" (2003, 4). While Herskovits underscored the importance of the research among the Saramaca, his observations of the creoles in Paramaribo anticipated much of his subsequent interest in cultural change (see Baron 1994, 178–218). The significance of Herskovits's observations of cultural forms among the Paramaribo Creoles for understanding *The Root of Roots: or, How Afro-American Anthropology Got Its Start* is overlooked by the Prices.

In *Suriname Folk-lore* ([1936] 1968), written with Frances S. Herskovits several years after their two field trips, various metaphors were used for different kinds of combinatorial processes through which creole cultural forms developed from dual sources. They used metaphors that rendered how the constitutive components of these forms were alternatively compounded within a new entity, united while retaining some degree of independent identity, or coexisted as readily identifiable and relatively discrete elements.

The traditional dress of Paramaribo Creole women was described with metaphors speaking to different kinds of combinatorial processes. While one component of the *koto yaki* (a costume used for ceremonies and social dances) embodied mutual absorption of European and African elements, another apparently maintained the identities of distinctive historical sources. Components evidencing the most African influence include a head kerchief, often vividly colored, and a voluminous skirt of matching pattern. The blouse is described as "European, for clothing the upper part of the body is a European conceit" (Herskovits and Herskovits [1936] 1968, 4). The skirt includes a ruffle turned up and fastened at the waist with a drawstring, above a substantial pad, known as the *famiri* or "family." Its "effect" is described as "a very generous bustle"; consequently, the Herskovitses note, "the *famiri* is often identified with the European costume of the eighteenth century" (4). They offered an alternative view of its provenance, contending that it should not be viewed as either exclusively European or African. They noted that "women in Africa are given to the use of draperies and padding about the waist to emphasize the broadness of hips and buttocks, and it may well be in this, as in many other instances, the merging of two characteristics somewhat similar aboriginally has occurred to form a unified cultural trait in the civilization of the Suriname Negroes" (4). While the bustle of the *koto yaki* is described as the "merging" of components from two cultural sources, a different metaphor is used for the skirt as a whole. It is described as a "blending" of African and European fashions, but the Herskovitses do not elaborate about the combinatorial processes that presumably maintained, to some degree, the identities of its European and African components.

"Merger" is not an apposite metaphor for the *famiri* since, according to the *Oxford English Dictionary*, to merge is to "cause something to be absorbed into something else, so as to lose its character and identity." In this case, there was apparently neither a loss of identity of the constitutive components nor mutual absorption. As for "blending" (the metaphor used for the skirt), it has been defined as an intimate and harmonious mixing which obscures the individuality of each component. This metaphor seems more appropriate to the combinatorial processes shaping the *koto yaki*, where the relationships of different historical sources are ambiguous and their individual identities difficult to discern.

"Coalescence" was another metaphor used by the Herskovitses for a process through which a cultural element is shaped by dual or multiple sources from other cultures. While opening and closing formulae were described toward the outset of a discussion of Creole folk tales as "one of the deep-seated African characteristics of folk-tales that have persisted in all portions of the New World," the Herskovitses conceded toward the conclusion of their consideration of this topic that they "have not claimed that the endings to Negro tales are not European in provenience" ([1936] 1968, 144). They note that in the Grimm brothers collections "endings reminiscent" of those in Suriname Creole tales are present, and they might be "best regarded as representing a coalescence of African and European cultural elements" (144). By definition, to coalesce is to unite or come together, so as to form one. Coalescence does not necessarily entail the loss of identity of individual components—coalesced entities may be united as an association or coalition, neither of which implies full incorporation in one body. The Herskovitses were, by their own admission, uncertain ("may, perhaps, be best regarded," they said, hesitatingly) about whether, in fact, European and African closing formulae came together as a "coalescence." It is a congenial metaphor for such a situation since it allows for the possibility of alternative interactions in the creolization process.

Components from two cultural sources were also said to combine in Suriname through what the Herskovitses called a "telescoping" process. By definition, telescoping refers to a process whereby one thing fits or slides into another, as in the tubes of a telescope. As a Herskovitsian metaphor, it is well suited for rendering the persistence of components of distinct origins that fit well together and maintain their original attributes (Herskovits [1936] 1968, 36). *Trefu* is an inherited prohibition against performance of "an act . . . hateful to some supernatural agent against which the destiny of the individual is associated," usually involving abstinence from certain foods. The term "trefu" was transmitted by Jews, who were present in Suriname since the earliest days of colonization (Herskovits [SCHP], Personal Diary—Surinam, July 18, 1928). While other scholars contended that the institution of *trefu* as a whole derived from "the same Hebrew sources as the word itself," the Herskovitses claimed that the "institution is African, the world of Hebrew origin, and the resulting integration in Surinam Negro life is to be accounted for by a process of telescoping" ([1936] 1968, 36). This same metaphor was also used for a process shaping an ambivalent attitude toward twins, viewed as "the manifestation of a telescoping of two distinct attitudes toward twins which derive from different regions of West Africa—one of worship, the other of abhorrence" (42).

The Herskovitses never explained their rationales for the use of metaphors to describe cultural forms of dual provenance and the processes that created them. However, their choices of different metaphors seem to reflect their efforts to craft conceptual handles for the combinatorial processes, derivations, and creolized character of the cultural forms observed in Suriname. During the decade following his second field trip to Suriname in 1929, Herskovits attempted to develop a conceptual framework conjoining the analysis of provenance, cultural change, and the results of cultural contact. This project was closely linked to his deep involvement with other anthropologists in the development of acculturation studies.

The analysis of creolized cultural forms and processes in Suriname was shaped primarily by a diffusionist Boasian perspective, which entailed tracing the historical relationships of cultural elements found in different regions. Herskovits's theoretical concerns shifted during the 1930s as he became as interested in cultural *change* as in persistence and continuity in culture. While his continuing interest in exploring cultural continuities with Africa among New World Blacks set him apart from other anthropologists, in other respects his work incorporated what George Stocking describes as a "change in emphasis between the central components of Boasian analysis—from 'elements' to 'processes' and 'patterns' in the context of a simultaneous shift in analytic perspective from the diachronic to the synchronic" (1976, 15). The focus of anthropology shifted to "the dynamic changes in society that may be observed at the present time" (Stocking 1976, 15).

For several years following his two field trips to Suriname, Herskovits devoted much of his research to constructing, link by link, what he called a "chain of evidence" (1932, 37) of specific correspondences between cultural elements of New World Blacks and Africans. Exhaustive research in existing ethnographic materials, a first field trip to West Africa, and evaluation of the results of the Suriname field trips revealed widespread continuities in folklore, language, and religion. While always greatly interested in identifying the purest African retentions, his scholarship during this period became increasingly directed toward analyzing what happens to African cultural elements when they are not maintained in apparent purity. He delineated gradations between different New World Black cultures in the intensity of their retentions of African cultural elements and analyzed the processes that resulted in the retention of some elements in apparent purity, the rejection of others, and the transformation of yet others into what we would now call creolized forms, through their combination with cultural elements of dual or multiple provenance.

During his first field trip to West Africa in 1932, Herskovits was struck by the impact of interpenetrating cultures and internal change. While the field trip was concentrated in Dahomey (now known as Benin), he also traveled in Nigeria and recorded trenchant observations in field diaries and correspondence. Shortly after his return from Suriname three years before, he suggested to Elsie Clews Parsons that the culture of the Maroons in the "deep interior" was "more African than the West African cultures of today," viewing it as "analogous to the . . . balladry of the Tennessee mountaineers" (Herskovits [NUHP], correspondence, Herskovits/Parsons, November 11, 1929). Comparisons of the cultural elements of Suriname Maroons and the West African source cultures he had seen firsthand in Africa revealed the latter to have undergone considerable internal change, while most of the cultures of Suriname Maroons seemed frozen in time. On a quick trip through Northern Nigeria, Herskovits perceived that culture contact had had a profound effect. He wrote to Franz Boas that he could "conceive of nowhere better to study acculturation; the Mohammedan influence from the north, the aboriginal cultural elements persisting in spite of the Mohammedan" (Boas 1972, correspondence, Herskovits/Boas, April 7, 1931).

The West African field experience intensified Herskovits's interest in acculturation and cultural change. Seemingly pure African retentions in the Americas were now seen as archaic forms of African cultural elements that, in Africa, underwent change over two centuries. He also saw substantial evidence of the acculturative effects of Islam, as well as European colonialism. Back in the United States, Herskovits felt greater urgency about studying acculturation in process among New World Blacks.

Over the next decade, Herskovits engaged in major field research projects in Haiti and Trinidad, which served as laboratories for *in situ* studies of acculturation and culture change, continued to analyze his field data from Suriname and Dahomey, and exhaustively researched ethnographic materials from throughout the New World. He viewed New World Black cultures as paradigms for the study of acculturation and culture change and as sources for links in a chain of evidence connecting African and New World Black folklore, social institutions, language, religion, and customary behavior (Herskovits [NUHP], correspondence, Herskovits/John M. Cooper, August 13, 1933). His circum-Atlantic project provided a foundation for analysis of the African heritage of Blacks in the United States, eventually culminating in the publication of *The Myth of the Negro Past* in 1941.

As Herskovits turned to identifying Africanisms in the United States, he perceived acute obstacles for establishing specific African sources for a people with multiple African origins and centuries of interaction with Americans of European ancestry. Herskovits was only able to identify a few examples of a "localized" African provenance—day names, a drum of Gold Coast type collected in Virginia, and the *Place Congo* in New Orleans. African American cultural elements were found to have dual or multiple sources in Europe and Africa, and he ascribed African sources generally to West Africa as a whole rather than to specific African peoples: "The shifting about of slaves, and the policy of separating those of the same tribe, has operated to cause the retention of Africanisms in implications and inner structure rather than externals. That is why, when we search for intimations of definite sources of origin in the United States, we find a generalized expression of West African heritage, modified by or welded to customs derived from the European civilization of the masters" (Herskovits 1933, 260).

"Welded" is an apt metaphor for the processes that many aspects of African culture experienced in the United States, as they were transformed through cultural contact with Euro-Americans. Their specific African sources cannot be discerned due to the origins of slaves in various regions of West Africa—and, to a lesser extent, Central Africa as well.[4] "Welding" denotes an inseparable or intimate uniting, befitting the situation described by Herskovits, where Africanisms of generalized West African origin can only be identified through "implication" or "inner structure." By suggesting that some African cultural elements are "modified" rather than "welded," Herskovits set up an implicit contrast between situations where Africanisms are more readily discerned and those where they have been united through welding with European cultural elements.

"Convergence" first appeared as another Herskovitsian metaphor during this period, referring to processes of cultural contact that preserve the distinctive identities of component elements within a new belief system or cultural form. It was used in 1933 to describe a phenomenon found in New World Black Catholic cultures that he would label "syncretism" several years later. In "Cuba, as in Brazil," Herskovits wrote, "there is convergence of the aboriginal African gods with Catholic worship, a significant fact for the study of acculturation" (1933, 258). Citing Fernando Ortiz's *Los Negros Brujos* ([1917] 1995), he noted the identification of St. Barbara with Shangó, and Obatalá with the image of the crucified Christ (1933, 258). While distinct deities are identified with one another in these Afro-Caribbean religions, they do not lose their independent identities in the new belief system. A fresh approach to a controversy raging among folklorists for many years about whether the "spirituals" of Black Americans were "African" or "European" in origin was inspired by Herskovits's use of this convergence metaphor. This controversy was generally staked out in sharp dichotomies (see Wilgus 1959, 345–364). A view of spirituals as creolized forms with sources in both Africa and Europe remained outside of the grounds of discourse, even though some of those claiming European origins allowed for a measure of African influence in some formal features, and those who argued for African origins conversely conceded some extent of European influence.

After seeing how Herskovits used the term *convergence*, George Herzog expressed great interest in the concept of convergence as providing an alternative to reductive ascriptions of exclusively European or African origins for New World Black music or languages. As he prepared reviews of Guy B. Johnson's *Folk Culture on St. Helena Island* (1930) and George Pullen Jackson's *White Spirituals in the Southern Uplands* (1930), he suggested that convergence offers a new way of viewing the origin of spirituals: "I shall make the point that, after so much controversy about whether something is 'African' or not in origin, we are likely to lose sight of the possibility of convergence. To put it better, that a number of things may be difficult at present to ascribe to an African or a White origin, because there are parallels in both cultures. For instance, the habit of singing the line solo and have the chorus repeat it; very common in Africa (Cameroons, Congo, etc.). But Jackson mentions 'lining out of songs by the leader in the 17th century songs of New England'" (Herskovits [NUHP], correspondence, Herskovits/Herzog, April 12, 1934). Responding to Herzog, Herskovits encouraged this view "as far as music is concerned," agreeing that the "point of convergence should be strongly stressed" in Herzog's review (Herskovits [NUHP], correspondence, Herskovits/Herzog, April 12, 1934). Although he apparently agreed about the value of convergence as a metaphor, it did not reappear in his writings of the time as he continued to offer up new metaphors for the transformations of African cultural elements in the Americas.

Herskovits's writings at this time began to forcefully challenge a virtually universal assumption of the absence of African influences in the cultures of the United States. "What has Africa Given America?" published in the *New Republic* in 1933, set out arguments that would be elaborated at greater length in *The Myth of the Negro Past*. While it was "long understood" that contacts between cultures resulted in "mutual borrowings," Herskovits asserted this fundamental "principle" was either "blandly overlooked or emotionally denied" when it came to contacts between White and Black Americans ([1935] 1966, 168). His examples of African influences must have seemed startling in 1935, since they encompassed mainstream dimensions of American life experienced by Whites—including folk culture generally viewed as quintessentially Southern. It was almost unimaginably radical to make such claims at a time of pervasive ethnocentrism shaping both academic and popular constructions of American culture.

Discussing Southern foodways, Herskovits ascribed African influence to fried chicken, gumbo, and the "particularized use of yams, okra and rice" ([1935] 1966, 172). To make his case, he marshaled his broad comparative perspective, extending through the Caribbean and Africa, along with comparisons between New England and the South. He stated, "It is almost self-evident . . . that New England cooking is closer to the ancestral [British] than is that of Charleston or Savannah," as he asked, "May not the unknown element in the equation be the Negro?" (173). He reported seeing cooked foods for sale in markets in West Africa like those consumed in the South and proceeded to provide several examples of direct African influence: cooking in deep fat, fried foods, the African origins of the word "gumbo," and the "high seasoning" found in African, Caribbean and Southern American cooking (173).[5]

African influence was also seen in the "important role assigned to the art of proper behavior" in the South, where "mind your manners" is a "fundamental tenet" that shapes the region's "graciousness of life" (Herskovits [1935] 1966, 172). Herskovits noted, "Africans place the greatest of emphasis on good manners," and "proper behavior—in the sense of an ability to observe the minutiae of a code of politeness—is a first requirement in any social intercourse" (172). The "essence of African behavior" is seen in behavioral norms also valued in the "Southern-white code of politeness," including "respect for elders, the soft voice before one who is a power in the community [and] the excessive employment of terms of endearment or kinship in neighborly contacts" (172). In this article, Herskovits offered telling examples to show that "reasonable indication of revamped survivals of African tradition are not lacking" (174). The metaphor of "revamped" suggests the reworking of a tradition from its African sources by a folk process. By definition, "revamping" means a reworking, making something new from old materials, patching something up again. It can involve improvisation, suggesting a process of cultural creativity. This process engages both of the parties in culture contact, in the United States as elsewhere, as Herskovits indicated when he called for "much further investigation along these lines . . . if we are to have an undistorted concept of the roots from which our culture has grown" in a country where "both whites and Negroes took, both gave" (174). A culture shaped by such give and take may be viewed as profoundly creolized, rather than monolithically Black and White in cultural character and derivation.[6]

Another metaphor, "pouring into a mold," was used in a discussion of the influence of African languages upon American speech. Although slaves from different parts of West Africa spoke mutually unintelligible languages, Herskovits saw commonalities in "similar structural and idiomatic organization" and in the "phonetics of all these tongues" that were "about the same" ([1935] 1966, 171). In the New World, Blacks learned new words in the European languages of their masters, "spoke these words with a West African pronunciation, and poured their new vocabulary into the mold of West African grammatical and idiomatic forms" (171). "Pouring into a mold" as a metaphor speaks to perduring structures of African culture within which content of Euro-American origin is reshaped.

Herskovits suggested that Africa "gives" to America through cultural contact occurring in social interaction between Blacks and Whites. An example of such interaction is transmission of Black English by African American nurses to children in their care, setting in motion African influences in the speech of White Americans ([1935] 1966, 171). Through situating the transformation of cultural forms in actual social interaction, Herskovits represents cultural change as a process involving individual personalities, rather than as a diffusion of cultural elements abstracted from social life.

During the mid 1920s, Herskovits criticized A. L. Kroeber's view of culture as too "mechanical" and cautioned against the superorganic "objectification of culture" (1924, 26). He argued against the view of some diffusionists that culture is an objective force that can be abstracted from the agency of human actors (Willey and Herskovits 1927, 263). This movement in anthropological thought was pioneered by Edward Sapir, who paved the way for culture and personality studies in a 1917 article, "Do We Need the 'Superorganic?'" Sapir came to view culture as a "personality organization," rather than a "more or less mechanical sum of . . . generalized patterns of behavior abstracted by the anthropologist" (1934, 409–410). This view meshes with an approach to creole cultures (or any culture, for that matter) as emergent, rather than as consisting of fixed forms. For Sapir, "culture is not a 'thing,' monolithic and equally 'shared' by all those included within its boundaries. . . . In other words, culture is not fixed and static, but open-ended; it is not thinglike, but exists only as it is continually reinterpreted by creative personalities" (Handler 1986, 147). Since creole societies are relatively new social formations whose component populations engage in fluid relationships with each other, their open-endedness is more apparent than in older, more settled societies.

Field research in Haiti in 1934 fundamentally altered Herskovits's approach to acculturation, as he focused upon how individual personalities in Haiti experience a dual cultural legacy. While he had conceptualized culture as centered upon individual personalities for a number of years, his studies of New World Black cultures were still shaped by a diffusionist approach. After an "Aha!" experience in the field, he began to analyze the African cultural legacy in the Americas through the experience of individual personalities and put a psychological stamp on general acculturation theory. While he continued to construct "links in a chain of evidence" of Africanisms through tracing cultural elements, he now also began to adduce new kinds of patterns for the transformation of African cultures in the Americas, constructing new metaphors for these patterns.

Research during the first month had much of the same thrust as the Suriname field trip five years before. Herskovits considered how Haitian cultural elements corresponded to those of Africa, focusing upon how Haitian elements varied from presumed African sources. Then, one day, a discussion with his interpreters Leonce Joachim and Galbert Constance about the church's role in "matters of death and burial" revealed complexities in the relationships of Haitians to Catholicism and Vodou that would alter the course of his research. He wrote in his field diary that "Catholicism and Voodooism are even more mixed" than he had recognized, extending beyond *lwa* (Vodou deities) having names of saints and the "use of crucifixes and 'images' in Vodou rites." He discovered that "there is no clear line of demarcation between those who are Voduists and those who are Catholics," when Joachim and Constance told him that the *hungan* in the area [Mirebelais] "all go to church and take the sacraments." He learned soon afterwards, from another Haitian, that in Leogane, although *hungan* do not attend church, the *mambos* (priestesses) do, as do "all the rest of the people." Excited by this new information, Herskovits wrote that "if this is true from the point of view of internal psychological adjustment as it . . . seems to be true of the external adaptation of the two sets of beliefs, it can be one of the best acculturation finds that can be imagined" (Herskovits [SCHP], Diary—Haitian Field Trip, July 19, 1934).

As he began to assimilate his new understandings of Haitian culture, Herskovits formulated hypotheses about how Haitians reconcile their dual cultural legacies. A month later, he reflected upon the vacillating personalities of the individuals who served as his research sources. He wrote in his field diary of his intention to "uncover . . . the psychological substratum that will go far toward explaining the manner in which European and

African social and religious customs,—but mainly religious ones,—have combined to give to these people the duality of approach to so many situations" (Herskovits [SCHP], Diary—Haitian Field Trip, August 18, 1934). Writing to Elsie Clews Parsons shortly after returning from Haiti, he indicated that his primary research objective shifted during fieldwork from the recording of survivals to studying acculturative processes: "[The] problem changed—or changed itself—after we were in Haiti for only two or three weeks. The African survivals were so numerous, and so obvious, that they almost recorded themselves. But the thing that continued to fascinate us . . . particularly in the religious life, was the manner in which African and French traditions have been integrated in a single system. This has been noted, of course, for the Vodu cult, but I do not believe its ramifications, and its psychological significance to the people have ever been analyzed to any extent" (Herskovits [NUHP], correspondence, Herskovits/Parsons, October 8, 1934).

An appropriately ambiguous metaphor appeared in a letter to Fernando Ortiz about how African and European belief systems combined in Haiti. Remarking on parallels between Afro-Cuban and Haitian religions, Herskovits wrote about his fascination with how "Haitians, like your Cuban Negroes, have interlarded their aboriginal African tradition with beliefs and ceremonies drawn from Catholicism" (Herskovits [NUHP], correspondence, Herskovits/Ortiz, October 19, 1934). "Interlarding" means the mixing of fat with lean in alternating strips, a mingling or an interspersing. This term is suitably ambiguous for Herskovits's purposes, since it may involve a relatively predictable alternation of fat with lean, or, irregularly, a scattering through interspersal. Since he was uncertain at the time about the patterning of European and African components in Haitian culture, "interlarding" could suit conditions of regularity or scattering. Now that he was focusing upon how individual personalities experience acculturation, Herskovits was especially concerned with how Haitians were able to reconcile "African" and "European" dimensions of their culture, however they may have been ordered.

During the period Herskovits spent writing up the results of the Haitian field study as *Life in a Haitian Valley*, he was also formulating parameters for the study of acculturation as a member of the Committee on Acculturation of the Social Science Research Council. As the committee considered the definition of terms in acculturation studies, he insisted on foregrounding the role of the individual in the acculturative process and avoiding superorganicist language. Herskovits was adamant about distinguishing

between diffusion, which may involve indirect contact, and acculturation, seen as always involving firsthand contact. Heatedly objecting to a
component of an acculturation definition circulating among committee
members that allowed for indirect, non face-to-face contact, he wrote to
Ralph Linton, in handwritten comments bursting through the margins,
that indirect contact is "not *acculturation* but *diffusion:* [this] is important because personal element is lacking & is this not the reason that our
Committee exists—since we agreed that acculturation is a key element in
the study of the rel. bet. *culture & personality?*" In this letter, Herskovits
also questioned a statement that from an "objective" perspective, culture
can be "thought of in terms of culture elements or traits, abstracted patterns of behavior which may be named, described or dealt with apart from
the individuals in whose behavior they are apparent" (Herskovits [NUHP],
correspondence, Herskovits/Linton, October 16, 1935). His position about
traits demonstrates that Herskovits now resisted viewing cultures as
entities abstracted from human agency and behavior and should not be
uncritically seen as a "trait chaser," as he has been mischaracterized by
some anthropologists from subsequent generations. Herskovits's recom-
mended revisions were eventually incorporated in the "Memorandum for
the Study of Acculturation," which defined acculturation as "phenomena
which result when groups of individuals having different cultures come
into continuous first-hand contact, with subsequent changes in the original cultural patterns of either or both groups" (Redfield, Linton, Herskovits 1936, 149–150).[7] This definition, as we see, indicates that change may
involve "either" or "both" groups. Change for "both" groups is characteristic of creolization and fits as well with Fernando Ortiz's concept of transculturation, as a mutual exchange between cultures ([1947] 1995).[8]

Syncretism, the best known of the terms in the Herskovitsian acculturation lexicon, should be understood within the context of his interests
in culture and personality. It is a term that has been extensively used for
creolized cultural forms. Herskovits initially referred to syncretism as a
process of identification by individuals between two different belief systems. The term *syncretism* had been applied to belief systems since the
sixteenth century as the "attempted union or reconciliation of diverse or
opposite tenets or practices" (*Compact Edition of the Oxford English Dictionary*, 1971 ed., s.v. "syncretism"). For example, in the Haitian *humfort*
(temple of a Vodou priest), chromolithographic portraits of Catholic saints
are displayed. The saints represented in these portraits are identified with
lwa. The portraits are described by Herskovits in *Life in a Haitian Valley*

as "one of the most vivid instances of the mingling of African and European elements in Haitian belief, for they are the outward symbol of the psychological reconciliation that has been effected between the saints of the Church and the African deities" ([1937c] 1971, 282). They function as a "device to achieve an adjustment between two conflicting systems by emphasizing the resemblance between Catholic saints and African nature deities" (Herskovits [1937c] 1971, 282). Herskovits first used the term *syncretism* for this reconciliative device in an aptly titled article offering a comparative perspective, "African Gods and Catholic Saints in New World Negro Belief," which appeared the same year as *Life in a Haitian Valley*. "Syncretism" would be used to describe both the process of identification between two beliefs and creolized forms that are tangible manifestations of the reconciliation of two belief systems. It has a more precise meaning than "mingling," a metaphor of interspersal—a mixture uniting elements— used in *Life in a Haitian Valley* to characterize the chromolithographs as outward manifestations of the reconciliation of beliefs. "Mingling" as metaphor does, however, appropriately suggest maintenance of the identity of component elements—what would be found in a mixture, rather than a compound. In syncretisms, as well, elements from two belief systems are identified with one another without losing their individual identities.

"African Gods and Catholic Saints in New World Negro Belief" begins by contrasting the syncretisms of native peoples in Mexico, Central America, and the Southwest United States with those of New World Blacks. Among the latter, Herskovits identified a "more thoroughgoing assimilation of Christian and Pagan beliefs," in contrast with the "assimilation" found in Mexico and the Southwest, which has "generally taken the form of the survival of aboriginal custom in a system of belief and ritual practices the outer forms of which are predominantly Catholic" (Herskovits 1937b, 635). Among Blacks in Brazil, Cuba, and Haiti, on the other hand, "the exchange has been less one-sided, and the elements ancestral to the present-day organization of worship have been retained in immediately recognizable form" (635). In the latter case, there are "everywhere specific identifications . . . between African gods and Catholic saints" (321–322). These syncretisms thus are marked by *identification*, which Herskovits characterized as a psychological phenomenon in *Life in a Haitian Valley*. They are also viewed as a combination of African and European beliefs that involve mutual exchange. At the same time, as retentions, they maintain ancestral belief, as is suggested by the "mingling" metaphor used in *Life in a Haitian Valley*.

Drawing broader strokes, Herskovits also indicated that syncretisms illustrate how New World Blacks, "in responding to the acculturative process, have succeeded in achieving, at least in their religious life, a synthesis between aboriginal African patterns and the European traditions to which they have been exposed." A footnote to this statement quietly suggests that the term *syncretism* can be applied well beyond religion: "this synthesis marks practically all phases of the life of the Negro peasant" in Haiti, and "there is no reason to assume that a similar assimilation has not taken place in Cuba and Brazil" (Herskovits 1937b, 635–636). While this larger conceptualization of syncretism is here embedded in a footnote, a broader meaning was now surfacing. During the 1940s Herskovits would explicitly define syncretism as a major concept in his theory of acculturation, exemplified in New World Black religions but also present in other areas of culture.

For now, syncretism did not figure significantly in Herskovits's writings about acculturation theory. In 1938, he published *Acculturation, the Study of Culture Contact*, a transcultural study examining acculturation in various manifestations around the globe. It included his concept of *assimilation*, a term he used in explaining syncretism as a cultural process in "African Gods and Catholic Saints in New World Negro Belief." Following from Robert Park, Herskovits saw *assimilation* as a term broadly applicable to a wide variety of kinds of cultural contact, entailing the "process by means of which a synthesis of culture is achieved, whatever the degree of contact or amount of borrowing" ([1938] 1958, 13). From a creolist perspective, such a "synthesis" occurs in creolization processes taking place in any culture, potentially occurring wherever different groups come into face-to-face contact. This work also contained a justification for trait analysis, a method associated with diffusionism that Herskovits maintained throughout his search for Africanisms. He defended it as a vital means to the end of understanding acculturative processes, asserting that "the assignment of one element or another to a specific source merely clears the ground so that we can understand the kinds of things that were taken over or rejected, the ways in which they were integrated into the culture, and from this and the study of many acculturative situations, of the possibility of working out general principles of cultural change" ([1938] 1958, 28–29).

Life in a Haitian Valley employed metaphors to render the varieties of cultural forms that emerged out of processes bringing together African and European elements. Metaphors were also used to characterize Haitian culture as a whole, which was seen as maintaining a conflicted relationship to its dual historical legacy.

For acculturation studies, Haiti provided a kind of control situation where prolonged exposure to European culture was followed by "more than a century of consolidation of the original influences." The combination of African and European influences was viewed as a process "of selection, of working over, of revamping and recombining the elements of the contributing cultures, with the result that the ensuing combinations, though of recognizable derivation, differ from their aboriginal forms" (Herskovits [1937c] 1971, 301). "Consolidation," one of several tropes in this metaphorically packed passage, signifies a process through which two entities combine in a new form, remaining connected yet not necessarily fully united. In Haiti this consolidation occurred as a process of uniting and combining European and African traditions following the cessation of slavery and independence. The presence of foreigners greatly diminished until the American military occupation that began in 1915 and ended just before Herskovits's arrival in 1934. His view that the consolidation was incomplete is reflected in his reference to the revamping, selecting, recombining, and reworking that had occurred from the time of initial colonization.

"Amalgam," another key metaphor in *Life in a Haitian Valley*, conveys well the plasticity and fluidity of a culture experiencing the ongoing reworking of African and European elements. "Working the Amalgam" was the vividly processual title of a chapter describing the formation of Haitian culture during the colonial period as a result of the acculturative encounter of French settlers and African slaves. By definition, an amalgam is a soft mass created by chemical manipulation, an intimate, but plastic combination of any two or more substances. Harmonious combination, one of "amalgam's" figurative meanings, is not applicable to the Haitian situation, but plasticity is. Herskovits represents the development of Haitian culture as characterized by plasticity as African and European cultural elements combine, with African and European heritages joined in an unresolved relationship, evading a united state. Amalgamation is frequently used as a metaphor in discussing Vodou, seen as shaped by reciprocal interrelationships between Catholicism and African traditional religions, yet maintaining distinctive features of each belief system. Arguing against a received view of acculturation as a unidirectional process resulting in European domination, Herskovits contended that the incorporation by Vodou of elements of both Catholicism and African religions involved "amalgamation rather than . . . dominance" ([1937] 1971, 274).

Another seemingly contradictory metaphor for Haitian culture as a whole appeared as a section of *Life in a Haitian Valley* called "Haiti, a Cultural Mosaic." While "amalgam" suggests an entity susceptible to change because of its plasticity—suitable for an emergent, Creole culture—"mosaic" connotes fixity. Although mosaics are wholes made up of parts of clearly different origin, they have a fixed character, with their discrete, differentiated tesserae remaining in the same place. Herskovits does not explain his use of the "mosaic" metaphor in this book, but discusses it in *Acculturation, the Study of Culture Contact*. He speaks in the latter work of "an amalgam of culture such as can be seen in Mexico and Haiti and other parts of the world, where peoples who were once in continued contact with foreign bodies of tradition have made an adjustment . . . of adaptation to the fashions of living newly introduced. Perhaps this . . . is the result of more extended contacts between cultures, rather than the more conventionally accepted dictum that contact eventuates in extinction of one by the other" ([1938] 1958, 65).

However, elsewhere in this book Herskovits seems to contradict himself, stating that in "Haiti . . . conflicting traditions have never been resolved, but have been so adjusted to one another that a mosaic has resulted rather than an amalgam such as is found in Mexico" ([1938] 1958, 65). In another publication, "African Ethnology and the New World Negro," published in 1937, Herskovits viewed amalgamation as a stage on the way to the formation of a mosaic, reporting that he had "determined how the . . . [Haitians] amalgamated West African and European customs . . . to form the complex mosaic of the living culture (1937a, 10). But his uses of both "mosaic" and "amalgam" during this period seem confused, more elusive than allusive.

"Kaleidoscope," a powerful and richly evocative term, is yet another metaphor used for Haitian culture as a whole. Herskovits wrote of the transformation of French and African cultural elements as a result of acculturative contact over centuries. In Haiti, "where continuous contact between French and Africans resulted in a centuries-long consolidation of traditions, . . . the manner in which, in technology, social and economic organization, religion, music and the dance, the ancestral components have taken new form as a result of the movement of the historical kaleidoscope, can very readily be discerned" (Herskovits 1937a, 263). A kaleidoscope, shifting continuously in successive phases, conveys splendidly the ongoing transformations of cultural elements derived from Europe and Africa during "centuries of consolidation." If fits with Brathwaite's view of creolization as a process that results in "multiform orientations from or *towards* ancestral originals" (1974b, 7)—continuous emergence and interplay rather than constant and fixed relationships.[9]

Textiles provided other metaphors for Herskovits. At the outset of *Life in a Haitian Valley*, Herskovits indicated that he would reach far beyond mere acknowledgment of a dual legacy. He remarked, "It has been repeatedly stated that Haiti is the child of Africa and France. . . . [E]ven those who proclaim this emphatically fail too often to recognize the need for as detailed a knowledge as possible of how the strands of history were woven into the fabric of Haitian cultural life" (Herskovits [1937c] 1971, 15). Extending this "strands of history" metaphor, he also wrote of the need to "disentangle the varied sources" (253) of Haitian cultural institutions, identifying the provenance of elements of particular cultural forms. As he disentangled, he found a variety of ways in which cultural elements were retained in putative purity, displaced, adapted within new cultural patterns, and transformed as they combined in various ways with traits derived from another culture.

"Intermingling," as a metaphor, speaks to the possibility of different kinds of patterning in a new entity, including a mixture where elements of different provenance coexist, or a blend, where the identities of the parts that unite are obscured. The *caille*, a widespread vernacular house type, is offered as an example of the intermingling of cultural elements. As he had for the *koto yaki* in Suriname, Herskovits teases out "African" and "European" elements, as well as an Amerindian element, identified as isolable elements of distinctive provenance, coexisting alongside each other in a single cultural form.[10] He noted "purely African" thatching of twilled withes, but "entirely European furniture, since the African stool has given way to the European straight chair." The *ajupa*, an accessory field house, is seen as one of the few aboriginal contributions to present-day culture. Viewed as a whole, he also sees the *caille* as a coalescence, a unified object incorporating structural elements that were similar to one another in their source cultures. Since the rectangular floor plan and the roof are found in both West Africa and Europe, Herskovits suggested that "the house thus probably represents a coalescence of two dwelling forms that were originally not strikingly unlike each other" (Herskovits [1937c] 1971, 253–254).

"Coalescence" as metaphor had been used in *Suriname Folk-lore* for opening and closing formulae in folktales. It suited the patterning exhibited by the *caille* as it had opening and closing formulae: elements similar in origin unite in a new association, but they do not necessarily lose their original identities through incorporation in the new body.

In his conclusion to *Life in a Haitian Valley*, Herskovits asserted that his findings in Haiti provided vivid evidence of how African cultures did not give way to European cultures. Turning to the United States, he asked, "What of the belief in the United States that nothing of Africa remains?" In the United States, Blacks retain "certain African aspects of behavior" and belief "within a varying range" while assimilating American culture. He noted that it is not thought "strange that the descendants of British colonists . . . in New England should have retained certain speech or food habits of England," or that predominantly German Milwaukee "should have a flavor that is a carryover of the culture of Germany," or that Scandinavian, Jewish, Polish, and other traditions have not "entirely given way before the patterns that characterize the culture of the country as a whole." For all of these groups, parents "consciously and unconsciously handed down their knowledge, beliefs and habits of motor behavior to their children, which is . . . all that is meant, when it is pointed out that the Negro's heritage from the cultures of Africa has not been lost" (Herskovits [1937c] 1971, 308–309).

From a creolist perspective, the common American culture assimilated by African Americans could be seen as a product of interactions and combinatorial processes involving members of all cultural groups. In "What Has Africa Given America," Herskovits ([1935] 1966) showed how cultural forms viewed as "White" are, in fact, substantially shaped by African cultural influences. Now, however, his scholarship about African Americans was driven in large part by a mission to show that African Americans have retained an African heritage. Seventy-five years later such a contention does not seem revolutionary at all, but it was a radical, minority opinion at the time.

As he prepared to write *The Myth of the Negro Past*, Herskovits ([1941] 1958) faced the challenge of substantiating an African heritage for African Americans in the face of evidence that did not seem "African" at all on its surface. He turned to acculturation theory as he constructed a conceptual framework to show how African cultural elements are maintained, in modified form and in combination with elements derived from other sources. *Syncretism* appeared as a general term for the products of acculturative processes in a *"Preliminary Memorandum* on the Problem of African Survivals,"* which stated that "much of present-day Negro culture is, in the nature of the case, neither purely African nor purely European, but represents, in varying degrees, a syncretism of the dual heritage of Europe and Africa."[11] "Syncretism" was now broadly construed as referring to cultural forms and processes of dual provenance.

Textile metaphors reappeared in the *"Preliminary Memorandum,"* as Herskovits justified the need to understand the acculturative mechanisms that transformed African cultures in the United States: "In the tangled skein of American Negro culture history, the African threads are meaningless unless we arrive at a comprehension of the mechanisms whereby such Africanisms as may be discovered were perpetuated, and how they were rewoven with yarn from other sources" (Herskovits [NUHP], *Preliminary Memorandum* on the Problem of African Survivals," ca. January 1, 1940). The metaphors of skein and rewoven threads were intriguingly juxtaposed, but seemed somewhat contradictory. The cultural history of African Americans is represented as a disordered coil of unwoven threads, a "tangled skein." Herskovits claimed that it is necessary to sort our African threads amidst a mess of yarn. Elsewhere in his writings about Blacks in the United States, he indicated that the European sources (or "threads," if you will) are more prominent and easier to identify. The metaphor of rewoven threads apparently represents an interweaving of European and African cultural elements, through acculturative processes, for which "mechanisms" must be adduced. On the one hand, we have a "tangled skein," on the other, "interwoven threads." Perhaps he is saying that a pattern does exist, within a history that appears outwardly tangled.

Although Herskovits had long recognized that Africanisms would mainly be found beneath the surface of overt behavior, he was just beginning to conceive of an acculturative mechanism to account for retentions of "inner meanings" within adapted European "outer forms." Such "inner" dimensions of African American culture retained from Africa are viewed in *The Myth of the Negro Past* as "cultural intangibles," retained in "motor behavior" and within beliefs and values underlying diverse aspects of African American culture. "Cultural intangibles" included codes of polite behavior, a distinctive concept of time, and strategies to adjust to difficult situations through indirection, evasion, ridicule, and the feigning of stupidity. The "principle of indirection" entails the use of "subterfuge and concealment" as a "weapon" and "discretion" as a survival technique (Herskovits [1941] 1958, 151–156, see also Baron 1994, 658–666). Motor habits derived from Africa included accompaniments to song, planting techniques, and the carrying of burdens on the head. Herskovits drew from folklore for examples of cultural intangibles, including folk beliefs about the power of ancestors (collected by Newbell Niles Puckett), responses of congregants to preachers (which are compared to African polite behavior), and improvised songs by slaves, "which were positively impudent, but which, clothed in the right forms, would pass unnoticed, or even provoke a smile or laughter" (Herskovits [1941] 1958, 151, 152, 154).

While Herskovits's discussions of cultural intangibles constitute a relatively small portion of *The Myth of the Negro Past*, they are quite suggestive. A decade later in a discussion of Afro-American research strategies he would state that "much of socially sanctioned behavior lodges on a psychological plane that *lies below the level of consciousness*" in calling for the study of "motor habits," "aesthetic patterns," and "value systems" (Herskovits 1952, 153, cited in Mintz and Price [1976] 1992, 11). While Mintz and Price claim that "in spite of these pronouncements, neither Herskovits nor his students were able to advance very far beyond the level of overt forms or explicit beliefs when they actually tried to enumerate the shared characteristics of the people of Africa" (Mintz and Price [1976] 1992, 11), Herskovits actually does provide a number of African American examples of behavior "below the level of consciousness" in *The Myth of the Negro Past.*

A revelation during his 1939 field trip to Trinidad induced Herskovits to develop the concept of *reinterpretation*, which would eventually become a linchpin of his theory of culture change and acculturation. In Trinidad, Herskovits found a creole culture exhibiting many similarities to African American culture. The village where he worked, Toco, appeared more "Europeanized" than any of his other fieldwork venues in the New World. It is a Protestant community with a range of Protestant denominations comparable to those found in the United States. Within two weeks of his arrival, he knew that "one thing is certain: the situation we are studying here is different in many ways from any we have yet analyzed, it is different in a way that should make it possible for us to understand life in American southern communities far better than if we did not have the experience here" (Herskovits [SCHP], Diary—Trinidad Trip, June 26, 1939). Africanisms turned up unexpectedly, in unlikely combinations with European cultural elements:

> During the past few days we've had a lot of reel and bele songs, as well as the Baptist shouts, and today we took a few more of the "sentimental" songs, which live up to their name in the worst sense. As Fann [Frances. S. Herskovits] says, it is an amazing culture where the most African music is the Baptist song, and the most African tradition, worship of the ancestors, is carried on to French quadrilles and Irish reels! However, it strikes me that it is important to record these "sentimental" songs, since they not only figure prominently in the repertoire of the people, but are really amazingly good evidence that when Negroes wished to take over European music they were able to take it over

lock, stock and barrel, with no nonsense about "survivals." (Herskovits [SCHP], Dairy—Trinidad Trip, July 18, 1939)

A church service among Shouter Baptists strongly evoked similar services in Black Protestant churches in the Untied States. Restrained Protestant worship became more "African" in the course of the service: Sankey hymns were first sung slowly, then more fervently, as the tempo quickened and the singing became "jazzed." The songs were ornamented with simulated drumming, accompanied by the patting of feet and hand clapping. Possession and glossolalia also occurred. *Trinidad Village*, published in 1947, described how these field experiences led to the concept of *reinterpretation*. The Herskovitses wrote—metaphorically—of how field materials "eventually yielded, as if casting a sudden flair against indistinct masses, silhouetted for us in clear outline the means whereby transitions from African culture to ways of life preponderantly European had been achieved by Africans and their descendants. The shouter's sect, for example, revealed how African worship . . . had been shaped and reinterpreted to fit into the pattern of European worship" (Herskovits and Herskovits [1947] 1964, vi).

Reinterpretation was viewed as a phenomenon of cultural borrowing, a selective process determining the degree of acceptance of the new and retention of the old. It was defined as a "mechanism" that "permit[s] a people to retain the inner meanings of traditionally sanctioned modes of behavior while adopting new outer institutional forms" (Herskovits and Herskovits [1947] 1964, vi). Retention was now redefined in terms of the maintenance of meaning during acculturation rather than as preservation of elements of culture.

Explaining reinterpretation in psychological terms, Herskovits compared Trinidad to the rural South of the United States. In both places, slavery deprived Blacks of "psychological security by rendering meaningless traditional African institutions and their validating sanctions." A "disordered orientation" resulted, with ensuing "frustrations based upon the social and legal proscriptions of culturally sanctioned traditions of family life and worship." Reinterpretations act as compensatory mechanisms, providing "continuity and a measure of adjustment, affording psychological resilience" (Herskovits and Herskovits [1947] 1964, 4–6). He viewed resilience as a defining feature of the cultures of peoples of African descent in the Americas; and the concept of reinterpretation helped explain how resilience was achieved despite the repression of African tradition.

Writings of Herskovits that appeared prior to the development of his concept of reinterpretation had rendered various kinds of "reworkings" through metaphor. As he conceptualized reinterpretation, it suited a new objective of ascertaining the degree of reconciliation between different source cultures, enabling him to see how "cultural accommodation and cultural integration had been achieved" and moving him away from "the question of what Africanisms were carried over in unaltered form." Herskovits had come to recognize that "cultures of multiple origin do not represent a cultural mosaic, but rather become fully integrated," and he sought to "ascertain the degree to which these reconciliations had actually been achieved, and where, on the acculturative continuum, a given manifestation of the reworking of these elements might lie" ([1941] 1958, xxiii). By apparently rejecting the mosaic metaphor for cultures of multiple origin, he now saw creolized cultures as integrative of elements from different source cultures. This view of cultures of multiple origins as integrative and containing varying degrees of reconciliation of their component cultures is extremely suggestive for creolization studies. It represents such cultures as built up of component source cultures that do not remain as discrete entities in a fixed form (like a mosaic's tesserae) but are "reworked" in varying ways.

During the final stage of Herskovits's career (he died in 1963), he was more interested in the values, meanings, and functions of forms rather than in the preservation of forms per se. Form became a less important issue for Herskovits, since at its "essence . . . the reinterpretive process" entails "differentiating cultural form from cultural sanction. Under contact, a new form can be accorded a value that has a functioning role into which it can be readily fitted; or an old form can be assimilated to a new one" (Herskovits [1941] 1958, xxi–xxiii).

Syncretism had remained a key term in *The Myth of the Negro Past*, used variously for specific processes bringing together forms of African and European provenance, the reconciliation of beliefs, and an overarching process of syncretization in the New World. These diverse meanings appeared several years before Herskovits severely narrowed what he meant by the term as reinterpretation ascended in the Herskovitsian lexicon. A broadened conceptualization of syncretism would be developed by the French anthropologist Roger Bastide, who reclaimed it as a central concept in acculturation studies. He identified two types of syncretic structures, *les structures lineares* (linear structures) and *les structures rayonnantes* (radiating structures), which include complex groupings of sentiments, inclinations, and cognitive features. These types of structures correspond to two types of acculturation studies: "material acculturation," involving combinations of traits such as Herskovits identified in his analyses of African cultural elements in the Americas, and "formal acculturation," which includes psychological aspects of acculturation and processes of transformation in logic, perception, memory, and emotion, like in Herskovits's concept of reinterpretation (Bastide 1970, 137–148). Ideology might also be added to the components of radiating syncretic structures (see Baron 1977). Applied to the creolization process, a wider range of meanings associated with syncretism allows for both the combination of cultural forms from two or more cultures as tangible, material Creole forms (such as a food or a musical style) and the meanings, values, and ideologies associated with these forms.

A critical distinction between reinterpretation and syncretism adumbrated in *The Myth of the Negro Past* turns on the dichotomy in reinterpretation between "outer" form and "inner" meanings, values, and beliefs. While a cultural form may seem outwardly "European," its Africanness is revealed in its interpreted, embedded meaning. Reinterpretation is especially manifest in Black Protestantism, which lacks the syncretic forms that identify African gods and Catholic saints. Herskovits saw the "most striking and recognizable survivals of African religion" not in religious doctrine, but in "behavioristic aspects that, given overt expression, are susceptible of reinterpretation of a new theology while retaining their older established forms ([1941] 1958, 214). The Baptist church offered African Americans opportunities to reinterpret a number of elements of West African religious traditions. Herskovits contended that the slaves who came to the Untied States would have found the ritual of total immersion familiar, as part of a "water ritual."[12] While Black Baptists in the United States do not "run into the water under possession by African gods," possession does occur as the spirit descends when "the novitiate whose revelation has brought him to running stream or tidal cove is immersed" (234). Possession is viewed as "almost indistinguishable from the possession brought on by African water deities" (234).

Another, related example of reinterpretation among Baptists involves the biblical concept of "crossing the river Jordan," which "any African would find readily understandable," and plays an important role in Black religious imagery (Herskovits [1941] 1958, 234). While religion provided most of the examples of reinterpretation in *The Myth of the Negro Past*, Herskovits also sees it occurring in the "elasticity of the marriage concept," deriving from the adjustment of polygynous family structure to patterns based upon monogamy, an adjustment "made the more difficult by economic and psychological complications resulting from the nature of the historical situation" ([1941] 1958, 170). Reinterpretation is thus used to explain African American family structures and partnerships created outside of marriage as it is conceived in Euro-American cultures.

Metaphors rarely appeared in *The Myth of the Negro Past*, which interpreted the formation of creolized cultural forms within the conceptual framework of acculturation theory used by Herskovits at the time. On a few occasions, familiar metaphors like "coalesce" and "merger" reappeared. One new metaphor, "coagulate," was used to powerful effect in the concluding chapter to express how thickly African cultural heritage is maintained through reinterpretation, a process as inner as the flow of blood in the human body. This metaphor appeared as Herskovits set forth a rejoinder to one of the "myths" of the Negro past that held that African cultures were so savage and uncivilized that the "apparent superiority of European custom as observed in the behavior of the masters" caused them to "give up such aboriginal traditions as they may otherwise have desired to preserve" ([1941] 1958, 296). On the contrary,

> coming, then, from relatively complex and sophisticated cultures, the Negroes . . . met the acculturative situation in . . . the New World far differently than is customarily envisaged. Instead of representing isolated cultures, their endowments, however different in detail, possessed least common denominators that permitted a consensus of experience to be drawn on in fashioning new, though still Africanlike, customs.
>
> The presence of members of native ruling houses and priests and diviners among the slaves made it possible for the cultural lifeblood to coagulate through reinterpretation instead of ebbing away into the pool of European culture. (Herskovits [1941] 1958, 296, 297)

The compelling image of coagulating lifeblood conjoins form and process. It speaks to the dynamic maintenance of African cultural characteristics as new creolized cultural forms emerged through a process of reinterpretation. Through coagulation, blood is transformed from fluid to a solid mass. Out of the fluid *process* of reinterpretation, *new forms* emerged which retained the vital substance of African culture. The use of this metaphor at the conclusion to *The Myth of the Negro Past* occurred at a consummate moment in Herskovits's mission to substantiate an African heritage for New World Blacks through providing abundant evidence of the retention and transformation of African cultural forms.

By 1948, reinterpretation stood as an overarching, encompassing term for the acculturative processes examined by Herskovits over the past two decades. It was viewed as applicable to any culture, worldwide, in *Man and His Works*, a textbook that served as the most extensive exposition of his cultural theories. In this book, Herskovits represented reinterpretation as a universal process of cultural change that involves the "reading of old meaning into new forms, or the retention of old forms with new meanings" (1948a, 557). It includes changes internal to cultures, as well as those that are externally induced: "*Reinterpretation* marks all aspects of cultural change. It is the process by which old meanings are ascribed to new elements or by which new values change the cultural significance of old forms. It operates internally, from generation to generation, no less than in integrating a borrowed element into a receiving culture. But it is in the latter process that the phenomena is most easily to be studied" (1948a, 553).

Syncretism was now viewed as "one form" of reinterpretation, exemplified in the identification of African gods and Catholic saints. Field research in Trinidad induced Herskovits to differentiate between Catholic New World Black cultures, where adaptation to proselytization occurred "without inner conflict" through the identification of saints and African gods, and Protestant cultures like in Trinidad, where "reinterpretations of necessity were of a less direct and more subtle character" (Herskovits and Herskovits [1947] 1964, 304). In *Man and His Works*, Herskovits stated simply that "syncretism is one form of reinterpretation" (1948a, 553). Indicating that syncretism "is most strikingly exemplified by the reconciliations that have been effected by New World Negroes in the focal aspect of aboriginal African culture, religion" (1948a, 553), notably in the identification of African gods and Catholics saints, Herskovits seemed to allow for syncretisms in other domains of culture, but provided no examples outside of religion.

Representing reinterpretation as cultural creativity, Herskovits saw the concept as a central term for understanding cultural change. His revelation in Trinidad convinced him that maintaining older cultural elements is not a matter of preserving survivals, but a transformative undertaking integrating the new with the old. If we think of reinterpretation as an ongoing, universal process, it fits with a notion of creolization as an ever-emergent, creative process shaped and re-shaped by groups as they come into contact with one another.

Contemporary anthropologists misread (or selectively read) Herskovits as maintaining a static view of the maintenance of an African heritage in the Americas. Critiquing Herskovits's notion of syncretism and reinterpretation, Andrew Apter contends that his view of cultural resistance embodies a "passive sense of resisting change," which he associates with Herskovits's view of "cultural conservatism" ([1991] 2004, 179, 166). A closer reading of Herskovits's notion of "the force of cultural conservatism" reveals that he sees it operative transculturally as a result of the "transmission of habits, customs, beliefs and institutions from one generation to the next" (Herskovits [1945] 1966, 56). This "force of cultural conservatism" "gives to every way of life a *tenaciousness*, a *toughness* [my emphasis] . . . which comes to be of special importance in the study of Africanisms in the New World (56–57).

Apter sees syncretisms as utilized counterhegemonically by slaves and their descendents in the Americas, as the "syncretic revision of dominant discourses sought to transform the authority that these discourses upheld." Apter speaks of how "the religion of the masters" was "revised, transformed, and appropriated by slaves to harness its power within their universes of discourses" ([1991] 2004, 178). He correctly recognizes that Herskovits did not situate syncretism within a political context of resistance; and, indeed, Herskovits's notion of reconciliation in syncretism did entail adjustment, integration, and accommodation rather than appropriation as means of resistance. However, the totality of Herskovits's oeuvre can be seen as testifying to the resilience of Black Atlantic peoples whose very maintenance and reinterpretation of their ancestral heritage have been acts of resistance, social agency, and cultural creativity in the face of centuries of oppression and denial of the legitimacy of their culture—factors which recurrently appear in his scholarship. "Tenaciousness" and "toughness" in maintaining an ancestral culture should be seen as agentive, rather than simply as "passive" cultural conservatism, since agency, in the sense of what Laura Ahearn calls the "socioculturally mediated capacity to act" (2001, 130), can be expressed in any number of ways. Ahearn lists "oppositional agency, complicit agency, agency of power, [and] agency of intention" as various kinds of agency (2001, 130; see also Baron 2010, 65). Like many contemporary critics of Herskovits, Apter does not adequately allow for the Herksovitsian view of change, which conceptualizes the creative reworking of source cultures in manifold ways for a variety of purposes, including both the deliberate maintenance of older cultural forms and adaptation to new social and cultural circumstances. Their creative reworking of source cultures is most apparent in expressive culture, through folklore as well as religious practice, and since the earliest days of slavery in the New World it has engaged the processes that we now call creolization.

Creolization involves not only continuous cultural creativity that makes the new. It engages both past and present through ongoing reinterpretation of form and meaning transmitted from the past—as a remaking of the old—as well as the creation of new forms out of the conjunctions of two or more cultures. It can also mean choosing *not* to maintain an ancestral tradition or, alternatively, "anti-syncretism" (Palmié 1995), with assertion of the ancestral form and rejection of its creolized transformation. On this note, we are reminded again of Brathwaite's view of the dual orientation of creolization "from or *towards* ancestral originals" (1974a, 7).

Whether or not it is possible to adduce a relationship between a cultural form and its historical source (as, for example, an "Africanism"), ideological perspectives upon ancestral sources are of focal importance for creolization, especially among peoples with a legacy of disenfranchisement by slavery and colonialism. David Scott has suggested that Afro-American anthropology should be reoriented from "sustained preoccupation with the corroboration or verification of authentic pasts" to the "complex discursive field we may usefully call 'tradition,'" with "discourse" situated between "that event (Africa or slavery) and this memory" (1991, 278). While tradition is, as most folklorists would agree, critically important in relating past to present, Richard Price correctly maintains that it is also important to continue to consider historical evidence and memory of the past in the study of New World Black cultures (2006, 134).

Anthropologists of subsequent generations have frequently represented Herskovits as consumed by the search for Africanisms while neglecting change and transformation in New World Black cultures. In fact, he maintained dual emphases upon both the retention of an ancestral heritage—which he substantiated through the identification of cultural forms of African provenance—and the transformation of these forms through cultural processes we now call creolization. Throughout Herskovits's writings, we see abundant evidence of traditions both maintained and creatively adapted to new cultural circumstances, often under oppressive conditions. As Mintz has indicated, "what typified creolization was not the fragmentation of culture and the destruction of the very concept, but the creation and construction of culture out of fragmented, violent and disjunct pasts" (1996, 302). In the Americas, peoples of African descent exercised agency in retaining ancestral traditions and creating new cultural forms substantially based upon their African heritage. Herskovits felt that the resilience of New World Blacks in syncretizing traditions of dual provenance was itself an African legacy, stating that "on the most comprehensive level, the manner in which New World Negroes have syncretized African and European custom into a functioning culture different from either of its ancestral types points to *psychological resilience as a deep-rooted African tradition of adaptation*" (1948b, 10).

Creolization studies should deal with both past and present, integrally incorporating reference to the antecedent cultural forms transformed through creolization. Understanding of these forms, as well as their values and meanings, provides a full picture of new, creolized cultural formations. Metaphors offer potent, affectively rich, and conceptually suggestive means for characterizing the processes that rework cultural forms of dual and multiple provenance, their relationships to source cultures and one another, and the new cultural forms that result from creolized encounters. Creolization, which encompasses both form and process, is best rendered through metaphors that speak to states of both being and becoming.

In the early and middle period of his scholarship about peoples of African descent, Herskovits employed metaphor to varying degrees of effectiveness for a variety of combinations of forms of different cultural provenance. While he achieved a certain conceptual rigor in his refinement of the concept of reinterpretation for the changes in meanings and values that occur in the acculturative encounter, only the metaphors of his earlier scholarship rendered the varieties of combinations that brought forms together with varying degrees of fluidity and completeness through a creolization process that also maintained elements of the forms undergoing change. These metaphors warrant reclamation in folklore scholarship. The concept of syncretism should likewise be revisited, since it speaks to the identifications that individuals make between cultural forms of different origin. These identifications relate to matters of form as well as meaning and ideology. Creolization studies must conjoin analysis of form, content, and process much like the field of folklore, historically concerned with origins, growth, and diffusion of forms and directed in the late twentieth century toward processes of performance and emergence. Perhaps creolization can provide a twenty-first-century convergence, adapting conceptual approaches of diverse provenance to new ends, revivifying the theoretical base of folklore studies in a creole-like manner.

Notes

A previous version of this essay was presented at the 1995 American Folklore Society annual meeting in Lafayette, Louisiana, in the panel "Metaphors and Models of/for Creolization." I am indebted to Ana Cara for her valuable comments about earlier drafts.

1. Like the biological and physical sciences, the social sciences look to metaphors from other domains when they lack their own terms for rendering what they observe, experience, and propound as theoretical constructs. Victor Turner speaks of the virtues of metaphor for viewing society and culture dynamically—where the "social world is a world in becoming," in contrast with the "world in being," suggested by mechanistic metaphors (1974, 24–25). However, he warns of the limitations of organic metaphors, where "by invoking the idea 'becoming' one is unconsciously influenced by the ancient metaphor of organic growth and decay" (30). For Turner, "many social events do not have this 'directional character,'" which "becoming" suggests through its association with "genetic continuity, telic growth, cumulative development, progress, etc." (30). As a result the metaphor will "select, emphasize, suppress, or organize features of social relations in accordance with *plant* or *animal* growth processes, and in so doing, mislead us about the nature of the *human* social world, *sui generis*" (30).

2. Gundaker ties the dual and multiple character of creolization to its lack of dichotomies. She writes of the "dual and multiple factors" that occur in the creolization process, which "work against either/or, is/isn't polarization" (Gundaker 1998, 11).

3. Reisman (1970, 141) also speaks of oscillation as characteristic of creolization in his account of alternations between Creole and English standards of decorum.

4. Although Herskovits acknowledged that some slaves originated in Central Africa (and, to an even smaller extent, East Africa), he contended that West Africa represented by far the largest African source for African American culture ([1941] 1958, 39). Robert Farris Thompson's (1983) studies of African aesthetics in the traditional visual arts of peoples of African descent in the Americas point to substantial Central African influences.

5. While Herksovits pointed out an abundance of African influence upon American foodways in this article, he recognized other non-European influences. The creoleness of American culture is not derived solely from African and European sources, as Herskovits noted in occasional references to American Indian influences. After Walter White, secretary of the NAACP, read "What Has Africa Given America," he wrote an enthusiastic letter to Herskovits and described a book he was writing, "Negro Cookery of the United States and West Africa." He intended "to show why most of the contributions to American cuisine are Negro ones; . . . why, with a few exceptions, like the New England boiled dinner, the North has contributed nothing to the art of cooking; and why the slave owners and poor whites have contributed little" (Herskovits [NUHP], correspondence, White/ Herskovits, September 3, 1935).

In responding, Herskovits hoped that "you won't insist on taking the position that no other people except Negroes have made contributions to American cooking. The Indians, for example, have given us quite a bit—and just consider the joyous flapjack!" (Herskovits [NUHP], correspondence, Herskovits/White, September 9, 1935).

6. Cultures are selective in what they give and take, rejecting as well as accepting. In his analysis of creolization in Trinidad, Crowley states that "each member of each group accepts or rejects" the traditions of other groups "in varying degrees to suit particular needs and situations, which we may call differential acculturation." At the same time as "each individual and each group has been Creolized to greater or lesser degree in one or another aspect of his culture," each Trinidadian preserves "inviolate the traits and complexes of his parent culture or cultures" (Crowley 1957, 823–824).

Brathwaite discusses the rejection of European culture in the creolization process in colonial Jamaica, viewing "negative" creolization as expressions of ideology and nationalism. Brathwaite contends that "the idea of creolization as an ac/culturative, even an interculturative process between 'black' and 'white,' with the (subordinate) black absorbing 'progressive' ideas and technology from the white, has to be modified into a more complex vision in which appears the notion of *negative or regressive* creolization: a self-conscious refusal to borrow or to be influenced by the Other, and a coincident desire to fall back upon, unearth, recognize elements in the maroon or ancestral culture that will preserve or apparently preserve the unique identity of the group. This quality of consciousness is recognized in all modern societies as one of the roots of nationalism" (1977, 54–55).

7. The definition was immediately followed by a "Note" that differentiated it from other terms, as Herskovits had urged: "Under this definition, acculturation is to be distinguished from *culture-change*, of which it is but one aspect, and *assimilation*, which is at times but a phase of acculturation. It is also to be distinguished from *diffusion*, which, while occurring in all instances of acculturation, is not only a phenomenon which frequently takes place without the occurrence of the type of contact between peoples specified in the definition given above, but also constitutes only one aspect of the process of acculturation (Redfield, Linton, Herskovits 1936, 149–50).

8. Yelvington discusses the "critique" of the term "acculturation" associated with the concept of "transculturation." Malinowski, in his introduction to *Cuban Counterpoint*, stressed that transculturation involves "exchange between two cultures . . . both contributing their share" and contended that the term "acculturation" is "an ethnocentric word with moral connotations," where the "'uncultured' is to receive the benefits of 'our culture'; it is he who must change and become converted to 'one of us'" (Malinowski [1947] 1995, lviiii, lix, cited in Yelvington 2006, 71–72). Yelvington notes that Herkskovits "wrote to Ortiz, strenuously objecting to what he felt was a misunderstanding of his use of the term *acculturation*"(2006, 72).

9. Bernabé, Chamoiseau, and Confiant also use the kaleidoscope metaphor for creole societies as total societies. Creoleness is viewed as an "open specificity," which

expresses "a kaleidoscopic totality, that is to say: the *nontotalitarian consciousness of a preserved diversity*" (Bernabé, Chamoiseau, and Confiant 1990, 892).

10. John Vlach also describes the provenance of the *caille* as African, European, and Amerindian as "the result of a three-way interaction among Arawak Indians, French colonials, and African slaves." The Yoruba are viewed as the primary source for "the cultural amalgam that produced Haiti's architecture." Vlach locates the three cultural sources for this house type in other elements of the *caille* than Herskovits does, indicating that it "contains the gable door and porch of the Arawak *bohio*, the construction technique of French peasant cottages, and the spatial volume of a Yoruba two-room house" (1978, 125).

11. The *"Preliminary Memorandum* on the Problem of African Survivals" was submitted to Gunnar Myrdal, who directed the "Study of the Negro in America," a major study organized by the Carnegie Corporation of New York, which provided funding for *The Myth of the Negro Past.*

12. Acknowledging the impact of cultural contact with Native Americans, Herskovits notes that the "river cult" of the Cherokees, "also furthered this particular process of reinterpretation." He noted that Cherokee immersion took place at each new moon. Fasting occurred prior to Cherokee immersion, "something which in spirit is not too far removed from the restraints laid on the novitiate of any cult in Africa, or in the rites of certain 'shouting' sects where new members 'go to mournin' before baptism" (Herskovits 1958[1941], 234).

About Face

Rethinking Creolization

—ROGER D. ABRAHAMS

> A mixt is a natural body consisting of Elements of Mat-
> ter and the form of a Mixt. Mixture is the Union of Ele-
> ments altered, not corrupted, for the Elements remain
> in the mixt bodyes but the Qualities are so broken by
> the mutual reaction of contraries, and the matter so
> divided into minute parts, Shuffled together, that they
> are not discernible apart in any mixt body.
> —CHARLES MORTON, *Compendium physicae*, 1687

Creolization, Creolizing, Creolized

Creolization is a complex process of cultural mirroring and blending that
occurs when peoples come together for trade and other forms of exchange.
Creolizing is a process of mixing which maintains its precarious stability.
The mixt, the mixtury, is discrete, yet its forms may be purposely occluded
in out-of-the-ordinary practices marked by the simultaneous expression
of fear and desire. A mixtery of feelings and sense responses play off each
other at points of intense experience.

Creolization draws on an artful layering of meanings and styles from
different cultural resource banks: cultural archives without walls. Creolizing does not contain just any mixture of cultural styles or existential states;
creole creations develop their own stability, one that is recognizable, learnable, subject to replication and elaboration—like any other kind of artistic
or metaphysical experiences. Creole creations carry traces of earlier practices drawn upon by maestros and maestros who have learned to draw on
them in whatever strange combinations work. Because they arise at those

life-places in which the feelings of individuals are addressed, feelings of lack or need become central to the moment of possible transformation. Questions of individual or social health call for a drawing on unique congeries of practices and styles, whether by Big Men and Big Women, by warriors and by healers. Everyone involved in these moments of transformation take them very seriously, even when these transformations involve great fun.

Creolization invokes a cultural, social, political, and artistic imaginary with echoes of home or place of origin, a registering of a historical coming together resulting from the dispersion and relocation of peoples. The creolization process occurs as folks vigorously interact and perform for one another under borderland conditions, though these borders are not those of the expanding frontiers but of two or more groups seeking to establish exchanges of benefit to either or all parties. This culture draws from already established, customary, stylized, compositional activity. At these boundaries, a kind of consensus culture develops, not unlike the *lingua franca* that emerge in sites of trade and commerce. Nevertheless, in this process of admixture—in which vernacular creativity erupts—more than music, cooking and eating, and dancing and promenading take place. A new culture emerges.

However, those who do not share the sensibility of emergent creolized cultures hear only *noise*. So long as one regards cultures as linguistically, geographically, and institutionally distinct from others, neither the movement of peoples nor the way in which they express themselves is revealed to be problematic. This unusual state of affairs is rapidly complicated, however, by the breakdown of civil order and ritual purity brought on by the virtual inevitability of culture contact between contiguous communities. Rather than responding to the many sensory channels that new *mixturies* offer and rather than understanding them as a whole, those unfamiliar with creolized cultures perceive only a congeries of infelicities. Creole practices, however, have their own underlying principles; they may simultaneously voice the condition of political disempowerment while maintaining the language of social and cultural resistance.

Indeed, in class-ridden situations, creolized expressive forms take on a derisive charge leveled at elites and function as a form of resistance from below. Furthermore, creolized expressions are not without roots or ties. They are linked to particular historical moments in specific places. Moreover, creole styles are sufficiently formulated that they are given a name, are repeatable, and are subject to being improvised upon without losing their shape and the propulsive force that marked their creation.

Creolized formations, in other words, grow new allegiances. While they become identified with the neighborhood or precinct in which they develop, they are also portable and exportable to other performance sites, most notably in the case of touristic conditions. No doubt, simply living in contiguity establishes new kinds of intimacies, as well as distances, between communities. Creolization, as a cultural process, offers a way by which to negotiate and manifest cultural approximations and disassociations. The notes that follow (largely based on recent scholarship but also drawing from over forty years of research and fieldwork relating to creolization in the United States and the West Indies) focus on the breakdown of physical and cultural purity and on the emergence of in-between zones where creolization processes have free reign. Display events in these zones embody deep play, while substantially incorporating memory and commemoration, of liberation as well as oppression. Holidays, festivals, and entertainment venues are viewed as primary examples of "unstable" social and cultural zones where—both wretchedly at times and triumphantly at others—creole creativity flourished in asymmetrical fashion and (for some observers) festered as creole degeneracy. Today, "creole" and "creolization" have lost their stigma and, in fact, have become fashionable. Arguing for the importance of restricting "creolization" to refer to culturally specific situations in colonial and post-colonial societies, it is distinguished from "hybridity" and "cosmopolitanism," and I reflect on the pitfalls of conflating "creolization" and "cosmopolitanism" in order to encompass contemporary relationships between the local and global. The pairing of creolization with cosmopolitanism represents a misbegotten "about face."

On the edges of empires built upon trade and slavery, populated mainly by the dispossessed and disempowered, different communities encountered one another and created new cultural forms, styles, and populations. Considering how (and whether) the development of Creole languages models the emergence of Creole cultures, I discuss how multiple language codes are maintained. Creolization suggests that internal variation and continuous historical and cultural change are necessary dimensions of language and culture anywhere in the world. Further observations distinguish phenomena viewed as "creole" or "hybrid" in the broad context of today's postcolonial "global zone" and consider the social and political nuances that inform the use of these terms.

In-between Zones

Two or more groups living in borderland neighborhoods can lead to turf wars. An exotic distance operates in such zones, in which some combination of fear and exotic attraction arises. Exoticizing carries with it the creation of objects of desire, which not uncommonly are sexual. From this dangerous attraction comes a system for communication across the divide, including an imitation of one another's performance styles. Cultural performances—especially those invented by the newly displaced peoples as a defense against total oppression—cause a mixing of cultures, though not necessarily an alteration of the social status of either group. Music and dance, of course, are especially subject to imitation, especially if a zone of goods across borders is involved. One group's music becomes another's forbidden practice, especially if some kind of mystique is attached to the performances. This applies to religious and healing practices as well.[1]

An in-between entertainment zone commonly emerges in these conditions, creating spaces in which these transactions can now take place. Styles of music, dance, formal speaking, food and drink consumption, as well as sex become a part of the modus vivendi of the two communities. In such mutually agreed-upon zones of interaction, official rules of approach and avoidance are subject to constant negotiation. Whoever has learned the ways of the other acquires a new position of power. In exchange for becoming a cultural nobody, the entertainer, the guide, the pimp is given the power to articulate the displays in which exotic performances occur and the raw emotions of fear and desire are drawn upon. The more illicit, even illegal, the transaction is, the more it will be attached to practices of secrecy and to the power figures who control the exchange.[2]

The propinquity of peoples produces a highly charged and volatile social space, as well as a site for sexual congress. Here hybrid ways of life emerge, along with a hybrid population. Each group develops an ongoing wariness of these contact zones for similar reasons: the confusion of realms, the dilution of canons of purity and cleanliness, and the violation of social rules introduced in encounters by each group. In places where different groups meet regularly, a distinctive liberating force begins to operate. Although negotiated under distressing and unequal conditions, a consensus culture emerges, achieving a kind of stability as the groups continue to live in close proximity.[3]

Needless to say, the pursuit of empire was not conducive to operating with good manners; much less extensive was the trust between those most deeply involved in commercial exchange. The creole world operated away from precisely such civilizing norms most of the time. Creoles were often presumed to be the result of miscegenation. Moreover, they were perceived as indolent, lascivious, given to excesses of all sorts, such as engaging in sexual abandon and disregarding the Sabbath.

Most of those practices occurred at the edges of empires built on the commercial flow of goods. Dispossessed and disempowered peoples (including slaves and recently emancipated ex-slaves) are found at those points where metropolitan control is most easily tested. Noticing a sordid interest among higher-status settlers in their lives as pirates, thieves, or savages, these dispossessed peoples found ways of performing in select public venues, building or "elaborating" upon their stylistic differences in performances, in music making, praise and scandal singing of libels, in masking, processing, parading, in sports, and in healing practices. These performances commonly found a ready audience on those special occasions in which they were called upon to perform, and soon these dispossessed peoples found themselves imitated by the more inventive members of the higher-status groups who came to watch and listen.

In the New World, these betwixt and between sites took on a life of their own as new peoples and new cultural forms emerged. These peoples and their expressive styles were often stigmatized by the dominant group and ostracized by the subordinated one. Yet they thrived—not only within these in-between cultural niches, but also eventually beyond these zones.

In this part of the New World, these stylistic developments were strongly associated with shantytown neighborhoods populated primarily by ex-slaves. As a carryover of the sort of independence achieved by the African Americans in their slave holidays, they found themselves expressing their independence, however small that might be, in contrast to both the local *prominenti* and the metropolitan authorities in the Old World. Whereas a received historical view sees a kind of stylistic unity to the European powers at the time of initial colonial settlement, now we can see more and more the importance of various underworlds—some just imagined (as with thief culture in England) and some very real (as in the sex-trade practices that led to neighborhoods that came to be known as red-light districts or entertainment zones). Certain social imaginaries come to embody more than only difference, periodically expressed through liberation or independence and palpably evident on occasions when maroons and other outsiders make their way to town to enter into market exchanges, in the open or on the black market.

Creole/Hybrid

Emancipation was declared at a time when European markets for the crops produced by slave labor on Caribbean plantations were collapsing. Where large cosmopolitan populations had emerged during the period of successful trade, mixed-breed individuals born in the New World, most often referred to as Creoles, developed a social niche much more quickly than in those areas in which colonial identities persisted because of metropolitan indifference. As Creoles became leaders of independent nations and complex, stratified societies, creolization slowly lost its sense of opprobrium and became legitimate. The terms creole and creolization, which once connoted contamination and degradation, are now used in a less condemnatory sense. They and their near synonym, hybridity, receive a more kindly reception in the contemporary world of global trade and cosmopolitan sensibilities. A growing number of cultural observers have turned this set of terms into positive descriptors for the pluralistic communities that are emerging under current conditions of exchange and interaction (Hannerz 1987). This shift has been reinforced as the artistic styles developed under the old orders have proved to be marketable through new forms of mediated communication. Artists born into creole communities salvage and redeem (although not unambiguously) the words for colonial resilience and combinatory genius. These expatriates and cosmopolitan artists see the possibilities of maintaining the viability of creolization as a term of art, even as they are able to draw on the reservoir of historical experience found within such ex-slave formations.

Other commentators within the ranks of the post-colonial brigade, however, urge the use of the term "hybridity." Although that term sidesteps some of the semantic drag accruing to creolization, hybrid forms are far from uncontaminated by past usage. The sense of illicit and uncontrolled breeding maintained in creolization is bypassed by "hybridity," but not the implicit meanings of forced interbreeding. Perhaps the success of the term hybridity has as much to do with the critical success of the work of the Russian language philosopher Mikhail Bakhtin. By his definition, hybrid forms involve "a mixture of two social languages within the limits of a single utterance—an encounter, within an utterance, between two different linguistic consciousnesses, separated from one another by an epoch, by social differentiation, or by some other factor" (Bakhtin 1981, 358). Drawing on the term from this perspective, critics have been attracted to the usefulness of "hybridity" as a way of drawing attention to the idea of kidnapping cultural forms, translating them into the colonialists' language, and putting them into print, which formerly colonized peoples recognize in this post-colonial world.

Creolization and Language:
Internal Variation, Historical and Situational Change

Before *creolization* became a glamour term for describing all cultural con-junctions, the word was employed to describe the linguistic and social process by which different peoples came together under the harsh regime of export-oriented plantation agriculture.

Initially described as simply a mixture, creole languages and cultures proved to be far more complex. Indeed, a commonsense view of language history would say that all languages are the result of such mixture, a condition intensified once mercantilism produced its own set of practices. To be sure, there were no standard languages before the establishment of the modern nation-state, with its bureaucratic apparatus that could identify and insist upon the use of one or another local dialect, which, by the accident of history, became the standard because it was the language of those in hegemonic control. Within this system, and by contrast, creole languages were those which were "corruptions" of a European standard—bad, broken-down, bastardized ways of talking used by vagrant and marginal peoples, such as slaves. The notion of *appropriate* language, therefore, was nothing less than an invention, a product of the civilizing moment and an outgrowth of the four-stage theory of human development. Schools, dictionaries, bureaucratic organizations, mapping, national libraries, all represented themselves as cooling down the hubbub of the market crowds through the imposition of a reasoned set of interactional practices. Standard languages, in other words, represent one dimension of living by good (i.e., friendly) manners. Yet, to be sure, speaking equitably is by no means a universal norm within speech communities, nor is having a *palaver* the same as friendly conversation. Quite the contrary, palaver talk often invokes severe restrictions on who can talk to whom and when. In fact, the deeper the discussion, the more rules of accession and succession of talk are subject to being invoked.

The creolizing of language and culture emerges at boundaries, or "beaches," as Greg Dening calls them, with intense exchanges occurring in which the previous practices of those coming together are imitated and shared between them. A kind of consensus culture thus develops, operating apart from the mixing and matching of the interacting groups. This style of thought concerning creolization emerges from the commonsense notion that when regular trade is involved between those who do not speak the same language, a new one emerges, developed just for trade, such as a lingua franca, a pidgin or trade language. Creole languages and creolized societies involve such a further development of trade that a residential trade community emerges, broadening and intensifying the pidgin, making it into a fully formed language useful not only in trade but as a first language for those raised in such polyglot communities. In the main, this is a reconstruction of "what *must* have happened" from the fragments discoverable within a language still being produced, learned, and understood in the complex ways by which humans communicate in groups. In such a scheme, the old African languages were maintained at the margins, in isolated communities, or as a *koine*, an old language still in use in ritual situations, but not always understood by those who employ it, other than to maintain the magical character inhabited by past practices.

One way or another, creolization of language and culture must be understood in terms of a kind of social disintegration that occurred outside the boundaries of a home community, as the social imaginaries or habitus of one group—that is, its accumulated customary practices are put to work in a different situation calling for friendly communication. Because the creolization process takes bits and pieces of the expressive practices of others and combines them in an apparently willy-nilly fashion, creolization in the past has seemed to draw on a grab bag of linguistic and cultural practices. Language, therefore, has become one way of handling the problem of the remnants and ruins of historical or geographical others. Before the *bricoleur* and the artist were given the approval of cultural theorists, calling something creole or creolized was a quick and easy way of accounting for diversity without conferring any kind of official approval. But creolization accumulated positive valence in the vocabulary of vernacular creativity, as theorists drawing on French deconstructionist language, first as *assemblage* and then as *bricolage*, attained status, and the *bricoleur* was imagined as an artist.

Concretely, in the first reaction against structural functionalism in cultural analysis during the 1960s, fieldworkers studying the expressive production of plural communities were increasingly unwilling to impose a model based on an imposed, standard way of interacting. Instead, behavior and performance were described and judged in terms of their situational appropriateness. Local norms of interactions were privileged by taking an emic (native, indigenous) analytical approach, as opposed to an etic (externally derived) one. Ethnographers working in Afro-American and Afro-Caribbean communities embraced this shift of view. In creole cultures, especially, it was essential to begin not by normalizing standard language production, for example, but rather by recording and analyzing local varieties of speech in context.

Creolization suggests that internal variation and continuous historical and situational change are necessary dimensions of language and culture reportage. The number and range of language codes in any creole community are remarkably wide—so much so that speakers and performers often discuss the matter among themselves. Good talk and other kinds of artful presentation are ongoing topics of conversation in daily life; audience reaction during performances often centers on the quality of speech as well (Reisman 1970; Abrahams 1983).[4]

Most creolists attempt to study language convergences in order to understand how creolization actually works. But the study of Creole languages is always nested within a particular time and cultural moment of mixture, one which produced a firm positioning of a specific creole "language" with regard to its relation to some standard (i.e., written or ceremonially elaborated) language. It emerges then within a nest of hierarchical forms of speech in which creole forms are somehow subservient to those of the official language.

Ethnographers working in Creole communities discussed the range and intensity of various kinds of interaction: orating, bantering, singing and dancing, and performing the many ceremonies that percolate through creole life. From these reports, alternative perspectives on language were proposed that account for the range of situation-specific styles of communicating. Some form of standard broadcast English or school English was posited as one end of the spectrum; the other end was broad or broken patois, or old talk. These ways of speaking derived from historically distinct moments in the process by which Africans and Europeans were brought together, though an adequate account of the lingua franca (aka *sabir*) has yet to be written.

Common sense dictates that variety and change are to be anticipated in any expressive environment, especially in areas with populations constantly on the move. Each language and culture in any contact situation was presumed to enter into the expressive mix, even in situations of forced dislocation and enslavement. Fieldworkers discovered that the more intense

the occasion of interaction and performance, the more the creole populations drew upon the most archaic, or "African," expressive resources.

One of the greatest problems facing creole-speaking peoples in the
modern world has been that they have been socially stigmatized by the
fact that those linguistic forms closest to their African antecedents are
regarded as bad or broken talk. Folklorists and ethnographers emphasized
how mixed, mobile, and adaptive these populations have been. While
attempting to sidestep the stigma, this approach still elicits the old problem of language and cultural legitimacy. As the dean of Caribbeanists, Sidney Mintz, argued, "Creoles were people who moved beyond the cultural
and conceptual confines of their migrant parents, and became, for better
or for worse, hemispheric Americans of a new sort. . . . The new concept
of creolization has been borrowed without serious attention to what the
term meant, or to what historically specific processes it stood for. What
typified creolization was not the fragmentation of culture and the destruction of the very concept, but the creation and construction of culture out
of fragmented, violent, and disjunct pasts" (1994, 302). Certainly, by now,
the continuing vitality of contemporary creole cultures and languages is
hardly debatable.

Creole Moments and Cultural Flashpoints

Forms that popularly represent creolization arise out of particular historic and cultural matrices in which artistic invention is highly valued and
improvisation is customary. The performances comment directly on historical inequities and ongoing social and political conditions. Under conditions of political instability, they provide a means of expressing social
discontent, often through replaying historical injustices.

Creolization was in large measure a process occurring out of zones
of trade, where peoples with different presentational styles encountered
each other in the exchange of goods and services, including performances.
Here, in these trade centers, the *haves* and the *have-nots* were commonly
separated geographically in neighborhoods, and extreme differences were
dramatized. Within this mercantile world severe class distinctions were in
place, and the population of the free ports included slaves and ex-slaves,
maroons, mixed-breed peoples, and those who served as trade agents and
bankers: trade families encouraged to establish family enterprises in trade
communities that were semi-autonomous from local authorities.

Masters and their agents entered into this mixtury only insofar as they found themselves imitating slave practices, while attempting to intervene in those aspects of slave life they found most savage. Yet at the center of any mirroring one finds practices of licensed libel, songs and dances and plays which depict elites in embarrassing ways. In extremely class-ridden situations, these derisive forms are all the more important as a channel for resistance from below. In fact, precisely because the confrontation of African and European cultural styles arose during times in which Africans were enslaved, the stylistic encounter occurred between peoples who were unequal socially, politically, and economically.

However, it is this very inequality that is a precondition of most of those aspects of modernity exhibiting creolization. Creolization seems to arise in those cities and towns that were once plantation ports of call to which a great majority of the ex-slave population repaired. In the resulting neighborhoods, voluntary associations such as mutual aid and burial societies already engendered on the plantation emerged. Clinging to the few ways in which former slaves had achieved a modicum of liberty before emancipation—that is, in their Sunday markets and slave holidays—they chose to group themselves on principles of brotherhood and sisterhood. They developed these sharing organizations for the purpose of not only socializing but also ceremonializing, as in the seasonal festivities and in healing rites and in burials.

Each neighborhood so self-identified has a sense of its own uniqueness, and regards some of its celebratory flourishes as its signature style. These signatures have been elevated to embellish the local pride, not only of the neighborhood, but also of the civic entity in which they live. They celebrate on their side of town, but on calendared holidays, this celebration is carried out at the same time as the European-derived holidays. Both remain anchored in the calendar brought from the Old World. Thus Old Christmas, Carnival, Corpus Christi, and other such "Christian" holidays provide the occasion for all—Black and White—to celebrate. In the neighborhoods this generally means an elaborate elevation of their leaders (kings and queens for the day, captains, chairmen, chiefs), locating the leaders of their groups by the dramatic means of elevating them physically, or by taking the symbol of their power and raising it above the assembled crowd. The unique feature of this kind of performance or ritual is that it carries a narrative of its own invention within the composition of the song, dance, and other expressive forms. One can see, hear, and feel the residue of the styles and the sense-experience of the past now superimposed on each other. In

both the historical and contemporary sense, they mark times of passage
or at least high-intensity activity; the more the superimposition of past
styles, the deeper and more intense the experience of the participants is
potentiated.

At some point in the ongoing creolized activity, participants and well-
informed audiences can experience at a physical and sensual level the historical overlay "all the way from top to bottom." These are creole moments,
these cultural flashpoints in which a ramping up in mimetic intensity is
made apparent to all, performers and informed audience members as
well. Coherence is achieved because of the power and brilliance of the
performers, the artists, the ritual officers, and the healers, who seize the
moment and share it with all others coming together at that flashpoint.
What difference does it make that the conditions under which these cultures converged occurred because the performers, healers, ritual specialists happened to come from people who were historically dispossessed,
dislocated, or forced by the agents of empire to move on constantly or to
carry out work as enslaved populations?

The styles that emerge from these celebrating groups invite participation of non-members. They have a master-pulse system that encourages
all to sing and dance along, usually established through the sounds of a
Big Drum, a mastering sound on which other counter-pulses are superimposed. Though certain entertainments develop that draw on both sides
of town, the neighborhoods remain separated racially, politically, and
socially. The opposition of the high style and that of the neighborhood
groups provides the driving force for the event. Inevitably there are routine confrontations between the civic authorities and the revelers. The
event itself is heated from within, then, through the recognition of this
historical confrontative style.

As they were decolonized, these polities attempted to make the holidays
into a statement of national solidarity, giving the word out that in celebration "we are all one." Yet, the two strata keep Carnival or Christmas in their
own way, and the new nation is hardly united. Yet, the signature style of the
New World Black Atlantic neighborhood organizations becomes highly
visible and available for imitation across these boundaries. It is the resulting shared styles, then, that give the appearance of everyone celebrating
together. The celebration relies on the vernacular vigor based in the voluntary associations on both sides of town, but mainly in the neighborhoods.
All involved, Black and White, recognize that the event relies on vigorous
inventions on the Black Atlantic side of town. By hiring costumed singers

and other musicians and dancers from the neighborhoods, drawing them into the center of the official parade, the unity of that polity is given voice and body for the day. But few of the revelers doubt the origin of the signature styles and competitive events.

The more interesting story has to do with those who were actively involved in inventing a way of life adapted to the intensive staple-crop agriculture. They drew upon a mixture of customs and practices that went beyond the techniques of control and surveillance of the plantation. What is too seldom remarked upon in discussions of creolization is the degree of cultural transfer that occurred throughout this plantation world as a matter of course.

In contrast, it is the fear-inducing dimension of Creole productions that has often provided the greatest degree of fascination for onlookers ever since Creole cultures were first observed in the seventeenth century. Deep anxieties about disorder and dread of contagion saturate the texts written by observers of African America for three centuries and more. Terms such as "dunghill," "cesspool," and "shit-heap" resonate through the early descriptions of those outposts of empire. Such catch-phrases reflect a complex reaction to the formation of trade communities which were out of the regular control of those bureaucratic and cosmopolitan centers of civilization that were involved in overseas expansion and the creation of plantations. Creole encampments were met with revulsion by the very people responsible for their coming into being. As we value the creolization process with its secondary characteristics of artful conflation, improvisation, and spontaneous creativity, we must also bear in mind its converse dark side. To be sure, adaptive mixtures of historically distinct styles and systems of practice have been discovered now in one place, now another, in the creole communities of the New World. The honor due these developments is surely appropriate, but not at the expense of eliminating the historical lamination to be found in creole performances and celebrations.

In the end, the most distinctive feature of creole societies to outsiders was the inventiveness of the enslaved peoples. Seizing upon the gardening provision grounds given them to provide their own subsistence, the slaves produced surpluses. This surplus, along with the braided horse-collars, baskets and other such weaving, and the animals they had raised, which they sold at periodic markets in town, created a shadow economy. They demanded and were given time off at Crop-over, Christmas, and sometimes Carnival. They expanded these into the holidays that were even more wildly celebrated after Emancipation. On Emancipation Day, as in

Carnival and Christmas entertainments, the theme of expressive liberation is remembered and often reenacted in contemporary terms. This creative explosion lies at the heart of the process of creolization as it has been
discussed during the last half-century.

Memory and Commemoration

These festive observations involve a number of historical ironies. The
languages and styles that emerge at the most intense moments of festive celebrations are those that were regarded as especially aberrant and
corrupting—even diabolically inspired—under the plantation regime.
Descriptions of these moments were especially troubling insofar as they
obviously employed African styles of song, dance, and enthusiastic display.
And, as the expressive occasion became more intense, they drew upon
more deeply African styles (Abrahams and Szwed 1977; Gundaker 1998;
Malone 1996; Marks 1974). Consequently, secret understandings were
hinted at and revealed only to those within the circle of celebrants.

Today, these festivities have been translated into homecoming events for
people who have emigrated from the community. They also have become
national holidays, which amount to tourist attractions. These reenactments commonly call for singing, dancing, and costuming regarded as
unique to that particular place, time, and occasion. Here are born some
of the most enduring forms of vernacular expression by which the creole
world has put its stamp on international popular culture. These celebrations have provided the impetus for the development of song and dance
and other display forms, which have subsequently been adopted throughout the global *ecumene.*

Quintessential creole events involve serious play, an investment of time,
money, and sentiments. They are marked by excessive consumption, but
they build upon the labors of the rest of the year: planning the events,
designing the costumes, rehearsing, composing new songs or speeches on
the patterns of past performances. At Carnival in Trinidad and Tobago,
Mardi Gras in New Orleans and Memphis, Christmas sports on Nevis, St.
Kitts, and Jamaica, and the Bahamian Jonkonnu, for example, enslavement
and liberation are replayed. The cultural rupture created by the Middle
Passage lies at the heart of these events, minimally submerged in the official prize competitions and mock battles.

Such national celebrations are not unique to the Anglophone areas of the New World. Similar stories are told of Rio and Bahia, Port au Prince, and Buenos Aires, reported in the official web pages of the cities and nations throughout the Black Atlantic. As the results are often successful for nation-builders and for tourism, their narrative tends toward a triumphalist interpretation. Those promoting local civic pride give the message that, even in the face of a brutal past, the people have been able to persevere through creative expression. But for those who have played these festivities throughout their lives, the story also carries messages of loss of the old ways of celebrating, as the events have grown in scale and attracted outside investment. Individual performers and neighborhood groups attempt to keep the traditions alive. In the most extreme formulations, they conduct counter-festivities that comment negatively on the official ways of celebrating.

All-consuming high times engender the songs and dances, which embody the signature styles of each locale: scratch band, steel band, beguine, *belaire*, calypso, or winding, to name only a few. This singing and dancing, relocated to dance halls, rum shops, and juke joints, endows the entire year with reminders of the high moments of the festival. The year is threaded together through the replay of the victorious road march or calypso from Trinidad (Rohlehr 1990; Hill 1993). In the yards of many neighborhoods, next year's productions are conceived, new tunes and songs are written, and the stories of previous years' presentations are retold as the paraphernalia of the big time is repaired or made anew. Here renewal and replenishment provide the tone for the rest of the year.

It would be a mistake to see these uproarious times as the only events in the Black Atlantic that invoke the past. The more solemn oratorical and orderly marching display events, like Emancipation Day in its various apotheoses or the activities of the burial societies at the death of a member, all testify to stylish gravity. Ironically, the gravity of some of these occasions calls for an eccentric parade route. The two styles—the slow, stately, and ornamental and the riotous and freewheeling—are often juxtaposed, as in the Second Line in New Orleans or the Tea Meeting and Shakespeare Lessons in the ex-British Lesser Antilles. In the Second Line, the marching group accompanying the dead body of a community member is led to the graveyard by a brass band playing songs directing home the spirit of the departed. With the internment, the mourners become the celebrants, and the brass band plays with greater freedom and even abandon as the group winds its way back to the neighborhood via a purposely meandering route. With the Tea Meeting, the two styles of speechmaking, orderly and farcical, are juxtaposed within the same event and often performed against each at the same moment (Abrahams 1988; Burton 1997; Kinser 1990).

Overt memorial references to Africa, slave times, and emancipation occur within the performances themselves. The performances also remark on the activities of politicians and other leaders in more recent notable events. Far from reveling in the outrage of historical victimization, these celebrations remind the participants of the resilience of people of mixed parentage who repeatedly invent and reinvent display forms, which are portable and exportable. Indeed, the particular genius of creole performance and celebration arises from that combination of protean inventiveness and mobility.

The sauciness and swagger of many marchers command everyone's attention. No wonder that some outsiders have been troubled by this expansive display on the streets wherever these practices have been deployed in national celebrations. These forms have become part of the cultural equipment for living of many New World peoples seeking a usable past. Holidays observed by the descendants of slaves have embedded within their practices traces of historically identifiable motifs that were well understood to refer to Africa, the experience of the Middle Passage, and enslavement. Carnival and other representative African American holidays and public celebrations—Juneteenth, August Monday, the Family Reunion, the Million Man March—explicitly reenact a commitment to significant subversive possibilities. Coursing through the countryside, the town, and the city, these events underscore the adaptive and portable character of these gatherings and their potential to fuel social movements.

The power of performers and celebrants to knit together various styles and traditions into one moment of celebration stuns onlookers unused to such propulsive displays. In these acts, the history of the creole world is embodied, rehearsed, and replayed. Here are found the newest old creole styles of moving together: jumping up, breaking, strutting, and jamming. These mass dance-frenzies are commonly accompanied by groups of costumed figures, including the myriad kinds of clowns, and by more serious fraternal and military-style drill teams that perform in a stately manner.

The term creolization seeks to capture the recombinatory power of the cultures of what I dub mixtery, which the forced dislocation of Africans and European peasants translated into those mixed forms and styles that animate popular culture throughout the contemporary world. Without the agonizing history of dislocation taking place as the modern emporium economy emerged, the process of creolization becomes just one more name for the modernist or cosmopolitan project, which encourages the coming together and superimposition of peoples from many different parts of the world in a metropolitan polity. Creole vernacular forms can only be understood as products of this variety of peoples coming together, developing a lingua franca, and showing off vernacular forms taken from ports of call throughout these zones of commerce. I fear any erasure of the harsh history of the massive dislocations of peoples, whether enslaved or emancipated, and it seems counterproductive to erase the vernacular forms that develop as populations are creolized. These emergent vernacular forms can only be fully understood as they comment on and reenact this often violent past. That these reenactments are also carried out in a sea of laughter and celebration makes them especially interesting for those interested in exploring the range of human expressive possibilities.

Creolization and Cosmopolitanism

To the complications arising from the broadening of the term *creolization*, cultural critics now pair it with the hardly new idea of new (or neo-) *cosmopolitans*. The pairing of these two portmanteau terms seem to promise a new and pragmatic set of terms for practices by which the relationships between the global and the local may be described. Yet both are launched from a platform that begins not with totalizing economic, social, or geopolitical agendas but with something much simpler: the mystery of stylistic mixtures on the ground level, of situated expressive moments involving many people of widely different cultural practices.

The dynamics of the conflation of creolization and the new cosmopolitanism are not a casual outcome of post-colonialist discussion. Creole forms and performances, once regarded as bastardized or contaminated, are now presented as vigorous hybrid forms, especially as providing the basis of a popular form of enactment, one subject to the many impulses of purchase, collection, archiving. But when discussed in the context of Diasporas (forced or unforced) and cosmopolitanism, *mixtury* and *mixts* offer a needed cultural set of possibilities that escape official notice or legal censure. At such points of historical rupture, the practices of the displaced or disenfranchised peoples are part of the process of asserting hegemony over all things native and fine to the land.

The cosmopolitanism of the grand tour is now joined with the expulsions and dislocations of groups that become homeless and stateless. This is not a new phenomenon: the Moors left their imprint on the entire Iberian peninsula after the *reconquista*, the Druids and the Arthurian legends are invented with the "defeat" of the Gaelic-speaking peoples, and Native American places and practices stand at the center of those elements of American culture related to masculinizing the young warriors in preparation for future battle. Today a new kind of cosmopolitanism has evolved, one based on the creolization of styles and outcomes, one in which trade will result in international practices of civility. A new class of elites emerges able to command the lingua franca of the international marketplace.

Today, creole styles and practices have been scrubbed clean and given high value. In many places on the tourist trail, creolized forms of health practice, ritual behavior, as well as song, dance, and instrumental music have become regarded as distinctive, attractive, colorful, lively—and they can be commodified in many ways, now turned into souvenirs or mementos. All of this reformulates the creole production in such a way that all can enter into the experience of its world without tainting themselves. Hubbub and its intoxifications now become a desirable—perhaps even a necessary—by-product in a globalizing economy, which is driven by touristic criteria by which pleasure is produced and judged. A creolized world promotes the idea that anyone and everyone can *get down with each other* in moves which enhance individual experience (identities and understandings now relieved of the opprobrium heretofore visited on mixed-breed populations as they construct their identities).

In a liberal democratic environment, this is taken to be a record of vernacular vigor, cultural invention in spite of itself. When creole speakers, singers, dancers, ritual specialists, and healers do make a place for themselves, their space is bounded from without, lest the disorder they bring spill over into the dominant society. Yet from mobility and mixture comes creative innovation. Many of the emergent forms of display and celebration emanate from the streets and the yards of the most hard-bitten neighborhoods, which those in power continue to regard as contaminated and potentially contagious. Finally, the results of creole vernacular creativity come to public notice through their commodification—that is, their employment in a cosmopolitan literature intended for non-creole-speaking audiences. Post-colonial communities situated within the New World Order and its global economy find themselves living at the unraveling edges of empire. The creole world begins to capitalize on its cultural dynamic in which new forms and styles are produced out of the mix. A kind of cultural acceleration seems to be taking place, in which the creolized forms are taken into planning of a tourist economy.

Stories of dispossession and Diaspora have turned into big business. What was thought of as contaminated and marginal is now rediscovered, cleaned up, and given a reinscribed narrative formulation that enables these visitors to re-experience expulsion and enslavement. Here visitors on holiday enter into the local economy, and the stylistic forms engendered within the creole world are exported, the two movements occurring simultaneously.

In such cases or settings creolization runs the risk of becoming just another term hijacked by the global theorists in hopes of creating the new Utopia, the creolized cosmopolitan state in which local culture is only incidental. Like *Diaspora* and *cosmopolitan*, expressive conditions are posited that deny the importance of local vernacular styles so that a technologically driven set of styles may be invented in the studio, through the Internet, and the like, echoing the techniques developed by early modernists. Those who push such a perspective, the post-colonial theoreticians, are making a bid for the status of oracles.

In sum, *Creole* has undergone a transvaluation, which has caused it to gravitate away from a sociopolitical set of meanings toward a more neutral, global term without any connotations of power manipulation, surveillance, or control. In its new formulation it becomes a bellwether term, one which promises cultural equity, an end to class at least insofar as we all become fellow travelers on the Grand Tour. Does this promise political equities at the same time? Encounters between cosmopolitans reach a kind of equitable plateau.

In a world in which everyone, potentially, is disjoined, relieved of the burden of tradition by making all vernaculars available to anyone with the technological know-how to infuse and even invade everyone else's business, all peoples are in dispersal. The agonizing history of human power-based displacement or disjunction simply becomes the norm. So it seems to me at my age and place in life. The commercial, then the industrial, and now the "knowledge industry" give promise of eliminating the old distinctions between developed and undeveloped nation-states. The promises of universal access to cultural alternatives and, perhaps more significant, to the accrued archives of information given under the power regimes of the colonizing world would seem to guarantee cultural equity—but equity for whom?

We are left with the accrued anxieties of a creolizing world in which virtually everyone seems to have a bone to pick with past overseers. The overtly confrontational attitude arising from the conditions of creole communities does not effectively get non-creoles to listen to overloud messages reminding the reading world of the ways in which the history of dislocation and enslavement, economic hardship, and political marginalization is connected to any mixture of styles achieved through entertainment forms of display. We pursue the very idea of creolization at our own risk if we forget the more deleterious attitudes toward racial admixture, which heretofore have been implied by the term.

Notes

1. For the moment, I am finessing the problem of gendering, which also is important in creolizing processes. Both religious and healing practices are built on private consultations, leading to clientage arrangements between individuals, who are often experienced women. Steven Feierman has argued, in personal conversations, that African market healers develop clientage that follows no other political or economic lines of power arrangement. Raquel Romberg's important pair of books (2003b, 2009) on a Puerto Rican witch details one such transcultural healing arrangement, as does Richard Price's latest work with his Saramaka friend Tooy (Price 2008). This geographical opening up of channels subject to creolizing should probably be considered a different kind of creolization as it is more private and more eccentric. The end products of creolization differ, then, from one situation to another, especially when secrecy becomes a factor.

2. The proliferation of kinds of sexualized interactions is made more and more public by both the development of the Internet and of telephonic styles of interaction. The movement of money is taken from the realm of face-to-face canons of acceptable behavior. And the creation of sex tourism further complicates the idea of creolization. I don't believe that theorists of the creole world would maintain interest in these subjects, but time will tell.

3. These matters come to public notice the more historical documents reveal how widespread the sexual congress between slaves and masters came to matter in other domains of the law. The Jefferson/Hemings situation, for instance, has recently been expanded by a careful combing of the documentary remains and the development of DNA technology. See here the summarizing work of Annette Gordon-Reed (2009). And this is just the most notorious American example of the problem. The importance of family stories should no longer be discounted as the result of gossip. In Caribbean outposts, there are many family stories of such racial mixtures having to do with

Alexander Hamilton, Empress Josephine, Lord Rochester's wife, the madwoman in the attic in *Jane Eyre*, among others.

4. Though I have argued in favor of the usefulness of the idea of the creole continuum, this no longer seems to carry much vigor, due to its politically dated origins and the lack of the broad data that would give bulk to the model (but see Bickerton 1975; DeCamp 1971, 1986). I continue to find useful the distinctions between *sweet talk* and *bad talk* and the suggestion that the range of codes revealed in my discussions with my assistants and friends, which leaned toward the further opposition between respectability and reputation norms, which I summarized in Abrahams 1983; see also Brown 2003; Burton 1997; McAlister 2002. The radical distinction between canons of respectability and reputation has been justly and intelligently questioned on the grounds of its structuralist simplicities.

References

Abel, Antoine. 1977. *Contes et poèmes des Seychelles. Poésie/prose Africaine*. Paris: Pierre Jean Oswald.

———. 1981. *Contes des Seychelles*. Illustrated by C. Vicini. Contes Du Monde Entier. Paris: CLE International.

Abrahams, Roger D. 1983. *The Man of Words in the West Indies: Performance and the Emergence of Creole Culture*. Baltimore: Johns Hopkins University Press.

———. 1992. *Singing the Master: The Emergence of African-American Culture in the Plantation South*. New York: Penguin Books.

———. 1998. "Antick Dispositions and the Perilous Politics of Culture: Costume and Culture in Jacobean England and America." *Journal of American Folklore* 111 (440): 115–132.

———. 2002a. "Criolian Contagion." Invited speaker. Caribbean Speaker Series. Swarthmore College.

———. 2002b. Panel discussant. "Creolization: Mapping New Territories in Creolization." American Folklore Society meeting. Rochester, NY.

———. 2003. "Questions of Criolian Contagion." *Journal of American Folklore* 116 (459): 73–87.

Abrahams, Roger D., Nick Spitzer, John F. Szwed, and Robert Farris Thompson. 2006. *Blues for New Orleans: Mardi Gras and America's Creole Soul*. Philadelphia: University of Pennsylvania Press.

Abrahams, Roger D., and John F. Szwed, eds. 1983. *After Africa: Extracts from British Travel Accounts and Journals of the Seventeenth, Eighteenth, and Nineteenth Centuries*. New Haven: Yale University Press.

Abu-Lughod, Lila. 1990. "The Romance of Resistance: Tracing Transformations of Power through Bedouin Women." *American Ethnologist* 17 (1): 41–55.

Accouche, Samuel. 1976. *Ti anan en foi en soungoula: Creole Stories from the Seychelles*. Köln (Cologne): Annegret Bollée.

Agnew, Jean-Christophe. 1986. *Worlds Apart*. Cambridge: Cambridge University Press.

Ahearn, Laura M. 2001. "Language and Agency." *Annual Review of Anthropology* 30:109–137.

Aijmer, Goran, ed. 1995. *Syncretism and the Commerce of Symbols*. Goteborg, Sweden: IASSA.

Alaja-Browne, Afolabi. 1989. "A Diachronic Study of Change in Juju Music." *Popular Music* 8 (3): 231–242.

Alberdi, Juan Bautista. 1984. *Bases y puntos de partida para la organización política de la República Argentina*. 2nd ed. Buenos Aires: Eudeba.

Alegría-Pons, José Francisco. 1988. "Aspectos de la religiosidad popular en Puerto Rico." Exhibition catalog. San Juan, Puerto Rico: Centro de Estudios Avanzados de Puerto Rico y el Caribe. Appeared also in *La Revista del Centro de Estudios Avanzados de Puerto Rico y el Caribe* 7:105–109.

Alexis, Jacques Stephen. 1959. *L'espace d'un cillement*. Paris: Gallimard.

Allen, Carolyn. 2002. "The Problem of Definition." In *Questioning Creole: Creolisation Discourses in Caribbean Culture*, edited by V. A. Shepherd and G. L. Richards, 47–63. Kingston, Jamaica: Ian Randle.

Alleyne, Mervyn C. 1973. "Language and Society in St. Lucia." In *Consequences of Class and Color: West Indian Perspectives*, edited by David Lowenthal and Lambros Comitas, 198–212. Garden City, NY: Doubleday.

———. 1985. "A Linguistic Perspective on the Caribbean." In *Caribbean Contours*, edited by Sidney Mintz and Sally Price, 155–180. Baltimore: Johns Hopkins University Press.

The American Heritage Dictionary of the English Language. 2000. 4th ed. New York: Houghton Mifflin Company.

Andrews, George Reid. 1980. *The Afro-Argentines of Buenos Aires, 1800–1900*. Madison: University of Wisconsin Press.

Annan, Ivan. 1964. *Folk Music of Ghana*. LP and accompanying booklet. New York: Folkways Records (FW 8859).

Appadurai, Arjun. 1990. "Disjuncture and Difference in the Global Cultural Economy." *Theory: Culture & Society* 7 (2–3): 295–310.

———. 1996. *Modernity at Large: Cultural Dimensions of Globalization*. Minneapolis: University of Minnesota Press.

Apter, Andrew. 1991. "Herskovits's Heritage: Rethinking Syncretism in the African Diaspora." *Diaspora* 1 (3): 235–260.

———. [1991] 2004. "Herskovits's Heritage: Rethinking Syncretism in the African Diaspora." In *Syncretism in Religion: A Reader*, edited by Anita M. Leopold and Jeppe S. Jensen, 160–184. London: Equinox.

———. 2002. "On African Origins: Creolization and *Connaissance* in Haitian Vodou." *American Ethnologist* 29 (2): 233–260.

Aptheker, Herbert. 1946. *The Negro People: A Critique of Gunnar Myrdal's An American Dilemma*. New York: International Press.

Aranzadi, Isabela de. 2009. *Instrumentos musicales de las etnias de Guinea Ecuatorial*. Madrid: Apadena.

Archibald, Adams George. 1889–91. "Story of Deportation of Negroes from Nova Scotia to Sierra Leone." *Collections of the Nova Scotia Historical Society* 7:129–154.

Archivo General de Puerto Rico. 1865. Fondo Gobernadores Españoles. Box 283. Documents about a woman in Moca. Letters exchanged between the bishop, parish priest, and governor about a miraculous figure followed by prosecution of owner. San Juan, Puerto Rico.

Arrom, José Juan. 1971. *Certidumbre de América*. Madrid: Gredos.

Ashcroft, Ed, and Richard Trillo. 1999. "Sierra Leone: Palm-Wine Sounds." In *World Music: The Rough Guide*. Vol. 1: *Africa, Europe, and the Middle East*, edited by

Simon Broughton, Mark Ellingham, and Richard Trillo, 634–637. London: Rough Guides.

Ashley, L. R. N. 1977. "Rhyme and Reason: The Methods and Meanings of Cockney Rhyming Slang, Illustrated with Some Proper Names and Some Improper Phrases." *Names* 25 (3): 124–154.

Augé, Marc. 1999. *The War of Dreams: Studies in Ethno Fiction.* London: Pluto Press.

Auleear, Dawood, and Lee Haring. 2006. *Indian Folktales from Mauritius.* Chennai, India: National Folklore Support Centre.

Avalle-Arce, Juan Bautista. 1964. *El Inca Garcilaso en sus "Comentarios" (Antología vivida).* Madrid: Gredos.

Baissac, Charles. [1880] 1976. *Étude sur le patois créole mauricien.* Geneva: Slatkine.

———. 1887. *Folklore de l'île Maurice.* Paris: G. P. Maisonneuve et Larose.

Baker, Phillip, and Peter Mühlhäusler. 2007. "Creole Linguistics from Its Beginnings, through Schuchardt to the Present Day." In *Creolization: History, Ethnography, Theory*, edited by Charles Stewart, 84–107. Walnut Creek, CA: Left Coast Press.

Bakhtin, Mikhail M. 1968. *Rabelais and His World.* Translated by Hélèn Iswolski. Cambridge, MA: MIT Press.

———. 1981. *The Dialogic Imagination.* Edited by Michael Holquist. Austin: University of Texas Press.

Bakunin, Michael. 1972. *Bakunin on Anarchy: Selected Works by the Activist-Founder of World Anarchism.* Translated, edited, and introduced by Sam Dolgoff. With a preface by Paul Avrich. New York: Vintage.

Balutansky, Kathleen M., and Marie-Agnès Sourieau, eds. 1998. *Caribbean Creolization: Reflections on the Cultural Dynamics of Language, Literature, and Identity.* Gainesville: University Press of Florida.

Barat, Christian, Michel Carayol, and Claude Vogel. 1977. *Kriké kraké: Recueil de contes créoles réunionnais.* Travaux de l'Institut d'Anthropologie Sociale et Culturelle de l'Océan Indien. Paris/St Denis: CNRS.

Baron, Robert. 1977. "Syncretism and Ideology: Latin New York Salsa Musicians." *Western Folklore* 36:209–225.

———. 1994. "Africa in the Americas: Melville J. Herskovits' Folkloristic and Anthropological Scholarship, 1923–1941." PhD diss., University of Pennsylvania.

———. 2003. "Amalgams and Mosaics, Syncretisms and Reinterpretations: Reading Herskovits and Contemporary Creolists for Metaphors of Creolization." *Journal of American Folklore* 116 (459): 88–115.

———. 2008. "Major League Tassa: Indo-Caribbean Drumming and Accompanying Dancers from Queens, New York." Program notes for concert in Homegrown Series. Washington, DC: American Folklife Center, Library of Congress.

———. 2010. "Sins of Objectification? Agency, Mediation, and Community Cultural Self-Determination in Public Folklore and Cultural Tourism Programming." *Journal of American Folklore* 123 (487): 63–91.

Baron, Robert, and Nick Spitzer. 2007. "Cultural Continuity and Community Creativity in a New Century: Preface to the Third Printing." In *Public Folklore*, edited by Robert Baron and Nick Spitzer, 388–396. Jackson: University Press of Mississippi.

Bass, Ruth. 1990. "The Little Man." In *Mother Wit from the Laughing Barrel*, edited by Alan Dundes, 388–396. Jackson: University of Mississippi Press.

Bastide, Roger. 1960. *The African Religions of Brazil.* Repr., Baltimore: Johns Hopkins University Press, 1978.
———. 1970. *Le Prochain et le lointain.* Paris: Cujas.
Bateson, Gregory. 1975. "Some Components of Socialization for Trance." *Ethos* 3 (2): 143–155.
Bauman, Richard, and Charles L. Briggs. 2003. *Voices of Modernity: Language Ideologies and the Politics of Inequality.* Cambridge: Cambridge University Press, 2003.
Bavoux, Claudine. 1994. "A propos des devinettes créoles de l'Océan Indien et du mythe des origines malgaches. Questions de méthodologie." *Études Créoles* 17 (2): 48–60.
Beaujard, Philippe. 1991. *Mythe et société à Madagascar (Tanala de l'Ikongo): Le chasseur d'oiseaux et la princesse du ciel.* With a preface by Georges Condominas. Paris: L'Harmattan.
Beckwith, Martha. 1929. *Black Roadways: A Study of Jamaican Folk Life.* Chapel Hill: University of North Carolina Press.
Ben-Amos, Dan. 1976. "Analytical Categories and Ethnic Genres." In *Folklore Genres*, edited by Dan Ben-Amos, 215–242. Austin: University of Texas Press.
Bender, Wolfgang. 1989. "Ebenezer Calender—An Appraisal." In *Perspectives on African Music*, edited by Wolfgang Bender, 42–70. Bayreuth African Studies Series 9. Bayreuth: Bayreuth University.
———. 1991. *Sweet Mother: Modern African Music.* Chicago: University of Chicago Press.
Bendix, Regina, and Dorothy Noyes, eds. 1998. "Introduction: In Modern Dress: Costuming the European Social Body, 17th–20th Centuries." Special issue, *Journal of American Folklore* 3:107–114.
Benga, Ndiouga A. 2002. "The Air of the City Makes Free: Urban Music from the 1950s to the 1990s in Senegal Variété, Jazz, Mbalax, Rap." In *Playing with Identities in Contemporary Music in Africa*, edited by Mai Palmberg and Annemette Kirkegaard, 75–85. Uppsala: Nordiska Afrikainstitutet.
Benitez-Rojo, Antonio. 1992. *The Repeating Island: The Caribbean and the Postmodern Perspective.* Durham, NC: Duke University Press.
Berlin, Ira. 1996. "From Creole to African: Atlantic Creoles and the Origins of African American Society in Mainland North America." *William and Mary Quarterly*, 3rd ser., 53: 251–288.
Berlin, Ira, and Philip Morgan, eds. 1993. *Cultivation and Culture: Labor and the Shaping of Slave Life in the Americas.* Charlottesville: University of Virginia Press.
Bernabé, Jean, Patrick Chamoiseau, and Raphaël Confiant. 1989. *Éloge de la créolité/In Praise of Creoleness.* Paris: Gallimard.
———. 1990. "In Praise of Creoleness." *Callaloo* 13:866–909.
Bettelheim, Judith. 1979. "The Afro-Jamaican Jonkonnu Festival: Playing the Forces and Operating the Cloth." PhD diss., Yale University.
———. 1999. "Gumbay: A Name and a Drum." African Caribbean Institute of Jamaica. *ACIJ Research Review* (), no. 4:3–15.
Bhabha, Homi K. 1994a. *The Location of Culture.* New York: Routledge.
———. 1994b. "Of Mimicry and Man: The Ambivalence of Colonial Discourse." In his *The Location of Culture*, 85–92. London: Routledge.

Bickerton, Derek. 1975. *Dynamics of a Creole System*. Cambridge: Cambridge University Press.

Bilby, Kenneth M. 1981a. "The Kromanti Dance of the Windward Maroons of Jamaica." *Nieuwe West-Indische Gids* 55 (1–2): 52–101.

———. 1981b. *Music of the Maroons of Jamaica*. LP and accompanying booklet. New York: Folkways Records (FE 4027).

———. 1984. "The Treacherous Feast: A Jamaican Maroon Historical Myth." *Bijdragen tot de Taal-, Land- en Volkenkunde* 140:1–31.

———. 1992. *Drums of Defiance: Maroon Music from the Earliest Free Black Communities of Jamaica*. CD and accompanying booklet. Washington, DC: Smithsonian Folkways (SF 40412).

———. 1997. "Swearing by the Past, Swearing to the Future: Sacred Oaths, Alliances, and Treaties among the Guianese and Jamaican Maroons." *Ethnohistory* 44 (4): 655–689.

———. 1999. "Gumbay, Myal, and the Great House: New Evidence on the Religious Background of Jonkonnu in Jamaica." African Caribbean Institute of Jamaica. *ACIJ Research Review*, no. 4:47–70.

———. 2001. "Commentary." In *The South and the Caribbean*, edited by Douglas Sullivan-Gonzales and Charles Reagan Wilson, 116–125. Jackson: University Press of Mississippi.

———. 2005. *True-Born Maroons*. Gainesville: University Press of Florida.

———. 2007. "More than Met the Eye: African-Jamaican Festivities in the Time of Belisario." In *Art and Emancipation in Jamaica: Isaac Mendes Belisario and His Worlds*, edited by Tim Barringer, Gillian Forrester, and Barbaro Martinez-Ruiz, 120–135. New Haven: Yale Center for British Art and Yale University Press.

Blanchy, Sophie, Zaharia Soilihi, Noël J. Gueunier, and Madjidhoubi Said. 1993. *La maison de la mère: Contes de l'île de Mayotte*. Illustrated by Gilles Joisseaux. Paris: L'Harmattan.

Blier, Suzanne Preston. 1996. *African Vodun: Art, Psychology, and Power*. Chicago: University of Chicago Press.

Blyden, Nemata Amelia. 2000. *West Indians in West Africa, 1808–1880: The African Diaspora in Reverse*. Rochester, NY: University of Rochester Press.

Boas, Franz. 1972. *The Professional Correspondence of Franz Boas*. Microfilm ed. Wilmington, DE: Scholarly Resources.

Bolland, Nigel. 1992. "Creolization and Creole Societies: Cultural Nationalist View of Caribbean Social History." In *Intellectuals in the Caribbean*. Vol. 1, edited by Alistair Hennessy, 50–79. London: Macmillan Caribbean.

———. 1997. *Struggles for Freedom: Essays on Slavery, Colonialism, and Culture in the Caribbean and Central America*. Belize: Angelus Press.

Borgatti, Jean M. 1990. "Portraiture in Africa." *African Arts* 23 (3): 34–39, 101–102.

Borges, Jorge Luis. 1926. *El tamaño de mi esperanza*. Buenos Aires: Proa.

———. [1932] 1962. "The Argentine Writer and Tradition." In *Labyrinths, Selected Stories and Other Writings*, edited by Donald A. Yates and James E. Irby, 177–185. New York: New Directions.

———. 1964. "The Spanish Language in South America—A Literary Problem. El Gaucho Martín Fierro." A lecture delivered to the Department of Spanish, University of Bristol, February 22, 1963. London, Canning House.

———. 1974. *Obras completas, 1923–1972*. Buenos Aires: Emecé.

———. 1981. *A Reader.* Edited by Emir Rodríguez Monegal and Alastair Reid. New York: E. P. Dutton.

———. 1984. *Evaristo Carriego, A Book about Old-Time Buenos Aires.* Translated, with Introduction and Notes, by Norman Thomas Di Giovanni, with the assistance of Susan Ashe. New York: E. P. Dutton.

Brandon, George. 1993. *Santería from Africa to the New World: The Dead Sell Memories.* Bloomington: Indiana University Press.

Brathwaite, Edward Kamau. 1971. *The Development of Creole Society in Jamaica.* Oxford: Claredon Press.

———. 1974a. *Caribbean Man in Space and Time: A Bibliographical and Conceptual Approach.* Mona, Jamaica: Savacou Publications.

———. 1974b. *Contradictory Omens: Cultural Diversity and Integration in the Caribbean.* Mona, Jamaica: Savacou Publications.

———. 1977. "Caliban, Ariel, and Unprospero in the Conflict of Creolization: A Study of the Slave Revolt in Jamaica." In *Comparative Perspectives on Slavery in New World Plantation Societies*, edited by Vera Rubin and Arthur Tuden. Annals of the New York Academy of Science, vol. 292:41–62.

———. 1984. *The History of the Voice: The Development of Nation Language in Anglophone Caribbean Poetry.* London: New Beacon Books.

Brereton, Bridget, and Kevin A. Yelvington, eds. 1999. *The Colonial Caribbean in Transition: Essays in Post-emancipation Social and Cultural History.* Barbados and Gainesville: The Press University of the West Indies and University Press of Florida.

Briggs, Charles. 1993. "Metadiscursive Practices and Scholarly Authority in Folkloristics." *Journal of American Folklore* 106 (422): 387–434.

———. 2002. "Linguistic Magic Bullets in the Making of a Modernist Anthropology." *American Anthropologist* 104:481–498.

Brown, David H. 2003. *Santería Enthroned: Art, Ritual, and Innovation in an Afro-Cuban Religion.* Chicago: University of Chicago Press.

Brown, Ras Michael. 2002. "Walk in the Feenda: West-Central Africans and the Forest in the South Carolina–Georgia Lowcountry." In *Central Africans and Cultural Transformations in the American Diaspora*, edited by Linda M. Heywood, 289–318. New York: Cambridge University Press.

Browne, Katherine E. 2004. *Creole Economics: Caribbean Cunning under the French Flag.* Austin: University of Texas Press.

Burton, Richard D. E. 1997. *Afro-Creole: Power, Opposition, and Play in the Caribbean.* Ithaca, NY: Cornell University Press.

Cabrera, Lydia. 1954. El Monte. Repr., Miami: Ediciones Universal, 1975.

Campbell, James T. 2006. *Middle Passages: African American Journeys to Africa, 1787–2005.* New York: Penguin Press.

Campbell, Mavis C. 1990. *Nova Scotia and the Fighting Maroons: A Documentary History.* Williamsburg, VA: College of William and Mary.

———. 1992. "Early Resistance to Colonialism: Montague James and the Maroons in Jamaica, Nova Scotia, and Sierra Leone." In *People and Empires in African History: Essays in Memory of Michael Crowder*, edited by J. F. Ade Ajayi and J.D.Y. Peel, 89–105. London: Longman.

———. 1993. *Back to Africa: George Ross and the Maroons, from Nova Scotia to Sierra Leone.* Trenton, NJ: Africa World Press.

Cantwell, Robert. 1993. *Ethnomimesis: Folklore and the Representation of Culture.* Chapel Hill: University of North Carolina Press.

Cara, Ana C. 2002. "Creole Noise vs. Baroque Excesses." Invited paper. Voice/Over: Cultural Transmission as Translation, Exchange, and Reproduction. A symposium in honor of Roger D. Abrahams. University of Pennsylvania, Philadelphia.

———. 2003. "The Poetics of Creole Talk: Toward an Aesthetic of Argentine Verbal Art." *Journal of American Folklore* 116 (459): 36–56.

Cara-Walker, Ana. 1983. "The Art of Creole Expression in Argentina." Ph.D. diss., University of Pennsylvania.

———. 1986. "Borges' Milongas: The Chords of Argentine Verbal Art." In *Borges, the Poet,* edited by Carlos Cortínez, 280–295. Fayetteville: University of Arkansas Press.

———. 1987. "Cocoliche: The Art of Assimilation and Dissimulation among Italians and Argentines." *Latin American Research Review* 12:37–67.

Carayol, Michel. 1980. "La littérature orale réunionaise." In *L'encyclopédie de la Réunion,* vol. 7, Robert Chaudenson, gen. ed., 9–36. Saint-Denis: Livres-Réunion.

Carayol, Michel, and Robert Chaudenson, comps., in collaboration with P. Doomun. 1978. *Les aventures de Petit-Jean: Contes créoles de l'Océan Indien.* Illustrated by Marylène Vogel. Fleuve et Flamme. Paris: EDICEF.

Caro Costas, Aida R. 1983. "The Organization of an Institutional and Social Life." In *Puerto Rico: A Political and Cultural History,* edited by Arturo Morales Carrión, 25–40. New York: W. W. Norton.

Carter, Isabel Gordon. 1933. "Some Songs and Ballads from Tennessee and North Carolina." *Journal of American Folklore* 46 (179): 22–50.

Cassidy, Frederick K., and Ralph Lepage. 2002. *Dictionary of Jamaican English.* Cambridge: Cambridge University Press.

Césaire, Ina. 1985. *Mémoires d'isles.* Paris: Editions Caribéennes.

Césaire, Suzanne. 1942. "Misère d'une poésie: John Antoine-Nau." *Tropiques* 4:48–50.

Chagnoux, Hervé, and Ali Haribou. 1990. *Les Comores.* 2d ed. Que Sais-Je? Paris: Presses Universitaires de France.

Chamberlin, J. Edward. 1993. *Come Back to Me My Language.* Champaign: University of Illinois.

———. 2003. *If This Is Your Land, Where Are Your Stories? Reimagining Home and Sacred Space.* Toronto: Knopf Canada.

Chamoiseau, Patrick. 1992. "Les nègres marrons de l'en ville." *Antilla,* no. 473:29–33.

———. 1986. *Chronique des sept misères.* Paris: Gallimard.

———. 1997. *L'esclave vieil homme et le molosse.* Paris: Gallimard.

———. 1997. *Texaco.* New York: Pantheon.

———. 2002. *Livret des villes du deuxième monde.* Paris: Monum.

Chamoiseau, Patrick, and Raphaël Confiant, eds. 1991. *Lettres Créoles, Tracées antillaises et continentales de la littérature.* Paris: Hatier.

Chaudenson, Robert. 2001. *Creolization of Language and Culture.* Revised in collaboration with Salikoko S. Mufwene. London: Routledge.

Chernoff, John Miller. 1979. *African Rhythm and African Sensibility.* Chicago: University of Chicago Press.

——. 1985a. "Africa Come Back: The Popular Music of West Africa." In *Repercussions: A Celebration of African-American Music*, edited by Geoffrey Haydon and Dennis Marks, 152–178. London: Century.

——. 1985b. *Master Drummers of Dagbon*. Vol. 1. LP album/CD. Cambridge, MA: Rounder Records (Rounder 5016).

Clark, Vé Vé A. 1991. "Diaspora Literature and Marasa Consciousness." In *Comparative American Identities: Race, Sex, and Nationality in the Modern Text*, edited by Hortense J. Spillers, 40–61. New York: Routledge.

Clarke, Robert. 1843. *Sierra Leone: A Description of the Manners and Customs of the Liberated Africans*. London: James Ridgway.

Clifford, James. 1997. *Routes: Travel and Translation in the Late Twentieth Century*. Cambridge, MA: Harvard University Press.

Cohen, Robin, and Paola Toninato. 2010. "The Creolization Debate: Analyzing Mixed Identities and Cultures." In *The Creolization Reader: Studies in Mixed Identities and Cultures*, edited by Robin Cohen and Paola Toninato, 1–21. New York: Routledge.

Collins, John. 1985a. *African Pop Roots*. London: W. Foulsham.

——. 1985b. *Musicmakers of West Africa*. Washington, DC: Three Continents Press.

——. 1987. "Jazz Feedback to Africa." *American Music* 5 (2): 176–193.

——. 1989. "The Early History of West African Highlife Music." *Popular Music* 8 (3): 221–230.

——. 1994. "The Ghanaian Concert Party: African Popular Entertainment at the Cross Roads." PhD diss., State University of New York, Buffalo.

——. 2004. "The Impact of African-American Performance on West Africa from 1800." Paper presented at the Nineteenth International Conference of the Vereinigung von Afrikanisten, University of Hannover, Germany.

——. 2007. "Pan African Goombay Drum-Dance Music: Its Ramifications and Development in Ghana." *Legon Journal of the Humanities* 18:179–200.

Coluccio, Felix. 1981. *Diccionario folklórico argentino*. Buenos Aires: Editorial Plus Ultra.

Comaroff, Jean, and John Comaroff, eds. 1993. *Modernity and Its Malcontents*. Chicago: University of Chicago Press.

Condé, Maryse. 1989. *Crossing the Mangrove*. Repr., New York: Doubleday, 1995.

——. 1999. "On the Apparent Carnivalization of Literature from the French Caribbean". In *Representations of Blackness and the Performance of Identities*, edited by Jean Muteba Rahier, 91–97. Westport: Bergin & Garvey.

Condé, Maryse, and Madeleine Cottenet-Hage, eds. 1995. *Penser la créolité*. Paris: Éditions Karthala.

Connerton, Paul. 1989. *How Societies Remember*. Cambridge: Cambridge University Press.

Coplan, David. 1978. "Go to My Town, Cape Coast! The Social History of Ghanaian Highlife." In *Eight Urban Musical Cultures: Tradition and Change*, edited by Bruno Nettl, 96–114. Urbana: University of Illinois Press.

——. 1982. "The Urbanization of African Music: Some Theoretical Observations." *Popular Music* 2:112–129.

Cowley, John. 1996. *Carnival, Canboulay, and Calypso*. Cambridge: Cambridge University Press.

Crowley, Daniel J. 1957. "Plural and Differential Acculturation in Trinidad." *American Anthropologist* 59:817–824.

Cummings, Susan. 2006. "Sierra Leone's Refugee All Stars." *The Beat* 25 (5): 38–41.

Cuney-Hare, Maud. 1918. "The Drum in Africa." *The Metronome* 34 (8): 50–53.

———. 1936. *Negro Musicians and Their Music.* Washington, DC: Associated Publishers.

Curtis, Wayne. 2009. "Houses of the Future." *Atlantic Monthly* 304 (4): 56–67.

Dagan, Esther A., ed. 1993. *Drums: The Heartbeat of Africa.* Montreal: Galerie Amrad African Art Publications.

Dandouau, André. 1922. *Contes populaires des sakalava et des tsimihety de la région d'Analalava.* Algiers: Jules Carbonel.

Davis, Stephen. 1988. "Alpha Blondy: Africa's Reggae Superstar." *Reggae & African Beat* 7 (1): 33–35.

Dawdy, Shannon Lee. 2009. *Building the Devil's Empire: French Colonial New Orleans.* Chicago: University of Chicago Press.

Dayan, Joan. 1995. *Haiti, History, and the Gods.* Berkeley: University of California Press.

DeCamp, David. 1971. "Introduction: The Study of Pidgin and Creole Languages." In *Pidginization and Creolization of Languages,* edited by Dell Hymes, 13–39. London: Cambridge University Press.

———. 1986. *Language and Liberation: Creole Language Politics in the Caribbean.* London: Karia Press.

De Certeau, Michel. 1984. *The Practice of Everyday Life.* Berkeley: University of California Press.

Decros, Marie Christine. 1978. "Contes réunionnais, textes et traductions." Mémoire de maîtrise, Centre Universitaire de la Réunion.

Defoe, Daniel. 1750. *Madagascar: Or, Robert Drury's Journal. "A Vocabulary of the Madagascar Language."* London: M. Sheepey.

de L'Estoile, Benoît. 2007. *Le Goût des autres: De l'exposition coloniale aux arts premiers.* Paris: Flammarion.

Deleuze, Giles, and Félix Guattari. 1986. *Kafka: Toward a Minor Literature.* Minneapolis: University of Minnesota Press.

Desmangles, Leslie G. 1992. *The Faces of the Gods: Vodou and Roman Catholicism in Haiti.* Chapel Hill: University of North Carolina Press.

Diawara, Manthia. 1998. *In Search of Africa.* Cambridge, MA: Harvard University Press.

Dixon-Fyle, Mac. 2006. "Rescuing the Footnoted: Immigrant Krio Travails on the Niger, 1865–1926." In *New Perspectives on the Sierra Leone Krio,* edited by Mac Dixon-Fyle and Gibril Cole, 107–131. New York: Peter Lang.

DjeDje, Jacqueline Cogdell. 1998. "Remembering Kojo: History, Music, and Gender in the January Sixth Celebration of the Jamaican Accompong Maroons." *Black Music Research Journal* 18 (1–2): 67–120.

Domínguez, Virginia R. 1986. *White by Definition: Social Classification in Creole Louisiana.* New Brunswick, NJ: Rutgers University Press.

Dorson, Richard M. 1972. "The Use of Printed Sources." In *Folklore and Folklife, an Introduction,* edited by Richard M. Dorson, 465–477. Chicago: University of Chicago Press.

Douglas, Mary, 2002. *Purity and Danger: An Analysis of Concepts of Pollution and Taboo.* New York: Routledge.

Drake, St. Clair. 1987–1990. *Black Folk Here and There: An Essay in History and Anthropology.* 2 vols. Los Angeles: Center for Afro-American Studies, University of California.

Drake, St. Clair, and Horace M. Cayton. 1945. *Black Metropolis: A Study of Negro Life in a Northern City.* Chicago: University of Chicago Press.

Drewal, Henry John, John Pemberton III, and Rowland Abiodun. 1989. *Yoruba: Nine Centuries of African Art and Thought.* New York: Center for African Art in Association with H. N. Abrams.

Drewal, Margaret Thompson, 1990. "Portraiture and the Construction of Reality in Yorubaland and Beyond." *African Arts* 23 (3): 40–49.

Droogers, André. 1989. "Syncretism: The Problem of Definition, the Definition of the Problem." In *Dialogue and Syncretism: An Interdisciplinary Approach,* edited by Hendrik Vroom, Jerald Gort, Rein Fernhout, and Anton Wessels, 7–25. Grand Rapids, MI: Eerdmans and Rodopi.

Drummond, Lee. 1980. "The Cultural Continuum: A Theory of Intersystems." *Man* (n.s) 15:352–374.

Duany, Jorge. 1985. "Ethnicity in the Spanish Caribbean: Notes on the Consolidation of Creole Identity in Cuba and Puerto Rico, 1762–1868." *Ethnic Groups* 6 (2–3): 93–123.

———. 1998. "La religiosidad popular en Puerto Rico: Una perspectiva antropológica." In *Vírgenes, magos y escapularios: Imaginería, etnicidad y religiosidad popular en Puerto Rico,* edited by Ángel Quintero Rivera, 175–192. Río Piedras: Centro de Investigaciones Sociales de la Universidad de Puerto Rico, Centro de Investigaciones Académicas de la Universidad del Sagrado Corazón, and Fundación Puertorriqueñas de las Humanidades.

Du Bois, W. E. B. 2009. *The Souls of Black Folk.* New York: Oxford University Press, 2009.

Dundes, Alan, ed. 1968. *Every Man His Way: Readings in Cultural Anthropology.* Englewood Cliffs, NJ: Prentice-Hall.

———. 1971. "The Making and Breaking of Friendship as a Structural Frame in African Folk Tales." In *Structural Analysis of Oral Tradition,* edited by Pierre Maranda and Elli Köngäs Maranda, 171–185. Philadelphia: University of Pennsylvania Press.

Dunham, Katherine. 1946. *Journey to Accompong.* New York: Henry Holt.

Duran, Lucy. 1992. "Goumbe Go!" *Folk Roots,* no. 109:43–45.

Eaton, Mick, ed. 1979. *Anthropology—Reality—Cinema: The Films of Jean Rouch.* London: British Film Institute.

Eco, Umberto. 1962. *The Open Work.* Repr., Cambridge: Harvard University Press, 1989.

———. 1986. *Semiotics and the Philosophy of Language.* Bloomington: Indiana University Press.

El tango en Broadway. [1934] 2002. Directed by Louis J. Gasnier. International DVD Group.

Ellis, Kate, Stephen Smith, and Nick Spitzer. 2007. *Routes to Recovery: American Radio Works.* St. Paul, MN: American Public Media.

Ellison, Ralph. 2002. *Living with Music: Ralph Ellison's Jazz Writing.* Edited by Robert O'Meally. New York: Modern Library.

Encyclopedia Britannica. 1910. Vol. 7, 11th ed. New York: Encyclopedia Britannica Company.

Enwezor, Okwui, Carlos Basualdo, Ute Meta Bauer, Suzanne Ghez, Sarat Maharaj, Mark Nash, and Octavio Zaya, eds. 2002. *Créolité and Creolization: Documenta11_Platform3.* Ostildern-Ruit: Hatje Cantze Publishers.

Epstein, Dena J. 1973. "African Music in British and French West Indies." *Musical Quarterly* 59:61–91.

———. 2003. *Sinful Tunes and Spirituals: Black Music to the Civil War.* Silver Anniversary Edition. Urbana: University of Illinois Press.

Eriksen, Thomas Hylland. [2003] 2010. "Creolization and Creativity." In *The Creolization Reader: Studies in Mixed Identities and Cultures,* edited by Robin Cohen and Paola Toninanto, 68–81. New York: Routledge.

Fabian, Johannes. 2001. "Culture with an Attitude." In his *Anthropology with an Attitude: Critical Essays,* 87–100. Stanford: Stanford University Press.

Fabian, Johannes, and Ilona Szombati-Fabian. 1980. "Folk Art from an Anthropological Perspective." In *Folk Art in America,* edited by Scott T. Swank and Ian M. G. Quimby, 247–292. New York: W. W. Norton.

Falola, Toyin. 1999. *Yoruba Gurus: Indigenous Production of Knowledge in Africa.* Trenton, NJ: Africa World Press.

Fanon, Frantz. 1952. *Black Skin White Masks.* New York: Grove Press.

Faublée, Jacques. 1947. *Récits bara.* Travaux et Mémoires de l'Institut d'Ethnologie. Paris: Institut d'Ethnologie, Musée de l'Homme.

Feld, Steven. 1994. "From Schizophonia to Schismogenesis: On the Discourses and Commodification Practices of 'World Music' and 'World Beat.'" In *Music Grooves: Essays and Dialogues,* by Steven Feld and Charles Keil, 257–289. Chicago: University of Chicago Press.

Fernandez, James W. 1986. *Persuasions and Performances: The Play of Tropes in Culture.* Bloomington: Indiana University Press.

Fernández Latour de Botas, Olga. 1969. *Folklore y poesía argentina.* Buenos Aires: Editorial Guadalupe.

Fernández Olmos, Margarite, and Lizabeth Paravisini-Gebert, eds. 2003. *Creole Religions of the Caribbean: An Introduction from Vodou and Santería to Obeah and Espiritismo.* New York: New York University Press.

Floyd, Samuel A., Jr. 1996. *The Power of Black Music: Interpreting Its History from Africa to the United States.* New York: Oxford University Press.

Fontoynont, Dr. Maurice, and Raomandahy. 1937. *La Grande Comore.* Mémoires de l'Académie Malgache. Tananarive: Imprimerie Moderne de l'Émyrne, Pitot de la Beaujardière.

Frazer, Sir James George. [1901] 1960. *The Golden Bough: A Study in Magic and Religion.* New York: Macmillan.

Fusco, Coco. 1995. *English Is Broken Here: Notes on Cultural Fusion in the Americas.* New York: New Press.

Gallob, Karen W. 1987. "An Anthropological Study of Incongruity, Play, and Identity in Mauritian Verbal Humor." PhD diss., University of Colorado.

Galloway, Shirley. 1996. "The Mimic Men: A World Without a Center." http://www. cyberpat.com/shirlsite/essays/naipaul.html (accessed November 14, 2004).

Gates, Henry Louis. 1988. *The Signifying Monkey: A Theory of African-American Literary Criticism.* Oxford: Oxford University Press.

George, Claude. 1904. *The Rise of British West Africa.* London: Houlston and Sons.

GEREC. 1982. *Charte culturelle créole.* Schoelcher, Martinique: Centre Universitaire Antilles-Guyane.

Giegengack, Robert, and Kenneth R. Foster. 2006. "Physical Constraints on Reconstructing New Orleans." In *Rebuilding Urban Places after Disaster: Lessons from Hurricane Katrina,* edited by Eugenie Birch and Susan Wachter, 13–33. Philadelphia: University of Pennsylvania Press.

Gilroy, Paul. 1993. *The Black Atlantic: Modernity and Double Consciousness.* Cambridge: Harvard University Press.

Glissant, Edouard. 1956. *Soleil de la conscience.* Paris: Seuil.

——. 1989. *Caribbean Discourse.* Charlottesville: University Press of Virginia.

——. 1990. *Poétique de la Relation.* Paris: Gallimard.

——. [1990] 1997. *Poetics of Relation.* Translated by Betsy Wing. Ann Arbor: University of Michigan Press.

——. 1993. *Tout-Monde.* Paris: Gallimard.

——. 1996. *Faulkner, Mississippi.* Paris: Stock.

——. 1997. *Traité du Tout-Monde.* Paris: Gallimard.

Goffman, Erving. 1974. *Frame Analysis: An Essay on the Organization of Experience.* Cambridge, MA: Harvard University Press.

Gomez, Michael A. 1998. *Exchanging Our Country Marks: The Transformation of African Identities in the Colonial and Antebellum South.* Chapel Hill: University of North Carolina Press.

——. 2006. "Diasporic Africa: A View from History." In *Diasporic Africa: A Reader,* edited by Michael A. Gomez, 1–23. New York: New York University Press.

Goodman, Nelson. 1979. "Metaphor as Moonlighting." In *On Metaphor,* edited by Sheldon Sacks, 175–180. Chicago: University of Chicago Press.

Görög-Karady, Veronika, and Christiane Seydou, comps. and eds. 2001. *La fille difficile, un conte-type africain.* Paris: CNRS Editions.

Gort, Jerald, Hendrik Vroom, Fernhout Rein, and Anton Wessels, eds. 1989. *Dialogue and Syncretism: An Interdisciplinary Approach.* Grand Rapids, MI: Eerdmans and Rodopi.

Graham, Effie. 1912. *The "Passin' On" Party.* Chicago: A. C. McClurg.

Grant, John N. 2002. *The Maroons in Nova Scotia.* Halifax: Formac.

Grimshaw, Allen D. 1971. "Some Social Forces and Some Social Functions of Pidgins and Creole Languages." In *Pidginization and Creolization of Languages,* edited by Dell Hymes, 427–445. London: Cambridge University Press.

Grosfoguel, Ramón, Frances Negrón-Muntaner, and Chloe Georas. 1997. "Beyond Nationalist and Colonialist Discourses: The Jaiba Politics of the Puerto Rican Ethno-Nation." In *Puerto Rican Jam: Essays on Culture and Politics,* edited by Frances Negrón-Muntaner and Ramón Grosfoguel, 1–38. Minneapolis: University of Minnesota Press.

Gueunier, Noël J. 1990a. *Contes de la côte ouest de Madagascar.* In collaboration with J. M. Katupha, illustrated by Razafintsalama. Capricorne. Antananarivo and Paris: Éditions Ambozontany, Éditions Karthala.

———. 1990b. *La belle ne se marie point: Contes comoriens en dialecte malgache de l'île de Mayotte.* Paris: Peeters.

———. 1994. *L'oiseau chagrin: Contes comoriens en dialecte malgache de l'île de Mayotte.* Compiled by Noël J. Gueunier and Madjidhoubi Said, translated by Noël J. Gueunier, illustrated by Razafintsalama. Asie et Monde Insulindien. Paris: Peeters.

Gueunier, Noël. J., and Madjidhoubi Said, comps. 2001. *Le coq du roi: Contes comoriens en dialecte malgache de l'île de Mayotte.* Translated by Noël J. Gueunier, illustrated by Razafintsalama. Asie et Monde Insulindien. Paris: Peeters.

Gundaker, Grey. 1993. "Tradition and Innovation in African American Yards." *African Arts* 26 (2): 58–71, 94–96.

———. 1994a. "African American History, Cosmology, and the Moral Universe of Edward Houston's Yard." *Journal of Garden History* 14 (3): 179–205.

———. 1994b. "Halloween in Two Southern Settings." In *Halloween: Festivals of Life and Death,* ed. Jack Santino, 247–260. Knoxville: University of Tennessee Press.

———, ed. 1998a. *Keep Your Head to the Sky: Interpreting African American Home Ground.* Charlottesville: University Press of Virginia.

———. 1998b. *Signs of Diaspora/Diaspora of Signs: Literacies, Creolization, and Vernacular Practice in African America.* New York: Oxford University Press.

———. Forthcoming. "Face Like a Looking Glass: Ritual Figuration and Landscape in Special African American Yards." In *Materialities, Meanings, and Modernities of Rituals in the Black Atlantic,* edited by Akin O. Sauders and Paula Sauders. Bloomington: Indiana University Press.

Gundaker, Grey, and Judith McWillie. 2006. *No Space Hidden: The Spirit of African American Yards.* Knoxville: University of Tennessee Press.

Guralnick, Peter. 1995. *Last Train to Memphis: The Rise of Elvis Presley.* New York: Little Brown and Co.

Guy, Donna J. 1991. *Sex and Danger in Buenos Aires: Prostitution, Family, and Nation in Argentina.* Lincoln: University of Nebraska Press.

Hafstein, Vladimar Tr. [2001] 2005. "Biological Metaphors in Folklore Theory: An Essay in the History of Ideas." In *Folklore: Critical Concepts in Literary and Cultural Studies,* edited by Alan Dundas, 407–435. London and New York: Routledge.

Hall, Stuart, ed. 1997. *Representation: Cultural Representations and Signifying Practices.* London: Sage.

———. 2003a. "Créolité and the Process of Creolization." In *Créolité and Creolization: Documenta11_Platform3,* edited by Okwui Enwezor, Carlos Bausaldo, Ute Meta Bauer, Susanne Ghez, Sarat Maharaj, Mark Nash, and Octavio Zaya, 27–41. Ostfildern-Ruit, Germany: Hatje Cantz Publishers.

———. 2003b. "Creolization, Diaspora, and Hybridity in the Context of Globalization." In *Créolité and Creolization: Documenta 11_Platform 3,* edited by Okwui Enwezor, Carlos Bausaldo, Ute Meta Bauer, Susanne Ghez, Sarat Maharaj, Mark Nash, and Octavio Zaya, 185–198. Documenta. Ostfildern-Ruit, Germany: Hatje Cantz Publishers.

Hampton, Barbara L. 1977. "The Impact of Labor Migration on Music in Urban Ghana: The Case of Kpehe Gome." PhD diss., Columbia University, New York.

———. 1979–1980. "A Revised Analytical Approach to Musical Processes in Urban Africa." *African Urban Studies* 6:1–16.

———. 1983. "Toward a Theory of Transformation in African Music." In *Transformation and Resiliency in Africa*, edited by Pearl T. Robinson and Elliott P. Skinner, 211–229. Washington, DC: Howard University Press.

Hancock, Ian F. 1971. "A Survey of the Pidgins and Creoles of the World." In *Pidginization and Creolization of Languages*, edited by Dell Hymes, 509–523. London: Cambridge University Press.

———. 1977. "Appendix: Repertory of Pidgin and Creole Languages." In *Pidgin and Creole Linguistics*, edited by Albert Valdman, 362–391. Bloomington: Indiana University Press.

Handler, Richard. 1986. "Vigorous Male and Aspiring Female: Poetry, Personality, and Culture in Edward Sapir and Ruth Benedict." In *Malinowski, Rivers, Benedict, and Others: Essays on Culture and Personality*, edited by George W. Stocking Jr., 127–155. Madison: University of Wisconsin Press.

Handler, Richard, and Eric Gable. 1997. *The New History in an Old Museum: Creating the Past at Colonial Williamsburg*. Durham, NC: Duke University Press.

Hankins, John Ethan, and Stephen Maklansky, eds. 2002. *"Raised to the Trade": Creole Building Arts of New Orleans*. New Orleans: New Orleans Museum of Art.

Hannerz, Ulf. 1987. "The World in Creolisation." *Africa* 57:546–558.

———. 1989. "Notes on the Global Ecumene." *Public Culture* 1 (2): 66–75.

———. 1990. "Cosmopolitans and Locals in World Culture." In *Global Culture. Nationalism, Globalization, and Modernity*, edited by Mike Featherstone, 237–251. London: Routledge.

———. 1996. *Transnational Connections: Culture, People, Places*. London: Routledge.

———. 2006. "Theorizing through the New World? Not Really." *American Ethnologist* 33:563–565.

Haring, Lee. 1972. "A Characteristic African Folktale Pattern." In *African Folklore*, edited by Richard M. Dorson, 165–179. Garden City, NY: Doubleday Anchor.

———. 1982. *Malagasy Tale Index*. FF Communications. Helsinki: Suomalainen Tiedeakatemia.

———. 1985. "The Water-Spirits of Madagascar." *Cross Rhythms*, no. 2:157–175.

———. 1992. *Verbal Arts in Madagascar: Performance in Historical Perspective*. Publications of the American Folklore Society. Philadelphia: University of Pennsylvania Press.

———. 2004a. "Creolization as Agency in Woman-Centered Folktales." In *Fairy Tales and Feminism: New Approaches*, edited by Donald Haase, 169–177. Detroit: Wayne State University Press.

———. 2004b. "Cultural Creolization." *Acta Ethnographica Hungarica* 49 (1–2): 1–38.

———. 2007a. "Framing in Narrative." In *The Arabian Nights in Transnational Perspective*, edited by Ulrich Marzolph, 135–153. Detroit: Wayne State University Press.

———. 2007b. *Stars and Keys: Folktales and Creolization in the Indian Ocean*. Bloomington: Indiana University Press.

Harney, Stefano. 1996. *Nationalism and Identity: Culture and the Imagination in a Caribbean Diaspora.* Kingston: University of the West Indies.

Harrev, Flemming. 1987. "Gumbe and the Development of Krio Popular Music in Freetown, Sierra Leone" (revised edition, 1998). Paper presented at the Fourth International Conference of the International Association for the Study of Popular Music, Accra, Ghana, August.

———. 1993. "The Origin of Urban Music in West and Central Africa" (revised edition, 1997). Paper presented at the Twenty-third World Conference of the International Council for Traditional Music, Berlin.

———. 2001. "The Diffusion of Gumbe, Assiko, and Maringa in West and Central Africa." Paper presented at the Twelfth Triennial Symposium of the Arts Council of the African Studies Association, St. Thomas, U.S. Virgin Islands, April.

Harris, Roxy, and Ben Rampton. 2002. "Creole Metaphors in Cultural Analysis: On the Limits and Possibilities of (Socio-)Linguistics." *Critiques of Anthropology* 22:31–51.

Hart, Richard. 2002. *Slaves Who Abolished Slavery: Blacks in Rebellion of 1985.* Kingston, Jamaica: University of the West Indies Press.

Hearn, Lafcadio. [1890] 2001. *Two Years in the French West Indies.* New York: Interlink Books.

Hernández, José. [1872] 1953. *Martín Fierro.* Buenos Aires: Editorial Kapelusz.

———. 1974. *The Gaucho Martín Fierro.* Translated by Frank G. Carrino, Alberto J. Carlos, and Norman Mangouni. Albany: State University of New York Press.

Herskovits, Melville J. Papers. Northwestern University Archives (NUHP). Evanston, IN.

———. Papers. Schomburg Center for Research in Black Culture Archives (SCHP). New York Public Library, New York.

———. 1924. Review of "Anthropology" by A. L. Kroeber. *The New Republic* 38 (482): 25–26.

———. 1932. "Wari in the New World." *Journal of the Royal Anthropological Institute* 62:23–37.

———. 1933. "On the Provenience of New World Negroes." *Social Forces.* 12:247–262.

———. [1935] 1966. "What Has Africa Given America?" In *The New World Negro*, by Melville J. Herskovits, edited by Frances S. Herskovits, 168–174. Bloomington, IN: Minerva Press.

———. 1937a. "African Ethnology and the New World Negro." *Man* 38:9–10.

———. 1937b. "African Gods and Catholic Saints in New World Negro Belief." *American Anthropologist* 39 (4, pt. 1): 635–643.

———. [1937c] 1971. *Life in a Haitian Valley.* New York: Anchor.

———. 1937d. "The Significance of the Study of Acculturation for Anthropology." *American Anthropologist* 39:259–264.

———. [1938] 1958. *Acculturation: The Study of Culture Contact.* Gloucester, MA: P. Smith.

———. [1941] 1958. *The Myth of the Negro Past.* Boston: Beacon Press.

———. [1945] 1966. "Problem, Method, and Theory in Afroamerican Studies." In *The New World Negro*, by Melville J. Herskovits, edited by Frances S. Herskovits, 43–61. Bloomington, IN: Minerva Press.

———. 1948a. *Man and His Works.* New York: A. A. Knopf.

———. 1948b. "The Contribution of Afroamerican Studies to Africanist Research."
American Anthropologist 50:1–10.

———. 1952. "Some Psychological Implications of Afroamerican Studies." In
Acculturation in the Americas, edited by Sol Tax, 153–155. Chicago: University of
Chicago Press.

———. 1966. *The New World Negro*. Edited by Frances S. Herskovits. Bloomington, IN:
Minerva Press.

Herskovits, Melville J., and Frances S. Herskovits. [1936] 1968. *Suriname Folk-lore*.
New York: AMS Press.

———. [1947] 1964. *Trinidad Village*. New York: Octogon Books.

Hill, Donald R. 1993. *Calypso Callaloo: Early Carnival Music in Trinidad*. Gainesville:
University Press of Florida.

Hinds, Allister. 2001. "Deportees in Nova Scotia: The Jamaican Maroons, 1796–1800."
In *Working Slavery, Pricing Freedom: Perspectives from the Caribbean, Africa, and
the African Diaspora*, ed. Verene A. Shepherd, 206–222. New York: Palgrave.

Hintzen, Percy. 2002. "Race and Creole Ethnicity in the Caribbean." In *Questioning
Creole: Creolisation Discourses in Caribbean Culture*, edited by Verene A. Shepherd
and Glen L. Richards, 92–110. Kingston, Jamaica: Ian Randle.

Holas, Bohumil. 1953. "La Goumbé: Une association de jeunesse musulmane en basse
Côte d'Ivoire." *Kongo-Overzee* 19 (2–3): 116–129.

Holbek, Bengt. 1976. "Games of the Powerless." *Unifol (København) Arsberetning*, 10–33.

Holm, John A., with Allison W. Shilling, eds. 1982. *Dictionary of Bahamian English*.
Cold Springs, NY: Barnhart.

Horton, Christian Dowu Jayeola. 1999. "The *Gumbe* and the Feedback Process." In
Turn Up the Volume! A Celebration of African Music, edited by Jacqueline Cogdell
DjeDje, 230–235. Los Angeles: UCLA Fowler Museum of Cultural History.

Houlberg, Marilyn, 2005. "Magique Marasa: The Ritual Cosmos of Twins and Other
Sacred Children." In *Fragments of Bone: Neo-African Religions in a New World*,
edited by Patrick Bellegarde-Smith, 13–31. Urbana: University of Illinois Press.

Howard, Philip A. 1998. *Changing History: Afro-Cuban Cabildos and Societies of Color
in the Nineteenth Century*. Baton Rouge: Louisiana University Press.

Howells, A. W. 1909. *Akanse Iwaasu Nipa ti Ijo Goombay, ati iwaasu miran ni Ile
Olorun St. John's Aroloya Lagos*. London: James Townsend and Sons.

Huerga, Álvaro, comp. 1989. *Damián López de Haro: Constituciones Sinodales de
Puerto Rico 1645*. Ponce: Universidad Católica de Puerto Rico.

Hugill, Stan. 1967. *Sailortown*. New York: E. P. Dutton.

Hurston, Zora Neale, 1942. *Dust Tracks on a Road*. Philadelphia: Lippincott Brothers.
Repr., New York: Harper and Harper Perennial Classics, 2003.

Hyatt, Harry Middleton. 1978. *Hoodoo—Conjuration—Witchcraft—Root Work*. 5 vols.
Hannibal, MO: Western Publishing.

Hymes, Dell. 1971. *Pidginization and Creolization of Languages*. New York: Cambridge
University Press.

———. 1972a. "The Contribution of Folklore to Sociolinguistic Research." In *Toward
New Perspectives in Folklore*, edited by Americo Paredes and Richard Bauman,
42–50. Austin: University of Texas Press.

———. 1972b. "Models of the Interaction of Language and Social Life." In *Directions in Sociolinguistics: The Ethnography of Communication*, edited by John J. Gumperz and Dell Hymes, 35–71. New York: Holt, Rinehart and Winston.

———. 1975. "Breakthrough into Performance." In *Folklore, Performance, and Communication*, edited by Dan Ben-Amos and Kenneth S. Goldstein, 11–74. The Hague: Mouton.

Impey, Angela. 1998. "Popular Music in Africa." In *The Garland Encyclopedia of World Music*. Vol. 1: *Africa*, edited by Ruth M. Stone, 415–437. New York: Garland.

Jackson, George Pullen. 1933. *White Spirituals of the Southern Uplands*. Chapel Hill: University of North Carolina Press.

Jackson, John. 2005. *Real Black: Adventures in Racial Sincerity*. Chicago: University of Chicago Press.

James, C.L.R. 1993. *Beyond a Boundary*. With an introduction by Robert Lipsyte. Durham: Duke University Press.

Johnson, Guy B. 1930. *Folk Culture on St. Helena Island, South Carolina*. Chapel Hill: University of North Carolina Press.

Jones, Howard Mumford. 1964. *O Strange New World*. New York: Viking Press.

Jordan, William Chester. 1993. *Women and Credit in Pre-Industrial and Developing Societies*. Philadelphia: University of Pennsylvania Press.

Joubert, Jean-Louis, Amina Osman, and Liliane Ramarasoa. 1993. *Littératures francophones de l'Océan Indien. Mauritius?* Rose Hill, Mauritius: Éditions de l'Océan Indien.

Jourdan, Christine. 1991. "Pidgins and Creoles: The Blurring of Categories." *Annual Review of Anthropology* 20:187–209.

Joyce, James. 1976. *The Portable James Joyce*. New York: Penguin Books.

Joyner, Charles. 1984. *Down by the Riverside: A South Carolina Slave Community*. Urbana: University of Illinois Press.

Kapchan, Deborah. 1993. "Hybridization and the Market Place: Emerging Paradigms in Folkloristics." *Western Folklore* 52 (2–4): 303–326.

Kapchan, Deborah, and Pauline Turner Strong, special eds. 1999. *Journal of American Folklore: Theorizing the Hybrid* 112, Summer issue, no. 445.

Kemble, Frances Anne. 1984. *Journal of a Residence on a Georgia Plantation in 1838–1839*. Athens: University of Georgia Press.

Khan, Aisha. 2001. "Journey to the Center of the Earth: The Caribbean as Master Symbol." *Cultural Anthropology* 16 (3): 271–302.

———. 2007a. "Creolization Moments." In *Creolization: History, Ethnography, Theory*, edited by Charles Stewart, 237–253. Walnut Creek, CA: Left Coast Press.

———. 2007b. "Good to Think? Creolization, Optimism, and Agency." *Current Anthropology* 48:655–673.

Kinser, Samuel. 1990. *Carnival, American Style: Mardi Gras in New Orleans and Mobile*. Chicago: University of Chicago Press.

Klein, Guus de. 1999. "Guinea-Bissau: The Backyard Beats of Gumbe." In *World Music: The Rough Guide*. Vol. 1: *Africa, Europe, and the Middle East*, edited by Simon Broughton, Mark Ellingham, and Richard Trillo, 499–504. London: Rough Guides.

Köelle, Sigismund Wilhelm. 1854. *Polyglotta Africana: Or, a Comparative Vocabulary of Nearly Three Hundred Words and Phrases, in More than One Hundred Distinct African Languages.* London: Church Missionary House.

Kogan, Lee. 1998. *The Art of Nellie Mae Rowe: Ninety-nine and a Half Won't Do.* New York: University Press of Mississippi in association with the Museum of American Folk Art.

Konaté, Yacouba. 1987. *Alpha Blondy: Reggae et société en Afrique noire.* Paris: Karthala.

Kozinski, Jerzy. 1965. *The Painted Bird.* London: Bantam Books.

Kristeva, Julia. 1980. *Desire in Language: A Semiotic Approach to Literature and Art.* edited by Leon S. Roudiez. Translated by Leon S. Roudiez, Thomas Gora, and Alice Jardine. New York: Columbia University Press.

———. 1984. *Revolution in Poetic Language.* Translated by Margaret Waller, with an introduction by Leon S. Roudiez. New York: Columbia University Press.

Kundera, Milan. 2006. *The Curtain.* New York: Harper-Collins.

Kup, A. P. 1975. *Sierra Leone: A Concise History.* New York: St. Martin's Press.

Kutzinski, Vera. 1993. *Sugar's Secret: Race and the Erotics of Cuban Nationalism.* Charlottesville: University Press of Virginia.

La Selve, Jean-Pierre. 1995. *Musiques traditionnelles de la Réunion.* Saint-Denis: Azalées Éditions.

Labov, William. 1969. "Contraction, Deletion, and Inherent Variability of the English Copula." *Language* 45 (4): 715–762.

Lacan, Jacques. 2006. *Écrits, the First Complete Edition in English.* Translated by Bruce Fink, collaborators Héloïse Fink and Russell Grigg. New York: W. W. Norton.

Laferrière, Dany. 1996. *Pays sans chapeau.* Québec: Lanctot.

Landa, Manuel M. de. 1997. *A Thousand Years of Nonlinear History.* New York: Swerve.

Latour, Bruno. 1993. *We Have Never Been Modern.* Cambridge, MA: Harvard University Press.

Latrobe, Benjamin Henry. [1818–1920] 1951. *Impressions Respecting New Orleans; Diary and Sketches, 1818–1820.* New York: Columbia University Press.

Lawton, Samuel Miller. 1939. "The Religious Life of South Carolina Coastal and Sea Island Negroes." PhD diss., George Peabody College for Teachers, Nashville, TN.

Le Clézio, J.M.G., and J. Le Clézio. 1990. *Sirandanes, suivies d'un petit lexique de la langue créole et des oiseaux.* Paris: Seghers.

LeFalle-Collins, Lizetta. 1987. *Home and Yard: Black Folk Life Expressions in Los Angeles.* Los Angeles: California Afro-American Museum.

Leiris, Michel. 1934. *L'Afrique fantôme.* Paris: Gallimard.

———. 1992. *Zebrage.* Paris: Gallimard.

Lester, Julius. 1972. *The Knee High Man and Other Tales.* New York: Dial Press.

Lévi-Strauss, Claude. 1985. "New York in 1941." In his *The View from Afar*, 258–267. New York: Basic Books.

Lionnet, Françoise. 1992. "Logiques Métisses: Cultural Appropriation and Postcolonial Representations." *College Literature* 19 (3): 100–120.

Lipsitz, George. 1990. *Time Passages: Collective Memory and American Popular Culture.* Minneapolis: University of Minnesota Press.

Livingston, Paisley. 1992. *Models of Desire, Rene Girard and the Psychology of Mimesis.* Baltimore: Johns Hopkins University Press.

Lockett, James D. 1999. "The Deportation of the Maroons of Trelawny Town to Nova Scotia, then back to Africa." *Journal of Black Studies* 30 (1): 5–14.

Lohman, Jonathan. 1999. "It Can't Rain Everyday: The Year-Round Experience of Carnival." Studies of Carnival in Memory of Daniel J. Crowley. Special issue edited by Peter Tokofsky. *Western Folklore* 58 (3–4): 279–298.

Lombard, Jacques. 1976. "'Zatovo qui n'a pas été créé par dieu': Un conte sakalava traduit et commenté." *ASEMI* 7 (2–3): 165–223.

Londres, Albert. 1928. *The Road to Buenos Ayres.* Translated by Eric Sutton. New York: Boni and Liveright.

Long, Edward. 1774. *History of Jamaica.* Vol. 2. London: T. Lowndes.

López Cantos, Ángel. 1992. *La religiosidad popular en Puerto Rico (siglo XVIII).* Santurce, Puerto Rico: Centro de Estudios Avanzados de Puerto Rico y el Caribe.

López Valdés, Rafael L. 1985. *Componentes Africanos en el Etnos Cubano.* La Habana, Cuba: Editorial de Ciencias Sociales.

———. 1995. Conversation with the author. San Juan, Puerto Rico.

Lovejoy, Paul. 1997. "The African Diaspora: Revisionist Interpretations of Ethnicity, Culture, and Religion under Slavery." *Studies in the World History of Abolition and Emancipation* 2 (1): 1–24.

Ludmer, Josefina. 1988. *El género gauchesco: Un tratado sobre la patria.* Buenos Aires: Sudamericana.

Lusk, Jon. 1999. "Goombay Roots: Jon Lusk Talks to John Collins about a Ghanaian Bicentenary." *Folk Roots*, no. 191:16–17.

Lynn, Martin. 1984. "Commerce, Christianity, and the Origins of the 'Creoles' of Fernando Po." *Journal of African History* 25:257–278.

———. 1992. "Technology, Trade, and 'A Race of Native Capitalists': The Krio Diaspora of West Africa and the Steamship, 1852–95." *Journal of African History* 33:421–440.

MacGaffey, Wyatt, 1986. *Religion and Society in Central Africa.* Chicago: University of Chicago Press.

MacGaffey, Wyatt, Michael Harris, and David Driskell. 1993. *Astonishment and Power: The Eyes of Understanding: Kongo Minkisi.* Washington, DC: Smithsonian Institution Press.

Mafud, Julio. 1973. *Psicología de la viveza criolla: Contribuciones para una interpretación de la realidad social argentina y americana.* 5th ed. Buenos Aires: Americalee.

Malinowski, Bronislaw. [1947] 1995. Introduction to Fernando Ortiz's *Cuban Counterpoint: Tobacco and Sugar*, translated by Harriet de Onís. Durham, NC: Duke University Press.

Mallet, Robert. 1961. *Histoires et légendes du pays de Madagascar.* Antananarivo: Éditions du CALAM.

Malone, Jacqui. 1996. *Steppin' on the Blues: The Visible Rhythms of African American Dance.* Urbana: University of Illinois Press.

Marimoutou , Jean Claude Carpanin. 2003. "Literature, the Imaginary, and Creolization: Texts and Intertexts." Translated by Miranda Robbins. In *Créolité and Creolization: Documenta11_Platform3*, edited by Okwui Enwezor, Carlos Bausaldo,

Ute Meta Bauer, Susanne Ghez, Sarat Maharaj, Mark Nash, and Octavio Zaya. 225–239. Ostfildern-Ruit, Germany: Hatje Cantz.

Marks, Morton. 1974. "Uncovering Ritual Structures in Afro-American Music." In *Religious Movements in Contemporary America*, edited by Irving I. Zaretsky and Mark P. Leone, 60–134. Princeton: Princeton University Press.

Martí, José. [1891] 1996. "Nuestra América." In *Voces de Hispanoamérica*. 2nd ed., edited by Raquel Chang-Rodriguez and Malva E. Filer. 237–242. Boston: Heinle & Heinle Publishers.

Martínez Estrada, Ezequiel. [1940] 2001. *La cabeza de Goliat*. Barcelona: Editorial Losada.

Matory, James Lorand. 2005. *Black Atlantic Religion: Tradition, Transnationalism, and Matriarchy in the Afro-Brazilian Candomblé*. Princeton: Princeton University Press.

———. 2006. "The 'New World' Surrounds an Ocean: Theorizing the Live Dialogue between African and African American Cultures." In *Afro-Atlantic Dialogues: Anthropology in the Diaspora*, edited by Kevin A. Yelvington, 151–192. Santa Fe, NM: School of American Research Press.

Matson, Henrietta, 1893. *The Mississippi Schoolmaster*. Boston: Congregational Sunday-School & Publishing Company.

Maurer, Bill. 1997. *Recharting the Caribbean*. Ann Arbor: University of Michigan Press.

McAlister, Elizabeth. 2002. *Rara! Vodou, Power, and Performance in Haiti and Its Diaspora*. Berkeley: University of California Press.

McDermott, R. P. 1988. "Inarticulateness." In *Linguistic in Context*, edited by Deborah Tannen, 37–68. Norwood, NJ: Ablex.

McDonald, Roderick. 1993. *The Economy and Material Culture of Slaves: Goods and Chattels on Sugar Plantations of Jamaica and Louisiana*. Baton Rouge: Louisiana State University Press.

———. 2001. *Between Slavery and Freedom: Special Magistrate John Anderson's Journal of St. Vincent during the Apprenticeship*. Philadelphia: University of Pennsylvania Press.

McWhorter, John H. 2000. *The Missing Spanish Creoles*. Berkeley: University of California Press.

McWillie, Judith. 1989. *Another Face of the Diamond: Pathways through the Black Atlantic South*. New York: INTAR Latin American Gallery.

———. 1998. "Art, Healing, and Power in the Afro-Atlantic South." In *Keep Your Head to the Sky: Interpreting African American Home Ground*, edited by Grey Gundaker, 65–92. Charlottesville: University Press of Virginia. .

Megill, Donald D., and Richard S. Demory. 1996. *Introduction to Jazz History*. Upper Saddle River, NJ: Prentice-Hall.

Mehan, Hugh, and Houston Wood. 1975. *The Reality of Ethnomethodology*. New York: John Wiley & Sons.

Meillassoux, Claude. 1968. *Urbanization of an African Community: Voluntary Associations in Bamako*. American Ethnological Society Monograph 45. Seattle: University of Washington Press.

Memmi, Albert. 1957. *The Colonizer and the Colonized*. Boston: Beacon Press.

Métraux, Alfred. 1959. *Voodoo in Haiti*. New York: Oxford University Press.

———. 1972. *Voodoo in Haiti*. Translated by Hugo Charters. New York: Schoken Books.

Meyer, Andreas. 1997. *Afrikanische Trommeln: West-und Zentralafrika*. Berlin: Museum für Völkerkunde.

Michel-Andrianarahinjaka, Lucien X. 1986. *Le système littéraire betsileo*. Fianarantsoa: Éditions Ambozontany.

Mintz, Sidney. 1960. "The House and the Yard among Three Caribbean Peasantries." *VIe congres international des Sciences Anthropologiques et Ethnologiques* 2:590–596.

———. 1966. "The Caribbean as a Socio-Cultural Area." *Cahiers d'Histoire Mondiale* 9:912–937.

———. 1971a. "Men, Women, and Trade." *Comparative Studies in Society and History* 13:247–269.

———. 1971b. "The Socio-Historical Background to Pidginization and Creolization." In *Pidginization and Creolization of Languages*, edited by Dell Hymes, 486–496. Cambridge: Cambridge University Press.

———. 1974. *Caribbean Transformations*. New York: Columbia University Press.

———. 1985. "From Plantations to Peasantries in the Caribbean." In *Caribbean Contours*, edited by S. W. Mintz and Sally Price, 127–153. Baltimore: Johns Hopkins University Press.

———. 1996. "Enduring Substances, Trying Theories: The Caribbean Region as Oikumene." *Journal of the Royal Anthropological Institute* 2:289–311.

———. 1998. "The Localization of Anthropological Practice: From Area Studies to Transnationalism." *Critique of Anthropology* 18:117–133.

Mintz, Sidney, and Douglas Hall. 1970. The Origins of the Jamaican Internal Marketing System. Reprinted in *Caribbean Slave Society and Economy: A Student Reader*, edited by Hilary Beckles and Verene Shepherd. London: James Currey Publishers, 1991.

Mintz, Sidney W., and Richard Price. 1976. "An Anthropological Approach to the Afro-American Past: A Caribbean Perspective." Manuscript. Philadelphia: Institute for the Study of Human Issues.

———. 1992. *The Birth of an African-American Culture: An Anthropological Perspective*. Boston: Beacon Press.

Misir, Prem, ed. 2006. *Cultural Identity and Creolization: The Multiethnic Caribbean*. Lanham, MD: University Press of America.

Mitchell-Kernan, Claudia. 1973. "Signifying." In *Mother-Wit from the Laughing Barrel: Readings in the Interpretation of Afro-American Folklore*, edited by Alan Dundes, 310–328. Englewood Cliffs: Prentice-Hall.

Montuschi, Eleonora. 1995. "What Is Wrong with Talking of Metaphors in Science?" In *From a Metaphorical Point of View: A Multidisciplinary Approach to the Cognitive Content of Metaphor*, edited by Zdravko Radman, 309–327. Berlin: Walter de Gruyter.

Moore, Robin. 1997. *Nationalizing Blackness: Afrocubanismo and Artistic Revolution in Havana, 1920–1940*. Pittsburgh: University of Pittsburgh Press.

Mörner, Magnus. 1967. *Race Mixture in the History of Latin America*. Boston: Little, Brown and Company.

Moya, Ismael. 1959. *El arte de los payadores*. Buenos Aires: Editorial P. Berruti.

———. 1972. *Didáctica del Folklore*. 3d ed. Buenos Aires: Compañía General Fabril.

Mullin, Michael. 1992. *Africa in America: Slave Acculturation and Resistance in the American South and the British Caribbean, 1736–1831*. Urbana: University of Illinois Press.

Munasinghe, Viranjini. 2006. "Theorizing World Culture through the New World: East Indians and Creolization." *American Ethnologist* 33:549–552.

Munasinghe, Viranjini, and Ulf Hannerz, Aisha Khan, John Tomlinson, Deborah A. Thomas, Vicente M Diaz, Daniel A. Segal, Verena Stolcke, and Pauline Turner. 2006. "Locating or Liberating Creolization." A forum in *American Ethnologist* 33 (4): 549–592.

Murga, Vicente, and Álvaro Huerga, comps. 1989. *Episcopologio de Puerto Rico III de Francisco de Cabrera a Francisco de Padilla (1611–1695)*. Ponce, Puerto Rico: Universidad Católica de Puerto Rico.

Murphy, Jeannette Robinson. 1899. "The Survival of African Music in America." *Popular Science Monthly* 55:660–672.

Myrdal, Gunnar. 1944. *An American Dilemma: The Negro Problem and Modern Democracy*. New York: Harper.

Naficy, Hamid. 1993. *The Making of Exile Cultures: Iranian Television in Los Angeles*. Minneapolis: University of Minnesota Press.

Naipaul, V. S. 1967. *The Mimic Men*. London: Penguin.

Nettleford, Rex M. 1970. *Mirror Mirror: Identity, Race, and Protest in Jamaica*. Jamaica: William Collins and Sangster.

Noiret, François. 2008. *Le mythe d'Ibonia, le grand prince*. Paris: Karthala.

Nooter, Mary H. 1993. Secrecy: "Art that Conceals and Reveals." *African Arts* 26 (1): 59.

Nunley, John W. 1987. *Moving with the Face of the Devil*. Urbana: University of Illinois Press.

Nunley, John W., and Judith Bettelheim, eds. 1998. *Caribbean Festival Arts*. St. Louis: Washington University Press.

Oldendorp, C.G.A. [1777] 1987. *C.G.A. Oldendorp's History of the Mission of the Evangelical Brethren on the Caribbean Islands of St. Thomas, St. Croix, and St. John*. Translated by Arnold R. Highfield and Vladimir Barac. Ann Arbor: Karoma Publishers.

Olwig, Karen Fog. 1993. *Global Culture, Island Identity: Continuity and Change in the Afro-Caribbean Community of Nevis*. Switzerland [Philadelphia] and Amsterdam, Netherlands: Harwood Academic Publishers.

Ortiz, Fernando. [1917] 1995. *Los Negros Brujos*. Havana: Editorial de Ciencias Sociales.

———. [1947] 1995. *Cuban Counterpoint: Tobacco and Sugar*. Translated by Harriet de Onís. Durham, NC: Duke University Press.

———. 1952. *Los intrumentos de la música afrocubana*. Vol. 3. Havana: Ministerio de Educación.

———. 2001. "The Afro-Cuban Festival 'Day of the Kings.'" In *Cuban Festivals: A Century of Afro-Cuban Culture*, edited by Judith Bettelheim, translated by Jean Stubbs, 1–41. Princeton: Marcus Weiner.

Ortiz Oderigo, Néstor. 1974. *Aspectos de la cultura africana en el Río de la Plata*. Buenos Aires: Editorial Plus Ultra.

Páez, Jorge. 1970. *El conventillo*. Buenos Aires: Centro Editor de América Latina S.A.

———. 1971. *Del truquiflor a la rayuela, Panorama de los juegos y entretenimientos argentinos.* La Historia Popular 57. Buenos Aires: Centro Editor de América Latina S.A.

Palmié, Stephan. 1995. "Against Syncretism: 'Africanizing' and 'Cubanizing' Discourses in North American Òrìsà Worship." In *Counterworks: Managing the Diversity of Knowledge,* edited by Richard Fardon, 80–104. London: Routledge.

———. 2002. *Wizards and Scientists: Explorations in Afro-Cuban Modernity and Tradition.* Durham, NC: Duke University Press.

———. 2006. "Creolization and Its Discontents." *Annual Reviews in Anthropology* 35:433–456.

———. 2007a. "The 'C-Word' Again: From Colonial to Postcolonial Semantics." In *Creolization: History, Ethnography, Theory,* edited by Charles Stewart, 66–83. Walnut Creek, CA: Left Coast Press.

———. 2007b. "Is There a Model in the Muddle? 'Creolization' in African Americanist History and Anthropology." In *Creolization: History, Ethnography, Theory,* edited by Charles Stewart, 178–200. Walnut Creek, CA: Left Coast Press.

Paredes, Américo. 1993. *Folklore and Culture on the Texas-Mexican Border.* Austin: CMAS Books, Center for Mexican American Studies, University of Texas.

Parsons, Talcott. 1985. *Institutions and Social Evolution: Selected Writings.* Edited by Leon H. Mayhew. Chicago: University of Chicago Press.

Patton, Sharon. 1998. *African-American Art.* New York: Oxford University Press.

Paulme, Denise. 1975. "Typologie des contes africains du décepteur." *Cahiers d'Études Africaines* 15 (60): 569–600.

Picart, Lennox O'Riley. 1996. "The Trelawny Maroons and Sir John Wentworth: The Struggle to Maintain Their Culture, 1796–1800." *Collections of the Royal Nova Scotia Historical Society* 44:165–187.

Piersen, William D. 1988. *Black Yankees: The Development of an Afro-American Subculture in Eighteenth-Century New England.* Amherst: University of Massachusetts Press.

Polk, Patrick. 2005. *Botánica Los Angeles: Latino Popular Religious Art in the City of Angels.* Los Angeles: UCLA Fowler Museum.

Polomé, Edgar C. 1982. "Creolization and Language Change." In *Language, Society, and Paleoculture,* 271–284. Palo Alto: Stanford University Press.

Pratt, Mary Louise. 1992. *Imperial Eyes: Travel Writing and Transculturation.* London: Routledge.

President Kirchner en Automotriz Volkswagen. 2007. Martes. Palabras del president de la nación, Néstor Kirchner, al término de su visita a la empresa automotriz Volkswagen, en la localidad de Pacheco, provnicia de Buenos Aires. October 16. http://www.casarosada.gov.ar/index.php?option=com_content&task=view&id=1287 (accessed March 23, 2010).

Price, Richard. 1973. *Maroon Societies: Rebel Slave Communities in the Americas.* Repr., Baltimore: The Johns Hopkins University Press, 1996.

———. 1983. *First Time: The Historical Vision of an Afro-American People.* Chicago: University of Chicago Press.

———. 1998. *The Convict and the Colonel.* Boston: Beacon Press.

———. 2001. "The Miracle of Creolization." *New West Indian Guide/Nieuwe West-Indische Gids* 75 (1–2): 35–64.

———. 2006. "On the Miracle of Creolization." In *Afro-Atlantic Dialogues: Anthropology in the Diaspora*, edited by Kevin A. Yelvington, 115–147. Santa Fe, NM: School of American Research Press.

———. 2008. *Travels with Tooy*. Chicago: University of Chicago Press.

———. 2009. "The Concept of Creolization." In *Cambridge World History of Slavery*, edited by David Eltis and Stanley L. Engerman. Cambridge, UK: Cambridge University Press.

Price, Richard, and Sally Price. 1997. "Shadowboxing in the Mangrove." *Cultural Anthropology* 12 (1): 3–36.

———. 2003. *The Root of Roots: Or, How Afro-American Anthropology Got Its Start*. Chicago: Prickly Paradigm Press.

Puckett, Newbell Niles. 1926. *Folk Beliefs of the Southern Negro*. Chapel Hill: University of North Carolina Press.

Quintero Rivera, Angel G. 1995. Conversation with the author. Universidad de Puerto Rico, Río Piedras, Puerto Rico.

———. 1998a. *Salsa, sabor y control! Sociología de la música "tropical."* Mexico: Siglo Veintiuno Editores.

———, ed. 1998b. *Vírgenes, magos y escapularios: Imaginería, etnicidad y religiosidad popular en Puerto Rico*. San Juan: Centro de Investigaciones Sociales de la Universidad de Puerto Rico, Centro de Investigaciones Académicas de la Universidad del Sagrado Corazón, and Fundación Puertorriqueñas de las Humanidades.

Ramdoyal, Ramesh. 1979. *Tales from Mauritius*. London: Macmillan Publishers.

———. 1981. *More Tales from Mauritius*. London: Macmillan Publishers.

Rankin, F. Harrison. 1836. *The White Man's Grave: A Visit to Sierra Leone, in 1834*. Vol. 1. London: Richard Bentley.

Rassoul, Abass, ed. 1992. *The Theology of Time by the Honorable Elijah Muhammad*. Hampton, VA: U.B. & U.S. Communications.

Rawick, George P., ed. 1972. *The American Slave: A Composite Autobiography*. 18 vols. Westport, CT: Greenwood Press.

Redfield, Robert, Ralph Linton, and Melville J. Herskovits. 1936. "A Memorandum for the Study of Acculturation." *American Anthropologist* 38:149–152.

Reisman, Karl. 1970. "Cultural and Linguistic Ambiguity in a West Indian Village." In *Afro-American Anthropology*, edited by Norman E. Whitten and John F. Szwed, 129–144. New York: Free Press.

———. 1974. "Contrapuntal Conversation in an Antiguan Village." In *Explorations in the Ethnography of Speaking*, edited by Richard Bauman and Joel Scherzer, 110–124. Repr., Cambridge: Cambridge University Press, 1989.

Rentink, Sonja. 2004. "Kpanlogo: Conflict, Identity Crisis, and Enjoyment in a Ga Drum Dance." MA thesis, University of Amsterdam.

Rhys, Jean. 1966. *Wide Sargasso Sea*. London: Penguin Books.

Roberts, Helen H. 1924. "Some Drums and Drum Rhythms of Jamaica." *Natural History* 24 (2): 241–251.

———. 1926. "Possible Survivals of African Song in Jamaica." *Musical Quarterly* 12 (3): 340–358.

Roberts, John Storm. 1998. *Black Music of Two Worlds*. 2nd ed. New York: Schirmer.

Robinson, N. Scott. 2003. "Frame Drums and Tambourines." In *Continuum Encyclopedia of Popular Music of the World*. Vol. 2: *Performance and Production*, edited by John Shepherd, David Horn, Dave Laing, Paul Oliver, and Peter Wicke, 362–372. London: Continuum.

Rohlehr, Gordon. 1990. *Calypso and Society in Pre-Independence Trinidad*. Port of Spain: privately printed.

———. 2004. "Calypso Reinvents Itself." In *The Creolization Reader*, edited by Robin Cohen and Paola Toninato, 170–184. Repr., New York: Routledge, 2010.

Román, Reinaldo Luis. 2000. "Conjuring Progress and Divinity: Religion and Conflict in Cuba and Puerto Rico, 1899–1956." PhD diss., University of California at Los Angeles.

Romberg, Raquel. 1998. "Whose Spirits Are They? The Political Economy of Syncretism and Authenticity." *Journal of Folklore Research* 35 (1): 69–82.

———. 2003a. "From Charlatans to Saviors: Espiritistas, Curanderos, and Brujos Inscribed in Discourses of Progress and Heritage." *Centro Journal* 15 (2): 146–173.

———. 2003b. *Witchcraft and Welfare: Spiritual Capital and the Business of Magic in Modern Puerto Rico*. Austin: University of Texas Press.

———. 2005. "Symbolic Piracy: Creolization with an Attitude?" *New West Indian Guide* 79 (3–4): 175–218.

———. 2009. *Healing Dramas: Divination and Magic in Modern Puerto Rico*. Austin: University of Texas Press.

Roseberry, William. 1989. "Balinese Cockfights and the Seduction of Anthropology." In his *Anthropologies and Histories: Essays in Culture, History, and Political Economy*, 17–29. New Brunswick: Rutgers University Press.

Rosenbaum, Art. 1995. *Shout Because You're Free: The African American Ring Shout Tradition in Coastal Georgia*. Athens: Georgia University Press.

Rouch, Jean. 1961. "Second Generation Migrants in Ghana and the Ivory Coast." In *Social Change in Modern Africa*, edited by Aidan Southall, 300–304. London: Oxford University Press.

———. 2003. *Ciné-Ethnography*. Edited and translated by Steven Feld. Minneapolis: University of Minnesota Press.

Rouch, Jean, and Enrico Fulchignoni. 2003. "Ciné-Anthropology: Jean Rouch with Enrico Fulchignoni." In *Ciné-Ethnography*, edited and translated by Steven Feld, 147–187. Minneapolis: University of Minnesota Press.

Rutledge, Archibald. 1938. *It Will Be Daybreak Soon*. New York: Fleming Revell.

Sahlins, Marshall. 1972. *Stone Age Economics*. Chicago: University of Chicago Press.

Saint-Aude, Magloire. 1970. *Dialogue de mes Lampes-Tabou-Dèchu*. Port-au-Prince: Première Personne.

Salm, Steven J., and Toyin Falola. 2002. *Culture and Customs of Ghana*. Westport, CT: Greenwood.

Sam-Long, Jean-François. 1988. *Zoura, femme bon dieu. Lettres Ultramarines*. Paris: Éditions Caribéennes.

Sapir, Edward. 1917. "Do We Need a 'Superorganic'"? *American Anthropologist* 19:441–447.

———. 1934. "The Emergence of the Concept of Personality in the Study of Culture." *Journal of Social Psychology* 5:408–415.

Sapir, J. David. 1977. "The Anatomy of Metaphor." In *The Social Use of Metaphor: Essays in the Anthropology of Rhetoric*, edited by J. David Sapir and J. Christopher Crocker, 3–32. Philadelphia: University of Pennsylvania Press.

Sapir, J. David, and J. Christopher Crocker, eds. 1977. *The Social Use of Metaphor: Essays in the Anthropology of Rhetoric*. Philadelphia: University of Pennsylvania Press.

Sargeant, Winthrop. 1946. *Jazz: Hot and Hybrid*. New York: E. P. Dutton.

Sarmiento, Domingo Faustino. [1845] 1961. *Facundo*. New York: Doubleday and Company.

Saxon, Lyle, Robert Tallant, and Edward Dreyer. 1945. *Gumbo Ya-Ya: A Collection of Louisiana Folktales*. Baton Rouge: Louisiana Library Commission.

Schaeffner, André. 1964. "Le tambour-sur-cadre quadrangulaire chez les Noirs d'Afrique et d'Amérique." In *Les Colloques de Wégimont*, vol. 4, 229–248. Paris: Société d'Édition "Les Belles Lettres."

Schegloff, Emanuel, and Harvey Sack. 1973. "Opening Up Closings." *Semiotica* 8:289–327.

Schmidt, Cynthia. 1998. "Kru Mariners and Migrants of the West African Coast." In *The Garland Encyclopedia of World Music*, vol. 1: *Africa*, edited by Ruth M. Stone, 370–382. New York: Garland.

Schrive, Maurice. 1989. "Recherche sur l'origine d'un conte betsimisaraka. L'histoire racontée semble se passer sur les plateaux du centre de l'île." Conference presentation. Antananarivo. Colloque international d'histoire malgache.

Schuchardt, Hugo 1928. *Schuchardt-Brevier: E in Vademecumd er allgemeinen Sprachwissenschaft*. Edited by Leo Spitzer. Halle: Niemeyer.

Schwartz, Henry, and Sangeeta Ray, eds. 2000. *A Companion to Postcolonial Studies*. Maldemn, MA: Blackwell Publishers.

Schwarz-Bart, Simone. 1972. *Pluie et vent sur Télumée Miracle*. Paris: Sevil.

Scott, David. 1991. "This Event, This Memory: Notes on the Anthropology of African Diasporas in the New World." *Diaspora* 1:261–284.

———. 1997. "An Obscure Miracle of Connection: Discursive Tradition and Black Diaspora Criticism." *Small Axe* 1:19–38.

Shain, Richard M. 2002. "Roots in Reverse: *Cubanismo* in Twentieth-Century Senegalese Music." *International Journal of African Historical Studies* 35 (1): 83–101.

Shepherd, Verene A., and Glen L. Richards, eds. 2002. *Questioning Creole: Creolisation Discourses in Caribbean Culture*. Kingston, Jamaica: Ian Randle.

Shohat, Ella, and Robert Stam. 1994. *Unthinking Eurocentrism: Multiculturalism and the Media*. New York: Routledge.

Shukla, Pravina. 2000. Exhibition review of *The Art of Nellie Mae Rowe: Ninety-Nine and a Half Won't Do*, Museum of American Folk Art. *Journal of American Folklore* 113 (447): 90–92.

Sibthorpe, A.B.C. 1868. *The History of Sierra Leone*. London: Elliot Stock.

Silverstein, Leni. 1995. "The Celebration of Our Lord of the Good End: Changing State, Church, and Afro-Brazilian Relations in Bahia." In *The Brazilian Puzzle: Culture on the Borderlands of the Western World*, edited by David J. Hess and Roberto A. DaMatta, 134–151. New York: Columbia University Press.

Smith, Felipé. 2003. "Coming of Age in Creole New Orleans: An Ethnohistory." In *Problematizing Blackness: Self-Ethnographies by Black Immigrants to the United States*, edited by Percy C. Hertzen and Jean Muteba Rahier, 113–128. New York: Routledge.

Smith, M. G. 1957. "The African Heritage in the Caribbean." In *Caribbean Studies: A Symposium*, edited by Vera Rubin, 34–46. Mona: Institute for Social and Economic Research, University College of the West Indies.

———. 1965. *The Plural Society in the British West Indies.* Berkeley: University of California Press.

Smith, Michael D. 1994. *Mardi Gras Indians.* Gretna, LA: Pelican Publishing Company.

Smith Omari, Mikelle. 1989. "The Role of the Gods in Afro-Brazilian Ancestral Ritual." *African Arts* 23 (1): 54–61, 103–104.

Smitherman, Geneva. 1994. *Black Talk: Words and Phrases from the Hood to the Amen Corner.* Boston: Houghton Mifflin.

Sobel, Mechal. 1979. *Trablin' On: The Slave Journey to an Afro-Baptist Faith.* Westport, CN: Greenwood. Repr., Princeton: Princeton University Press, 1998.

Soskice, Janet Martin, and Rom Harré. 1982. "Metaphor in Science." In *From a Metaphorical Point of View: A Multidisciplinary Approach to the Cognitive Content of Metaphor*, edited by Zdravko Radman, 289–307. Berlin: Walter de Gruyter.

Spencer-Walters, Tom. 2006. "Creolization and Kriodom: (Re)Visioning the 'Sierra Leone Experiment.'" In *New Perspectives on the Sierra Leone Krio*, edited by Mac Dixon-Fyle and Gibril Cole, 223–255. New York: Peter Lang.

Spitzer, Leo. 1974. *The Creoles of Sierra Leone: Responses to Colonialism, 1870–1945.* Madison: University of Wisconsin Press.

Spitzer, Nick. 1979. *La-La: Louisiana Black French Music.* Notes to Maison de Soul Records LP 1004.

———. 1982. "Coastal Louisiana: 'South of the South.'" *Southern Exposure* 10 (3): 56–59.

———. 1984. *Zydeco: Creole Music and Culture in Rural Louisiana.* Documentary film. Berkeley: Flower Films.

———. 1986. "Zydeco and Mardi Gras: Creole Identity and Performance Genres in Rural French Louisiana." PhD diss., University of Texas, Austin.

———. 1989. "Zydeco." In *Encyclopedia of Southern Culture*, edited by Charles R. Wilson and William Ferris, 1037–1038. Chapel Hill: University of North Carolina Press.

———. 1992. "Cultural Conversation: Metaphors and Methods in Public Folklore." In *Public Folklore*, edited by Robert Baron and Nicholas R. Spitzer, 77–107. Repr., Washington, DC: Smithsonian Institution Press, 1996.

———. 1995. "Black Creoles of Louisiana." In *Encyclopedia of World Cultures*, vol. 1, *North America*, edited by Timothy J. O'Leary and David Levinson, 36–40. Boston: G. K. Hall & Company.

———. 2002. "The Aesthetics of Work and Play in Creole New Orleans." In *Raised to the Trade: Creole Building Arts of New Orleans*, edited by John Ethan Hankins and Stephen Maklansky, 96–130. New Orleans: New Orleans Museum of Art.

———. 2003. Interview with blues guitarist and singer Taj Mahal for *American Routes*, July 3. New Orleans, American Public Media.

————. 2005a. Interview with pianist and producer Allen Toussaint for *American Routes*, September 19. New Orleans, American Public Media.

————. 2005b. "Rebuilding the Land of Dreams." Notes to *Our New Orleans: A Benefit Album 2005*. New York: Nonesuch Records.

————. 2005c. Interview with Creole pianist Eddie Bo. Broadcast on *American Routes*, November 2. New Orleans, American Public Media.

————. 2006. "Rebuilding the 'Land of Dreams' with Music." In *Rebuilding Urban Places after Disaster: Lessons from Hurricane Katrina*, edited by Eugenie Birch and Susan Wachter, 305–328. Philadelphia: University of Pennsylvania Press.

————. 2007a. Interview with Rebirth Brass Band leader Philip Frazier. Courtesy Matt Sakakeeny from *American Routes*, August 22. New Orleans, American Public Media.

————. 2007b. Interview with social aide and pleasure club member Edward Buckner for *American Routes*, August 19. New Orleans, American Public Media.

————. 2008. "Tremé Sidewalk Steppers and Rebirth Brass Band Second Line." Feature on *American Routes: Songs and Stories from the Road*. Minneapolis: High Bridge Company.

————. 2009. Interview with pianist and producer Allen Toussaint for *American Routes*, April 20. New Orleans, American Public Media.

————. 2010. Interview with Creole fiddler Cedric Watson for *American Routes*, January 25. New Orleans, American Public Media.

Spivak, Gayatri Chakravorty. 1990. *The Postcolonial Critic: Interviews, Strategies, Dialogues*. New York: Routledge.

Steere, Edward. 1870. *Swahili Tales, as Told by Natives of Zanzibar, with an English Translation*. London: Bell and Daldy.

Stewart, Charles. 1995. "Relocating Syncretism in Social Science Discourse." In *Syncretism and the Commerce of Symbols*, edited by Goran Aijmer, 13–37. Goteborg, Sweden: IASA.

————. 2007. "Creolization: History, Ethnography, Theory." In *Creolization: History, Ethnography, Theory*, edited by Charles Stewart, 84–107. Walnut Creek, CA: Left Coast Press.

Stewart, Charles, and Rosalind Shaw, eds. 1994. *Syncretism/Anti-syncretism: The Politics of Religious Synthesis*. London and New York: Routledge.

Stewart, Gary, and John Amman. 2007. *Black Man's Grave: Letters from Sierra Leone*. Berkeley Springs, WV: Cold Run Books.

Stocking, George W., Jr. 1976. "Ideas and Institutions in American Anthropology: Thoughts Towards a History of the Interwar Years." In *Selected Papers from the American Anthropologist*, edited by George W. Stocking Jr., 1–52. Washington, DC: American Anthropological Association.

Stoller, Paul. 1995. *Embodying Colonial Memories: Spirit Possession, Power, and the Hauka in West Africa*. New York: Routledge.

Strmel, Damir, and Peggy Ann Wachtel. 1988. "Kimati Dinizulu—Pan-African Polyrhythms." *Ear* 13 (4): 25.

Stuckey, Sterling. 1987. *Slave Culture: Nationalist Theory and the Founding of Black America*. New York: Oxford University Press.

Stuempfle, Stephen. 1995. *The Steelband Movement: The Forging of a National Art in Trinidad and Tobago*. Philadelphia: University of Pennsylvania Press.

Suárez, Casiano. 1988. *Dichos del truco, Historia, formas de jugarlo, reglamentos*. Buenos Aires: Editora Selene.

Sublette, Ned. 2004. *Cuba and Its Music: From the First Drums to the Mambo*. Chicago: Chicago Review Press.

Sweet, James H. 2003. *Recreating Africa: Culture, Kinship, and Religion in the African-Portuguese World: 1441–1770*. Chapel Hill: University of North Carolina Press.

Szwed, John F. 1992. "Vibrational Affinities." In *The Migration of Meaning*, edited by Judith McWillie and Inverna Lockpez, 59–67. New York: INTAR Gallery.

———. 2003. "Metaphors of Incommensurability." *Journal of American Folklore* 116 (453): 9–18.

———. 2005. *Crossovers: Essays on Race, Music, and American Culture*. Philadelphia: University of Pennsylvania Press.

Szwed, John, and Morton Marks. 1988. "Afro-American Transformations of European Set Dances and Dance Suites." *Dance Research Journal* 20:29–36.

Taussig, Michael. 1987. *Shamanism and Colonialism and the Wild Man: A Study of Terror and Healing*. Chicago: University of Chicago Press.

———. 1993. *Mimesis and Alterity, A Particular History of the Senses*. New York: Routledge.

———. 1997. *Magic of the State*. New York: Routledge.

———. 1999. *Defacement: Public Secrecy and the Labor of the Negative*. Stanford: Stanford University Press.

Taylor, Douglas Macrae. 1964. Review of Antoon Donicie and Jan Voorhoeve. *Sarama Kaanse Woordenschat. International Journal of American Linguistics* 30:434–439.

Thieme, Darius. 1969. "A Descriptive Catalogue of Yoruba Musical Instruments." PhD diss., Catholic University of America, Washington, DC.

Thioub, Ibrahima, and Ndiouga A. Benga. 1999. "Les groups de musique 'moderne' des jeunes Africains de Dakar et de Saint-Louis, 1946–1960." In *Fêtes urbaines en Afrique: Espaces, identités et pouvoirs*, edited by Odile Goerg, 213–227. Paris: Karthala.

Thomas, T. Ajayi. 1992. *History of Juju Music*. New York: Thomas Organization.

Thompson, Robert Farris. 1971. *Black Gods and Kings: Yoruba Art at UCLA*. Repr., Bloomington : Indiana University Press, 1976.

———. 1983. *Flash of the Spirit: African and Afro-American Art and Philosophy*. New York: Random House.

———. 1988a. "The Circle and the Branch: Renascent Kongo-American Art." In *Another Face of the Diamond*, edited by Judith McWillie and Inverna Lockpez. New York: INTAR Latin American Gallery.

———. 1988b. "Recapturing Heaven's Glamour: Afro-Caribbean Festival Arts." In *Caribbean Festival Arts*, edited by John Nunley and Judith Bettelheim, 17–29. Seattle: University of Washington Press.

———. 1989. "The Song that Named the Land: The Visionary Presence of African American Art." In *Black Art: Ancestral Legacy*, edited by Robert V. Roselle, Alvia Wardlaw, and Maureen A. McKenna, 97–141. Dallas, TX: Dallas Museum of Art.

——. 1993. *Face of the Gods: Art and Altars of Africa and the African Americas.* New York: Museum for African Art.

——. 1998. "Bighearted Power: Kongo Presence in the Landscape and Art of Black America." In *Keep Your Head to the Sky: Interpreting African American Home Ground*, edited by Grey Gundaker, 37–64. Charlottesville: University of Virginia Press.

——. 2005. *Tango: Art History of Love.* New York: Pantheon.

Thompson, Robert Farris, and Fr. Joseph Cornet. 1981. *The Four Moments of the Sun: Kongo Art in Two Worlds.* Washington, DC: National Gallery of Art.

Thornton, John. 1992. *Africa and Africans in the Making of the Atlantic World, 1400–1680.* Cambridge: Cambridge University Press.

——. 2000. "War, the State, and Religious Norms in "Coromantee" Thought: The Ideology of an African American Nation." In *Possible Pasts: Becoming Colonial in Early America*, edited by Robert Blair St. George, 181–200. Ithaca, NY: Cornell University Press.

Todd, Loreto. 1974. *Pidgins and Creoles.* Boston: Routledge and Kegan Paul Ltd.

Tokofsky, Peter, ed. 1999. "Studies of Carnival in Memory of Daniel J. Crowley." Special issue of *Western Folklore* 58 (3–4): 195–318.

Toll, Robert C. 1974. *Blacking Up: The Minstrel Show in Nineteenth-Century America.* New York: Oxford University Press.

Toussaint, Allen. 2009. *The Bright Mississippi.* New York: Nonesuch Records.

Trouillot, Michel-Rolph. 1991. "Anthropology and the Savage Slot: The Poetics and Politics of Otherness." In *Recapturing Anthropology*, edited by Richard G. Fox, 17–44. Santa Fe: School of American Research Press.

——. 1992. "The Caribbean Region: An Open Frontier in Anthropological Theory." *Annual Review of Anthropology* 21:19–42.

——. 1998. "Culture on the Edges: Creolization in the Plantation Context." *Plantation Society in the Americas* 5 (1): 8–28.

Turner, Edith, with William Blogett, Singleton Kahona, and Fideli Benwa. 1992. *Experiencing Ritual: A New Experience of African Healing.* Philadelphia: University of Pennsylvania Press.

Turner, Victor. 1974. *Dramas, Fields, and Metaphors: Symbolic Action in Human Society.* Ithaca, NY: Cornell University Press.

Uther, Hans-Jörg. 2004. *The Types of International Folktales: A Classification and Bibliography.* Editorial staff Sabine Dinslage, Sigrid Fährmann, Christine Goldberg, and Gudrun Schwibbe. FF Communications No. 284. Helsinki: Suomolainen Tiedeakatemia.

Vally-Samat, Renée. 1962. *Contes et légendes de Madagascar.* Paris: Fernand Nathan.

Vappie, Don, Glen Pitre, and Michel Benoit. 2006. *American Creole.* Color film. Cut Off LA: Bayou Films.

Vaxelaire, Daniel, director. 1993. *Contes des Mascareignes.* Saint-Denis (Réunion): Azalées Éditions.

Vergès, Françoise. 2003. "Kiltir Kreol: Processes and Practices of Créolité and Creolization." In *Créolité and Creolization: Documenta11_Platform3*, edited by Okwui Enwezor, Carlos Bausaldo, Ute Meta Bauer, Susanne Ghez, Sarat Maharaj, Mark Nash, and Octavio Zaya, 179–184. Ostifildern-Ruit, Germany: Hatje Cantz.

Vernon, B. J. 1848. *Early Recollections of Jamaica*. London: Whittaker.

Vidal, Jaime R. 1994. "Citizens Yet Strangers: The Puerto Rican Experience." In *Puerto Rican and Cuban Catholics in the U.S., 1900–1965*, edited by Jay P. Dolan and Jaime R. Vidal, 11–134. Notre Dame, IN: University of Notre Dame Press.

Vidal, Teodoro. 1986. *San Blas en la tradición puertorriqueña*. San Juan: Ediciones Alba.

———. 1989. *Tradiciones en la brujería puertorriqueña*. San Juan: Ediciones Alba.

Vlach, John Michael. 1978. *The Afro-American Tradition in the Decorative Arts*. Cleveland: Cleveland Museum of Art.

Vogel, Susan, ed. 1991. *Africa Explores: Twentieth-Century African Art*. New York: Center for African Art in Association with Munich, Prestel.

Volosinov, V. N. 1971. "Reported Speech." In *Readings in Russian Poetics*, edited by Ladislav Matejka and Krystyna Pomorska, 149–175. Cambridge, MA: MIT Press.

Voorhoeve, Jan, and Ursy Lichtveld, eds. 1975. *Creole Drum: An Anthology of Creole Literature in Surinam*. New Haven: Yale University Press.

Walcott, Derek. 1970. *Dream on Monkey Mountain and Other Plays*. New York: Farrar, Strauss and Giroux.

———. 1974. "The Caribbean: Culture or Mimicry?" *Journal of Interamerican Studies and World Affairs* 16 (1): 3–13.

———. 1992. *The Antilles: Fragments of Epic Memory*. London: Faber.

Ward, Ned. [1712] 1933. "Jamaica." In *Five Travel Scripts Commonly Attributed to Edward Ward, reproduced from the earliest editions extant with a bibliographical note by Howard William Troyer*, 1–16. New York: Published for the Facsimile Text Society by Columbia University Press.

Ware, Naomi. 1978. "Popular Music and African Identity in Freetown, Sierra Leone." In *Eight Urban Musical Cultures: Tradition and Change*, edited by Bruno Nettl, 296–320. Urbana: University of Illinois Press.

Warner-Lewis, Maureen. 2003. *Central Africa in the Caribbean: Transcending Time, Transforming Cultures*. Jamaica, Barbados, Trinidad: University of the West Indies Press.

Warren, Edward. 1885. *A Doctor's Experiences in Three Continents*. Baltimore: Cushings and Bailey.

Waterman, Christopher Alan. 1990. *Jùjú: A Social History and Ethnography of an African Popular Music*. Chicago: University of Chicago Press.

West, Cornel. 1993. *Beyond Eurocentrism and Multiculturalism*. Vol. 2: *Prophetic Reflections: Notes on Race and Power in America*. Monroe, ME: Common Courage Press.

Westmacott, Richard. 1991. "Pattern and Practice in Traditional African-American Gardens in Rural Georgia." *Landscape Journal* 10 (2): 87–104.

———. 1992. *African-American Gardens and Yards in the Rural South*. Knoxville: University of Tennessee Press.

Wilgus, D. K. 1959. *Anglo-American Folksong Scholarship since 1898*. New Brunswick, NJ: Rutgers University Press.

Willey, Malcolm, and Melville J. Herskovits. 1927. "Psychology and Culture." *Psychological Bulletin*. 24:253–283.

Williams, Brackette. 1991. *Stains on My Name, War in My Veins: Guyana and the Politics of Cultural Struggle*. Durham, NC: Duke University Press.

Williams, Raymond. 1980. "Base and Superstructure in Marxist Theory." In his *Problems in Materialism: Selected Readings*, 31–49. London: Verso.

Winks, Robin W. 1971. *The Blacks in Canada*. New Haven: Yale University Press.

Wittgenstein, Ludwig. 1973. *Philosophical Investigations*. 3rd English ed. New York: Prentice-Hall.

Wyse, Akintola. 1989. *The Krio of Sierra Leone: An Interpretive History*. Freetown: W. D. Okrafo-Smart and Company.

Yelvington, Kevin. 2001. "The Anthropology of Afro-Latin America and Caribbean: Diasporic Dimensions." *Annual Review of Anthropology* 30:227–260.

———, ed. 2006. *Afro-Atlantic Dialogues: Anthropology in the Diaspora*. Santa Fe, NM: School of American Research Press.

Young, Jason R. 2007. *Rituals of Resistance: African Atlantic Religion in Kongo and the Lowcountry of South Carolina in the Era of Slavery*. Baton Rouge: Louisiana State University Press.

Young, Robert J. C. 1995. *Colonial Desire: Hybridity in Theory, Culture, and Race*. London: Routledge.

Contributors

Roger D. Abrahams is now retired from the faculty of the University of Pennsylvania, where he was the Hum Rosen Professor of Folklore and Folklife. He has written widely in folklore history, theory, Anglo-American balladry, and various sites in the Black Atlantic World. His next book will be *Mapping the Black Atlantic*.

Robert Baron directs the Folk Arts Program of the New York State Council on the Arts (NYSCA) and has served as folklore administrator of the National Endowment for the Humanities and as senior research specialist in the Education Division of the Brooklyn Museum. He has carried out field research in Haiti, St. Lucia, and Japan and among Caribbean communities in the northeastern United States. His publications include *Public Folklore*, edited with Nick Spitzer, and a number of articles about Black Atlantic folklore, public folklore, the history of folklore studies, and museum studies. Baron has been a non-resident fellow in the W. E. B. Du Bois Institute for African and African American Research at Harvard, a Fulbright senior specialist in Finland and the Philippines, and a Smithsonian fellow in Museum Practice. In 2002, he received the Benjamin A. Botkin Award for Outstanding Achievement in Public Folklore from the American Folklore Society. He holds a PhD in folklore and folklife from the University of Pennsylvania.

Kenneth Bilby is director of research at the Center for Black Music Research and research associate in the Department of Anthropology at the Smithsonian Institution. Bilby earned his PhD in anthropology from Johns Hopkins University and his MA in anthropology from Wesleyan University. He has undertaken anthropological and ethnomusicological research in Sierra Leone and in several parts of the Caribbean, including Jamaica, French Guiana, Suriname, Dominica, St. Vincent, Belize, and the Bahamas. His extensive fieldwork with Maroon peoples in both Jamaica and the Guianas has resulted in numerous articles, book chapters, and other publications. He has also compiled and/or produced fifteen albums (LPs and/or CDs), several of which feature his own field recordings. Bilby was a Guggenheim fellow (2004–2005), scholar-in-residence at the Schomburg Center for Research in Black Culture (2003), visiting professor of music and anthropology at Bard College (2000–2002), and curator (1991–1992, 1997) and research associate (1993–present) with the Smithsonian Institution. He received the Caribbean Studies Association Gordon K. Lewis Memorial Award for Caribbean Scholarship in 1996 for the book *Caribbean Currents: Caribbean Music from Rumba to Reggae* (co-authored with Peter Manuel and Michael Largey) and the Wesley-Logan Prize of the American Historical Association in 2006 for his book *True-Born Maroons*.

Ana C. Cara is a professor at Oberlin College, where she instituted and chaired the Department of Hispanic Studies and teaches in Latin American studies, comparative literature, anthropology, and dance. She has conducted extensive fieldwork in Argentina, as well as field studies in the Caribbean and among Latino populations in the United States. Her publications focus on Jorge Luis Borges, Argentine creolization, tango, and other Latin American topics. She has been a research associate at the Center for Latin American Studies at the University of California at Berkeley and teaches in the Comparative Literature Masters Program at the Universidad Nacional de Córdoba, Argentina. She holds a PhD in folklore and folklife from the University of Pennsylvania.

J. Michael Dash, born in Trinidad, has worked extensively on Haitian literature and French Caribbean writers, especially Edouard Glissant, whose works, *The Ripening* (1985), *Caribbean Discourse* (1989), and *Monsieur Toussaint* (2005), he has translated into English. After twenty-one years at the University of the West Indies, Jamaica, where he was a professor of Francophone literature and chair of Modern Languages, he is now a professor of French at New York University after having been director of the Africana Studies Program. His publications include *Literature and Ideology in Haiti* (1981), *Haiti and the United States* (1988), *Edouard Glissant* (1995), and *The Other America: Caribbean Literature in a New World Context* (1998). He has also translated *The Drifting of Spirits* (1999) by Gisèle Pineau. His most recent books are *Libeté: A Haiti Anthology* (1999) with Charles Arthur and *Culture and Customs of Haiti* (2001). He is at present completing a book on the Francophone Caribbean in the 1940s.

Grey Gundaker teaches American studies and anthropology at the College of William and Mary. With graduate degrees from Teachers College, Columbia, and Yale, her interests include literacies, sign systems, and material and expressive culture in the African diaspora, especially within what is now the United States. Currently her research explores relationships among race, notions of the Garden, and civilization in the African Atlantic world.

Lee Haring is Emeritus Professor of English at Brooklyn College of the City University of New York. He has taught in graduate folklore programs at the University of California at Berkeley, the University of Pennsylvania, and the University of Connecticut. After early study of seventeenth-century English poetry, he took up the study of folklore, producing two recordings of American folk music. As a founding faculty member of Friends World College, the round-the-world study program, he resided in Kenya, where he began studying East African traditions. In 1975–76 he served the University of Madagascar as a Fulbright senior lecturer in American folklore and civilization. Extensive library research on Malagasy culture led to his *Malagasy Tale Index*, a comprehensive analysis of folktales; the translation of *Ibonia, Epic of Madagascar*; and *Verbal Arts in Madagascar*, a study of four genres of oral literature. Awarded a second Fulbright grant, this time for research and teaching of folklore in the Indian Ocean island of Mauritius, he conducted folklore fieldwork and began the study of the cultural interrelations of the Southwest Indian Ocean islands. His book *Stars and Keys: Folktales and Creolization in the Indian Ocean* shows those interrelations, through translating and commenting on a hundred stories from Madagascar, Mauritius, Réunion, the Comoros, and Seychelles. In an attempt to deprofessionalize folklore research, he has published the bilingual field manual (English, Kreol) *Collecting Folklore in Mauritius* and two tale collections.

Raquel Romberg is the author of *Witchcraft and Welfare: Spiritual Capital and the Business of Magic in Modern Puerto Rico* and *Healing Dramas: Divination and Magic in Puerto Rico* as well as several articles on Afro-Latin religions, Spiritism, and creolization. She teaches anthropology at Temple University.

Nick Spitzer is professor of anthropology and American studies at Tulane University. He is also an adjunct research professor in anthropology and urban studies at the University of New Orleans. Spitzer is known for work on the expressive culture of Gulf Coast communities, cultural creolization, American vernacular music, and public folklore. Spitzer is producer of public radio's *American Routes*, distributed nationally by American Public Media. He received a PhD in anthropology from the University of Texas and was founding director of the Louisiana Folklife Program, as well as senior folklife specialist at the Smithsonian Institution. Nick's film *Zydeco* has been broadcast internationally, and he has been an artistic director from Carnegie Hall (*Folk Masters*) to the National Mall (*American Roots Independence Day Concerts*), as well as a contributor to NPR's *All Things Considered*, ABC's *Nightline*, and PBS's *Great Performances*. Spitzer was named Louisiana's Humanist of the Year in 2006 for his cultural efforts in the wake of catastrophic flooding. In 2007 he received a Guggenheim fellowship for new research on traditional creativity in south Louisiana Creole communities.

John F. Szwed is professor of music and jazz studies at Columbia University and John M. Musser Professor of Anthropology, African American Studies, and Film Studies Emeritus at Yale University. He also taught at the University of Pennsylvania, where he was director of the Center for Urban Ethnography and chair of the Department of Folklore and Folklife. His research includes field studies of Newfoundland, the Georgia Sea Islands, and Trinidad, and some of his publications are *Afro-American Anthropology; Space Is the Place: The Lives and Times of Sun Ra; So What: The Life of Miles Davis; Crossovers: Essays on Race, Music, and American Culture;* and *Alan Lomax: The Man Who Recorded the World.*

Index

Abel, Antoine, 192, 196

Abidjan, Côte d'Ivoire, 157, 158, 160, 173n22, 176–77n36

Abrahams, Roger D., 17, 18, 52, 178, 198

Accompong, Jamaica, 139, 144, 146, 147, 167, 169, 170n11–12

Accra, Ghana, 155, 156

acculturation, 12–13, 17, 20, 35, 43–44, 72, 73, 89, 113, 179, 244, 251, 257–59, 263–65, 267–69, 271, 273–77, 283n6–8

acriollarse, 212–13

Africa, 15, 17, 18n1, 28, 49, 70, 73–74, 76–77, 90, 98–101, 103n20, 135n20, 137–38, 142–43, 146, 148, 150–53, 158, 160, 162–64, 166, 166–67n2, 167–68n3, 169n5, 169n7, 170n8, 171n13, 172n20, 173n21, 174n23, 176n35, 180, 182, 189–90, 227n20, 235, 240, 250, 252–53, 255, 257–63, 269–73, 280, 282n5, 284n12, 300; Central and, 69, 99, 138, 152, 168n4, 282n4; East and, 179–83, 282n4; South and, 24, 164; West and, 24, 34, 69, 147–48, 151–52, 155, 160, 164, 170n8, 176n36, 256–59, 262, 270, 282n4–5

African American culture, 22, 23, 26, 29, 34–36, 40–42, 49–51, 64, 69, 71, 73, 84–87, 94, 98–103, 106n60, 108n79, 190, 217, 227n33, 258, 262, 272–73, 277, 282n4, 300. *See also* Afro-American culture; Negroes

African Americans (Black Americans), 14, 26, 39, 41–43, 52, 56–57, 73, 94, 126, 148, 257, 259, 260, 271–72, 276, 289. *See also* Negroes

African culture, 7, 13, 15, 20, 22–26, 28, 32–41, 43, 49–50, 57, 65, 70–74, 76–79, 85, 87–88, 90, 94, 96, 100–101, 102n7, 108n81, 109, 111–12, 116, 118, 124–28, 134–37, 160, 180–85, 188, 191–93, 196, 207, 210–11, 212n24, 230–32, 240, 243–44, 250, 252–64, 266–82, 284, 292, 294–95, 298, 304n1; Central and, 77, 99; East and, 77, 180; West and, 40, 43, 52, 60–61, 77, 143, 147, 154, 163, 182, 258–59, 262, 269, 276

African Diaspora, 39, 52, 68–69, 72–73, 79, 80, 85, 100, 136n27, 189

Africans, 23, 71, 73, 76–77, 79, 80, 115, 137–38, 148–49, 157, 162, 169n7, 179–80, 250, 261, 269, 274, 293, 295, 300

Afro-American culture, 75, 77, 101, 147, 155, 160, 254, 273, 280, 293. *See also* African American culture

Afro-Caribbean (African Caribbean) culture, 22, 42, 49, 55, 79, 109, 138, 251–52, 259, 293

Alberdi, Juan, 227n23

Alexis, Jacques Stephen, 16

Alleyne, Mervin, 126

allusion, 184, 185, 190, 193, 224

Americas, 20, 34, 38, 55, 61–63, 65, 210, 260, 262, 271, 282n5, 284n11, 297; Central and, 266; Latin and, 4, 5, 7, 11, 18n1, 46, 119, 207–9, 236, 266; Native and, 49; North and, 37, 57, 72, 83, 99, 139; South and, 24, 37, 114. *See also* United States

Amman, John, 148, 171n15. *See also* Stewart, Gary

analytical categories, 4, 225n4

Anancy, 99

CPSIA information can be obtained
at www.ICGtesting.com
Printed in the USA
FFOW01n1251271115
19001FF